Progressive New World

Progressive New World

How Settler Colonialism and
Transpacific Exchange
Shaped American Reform

Marilyn Lake

▌▌▌
Harvard University Press

CAMBRIDGE, MASSACHUSETTS • LONDON, ENGLAND
2019

Library of Congress Cataloging-in-Publication Data

Names: Lake, Marilyn, author.
Title: Progressive new world : how settler colonialism and Transpacific
exchange shaped American reform / Marilyn Lake.
Description: Cambridge, Massachusetts : Harvard University Press, 2019. |
Includes bibliographical references and index.
Identifiers: LCCN 2018006855 | ISBN 9780674975958 (alk. paper)
Subjects: LCSH: Progressivism (United States politics)—History. | Social
problems—United States—History. | Social problems—Australia—History. |
Racism—United States—History. | Racism—Australia—History. | Colonies—
Oceania—Administration. | Indians of North America—Government relations—
History. | Aboriginal Australians—Government relations—History.
Classification: LCC HT1523 .L285 2018 | DDC 361.1—dc23
LC record available at https://lccn.loc.gov/2018006855

In memory of Tracey Banivanua-Mar, 1974–2017
An inspiring colleague and fine historian

Contents

Progressive New World

Introduction

Settler Colonialism and Progressivism

The ideas of progressives & of the infinite perfectability of the human race belong to democratic ages. Democratic nations care little for what has been, but they are haunted by visions of what will be; in this direction then unbounded imagination . . .

ALFRED DEAKIN, Notebooks

"AUSTRALIA IS THE second New World," the Harvard philosopher Josiah Royce declared in the *Atlantic Monthly* in the first of two articles on his "wandering life in Australasia," written after his visit in 1888.[1] Arriving after a long sea voyage prescribed by his doctor, Royce carried a letter of introduction to the Liberal leader and future prime minister, Alfred Deakin. The two spent an intense week together, walking and talking in the Blue Mountains west of Sydney, engaged in conversations that lay the basis for a deep friendship and correspondence lasting more than twenty years.[2]

Their talks also proved crucial to the development of Royce's thought. His reflections on the character of these new communities in the southwest Pacific informed his thinking on the dynamics of social organization more generally. His southern sojourn shaped Royce's development as a progressive philosopher of community and his conception of the "ethical principle of loyalty" as the key bond on which community was built, an idea later elaborated in his 1908 book *The Philosophy of Loyalty.*[3]

Deakin and Royce were both born in frontier settlements suddenly enriched by the discovery of gold—Deakin in the self-governing British colony of Victoria in southeastern Australia and Royce in Grass Valley in California—and each had enrolled in his local university in 1871. Of his childhood, Royce recalled "a very frequent wonder as to what my elders meant when they said that this was a new community."[4] Deakin also pondered the implications of this distinctive historical condition and thought that insight should come from American writers: "In this new land we look to America . . . Hawthorne, Emerson."[5]

New lands, new communities, new worlds. These were shared American and Australian comforts and conceits. Transpacific identifications between them were framed by the chronology of settler colonialism. As Patrick Wolfe has noted, "Historically speaking, Australia followed the United States," but "as incubators and developers of modernity, Australian settlers would be in the vanguard of a number of democratic movements."[6] Australian historians have written of the "radical novelty of colonial liberalism" in its conception of society as "an association of sovereign individuals."[7] Royce was impressed by precisely this novelty, and he pondered the dynamic of political and social association. "Organization, if it succeeds," he concluded in his second paper for the *Atlantic Monthly*, "does so by virtue of the loyalty of the individuals, and the result must be in general normal and progressive."[8]

The building of a new community was the major theme in Royce's history of California, published in the American Commonwealths Series, edited by Horace Scudder, in 1886.[9] *California: From the Conquest in 1846 to the Second Vigilance Committee in San Francisco* told of the triumph of the community over the individual. Amid all the facts of the story, Royce wrote, "I have felt running through the one thread of the process whereby a new and great community first came to be conscious of itself. . . . The story begins with individuals and ends where the community begins to be what it ought to be, viz., all important as against individual doings and interests."[10] The challenge in the anarchy and violence of the lawless frontier had been to establish moral and political order. How that had been achieved was the question that his history, dedicated to his mother, "a California Pioneer of 1849," sought to answer. Subtitled "a study of American character," Royce's narrative, though recognizing Americans as conquerors, paid no heed to the dispossession and destruction of local Indian communities, a catastrophic process recently characterized as "genocide."[11]

It was the building of new communities and crafting of ideal social orders that were the focus of the animated discussions between Royce and Deakin in the Australian winter of 1888. Royce was intrigued by Australian colonists' "socialistic tendencies." Australia was not simply a second New World; it was a more progressive and adventurous one. In addition to a common English-speaking heritage, "one finds in Australasia a rapid growth taking forms that are partly novel. No English community elsewhere has sought to govern itself in just the way here exemplified. Here are pure democracies, with what an American must unhesitatingly call strongly socialistic tendencies."[12] The ownership of railways by the state was already a fact, not merely a theory. Colonists looked to governments to provide for their welfare and manifold needs—Royce cited Deakin's speech as chief secretary in support of the 1888 Victorian budget as evidence of the full range of state provision expected by electors.[13] "It was this undercurrent of idealistic socialism," Royce told his American readers in a third article, written for *Scribner's* in 1891, "that attracted most my attention."[14]

Soon another Australasian innovation would capture the imagination of progressive Americans. In 1893, New Zealand women became the first in the world to win the right to vote (but not stand for election) at the national level. Some American and Australian women had also been enfranchised locally, but it was Australian women's achievement of the right to vote and stand for election across the new Commonwealth of Australia, in 1902, that was hailed by American admirers as "the greatest victory ever won for women," an "object lesson" that would surely "help the cause of human liberty throughout the earth."[15]

According to Ida Husted Harper, historian of the American women's movement and biographer of Susan B. Anthony, Australian women's political victory was "the most important event in the history of the [world] movement toward woman suffrage."[16] One reason Australian women were successful in winning political power, Harper suggested in the *Washington Post*, was that "the socialistic experiment there [had] reached its greatest development and one of its features [was] the equal rights of women."[17]

When young Vida Goldstein traveled from Melbourne to Washington in 1902 as the Australasian delegate to the first International Woman Suffrage Conference, she was warmly welcomed by the American organizers as a "sister in language and in blood" and a harbinger of Australia's "new world's promise" and "path of experiment."[18] Ellen Wright Garrison greeted her as the youthful embodiment of modernity:

> To Australasia all the world gives ear;
> Youthful, audacious, unrestrained and free.
> No immemorial bonds of time's decree
> Shackle her progress nor excite her fear.
> She beckons elder nations in her path
> Of bold adventure and experiment.

Alice Stone Blackwell, secretary of the National American Woman Suffrage Association, also drew an analogy between Goldstein's youth and that of the nation she represented:

> Amid this bright progressive band
> Of women picked from every land,
> We have a youthful delegate
> To represent a youthful State.

The representative of Colorado women, enfranchised in 1893, expressed the hope that "Australian and American women [would] progress spiritually side by side on the upward path of our common race."[19]

The enfranchisement of women, it was commonly understood, represented a racial triumph as well as a democratic milestone.[20] American and Australian suffragists measured their progress in terms of their advancement beyond the condition of women deemed "traditional," "primitive," "savage," or "feudal." US suffrage leader Carrie Chapman Catt reassured the international conference that American women, despite their lack of political rights, were advanced in world terms, having escaped traditional "bonds" and "restrictions." They were "unquestionably . . . less bound by legal and social restrictions than the women of any other country," she told assembled delegates, "unless we except progressive Australia and New Zealand."[21]

Progressive New World offers a new history of progressivism as a transpacific project shaped by Australasian example and the shared experience and racialized order of settler colonialism. Such a perspective allows us to better understand progressivism's ambiguous character as simultaneously democratic and elitist, reformist and coercive, advanced and assimilationist, uplifting and repressive. Appraisals of the political character of progressivism have shifted over past decades, oscillating between stern critique of its elitism and warm sympathy for its democratic impulse.[22] The interpretative framework of settler colonialism helps make sense of, and brings into one analytical lens, progressivism's constitutive contradictions. The project of progressive reform was imbued with settler colonialism's "regime of race," which informed the ascendant politics of "whiteness."[23]

Take the example of the "Australian ballot," introduced in the self-governing colonies of Victoria, Tasmania, and South Australia from 1856 to combat coercion and corruption in elections.[24] This Australian version of the secret ballot was distinctive in introducing the use of a government-printed ballot paper, signed by electoral officials and distributed at the polling booth.[25] Some American reformers, such as Richard Dana in Massachusetts, where the Australian ballot was first introduced in the United States, also advocated the reform to purify the election process.[26] It quickly became evident, however, that the use of an official printed ballot paper, which had to be read and marked by electors in the privacy of a polling booth, made it more difficult for illiterates to cast a valid vote. Many advocates in the north and south of the United States began to promote the Australian ballot as a disenfranchisement measure to eliminate "ignorant" votes.[27]

In the southern states especially, the Australian ballot was promoted as a way to exclude African Americans from voting. Thus, the "father of Georgia disfranchisement" included the Australian ballot system in a list of the most effective ways of "eliminating Negroes from politics," while a Democrat campaign song in Arkansas in 1892 assured electors:

> The Australian Ballot works like a charm,
> It makes them think and scratch,
> And when a Negro gets a ballot
> He has certainly got his match.[28]

In less than eight years after its 1888 adoption in Massachusetts, some 90 percent of states had followed suit. Rarely in the history of the United States had a reform movement spread so quickly and successfully.[29] One result was a large decline in voter turnout and the effective exclusion of black electors from the political process.[30] Progressive reforms could have profoundly undemocratic outcomes.

Indigenous peoples in both Australia and the United States were usually excluded, as noncitizens, from voting at all. From the late nineteenth century into the twentieth century their communities were in sharp decline as they continued to be forced from their lands, massacred, infected with disease, and subjected to the removal of their children. Birthrates plummeted. Much theoretical work on settler colonialism has emphasized the displacement and destruction of indigenous peoples that underpinned settler colonialism—the "logic of elimination," in Wolfe's influential formulation.[31] But there is also the corollary. Indigenous societies were supplanted by settler communities, who resolved to bring into being new kinds of race-based polities that were not simply "facsimiles" of the old but self-consciously innovative pioneering democracies.[32]

From the mid-nineteenth century, in both Australia and the United States, white self-government was based on manhood suffrage, with settlers enjoying political rights not extended to working-class men in Britain until after World War I. Settler societies were not mere extensions of the Old World. Rather, they were engaged in inventing novel kinds of democratic societies. In defining settler colonialism as a distinctive formation, Lorenzo Veracini has emphasized that settlers were "founders of political orders" who carried their sovereignty with them.[33] Their assumption of sovereign right rested precisely on the denial of the sovereignty and territoriality of indigenous peoples whose lands they occupied.[34]

In the self-governing Australasian colonies of the late nineteenth and early twentieth centuries, governments elected by manhood (and increasingly womanhood) suffrage inaugurated a series of radical democratic experiments—including the Australian ballot, the eight-hour day, the abolition of plural voting, public ownership of utilities, a legal minimum wage, wages boards and arbitration courts, workers' compensation, the abolition of child labor, immigration restriction, the political enfranchisement of women, the first children's court, mothers' pensions and a maternity allowance, old age and invalid pensions—inaugurating a reform regime described by contemporaries as "state socialism."

Progressivism was defined by a shift away from a reliance on charity and philanthropy to remedy social ills toward a vision of the state as a vehicle for achieving social justice. Theodore Roosevelt was an influential convert, evident, for example, in his discussions with Vida Goldstein when she visited Washington in 1902. His interest in arbitration systems and a legislated minimum wage, as conveyed to Henry Demarest Lloyd, Carroll Wright, and Victor S. Clark; his decision to hold the First White House conference on "dependent children" in 1909; and his platform as presidential candidate for the Progressive Party in 1912 all spoke to Australian initiatives.

When Roosevelt espoused the cause of progressivism in 1912—a development he conceptualized as "industrial evolution" and "economic evolution"—his platform included a living wage, shorter hours, protective tariffs, the abolition of child labor, workers' compensation, and woman suffrage. "Individualism" was now excoriated as an outdated, even a "savage," force. "We stand for a living wage," declared Roosevelt at the First National Convention of the Progressive Party in Chicago, where he received a fifty-five-minute standing ovation. "We favor woman suffrage."[35]

Described as "one of the boldest visions in the history of mainstream American politics," this was a program condemned by conservative critics for its radical, even revolutionary, nature and by others as derivative, a mere imitation, a "flung-together program of so-called 'State Socialism,'" a mere rehash of Australasian policy.[36] "Novel as the Roosevelt views may appear," complained one critic, "they are neither new nor strange to any man informed of political currents throughout the world. In brief, they are a rehash of policies long in vogue in Australia and New Zealand."[37]

Charles Pearson had written about the success of state socialism in Australia in his influential work of prophecy, *National Life and Character: A Forecast*, which Roosevelt reviewed and recommended to friends in 1894. In Australia, Pearson had explained, "The State employees are an important element of the population; the State builds railways, founds and maintains schools, tries to regulate the wages and hours of labour, protects native industry, settles the population on the land, and is beginning to organise systems of State insurance."[38] "State Socialism" had succeeded, he wrote, "because it is all-embracing, and able to compel obedience." Superior to European models of social or work-based insurance, it had been "developed by the community for their own needs, and not by State departments for administrative purposes."[39] State payments came from general revenue. The democratic origins of Australasian state experiments were also emphasized by American commentators, such as Henry Demarest Lloyd and Victor S. Clark following their visits to Australia and New Zealand in the late nineteenth and early twentieth centuries.[40] "In a democracy," wrote Lloyd in *Newest England*, "in self-government, state-help is self-help."[41]

They were but two of the large group of American reformers, including single taxer Henry George, social commentator Frank Parsons, Californian investigator Harris Weinstock, Stanford professor David Starr Jordan, Ohio State professor M. B. Hammond, Wisconsin professor Richard Ely, Boston feminists Maud Wood Park and Mabel Willard, "ardent suffragist of San Antonio" Marin B. Fenwick, and Woman Christian Temperance Union leader Jessie Ackerman, who traveled across the ocean to see the state experiments for themselves. For Henry George, Australians were "not merely our kinsmen, but [a people who] in character, conditions and future possibilities come closer to us than any other." Returning from his tour in 1890, George told his fellow citizens "there is no country whose social and political development is so well worth the study of thoughtful Americans."[42]

Henry Demarest Lloyd, whose *Wealth against Commonwealth*—a scathing attack on Standard Oil and corporate corruption—was published in 1894, crossed the Pacific in 1899. "Australian democracy was so successful and progressive," he told an Adelaide journalist, "that Americans . . . could make a study of it and reap an advantage."[43] Lloyd proved an influential publicist and was treated as an expert on Australasian developments.[44] In *Newest England*, the Chicago journalist extolled "the democratic efflorescence in Australasia," a "renaissance of democracy" featuring progressive taxation, land reforms, old-age pensions, labor legislation, and public ownership of railways and utilities. Impressed, in particular, by the role of New Zealand's system of compulsory industrial arbitration in preventing strikes and upholding labor standards, Lloyd declared happily, "New Zealand was a white man's country if ever there was one."[45] Australasian state socialism, it was commonly understood, enlisted the services of the state to enshrine a white man's standard of living.

Victor S. Clark traveled south during 1903 and 1904 at the behest of the US Labor Bureau as part of a tour that included visits to Java and the Philippines. "New Zealand and Australia [were] the most interesting legislative experiment stations in the world," he declared, "and they experiment so actively because their political institutions are extremely democratic. They are doing what people in the United States might do were they able to enforce their will with equal directness through the ballot. Our government is organized on a more conservative basis, and the popular voice manifests itself less directly in legislation."[46]

New England suffragist Maud Wood Park, who had met Vida Goldstein on her lecturing tour in Boston in 1902, toured the east coast of Australia in 1909. Meeting Labor leader (and soon to be prime minister) Andrew Fisher, together with a number of Labor women at parliament house in Melbourne, she was struck by "women's equal standing in the industrial and political organization of the Labor party." The "sense of the political equality of women in a country where they are enfranchised was a deep-rooted conviction."[47] Jessie Ackerman, who traveled regularly to Australia, was also impressed by Labor women's activism:

> The working women have grandly and nobly risen to the discharge of their duty as citizens, so far as actual voting is concerned.... That the results have told is unmistakably written in political events.... It has altered the very course of a nation, and made a volume of history in a day as it were, all of which is due to the unrelenting, ever-acting agencies of organisation.[48]

Other American reformers learned about Australian developments—in labor law, the public ownership of utilities, and child and maternal welfare, for example—from Australian visitors to the United States, such as Catherine Helen Spence, who spread the word about mothers' pensions and the first juvenile court (in South Australia) at the Chicago World's Fair in 1893, and novelist Miles Franklin and her friend, Alice Henry, who worked with Margaret Dreier Robins at the National Women's Trade Union League from 1906 as editor of the journal *Life and Labor.*[49]

When Henry first stepped ashore in New York, arriving via England, she was given a warm reception. "I was taken in at once and made welcome," she recalled. "At once! At first! A favored visitor from far-away Australia. . . . It was an introduction to the social workers' world at its best and highest, with close connections to the Labor Movement."[50] In her several lectures to social workers, women's clubs, and suffrage societies, Henry discovered intense interest in how Australia dealt with neglected children, how wages boards worked to secure a living wage, and the use enfranchised women had made of the vote. "Australia was a word to rouse interest in all that circle and I arrived at a moment when Australia was beginning some of her most notable experiments in social legislation, and, Federation having been accomplished, Americans generally were feeling a sense of sisterly interest in this new young country."[51] That interest, she found, was shared by President Roosevelt, whom Henry, like Goldstein before her, met in Washington, where she passed on Australia's "impromptu greetings."[52]

Henry's friend H. B. Higgins, the esteemed president of the Commonwealth Court of Conciliation and Arbitration, was invited to visit the United States in 1914 by progressive activist Robert Valentine—former commissioner of Indian affairs, confidant of Roosevelt, and, by 1914, working as a self-styled "labor counselor." Valentine introduced Higgins to his stellar network of East Coast progressives, including jurists Oliver Wendell Holmes Jr., Louis Brandeis, Learned Hand, and Felix Frankfurter, and labor reformers Elizabeth Glendower Evans, Florence Kelley, and Josephine Goldmark, leaders of the feminist National Consumers League (NCL). Higgins and Frankfurter became close friends and confidants, the two joined in intimate and candid correspondence until shortly before Higgins's death in 1929.[53]

In the United States, Higgins was interviewed by reformers in a number of cities for a range of papers. He was commissioned by the *Harvard Law Review* to write about the Australian minimum wage and industrial arbitration court, an article reprinted by the NCL in its Minimum Wages Series.[54] The Australian jurist's ideas were also discussed in the *New Republic*, a journal founded shortly after his 1914 visit in which Herbert Croly, Walter Lippman, Felix Frankfurter, and Learned Hand promoted the legitimate role of trade unions and the imperative of a legal minimum wage. In his advocacy of the minimum wage and collective bargaining, Croly had shown, Higgins suggested to Frankfurter, that he had "caught" Australian ideas.[55]

By 1914, Higgins's path-breaking jurisprudence was widely cited in the United States, and he was welcomed as something of a celebrity. Professor Hammond had lauded the Australian jurist in the *American Economic Review* the year before as a world pioneer of "social democracy": "He has certainly expressed, at greater length and with greater clearness than has anyone else, the ideals which have animated the Australian people and the Australian lawmakers in placing on the statute books the body of social legislation which has drawn the eyes of all the world to Australasia, and which marks the most notable experiment yet made in social democracy."[56] In his famous Harvester judgment of 1907, Higgins had defined the minimum wage as a "living wage" sufficient to meet the needs of workers carefully defined as "human beings living in a civilized community," a white man's wage designed to combat the degradation and exploitation experienced by indentured laborers, "coolies," Pacific Islanders, and slaves. As Jerold Waltman has noted, the idea of a "living wage" was routinely acknowledged in the United States as an Australian invention. Progressive reformers often quoted with approval the Australian standard: a minimum wage is one supporting the "normal needs of the average employee regarded as a human being living in a civilized community."[57]

Theodore Roosevelt visited Higgins in his Washington hotel, telling him that he had "been urged by his 'progressive' friends" to meet him.[58] Roosevelt had long been an enthusiast for the settler democracies of the southwest Pacific. The racial dimension of his often-expressed "fellow feeling" was evident in his history of colonizing conquest, *The Winning of the West:* "The average Englishman, American or Australian of today who wishes to recall the feats of power with which his race should be credited in the shadowy dawn of its history may go back to the half-mythical glories of Hengist and Horsa."[59] The settlement of America and Australia were, Roosevelt insisted, key events in world history: "When these continents were settled they contained the largest tracts of fertile, temperate, thinly peopled country on the face of the globe. We cannot rate too highly the importance of their acquisition. Their successful settlement was a feat which by comparison utterly dwarfs all European wars of the last two centuries."[60]

In his review of Pearson's *National Life and Character*, Roosevelt had lauded the settler societies of North America and Australasia as democratic triumphs over European aristocracy:

> Had these regions been under aristocratic governments, Chinese immigration would have been encouraged precisely as the slave trade is encouraged of necessity by any slave-holding oligarchy, and the result would have been even more fatal to the white race; but the democracy, with the clear instinct of race selfishness, saw the race foe, and kept out the dangerous alien. The presence of the negro in our Southern States is a legacy from the time when we were ruled by a trans-oceanic aristocracy.[61]

In their espousal of the twin ideals of political equality and racial exclusion, these English-speaking democracies were extensions of the British world but also repudiations of the economic, social, and political hierarchies that defined Britain itself.

In the New World democracies, settler colonists made themselves and their societies anew. In Old World Britain, "they had been instructed to reverence rank, wealth, landed-proprietorship, state religions and vested interests," flamboyant New Zealand Labor secretary Edward Tregear explained in *Arena*, the radical Boston monthly edited by Benjamin Orange Flower, an enthusiastic convert to the antipodean "Program of Progress."[62] "Economically they had been taught to respect old trade-jargons about 'freedom of contract,' 'supply and demand,' 'liberty of the subject,'" wrote Tregear, "phrases subtly concocted for the repression of all upward industrial effort and for the support of financial privilege." The challenge for settler colonists was to build new political and social orders: "To disentangle themselves from such associations and to dare to think for themselves, then to translate their meditation into action, needed severe and arduous struggle, but it was on the true lines of national evolution and results full of promise have been achieved." The ultimate result of this combined struggle and evolution, Tregear told his American readers, was "'progressive legislation.'"[63]

Settler colonialism was constituted in a triangular system of relationships comprising metropolitan, settler, and indigenous agencies.[64] From the late nineteenth century, reformers in settler societies began to cast themselves as "progressive" in a temporal construction of "double difference"—distinguishing themselves both from Old World feudalism and from Stone Age savagery.[65] Thus did Sam Gompers report in his history of *The Eight-Hour Workday* that when the Australian workingman "inaugurated" shorter-hours reform in 1856, "the gloom of the effete monarchical and feudal institutions" was lifted, and "the darkness of ages" ended.[66] Gompers would in fact prove wary of state intervention in industrial relations, preferring "red-blooded rugged independence and will power" to state protection, which would emasculate American workingmen.[67] In Australia, by contrast, labor reformers advocated extensive state protections precisely to secure white workingmen's manhood in relations of class equality.

Manhood was a key value for nineteenth-century settler colonists, who prided themselves on their manly capacity for "self-government," a prevalent discourse whose salience depended on the settler colonial context.[68] In settler societies, working-class men sought to escape the oppressive and demeaning class relations of feudal, monarchical, aristocratic societies. "The labourer with us," Andrews Norton had asserted, "feels that he is a *man* and a *citizen*."[69] But the deepening class exploitation of the late nineteenth century—the "inhumanly long hours of labor and starvation wages" in Ida Van Etten's words—challenged such conceptions.[70] The virtuous republic was under siege by the new antidemocratic forces unleashed by industrial capitalism. The "wage-system of labor" was "crushing the manhood out of sovereign citizens," lamented George McNeill in *The Labor Movement: The Problem of Today.*[71] In this context, many American reformers, including Florence Kelley, Elizabeth Glendower Evans, and Walter Lippman, heralded Australian wages boards—first established in 1896—as ushering in a new era of "economic democracy."[72]

In formulating social and economic goals, reformers on both sides of the Pacific responded to common economic and industrial crises, including economic depression, bitter and widespread strikes, and mass unemployment. In the course of their confrontation with economic turmoil, American policy makers—public officials, social investigators, independent labor reformers, and union and business leaders—located themselves as never before in a larger, international context.[73] While sometimes referring to developments in Europe, the path to reform that beckoned most strongly, as Leon Fink has noted, was the "Australasian road."[74] American interest in industrial arbitration and the need to inscribe remedies to industrial conflict in law—evident in the 1894 Strike Commission; the US Industrial Commission; and local initiatives in Chicago, New York, Colorado, Kansas, and Wisconsin—has been largely ignored in the historiography and thus "lost to posterity."[75]

Reformers in both countries aimed to reinvigorate democracy and extend self-government—to white women, workers, citizens, and voters, but not to African Americans, "Asiatics," or Pacific Islanders, who would be segregated, excluded, or deported, or to surviving indigenous peoples and foreign immigrants, who would be assimilated and absorbed. In her collection of lectures, *Democracy and Social Ethics*, Jane Addams, founder of Hull House in Chicago, explained the challenge of working with local immigrant communities. As "primitive people" with "untrained minds," "South Italian peasants" needed appropriate training to prepare them for democracy.[76] The capacity for and right to exercise self-government were conceptualized in racialized settler-colonial terms.[77] Nonwhite races might, perhaps, gradually attain that capacity through education and training, both at home and in overseas territories.[78] An active state was an expansive state, and advancement rested on the project of assimilation at home and abroad.

One of Alfred Deakin's first acts as chief secretary in the Victorian government in 1886, two years before he met Royce, was to preside over the introduction of the Aborigines' Protection Act, which marked the beginning of "the assimilation era" in Australian policy with regard to Aboriginal peoples.[79] Proposed by the Aborigines' Protection Board, the act was in part an economic measure aimed at saving money and in part an initiative to defuse Aboriginal political activism on the Coranderrk reserve northeast of Melbourne.

The goal was to absorb the mixed-descent Aboriginal population into the white community. They would "merge the half-castes and quarter castes into the general population," Deakin told parliament. "Full blood" Aborigines were expected to soon "die out." They were "a nearly extinct race," Deakin observed, invoking the familiar evolutionary trope, "and therefore the expense attending their maintenance ought to become less and less."[80] Aborigines of mixed descent, once living among the general population, "might be educated to earn their own living" and thus become "useful members of society."[81] The effects of the act were rather less benign, causing the breakup of Aboriginal families and communities and thus exacerbating their loss of culture, language, ceremony, and land.

In the United States, the Dawes Act, passed just one year later, in 1887, was a key component of the federal government's new Indian assimilation campaign.[82] Its allotment policy similarly provided for the gradual breakup of reservations and the absorption of Indians into the white community under what has been criticized as a "vanishing policy."[83] Henry Dawes and like-minded legislators believed that the future for Native Americans required them to "follow the white man's road" in settling on individual homesteads alongside white settlers rushing to take up "surplus" land. The Dawes Act ultimately reduced federally recognized Native American landholdings by about ninety million acres, thus clearing the way for the rapid expansion of settler colonization across the continent and the exploitation of vast natural resources, "so handled," as Roosevelt put it, "to be in the interests of the actual settler."[84]

In Australia and the United States, it was assumed that surviving indigenous peoples must be trained—coerced if necessary—to live and work like white people. Historians of American progressivism have noted the focus of urban reformers on assimilating new immigrants to American culture—the process of "Americanization"—but they have generally not included the simultaneous programs in Indian assimilation in the same analytical frame. It is time to consider how the study of indigenous histories in the context of settler colonialism might illuminate more broadly our understanding of progressivism.[85]

Also in Australia and the United States, the assimilation and education policies directed at indigenous peoples—especially children, through boarding and mission schools—and the continuing appropriation of indigenous lands, through breaking treaties and breaking up reserves and reservations, were central to, indeed definitive of, the progressive vision of advancement, efficiency, and modernity. The attacks on indigenous cultures, language, and ceremony and the removal and training of Aboriginal and Native American children were not peripheral to progressive goals but a prime example of the broader strategy of "Putting Children First."[86] And just as children were considered the key to the national future, so white maternal authority escaped the bounds of the private domain to reshape public life.[87] Progressivism was a transnational reform movement focused on realizing its aims through nation building, state intervention, and the enactment of reform in family life, the home, and the workplace, domains increasingly defined as central to national life.

In the United States, "field matrons" were appointed with the significant responsibility of "civilizing" Indian families, especially in their own homes and communities. Commissioners of Indian affairs were pleased to report on their progress. In one place, where Indians who had "sturdily resisted all civilizing influences, especially schools," the field matron had gathered the children up and "obtained a strong hold for good upon every family." At another place, "sewing schools, weekly clubs and simple Sabbath services" had brought self-respect to young men and women. The field matrons had enabled "something hopeful and widening" in Native Americans' narrow lives of poverty, dirt, and degradation until they had at last dared to become "progressives."[88]

Across the Pacific, Australian women reformers also claimed a special role in progressive programs focused on the welfare of children, the protection of the home, and the care of "dependent" natives.[89] Radical activists such as Mary Bennett, Ada Bromham, Edith Jones, and Constance Cooke lobbied, with little success, for a supervisory role in the protectionist regimes that governed Aboriginal lives at the state level and recognition of Aboriginal women's rights as mothers. In the United States, where Indian affairs came under federal jurisdiction, the new programs in Indian assimilation initiated unprecedented levels of federal activism and a huge expansion in the federal bureaucracy. Long before the establishment of the Children's Bureau and the Women's Bureau, the Indian Service brought large numbers of women into the federal workforce to implement policies formulated in considerable part by female-dominated Indian reform groups.[90]

By 1898, women constituted 42 percent of all Indian Bureau employees and a full 62 percent in the Indian School Service. The Indian Bureau also employed for the first time large numbers of indigenous employees, men and women such as Marie Baldwin, in positions that sustained "the first generation of Native professional and white-collar

workers."[91] One effect was to forge solidarity between tribes and encourage an identity as "Indian" that would become the basis of a new
progressive cultural and political organization: the Society of American Indians (SAI).

Sometimes called the "Red Progressives," the SAI was formed in
1911 by Native intellectuals, including Charles Eastman, Thomas
Sloan, and Marie Baldwin, with the support of the progressive commissioner for Indian affairs, Robert Valentine—a close friend of Felix
Frankfurter and Theodore Roosevelt, for whom he campaigned in 1912.
A quintessential progressive in his vision, methods, and goals, Valentine also became a pioneer in the field of industrial relations in which
capacity he invited H. B. Higgins to Boston and Washington. Valentine's sudden death in 1916 from a heart attack, at the age of forty-six,
meant that his multifaceted progressive activism has since been little
remembered.

The story of transpacific reform campaigns can best be understood
through the lens of personal friendships, shared enthusiasms, and professional networks. Ideas circulated through conversation, conferences,
and correspondence. The interpretative framework of settler colonialism illuminates the subjective affinities of American and Australian reformers—their often-stated sense of "fellow feeling" and "racial
kinship"—and their sensibilities as "pioneers" of "new lands," as
"path-breakers" and builders of "new communities." "I know myself
what all the feelings are when you're young and in a young country
and feel that you're turning over the fly leaf to a new history," said
Tom, the protagonist of Victor S. Clark's short story "Chippeway
Country." Tom was not "just a frontiersman," Clark informs us; "he
was a pioneer."[92] And Clark was not just a writer and labor investigator;
he was also a devoted colonial administrator committed to building
modern communities in Puerto Rico, Hawaii, and the Philippines.

Settler colonialism shaped a sense of kinship across the Pacific.
Josiah Royce referred to Australians as "our southern fellow countrymen," while for Henry George they were "far southern kinsmen."[93]
Victor Clark hailed the "kindred Federation of the South Pacific."[94]
Newspaper reports and magazine stories encouraged identification
through shared histories. In a sketch of New South Wales in 1901,
the year of the founding of the Commonwealth of Australia, the

Washington Post reported that Australian "settlers, like American frontiers men at the present day, often had to work hard with a gun ready to hand, for natives . . . appeared to resist the continual encroachments on their hunting grounds, while the bush concealed numbers of white desperadoes."[95]

To Catherine Spence, on her lecture tour in 1893, the United States "felt more nearly of kin" than did Old World Europe. The United States and Australia were both the "children of Europe," she wrote. "Americans look on Australians as nearer to them than the English themselves, and wherever—in railway trains, or street cars, or at any gathering, or in private houses—it transpired that I was from Australia immediately eager questions were asked and a cordial welcome was offered."[96] Spence was invited to stay or enjoy a family's hospitality in more than forty private residences. Clearly she felt at home. A sense of self shaped by the triangular relations of settler colonialism animated subjective affinities, common ideals, and progressive political commitments.

Just as settlers in standard postcolonial narratives "pioneered" the "wilderness," so too progressives cast themselves as natural "pioneers" of labor reforms, women's rights, and children's services. "I have been surveyor and miner and many other things," declared New Zealand secretary of labor, Edward Tregear, "and always ahead of civilization—a pioneer."[97] Clara Barton, president of the American Red Cross Association, praised Susan B. Anthony at the first International Woman Suffrage Conference as "the woman who has trodden the trackless fields of the pioneer till the thorns are buried in roses."[98] Frederic C. Howe praised Wisconsin for its "progressive legislation" that made the state "so widely known as a pioneer."[99] Writing to Lord Bryce, H. B. Higgins thanked the English statesman for his praise and explained that his arbitration court judgments were "anxious and toilsome work": "I have to blaze my own track through the bush." Perhaps an Englishman might have found the labor legislation crude, because unprecedented, but these were, as Higgins explained, "new communities."[100]

Australians and Americans were proud to be citizens of "young nations," Carrie Chapman Catt observed, "untrammeled by tradition and custom." "It is well known that new countries are far more free from the mandates of custom and conventionality than old ones," she told the First International Woman Suffrage Conference, "and that dissenters from established usage are far more willing to adopt new ideas and extend new liberties than those bound by traditional belief."[101] Yet as Australian visitors frequently observed, Americans were shackled by conservative political institutions, whose elitist, undemocratic character was shaped in the late eighteenth century by the founders of a settler colonial republic forged more than one hundred years before.[102]

Transpacific comparisons highlighted the limits to Americans' readiness and ability to adopt new ideas and implement desired reforms. A federal constitution that inscribed states' rights and the principle of individual liberty, together with a long-established two-party system that marginalized minorities and women, entrenched formidable barriers to change. Individualism and voluntarism remained powerful creeds in American public life, as Catherine Spence found at the International Congress of Charities, Correction and Philanthropy in Chicago in 1893 and Victor Clark affirmed to his friend Edward Tregear ten years later. At every turn, American reformers were "horribly fettered by the shackles" of their constitution, as H. B. Higgins, fresh from battles at the Australian constitutional conventions, told his friend Felix Frankfurter.[103]

Convinced that "socialistic" action was "the trend of modern thought, in spite of protests from individualists," Catherine Spence was taken aback by the criticism she encountered at the Chicago congress, forced to assert that state assistance to relieve destitution should be regarded not as a form of pauperizing charity but as a fundamental modern "right."[104] Nine years later, Jane Addams advocated a new form of "social ethics," recognizing that the charitable relationship between benefactor and beneficiary institutionalized an inequality that belied the ideal of democracy. For Australian progressives, however, it was legislative enactment, not simply the espousal of "social ethics," that was necessary to secure social justice.

In 1918, Felix Frankfurter wrote wistfully to Higgins of "the difficulty of translating ideals into institutions" in his country.[105] Victor Clark blamed the preponderance of farmers in the United States for American conservatism, telling Edward Tregear that more than in Australia and New Zealand, the "hayseed" still ruled the United States.[106] He pointed out that contrary to the stereotype, Australia was a more urban nation than the United States, with 47 percent of Australians living in cities of more than four thousand people, compared with only 37 percent of Americans. Resistance to radical reform was deeply rooted in the great republic.

Despite significant achievements at the state and municipal levels in the United States before World War I, progressivism remained largely aspirational at the federal level until the re-alignment of political forces in the 1930s saw the introduction of comprehensive labor and welfare reform in the New Deal. Title IV (Aid to Dependent Children) of the Social Security Act nationalized mothers' pensions in 1935, while the Fair Labor Standards Act introduced the first minimum wage at the national level in 1938. In the same decade, the Collier reforms in Indian administration gestured toward an end to settler governance and a new era of self-determination.

Progressive New World charts the intellectual, political, and personal exchanges between progressive reformers in the United States and Australasia in the context of the triangular relations between Old World Europe, settler societies, and indigenous peoples. An examination of diaries, letters, memoirs, journal articles, and other writings allows us to examine the making of the subjective identifications and political ideals that animated progressive visions of reform and shaped many American reform initiatives.

The book opens with a kind of prehistory to progressivism: an account of the friendship between an American man of letters, Charles Eliot Norton, and English-Australian historian, journalist, and politician Charles Henry Pearson that explores the ways in which a shared moral revulsion and political outrage at the English class system fueled a passion for democracy in settler colonies. Tragically, its realization rested on the dispossession, displacement, and destruction of indigenous peoples, characterized by Pearson in *National Life and Character*, in a classic instance of disavowal, as "evanescent races" doomed to extinction.[107]

The book concludes with a discussion of indigenous engagement with progressivism in the early twentieth century, evident in the formation of the Society of American Indians—the "Red Progressives"—and the Australian Aboriginal Progressive Association, political mobilizations that testified not only to the power of progressivism as a political idea but also to its imaginative limits and repressive underpinnings.[108] Although largely ignored in histories of American Indian policy, the period between the 1890s and the 1920s was a time of survival, adaptation, resistance, and innovation.[109] Similarly, in Australia, these decades saw Aboriginal people's first modern political mobilizations, also conducted in the name of "progressivism."[110]

Even as "experts" continued to proclaim the imminent extinction of the native peoples of Australia and America—"the fate of the Australian Blacks will be that of the American Indian—they will vanish from the face of the earth" proclaimed visiting American anthropologist William Lloyd Warner in Australia on a research trip in the 1920s— this period saw the rise of indigenous political movements in Australia and the United States, demanding an end to settler governance and recognition of indigenous rights—to land, citizenship, their children, and culture—in differently imagined new worlds.[111]

Progressives might have cared little for what had been, as Alfred Deakin suggested, focusing their imaginings on the future. From an indigenous perspective, however, real advancement demanded a new engagement with the past; an acknowledgment of the historic injustice perpetrated in the name of progress; and a new respect for traditional peoples, their territories and cultures. Indigenous progressives demanded acknowledgment of the legacies of settler colonialism, and they called its white beneficiaries to account. They created their own self-styled "progressive" organizations to "talk back to civilization"— to demand recognition and redress, the return of "land in their own country," and equal citizenship rights for their peoples.[112]

CHAPTER ONE

Self-Government, Democracy, and White Manhood

IN 1873, Charles Henry Pearson, an English historian of the Middle Ages, returned to his recently acquired farm in the colony of South Australia and wrote to his American friend, Charles Eliot Norton, about matters of national character: "You like myself have a sort of double nature your's [sic] being the American-European as mine is the Australian-European."[1] In Pearson's view, their double allegiance to New World democracy and Old World civilization provided a personal bond and distinctive perspective on their shared condition as colonizers of new lands.

In his discussions with Norton about the alarming social condition of England—the great gap between the rich and the poor—we can trace Pearson's transformation from being "a liberal of the English type," as he first described himself, to being a "democratic liberal" of the progressive type.[2] In this he participated in the broader shift in Australian political culture toward what historians have called "social liberalism." No longer preoccupied with political despotism or individual liberty, democratic liberals were more concerned with redressing broader inequalities in social and economic power.[3]

In the story of Pearson's commitment to building a new society in Australia "along the lines of equality," we can chart the ways in which the settler ideal of democracy, shaped by "memories of class rule and intolerable wrong in the old country" and intense land hunger in the new, also drove "the elimination of the native."[4] The progressive New World was understood as both prize and vindication of colonizing conquest, as Theodore Roosevelt observed in his review of Pearson's *National Life and Character: A Forecast.*[5] Progressivism justified the possession of new lands.

The democratic passion for equality expressed a repudiation of Old World hierarchies and privilege but led in turn to new oppressions, evi-

dent in the exclusion of indentured and "coolie" labor and "Asiatics"
more generally, the expulsion of Pacific Islanders, the segregation of
African Americans, and the destruction of indigenous communities,
whose "inevitable disappearance" shaped dominant narratives of
settler nations.[6]

Charles Eliot Norton was first cousin to Francis Parkman, the famous historian of the Oregon Trail and Indian wars, to whom Roosevelt dedicated *Winning of the West*, praising the popular writer as one
to whom "Americans, who feel a pride in the pioneer history of their
country are so greatly indebted."[7] Roosevelt wrote privately to Parkman:
"Your works stand alone, and . . . they must be models for all historical treatment of the founding of new communities and the growth of
the frontier, here in the wilderness."[8]

In his several works of history, Parkman, though sympathetic to
individual Indians and tribes, cast Native Americans in general as savages, locked in their barbaric past, always prone to treachery and de-
ceit, and incapable of modernity.[9] Parkman had asked Norton to help
him convert his original essays on the Oregon Trail, first serialized in
the *Knickerbocker* magazine, into one complete volume. Norton liked
to recall the nights they met on the Boston wharf to work on "Parkman's epic of the American West."[10]

Five years after the publication of *Winning of the West*, Roosevelt
reviewed Pearson's *National Life and Character*, commending it as
"one of the most notable books of the end of the century," a work of
"deep and philosophic insight into the world-forces of the present."[11]
One of those historic forces was the spread of Western "civilization"
across the globe, with its seeming corollary of the "dying out" of indigenous peoples. Pearson's magnum opus was, in part, an elegy to
those he called the "evanescent races" of North America and Australia,
who, he observed in a classic discourse of disavowal, "died out as we
approached."[12] Indigenous peoples, wrote Pearson, who as a traveler had
personally witnessed the violence of the Plains Indian wars, seemed
to "wither away at mere contact with the European."[13] In his charac-
terization of encounters between settlers and indigenous peoples,
Pearson, like most of his contemporaries, engaged in what might be
described as "fantasy" serving as "protective fiction."[14] In the self-
innocenting narrative of evolutionary progress that informed these

national histories, the "red man" was "little more than a memory" even as the "white man" came into his rightful inheritance.[15]

Pearson and Norton became friends when the young English historian visited the United States in the late 1860s. Both men of learning and refinement, they were also passionate democrats, morally outraged at the political and social injustice institutionalized in aristocratic Britain. They shared the conviction that in the self-governing democracies of the New World, ordinary men—white men—might rescue their manhood.[16] The cost of their redemption was substantial. As Christina Snyder has written, American democracy "sought to empower ordinary white men by colonizing Indian country and redistributing its resources that in the Jacksonian period had required the forced removal of 100,000 Indians."[17] Subsequent dispossession saw American Indians lose most of their land.

In his travels across the United States, Pearson was pleased to find that even workingmen in the great republic enjoyed a manly self-respect that eluded his fellow countrymen at home. Norton was pleased to agree.[18] But not all men were so blessed. The manly right of self-government—that definitive rights-claim advanced by settler colonists—remained the preserve of "white men," who alone were considered fit to govern themselves and others. As a radical liberal politician in Victoria, Pearson later defined democracy, somewhat tautologically, as "self-government by men educated up to a common low level and trained by the habit of self-government."[19] Francis Parkman used a similar logic in criticizing universal suffrage: it should apply "only to those peoples who by character and training are prepared for it."[20] Only Anglo-Saxons were thus trained and habituated. Others were cursed, in Parkman's view, by "hereditary ineptitude."[21]

In settler societies, it was the discourse on self-government that came to define contours of racial difference.[22] In these societies, racial identity and claims to self-government were intertwined and mutually reinforcing.[23] Colonists were always, already, "civilized," but in their historic encounters with indigenous peoples and with African Americans, "Asiatics," and Islanders, they came to define themselves more specifically as "white men": democratic, upstanding, independent, self-governing, and the equals of fellow (white) men. This was the basis of their much vaunted "fellow feeling," to invoke one of Theodore

Roosevelt's favorite conceits.[24] Other races of men were thought to be inherently "dependent," "docile," "servile," "supine," or "degraded" and hence not fit for the responsibilities of self-government.[25]

When Pearson first met Norton, Boston was a favored destination for many English "lights of liberalism," keen to offer their support for the cause of the North in the Civil War.[26] For James Bryce, who would later write the great survey work *The American Commonwealth*, the Civil War was the crucial political struggle of the age, "a turning point, for good or evil, of the course of human affairs."[27] It was in Oxford and Cambridge "where the various fortunes of that tremendous struggle" were followed with such close interest and "the educated class sympathised to such a strong degree with the cause of the North." Goldwin Smith led the group that took that view, "which included three quarters of the best talent in Oxford."[28]

Goldwin Smith wrote to Norton to express his solidarity with the cause of the Union, deploring the "malignant exaltation" of the English upper class over the "misfortunes of the American Republic" and their support for the Confederates. The North did have friends in England, Smith assured Norton, even though "the aristocracy are against you almost to a man. The great capitalists are against you. . . . The clergy of the Establishment are against you as a Commonwealth founded in liberty of Conscience. The rich are mostly against you."[29] For his own part, Smith confided,

> [I have] fairly thought my way out of social and political feudalism, and out of the State Church which is its religious complement. . . . My intellect and heart are entirely with those who are endeavouring to found a good community on the sounder as well as happier basis of social justice and free religious conviction. . . . Most likely I should be more in my element, in some respects, at Boston than I am at Oxford.[30]

The following year, Smith embarked on an American lecture tour, declaring that in the United States lay the "hopes of man."[31]

In the stellar literary society of New England, these liberal Englishmen discovered manly company of a kind they relished: cultivated yet democratic, intellectual yet vigorous. In 1868, Pearson met Longfellow, Agassiz, Wendell Holmes, and Emerson, whose essay "The

American Scholar" had been acclaimed by Holmes as "our intellectual Declaration of Independence." James Russell Lowell, coeditor with Norton of the *North American Review,* displayed "a certain unfriendliness to Englishmen," Pearson noticed, but it was understandable, for "any American might well be excused for some disgust towards the mother country after the conduct of our wealthy classes during the Civil War."[32]

The topic of American manhood arose. Lowell told Pearson about the Maine lumbermen, "whose delight it was to drift over the rapids seated astride on pieces of timber, in constant peril of death, for the mere excitement of a plunge."[33] Norton would later eulogize Lowell as "the very best and most characteristic specimen of democratic manhood that New England has produced."[34] It was the vibrant manhood of these Americans that dazzled the English visitors, but it was Norton, the aristocrat in culture and democrat in politics, who, in Pearson's eyes, outshone them all.

The descendant of a leading Puritan family, which had lived for two centuries on American soil, Norton was an art historian, a man of letters, a translator of Dante, and a friend of English literary figures, including Charles Dickens, Arthur Hugh Clough, Mrs. Gaskell, the Brownings, and John Ruskin. In the 1850s, he had traveled extensively in Italy, studying the paintings of Giotto and Fra Angelico as well as Gothic architecture, exemplified by the cathedral at Orvieto—the perfect expression, he thought, of pure and manly simplicity. In the spirit of Ruskin in *The Stones of Venice,* Norton tended to read architecture as an expression of national character. In Gothic cathedrals, he saw the "prevalence of the democratic element in society" before it was overcome by Renaissance pomp and worldliness and art forms he condemned as corrupt and false.[35] The Vatican was to his mind characterized by vanity and gaudy spectacle. Norton praised the work of Michelangelo in the Sistine Chapel but criticized the Roman Catholic Church as "un-American."[36] "No theories of government and religion can be more diametrically in opposition than those prevalent at Rome and in America," Norton declared. "As an American, born into the most unlimited freedom consistent with the existence of society . . . regarding feeling, thought, and speech as having a natural privilege of liberty . . . it is difficult, even at a distance, to regard the system of the

Roman Church as being other than a skilful perversion of the eternal laws of right."[37] In his *Notes on Travel and Study in Italy*, Norton returned to the repressive effects of a totalitarian church, especially its inimical effect on the development of "manly character." A modicum of liberty was essential for the development of literature and art. "When political and spiritual despotism combine," Norton wrote, "a vacuum is produced in which thought and imagination die out, and all the qualities of manly character dwindle and decay."[38]

Charles Pearson shared Norton's obsession with the importance of manly character. He was born in 1830, in London, the son of Harriet Pearson and the Reverend John Norman Pearson and grandson of John Pearson, a member of the Clapham Sect, founder of the Bible Society, and an "intimate," as he liked to recall, of "Wilberforce, Zachary Macaulay, and the whole connection of Stephens, Venns, Thorntons and Babingtons."[39] Pearson's father was the oldest son of a family of seventeen children, of whom only seven survived infancy. A shy and timid man, he suffered, according to his son, from the early influences of asceticism, "in which the traditions of the old school and the influences of Calvinism were unpleasantly blended."[40] He failed in his academic ambitions and was forced to subside, as a minister of religion, on what his son called "ordinary clerical work." At the time of Charles's birth, his father was employed as principal of the Church Missionary College.

Charles Pearson was first educated at home, in a repressive atmosphere in which even innocent amusements were proscribed, before enrolling at Rugby, a year after the death of famed headmaster Thomas Arnold. Pearson later condemned the school for the superficiality of its attempts to modernize the curriculum and its self-conscious moralism—teaching boys to be "always feeling their moral muscles, always careful about their school-fellows' morality, and always mindful of the high mission which they took with them into the world as Rugby boys."[41] Pearson valued the playground most for what it taught about manliness and character: "The playground, which boys regard only as the means of turning out good cricket and football teams, is yet directly and indirectly invaluable in its effects upon character. It teaches manliness and subordination, loyalty and veracity. [In the classroom] a good deal of cheating was contrived at. . . . In the playground everything was straight."[42] According to his reckoning, only three of Arnold's pupils achieved eminence: his son Matthew, Arthur Stanley, and the poet Arthur Clough, whose sister and widow provided important connections for Pearson in the United States and Britain. Clough's sister, Anne, interested him in the cause of women's entry into higher education, while his widow, Blanche, provided valuable letters of introduction when he visited the United States in 1868.

When Pearson and Norton met again in England, they talked at length about the topic on which Norton was writing an article for the *North American Review*, "The Poverty of England."[43] Reviewing official reports on the poor law, public health, and agricultural employment, Norton expressed his shock at the misery and pauperism of the English working classes. The condition of society was not only deplorable, he wrote, but alarming. An unprecedented increase in wealth had been accompanied by a dramatic rise in poverty, "with its concomitants of suffering, pauperism, ignorance, immorality and crime." "No language can be too strong to characterize the disgrace and the danger to a civilized community of a state of society which thus perpetuates the misery of a great proportion of its members, which thus degrades humanity by condemning it to conditions, which inevitably generate ignorance and vice, and are the fruitful sources of crime."[44]

Pearson shared his visitor's outrage at the degrading economic, social, and political inequalities that shamed his country. Norton was pleased in turn to find an English friend so well-disposed to American democracy, as so many of his literary acquaintances dismissed his pride in his country as Yankee boasting.[45] They agreed that revolutionary change was surely imminent. "I quite agree with you," Pearson wrote to Norton, "in the resemblance between the state of things just now in England, and that which preceded the French revolution."[46]

"I cannot but believe," Norton wrote to his friend Chauncey Wright in the same year, "that the question is imminent whether the nation is to decline into a state of chronic decrepitude, or to be redeemed by a more or less violent revolution which shall . . . restore vigor and common life to the various classes which are now arrayed against each other."[47] He repeated the prediction of "violent revolution" in his article for the *North American Review*. The laws of political economy, he argued, might be useful in elucidating the accumulation and distribution of wealth but had nothing to say about the relations of men to one another. Indeed, it was "a truth too often forgotten that, in the present complex and unorganized condition of society, many of the laws of political economy, if applied without restriction to the regulation of human relations, work nothing but misery."[48]

The question was whether the evolution of democracy was taking too long in Britain: "The transference of this power is so slow, and the majority have become so brutalized, that the very process is full of danger." The resentment of the working class might be slow-burning, but "their discontent, though smothered and ineffectual at present, might easily be wrought into a fury against which all the defences of actual institutions would be as vain as were the walls of the Bastile against the passions of the mob of the Faubourg St Antoine."[49]

At the time of Norton's visit to England, there was a post-Reform election under way, but there seemed little cause for optimism. Liberal candidates despaired at the coercion and corruption of Tory tactics, citing the threat of the Duke of Marlborough in Woodstock, where George Brodrick was running for office. "I hope the manners of the Democracy will not be much worse," Goldwin Smith wrote to Norton. "Everywhere the families of the poor are being threatened with ejection from their homes if the head of the family will not vote against his conscience and the interest of his order at the landlord's wish."[50] The secret ballot, already in place in the Australian colonies, had not yet been introduced in England. Smith wrote to Norton of his disappointment with the Reform Act. "To me it is sad to see how overwhelming the influence of wealth still is and how the extension of the suffrage is nullified by the restriction of the voters' choice to candidates who can pay heavy expenses."[51]

Norton's visit confirmed his visceral hostility to the English class system. "Snobbish-looking men" offended his manly sensibilities.[52] The "selfishness of the upper classes" fostered "ignorance, misery and recklessness."[53] Englishmen fawned on "rank and position." Their drawing rooms teemed with "white cravatted flunkeys." Englishmen's consciousness of status and titles was a denial of manly equality. London, he concluded, was the center of "selfishness and flunkeyism." "American republicanism," by contrast, "represented a new and higher stage of human political development." The United States, proclaimed

Norton, echoing Goldwin Smith, was "the hope of the world."[54] Pearson agreed, but his growing commitment to building a new society along the lines of equality led him to focus on opportunities in Australia and sent him down a different political path.[55]

As a proselytizer of democracy and a liberal politician in the self-governing colony of Victoria, Pearson would champion an interventionist state and legislative action that would later become an inspiration for many American progressives. In a speech in Melbourne in 1878, he outlined his vision of a state that would attend to the social and industrial welfare of its citizens. Objections to "parliamentary interference" should not be allowed to prevent "the action of legislation" in addressing people's "needs" and recognizing their "rights." He advocated old-age and invalid pensions and legislation to protect workers. "He thought a great deal might be achieved by the Government in the direction of the organization of labor laws. Take such questions as regulations against overtime, regulations against excessive working of children or women, laws against the importation of foreign immigrants to glut the labor market." He spoke of his dream of "a democratic community . . . in which no man who wanted bread should starve; in which no man should be denied work who required it; in which no woman should be induced to sell herself through want; in which no man should be afraid to speak . . . through fear of his employer; in which the rights of the employed should not be encroached upon by a privileged class."[56] When Pearson entered parliament as the Liberal member for the gold-mining electorate of Castlemaine, he was in a position to propose legislation. "Are you leading the Victorian left?" inquired his old friend and benefactor Henry Sidgwick, writing from England.[57]

Pearson's identification with the aspirations of workingmen had deepened when he lived for a time in a colonial bush town, an experience that prompted him to write to Norton, "I cordially like democracy and democratic institutions."[58] He had first tried his luck as a colonist in 1864, when he took up land at the very edge of white settlement in South Australia. The brutally swift dispossession of indigenous peoples in the southeastern Australian colonies made land available for settlers at a relatively cheap price. Pearson had decided to settle near Mount Remarkable and "take a farm there as an experiment."[59]

He was charmed by the "primitive democracy" of the bush township and later told a Melbourne audience that in transforming him from "a liberal of the English type" into a radical democrat, it had been "the great change of his life."[60] But his material prospects faltered. Lacking farming experience and confronted by drought, his attempt at agriculture ended in ruin. He rented out the farm and prepared to return to England. News that his father had died, bequeathing him a small inheritance, meant a more leisurely trip home and a stopover in India.

Pearson's visit to Calcutta was troubling but clarifying. As with his friend Charles Norton, who had traveled to India from Boston a few years earlier, his encounters provoked conflicting feelings about colonialism and caste: disgust at the way in which the British treated the natives but also revulsion at the natives themselves. Norton had found the scenes of Indian degradation "painful," "not merely as a republican but as a man," and he deplored the vast inequalities of wealth that separated the natives from the British rulers.[61] He told his cousin Francis Parkman that "India was an anomaly among nations—a country governed by foreign rulers, who do not colonize it, filled with a population who are for the most part without national pride, without energy and indeed with few of those manly virtues upon which the prosperity and happiness of a people depend."[62] He told Charles Mills, "The degraded state of immense numbers of the natives, and the misery in which they live can hardly be exaggerated."[63]

Pearson was similarly shocked but also felt ashamed. He realized that he "could never have sympathized properly with the natives": "As it was, I left the country revolted by the brutality with which Europeans treated them, and yet feeling towards them myself as the Northerners in America are accused of feeling towards the blacks."[64] His reflection on his own "feelings of caste" was important in shaping his conviction that there was no place for caste distinctions in self-governing democracies built along lines of equality. The importation of "coolie" labor was thus an impossibility. In "some of us," Pearson recognized, "the feeling of caste is so strong" that the prospect of living and working side by side with "servile" races was unthinkable.[65]

Back in England, Pearson would write about his firsthand experience of democracy in the Australian colonies, with their "republican" Houses of Assembly, as he fondly described them, in a contribution to the volume *Essays on Reform*, compiled in support of the proposed extension to English suffrage in the 1867 Reform Act. The collection also served as a rejoinder to the attacks on Australian and American democracy in the House of Commons by a former New South Wales politician, the erstwhile radical but now deeply conservative Robert Lowe.[66] Described by his contemporary Leslie Stephen as "the most caustic and vigorous of living parliamentary orators," Lowe told parliament that his experience of New South Wales strongly confirmed that giving votes to the lower orders was injurious to good government.[67]

Essays on Reform was published as a reply to the case against democracy and the working classes made by Lowe and other critics of the extension of manhood suffrage. George Brodrick, Pearson's fellow student at Oxford and Liberal candidate for the House of Commons, contributed the first of the essays, "The Utilitarian Argument against Reform, as Stated by Mr Lowe," responding directly to the charges of the Conservative member of parliament (MP). Lord Houghton wrote "On the Admission of the Working Classes as part of our Social System; and on their Recognition for all Purposes as Part of the Nation." Leslie Stephen's subject was "The Choice of Representatives by Popular Constituencies," while A. V. Dicey contributed a piece on "The Balance of Classes." James Bryce drew on his Oxford history thesis to write on "The Historical Aspect of Democracy," while Goldwin Smith provided a glowing account of "The Experience of the American Commonwealth."

Pearson's essay commended "The Working of Australian Institutions." He began by discussing the English charge that Australians had become "Americanized." There seemed to be a general feeling in Britain, he noted, that Australian society was chiefly derived from gold diggers—"the refuse of California"—and the dregs of penal settlements, and that Australian institutions had been, "to sum up all evils in one significant word," "Americanized."[68] Pearson countered with the facts: the Australian colonies had diverse populations, but probably three-quarters of the adult population had migrated from Britain and carried with them the liberal ideas of the middle classes at home: "a strong feeling for an extended suffrage, a desire for cheap land on a simple tenure, and a determination not to repeat the experiment of a State Church."[69]

Moreover, fair elections were secured by the Australian innovation of the secret ballot: "Whatever theorists may say, the ballot works simply and effectively in Australia, there is no bribery at elections, and as the voting is by papers, there is no treating and no intimidation."[70] The "republican Houses of Assembly" were supported by an independent judiciary and intelligent public-minded newspapers: "I know no newspapers in the world more honourably free from invective, or personal attacks, or low scandal, than the Australian."[71]

Pearson expressed his free-trade doubts about protective tariffs and other measures designed to keep wages higher than in the rest of the world ("I know not that any class of men have a right as citizens of the world to more than the cosmopolitan level of profit"), but he loved the spirit of equality that drove the policy. He reported a growing disinclination in colonial families to put their daughters to service in houses where they would not be "treated as equals" and that the custom of "touching the hat" to strangers in broadcloth was not in favor in the colonies, adding that he wished to see it also "disused in England."[72]

It was the English dread of the abolition of class distinctions that provided the key, in his view, to "the English dread of Australian politics."[73] It was, conversely, the promise of equality that explained English liberals' attraction to the United States, as Goldwin Smith made clear in his contribution to *Essays on Reform* on the "American Commonwealth": "Equality has created in America a nation great both in peace and war, wealthy, intelligent, united, capable of producing statesmen and soldiers, yet itself superior to its ablest men."[74] Crucially, Smith emphasized, equality depended on the free "availability of land." Happily, America had "an outlet to the West," wrote Smith, and England in her colonies.[75]

Pearson took up the theme of land availability in the United States in an article in *Contemporary Review* the following year, pondering the new challenges posed for the republic and for relations between capital and labor by what Frederick Jackson Turner later called the "closing" of the frontier.[76] Twenty-five years before Turner delivered his seminal lecture at the World's Fair in Chicago, Pearson observed that Americans were rapidly becoming "cramped for land." When the New World ceased to provide an "outlet," he wondered, how would the mounting tensions between the classes and resulting population pressures be resolved? The continuing expansion of settler societies rested on the continuing dispossession of indigenous peoples, but land for the taking was fast running out.

Pearson had also begun to think about the increasing tensions between the sexes arising from women's claims to equality. Soon after completing his contribution to *Essays on Reform*, he accepted an invitation from Anne Clough to "give lectures to large classes of ladies at Liverpool and Manchester." Clough was a founding member and secretary of the North of England Council for Promoting the Higher Education of Women, a cause dear to Pearson's heart. In the following decade in Melbourne, he would accept the positions of headmaster of the new secondary girls' school, Presbyterian Ladies College (PLC), and council member of the University of Melbourne, where he would advocate women's admission to enrollment for degrees.[77]

Like most progressive thinkers, Pearson saw women's higher education as an index of a people's progress. "We can all understand," he said in his inaugural address at PLC, "how immeasurable the change is from the days when the men were hunters and warriors; the women drudges, hewers of wood, and drawers of water; the men absolute; the women submissive and dependent, gaining their wishes only by artifice."[78] PLC, he advised, was "a new experiment."[79] The first young woman to matriculate was Alfred Deakin's sister, Catherine. Soon after, Vida Goldstein, future suffrage leader, followed in her footsteps. At the same time in England, Anne Clough accepted an invitation from Henry Sidgwick to begin what would become her life's work as founding principal of Newnham College, Cambridge.

Sidgwick also offered Pearson a position at Cambridge as lecturer in modern history, where he agreed to teach for four desultory terms. His students were of average ability and took little interest in the syllabus, but for a time the stimulation of academic colleagues compensated for the tedium of teaching. These included his old teacher from King's College, F. D. Maurice, now professor of moral philosophy at Cambridge; Henry Fawcett, the Liberal MP who held the chair in political economy; and Leslie Stephen, his former schoolmate at King's.

Pearson joined Fawcett and his wife, the suffragist Millicent Garrett Fawcett, in forming a Republican Club, whose radical definition of republicanism revealed the influence of feminism as well as democracy on the group: "hostility to the hereditary principle as exemplified in monarchical and aristocratic institutions and to all social and political privileges depending upon difference of sex."[80] An accomplished scholar, Millicent Fawcett was intellectual partner and secretary to her blind husband. Her older sister Elizabeth was among the first organizers of a petition asking for household suffrage to be extended to women. Henry Fawcett had seconded John Stuart Mill's proposed amendment to the 1867 Reform Bill to introduce woman suffrage.

This was "the first age of emancipation of Cambridge," as J. M. Keynes wrote in an essay on the economist Alfred Marshall, when "Christian dogma fell away from the serious philosophical world of England, or at any rate Cambridge."[81] Sidgwick, who had subscribed to the Thirty-Nine Articles as a condition of the tenure of his fellowship, had just resigned in order to free himself from "dogmatic obligations."[82] Stephen renounced his religious belief in 1870. Pearson, too, longed to escape the "shadow of the English Church." His break with religious orthodoxy reinforced his desire to break with all the institutions of the past.[83] And in any case he believed that "good work will never come out of Oxford or Cambridge."[84] When his South Australian tenant wrote to say that he was giving up the lease, Pearson decided to pack up his books and return for good. His first attempt at living in the bush had not proven profitable, but as he happily said, it had "made a new man of me."[85]

Settler colonialism offered jaded or disappointed Englishmen the opportunity to make themselves anew, even as the original owners of the land faced irretrievable loss. When Pearson first traveled across the United States in 1868—"I have been beyond the Rocky Mountains," he wrote jubilantly to Norton—he stopped in Chicago, where he was introduced to Horace White, the editor of the Chicago Tribune.[86] The newspaperman arranged for Pearson to take the "first excursion train that travelled the overland route west," as far as Cheyenne, in Indian Territory. At the railroad center of Council Bluffs, Iowa, the passengers changed trains and began a more dangerous journey, entering the battlefields of the Plains Indian wars, where local tribes, resisting white settlement and their relocation to reservations, engaged in deadly battles with the US Army. Pearson and his companions on this New World journey were armed, fully aware of the danger they faced from

Indian warriors defending their lands. The natives had not conveniently withered away, as he and others would later fantasize.

Just four years earlier, Col. John M. Chivington had led the 3rd Colorado Cavalry in a savage attack on a Southern Cheyenne and Arapaho village, where at least 130 Indians, mostly women, died in what became known as the Sand Creek massacre. Indian retaliation followed. Writing of his journey, Pearson reported that "Indians were still troublesome along the line": "Every station had a corral for cattle and a sheltered rifle-pit, to which the garrison could retire in case of danger. . . . We ourselves carried rifles, and had a pilot engine sent on in front to warn us if there was danger."[87] It was an anxiety-inducing excursion for the genteel Englishman. Later that year, the 7th US Cavalry under the command of Lt. Col. George A. Custer, charged with bringing Indian raids to an end, led a surprise dawn attack against a Cheyenne village on the Washita River, killing more than one hundred men, women, and children.

When Pearson took the train along the same route three years later, "vanishing" Indians no longer seemed threatening. "No one was armed; no precautions were taken; and when a company of Indians appeared returning from the chase, the passengers looked fearlessly on them as on so many gipsies." Once fierce warriors now resembled picturesque vagrants. By contrast, the white men of the west, the nation builders, were, to Pearson's mind, impressive figures. The workers employed in constructing the new railroad were "the finest set of men" he had ever seen. (Roosevelt was also a great admirer of railroad men.) They were "armed to the teeth" and dealt out swift vigilante justice. In Cheyenne, Pearson went in the evening to a dancing saloon. "Every man was a Hercules armed, and the few women present were of lost character, but the evident desire to avoid quarrels was remarkable."[88] Despite the vigilantism, the omnipresence of guns did not, Pearson insisted, translate into uncontrolled violence. Among white men, he liked to think, self-control prevailed.

The fate of Native Americans was a subject of discussion among his companions. In his memoir, Pearson invoked literary sources to draw a contrast between the admirable manhood of white men and the degradation of "Red Indians": "Altogether these pioneer men seemed to deserve the reputation Bret Harte has given them much better than the degraded savages we saw here and there justified the romance with which Fennimore Cooper has invested the Red Indian." His friends in Cheyenne insisted on introducing Pearson to a local chief, the Sioux leader, Spotted Tail. "I was obliged to shake hands with the wretch," reported Pearson, "who, soon afterwards, took to the warpath again, and committed a whole series of murders."[89] Spotted Tail in fact chose to forgo fruitless wars against encroaching white men. He became active instead in seeking to educate his children and leading treaty negotiations with the federal government.

Clearly, from Pearson's point of view, the future lay not with the degraded, dispossessed, original owners of the country but with the hardy "pioneer men" clearing the wilderness and building railroads. Traveling in the United States not only shaped his understanding of history but also provided a handy income from journalism. He wrote articles for the *Spectator* on Yosemite Valley ("said by Emerson to be the only natural object that has not been over-praised") and San Francisco politics.[90] The subject that most interested him on the West Coast was the widespread opposition to Chinese immigration, a cause taken up by members of the Republican Party despite previously supporting free migration. He didn't pay much attention to the charge of Chinese immorality but was persuaded by the argument regarding low wages. And, given that "the Negro problem" had not yet been solved, it did not seem prudent that another "inferior race should grow up and multiply in the state." Pearson nevertheless enjoyed his visit to Chinatown in San Francisco, where he saw his first "joss house" and ventured into a teahouse. He refrained from trying the mysterious pastries, but his companion was more daring, pronouncing his delicacy a "compound of pork, lard and chocolate."[91]

The other impression of California that stayed with Pearson was the character of its white men, especially the easygoing confidence and the frank courtesy of the lower classes. "Perhaps the general prosperity has something to do with it," he ventured; "it is easy to be good-natured when you are well off, as Becky Sharpe felt that she could be virtuous upon three thousand a year." And perhaps the very prevalence of gun ownership made men more careful and courteous in their dealings. Whatever the reason, Californian workingmen, Pearson concluded, "had a certain self-respect," which made them "among the most agreeable companions I have known anywhere."[92]

From San Francisco, Pearson took ship across the Pacific. Arriving in Sydney Harbor, he was reassured by the beauty of the place: "As I steamed up the bay and saw the white houses crowning the hills on either side, the terraced gardens, the mountain spurs that run out into the sea, the old faith came back upon me that this was the loveliest home ever found by a large population." Subtropical Sydney was alluring, but colonial taste, he noted, tended to prefer stolid bourgeois Melbourne, "with its massive blue-stone palaces, banks and warehouse, standing square to the rectilinear streets which traverse hill and valley without swerve." Pearson compared the New World cities of Sydney, San Francisco, and Melbourne, to the advantage of the last: "It is vaster and more solid, with grander buildings and above all, with incomparably finer public grounds."[93]

In the Australian countryside, the spread of agricultural settlement was transforming the landscape. There were now houses and fences, churches and schools, where just a few years before, traces of former Aboriginal habitation were still evident on vast sheep pastures. Thinking comparatively of white men's opportunities in the New World, Pearson considered that "a poor man [had] a better chance of getting on in the United States than in Australia," but that his position in the colonies was "at least equally better than it was in England."[94] Settled back on his farm in South Australia, he received a welcome letter from Norton and responded with his own happy tidings. At the age of forty-two, he was engaged to be married. His future wife, Edith Butler, was just twenty years old.

Pearson had entered a time of rare contentment. Settled in the countryside, he combined the satisfactions of the life of a gentleman farmer with his old pleasure of reading medieval history. His work on the property was restricted to the role of supervisor, as he relied on hired hands to do most of the labor. "I rise at 7 walk about the farm before breakfast and just now take my gun to shoot cockatoos and crows," he reported to Norton.[95] Gun ownership was common on Australian as well as American frontiers of settlement, "a ubiquitous part of frontier life for more than one hundred years."[96]

Pearson enjoyed life as a gentleman farmer but wanted greater access to libraries and missed educational work and contact with students. He fretted about the lack of intellectual conversation but didn't regret his move to Australia: "The climate gives me an enjoyment of mere life which I know nowhere else and the view I look at from my window is among the most lovely I have seen anywhere." In any case, if he returned to England he would feel compelled to take a more active part in republican clubs and land leagues, but such activism, he feared, would bring him into collision with former friends. As they were "either old Conservatives or Liberals of the Pall Mall Gazette type who object to any reform that threatens the rights of property, the result will be that I shall be involved in much unpleasantness with little chance of seeing any good for my labours."[97] Pearson had become an activist committed to democratic reform.

Norton recommended he meet the wife of the governor of South Australia, American-born Jeannie Musgrave, daughter of the New York lawyer David Dudley Field. The governor, Sir Anthony Musgrave, was serving a three-and-a-half-year term between postings to British Columbia and Jamaica. "Your friend Mrs Musgrave is very popular in South Australia," Pearson duly reported to Norton. In his opinion, she provided "a great contrast in her vivacity and affability to the wives of recent Governors." Governor Musgrave was also popular, because he understood "that the colonies are capable of governing themselves."[98] Perhaps, though, he may have leaned a bit too much toward a laissez-faire approach, for much developmental work remained to be done in South Australia, particularly in the educational field. The government was opening up the land and building roads and railways, but the public education system was underdeveloped, and a university was yet to be established in Adelaide.

As Pearson warmed to the prospect of government-sponsored nation building, Norton became increasingly pessimistic about the commercial and materialist tendencies of industrializing America. He also became anxious about the arrival of large numbers of foreign immigrants and the "decline of the old New England type." Pearson, who cherished his memories of Boston, sympathized with Norton's sense of loss. The New Englander had been "the root of so much that was grand and good in American history from resistance to England to resistance to slavery, that one cannot but regret to see [him] disappear." Still, the character of the men of the West had been reassuring in their "infinite kindliness, strength and elasticity." His only concern was

that perhaps they lacked "moral fibre." The new type of American believed in "a corn and cotton millennium of the Mississippi valley and
would sacrifice niggers or national good faith to it cheerfully."[99] The
challenge was to imbue the new secular order with moral values, but
racial equality would not be one of them.

In 1874, Pearson accepted an appointment as lecturer at the University of Melbourne, and although his hopes for a richer literary life
were disappointed, his new position brought one pleasure: "a singularly
pleasant set of pupils, more hard-working and more manly than the
Cambridge men." He missed the intellectual companionship of former
friends but worried about their reactionary politics. Goldwin Smith,
now employed at Cornell University, had come out as an opponent of
woman suffrage. Pearson wrote Norton a long and impassioned letter
in condemnation of Smith's undemocratic arguments, in particular,
"the time-worn ones that have been employed in England dozens of
times to defend rotten boroughs, or [to oppose] the giving of votes to
artisans":

> How are women to be anything but illiberal and narrow when they
> are shut out from all political activity, except in the most dangerous
> form of all, power without responsibility, the influence exercised over
> the men of their families? And how are men to legislate properly for
> a class whose point of view they never quite understand. As . . .
> legislation by men has meant hitherto in England that the wife has
> no right over her property nor the mother over her children; that
> prostitution and the gang system are comparatively uncared for; that
> men monopolize the endowment of education and exclude women
> from the professions.[100]

As it happened, Goldwin Smith's misogynist rantings against women
and his opposition to female enfranchisement had forced his early departure from Cornell and his move across the border to take up residence in Canada.

At Harvard, Norton was preparing to take up the positions of lecturer, then founding professor in fine arts, enticed to join the expanding
faculty by his cousin, the energetic and reforming university president
Charles W. Eliot. The new position enabled him to immerse himself
ever more deeply in the European past, as he lamented the dearth of

an aesthetic sensibility in contemporary America. Not only were the friends now separated by continents and oceans, but their political orientation to the world had begun to diverge dramatically. Norton lived the life of a fine arts scholar, nostalgic for the Gothic glories of Europe. Pearson, the erstwhile historian of the Middle Ages, was now engaged by the urgent challenges of the present. Some "interesting questions in politics are cropping up," he wrote to Norton from his new home in Melbourne.[101]

As a journalist and member of the legislative assembly and minister for public instruction in the Victorian government, Pearson dedicated himself to bringing into being a progressive democracy, inspired by but hopefully surpassing in moral tone that which he had admired in the United States. In Australia he would promote the intervention of the state to bring social justice and equal opportunity to ordinary men and women. The disillusioned Englishman sought to abolish demeaning class distinctions in the new society he was helping to build in Australia. It was unmanly, he exhorted parliament, to deny the equality and equal citizenship of one's fellow countrymen.[102] And in making the case for land reform, he urged: "If there is one vested interest in the country which has to be respected it is the vested interest of labour—the interest of the hard-working man."[103]

Seeking an American audience for his ideas, Pearson published a series of articles on Australian politics in the *Nation*. He wanted to present the peculiarities of colonial self-government to former British colonists who knew British traditions but had rejected them in favor of republican institutions. He pointed with pride to the popularity of free, compulsory, and secular education in Victoria and argued the necessity for a progressive land tax that would prevent the aggregation of large estates in few hands. And with the experience of California in mind, he drew the attention of the *Nation*'s readers to the recent arrival of Chinese "coolie labourers" in the tropical north of Australia and the threat posed by contract labor to an egalitarian high-wage democracy. In 1881, he became an enthusiastic supporter of new immigration-restriction legislation aimed at the Chinese and an amendment disenfranchising Chinese men, who from the 1850s had enjoyed manhood suffrage in Victoria. The passage of the legislation, he told parliament, gave him the "greatest satisfaction."[104]

As cabinet minister during the 1880s, Pearson devoted himself to securing reforms in land taxation, education, and divorce; making public art galleries and museums more accessible; and ending discrimination against women. He contributed to building the collections of the public library and ended the ban on Sunday openings of the library and national gallery. The government of which he was a part extended generous support to agricultural and manufacturing industries and built infrastructure and railways. The democracy was the product of manhood suffrage, and despite the obstruction of the property-based legislative council, the conservative upper house, the government sought to cater to popular demands. Pearson looked forward to the time, he told Norton, when "the democracy sweeps all barriers to the moment's need away."[105]

In 1884, the year of Britain's Third Reform Act, he reminded fellow colonists that in Britain there was still one class "not represented in the House of Commons, and that is the great working class." Even with the passage of the legislation, 40 percent of men were left without a vote. In debate on a proposal to abolish plural voting for the legislative council, Pearson observed: "There was one other thing that astonished him on the part of the Legislative Council, and that was their want of manliness, their want of regard for their fellow-countrymen."[106] Their lack of manliness in failing to recognize workingmen as equal fellow citizens—their want of fellow feeling—undermined the ideal of democracy.

As a minister in the Victorian government, Pearson joined an experiment in "state socialism," as he would describe it in *National Life and Character*, that protected working men and women from the excesses of market capitalism, landlords, exploitation by "slave-driving" employers, and the degradation of unemployment and penury in old age. The operation of the market had to be subordinated to the democratic state, which put the welfare of citizens before the sanctity of contract and the rights of property. Railways and utilities were in public hands. The state had extended its reach, and government services were rapidly expanding.[107]

Such experiments had been able to proceed more readily in a "new country," Pearson told readers of the English *Speaker*, invoking the familiar binary, but the "Old World" could profitably make a study of their progress. "England, surely, is not the worse for being able to study the effects of manhood suffrage, vote by [secret] ballot, secular and free education . . . among a people half of whom were born under the shadow of the English Church and aristocracy."[108] The political experiments adopted by the self-governing colonies "deserve attention as an indication of what we may expect in the future." This was surely the way of progress.

In Australia, "State Socialism had succeeded," he argued, "because it [was] all-embracing." Superior to European models of social or work-based insurance, it had been developed by the community for their own needs, not imposed from on high.[109] Democracy made it possible for the state to become an effective agent of the community rather than an instrument of the privileged classes. Or as visiting American journalist Henry Demarest Lloyd put it at the end of the decade, "In a democracy, in self-government, state-help is self-help."[110]

A progressive new nation was coming into existence in the south seas. When Pearson taught at the University of Melbourne, he had expressed his delight in the bright students he encountered there, some of whom he invited to join a Debating Society modeled on the Oxford Union. Two of those students, Alfred Deakin and H. B. Higgins, future national leaders, who would become key figures in translating the progressive ideals of equality of opportunity and the common good into institutional realities in the new Commonwealth of Australia and taking them to the wider world.

On the publication of his magnum opus *National Life and Character* in 1893, Pearson wrote from London to tell Deakin of its "unexpected but . . . real success. . . . It has altogether been reviewed in some thirty papers." One of his American reviewers was Theodore Roosevelt, who also wrote personally to tell Pearson about the impact of his book among his circle in Washington: "I wish we could see you some time on this side of the water. There are many of us who would like to have the pleasure of telling you in person of the enjoyment which we owe to reading your book."[111] To English diplomat Cecil Spring Rice, who was fretting about the decline of the empire and future of India, Roosevelt enthused, "The Australians are building up a giant commonwealth, the very existence of which, like the existence of the United States, means an alteration in the balance of the world and goes a long way towards ensuring the supremacy of the men who speak our tongue and have our ideas of social, political and religious freedom and morality."[112]

Roosevelt would later become a convert to the Australian example of "state socialism," advocating the eight-hour day, a minimum wage, workers' compensation, mothers' pensions, and woman suffrage. What impressed Roosevelt most about Pearson's account of the world in 1893, however, were his figures on comparative birth rates, his startling claim regarding the rise of "the black and yellow races," and China's inevitable ascendancy as one of "the great powers of the world." While European populations were reaching a stationary state, the "teeming population of China" was expanding and spreading across the globe. Pearson's book alerted Roosevelt to these "world-forces of the present."[113]

From this time we can date Roosevelt's so-called imperial turn, but it would be wrong to see it as a new departure. Roosevelt was more aware than most that the American career of "colonizing conquest" had begun much earlier—that imperial ambition was inherent to settler colonialism—but in the mid-1890s, overseas expansion and military adventure abroad beckoned. Sadly for Pearson, who craved worldly recognition, he didn't get to read Roosevelt's warm letter or his favorable review, as he died suddenly in London, succumbing to a chest infection in early 1894. It would be left to his protégés, Alfred Deakin and H. B. Higgins, to translate his vision of an activist state into the newly federated nation-state inaugurated in 1901.

CHAPTER TWO

An Expansive State with Socialistic Tendencies

"WHAT SOCIALISTS you all are!" exclaimed the Harvard philosopher Josiah Royce to Australian Liberal leader Alfred Deakin as they rambled in the Blue Mountains in June 1888. "More government, then, not less, is your ideal. . . . Would you have the State do everything for the people?"[1] With popular sovereignty rampant, might not even labor agitators become a power in colonial legislatures? Royce inquired. The young Victorian chief secretary replied in an equally spirited manner that Australian labor organizations were already doing much to settle modern labor questions. They had established, for example, that trade unions "must exist" to represent workers, help achieve "fair dealing on a fair basis," and advance social welfare more generally. They had already won the eight-hour day and progressive factory legislation. In any case, "why should not the people organize for their own good, and make laws to that effect?"[2]

To other hikers along these muddy bush tracks, Deakin and Royce must have appeared a striking couple. Deakin was tall, dark, and handsome, Royce short, stout, red haired, and ruddy in complexion. But their animation would also have attracted the attention of fellow walkers. Both avid conversationalists, they were intellectually curious and forthright in their views. Royce was struck by Deakin's "frank and intelligent confidence in the power of the State to do a great deal for its subject." Importantly for Royce, Deakin's confidence was based on "practical experience." He was "a busy politician," proud of extending state railways, providing assistance to industry, and investing in public works as well as state libraries and museums.[3]

From 1883, Deakin had served as minister for public works and water supply and then as chief secretary in the Victorian government, working alongside his mentor, Charles Pearson, minister of public instruction. When Royce first arrived in Melbourne, bearing a letter of introduction from their mutual friend Richard Hodgson, who worked with William James at the Center for Psychical Research in Cambridge, Deakin, as chief secretary, was preoccupied with the challenge of Chinese immigration. An intercolonial conference on the subject was being planned for Sydney when Royce arrived in Melbourne.

After departing Australia at the end of June, Royce subscribed to the *Age*'s weekly publication, the *Leader*, and read Deakin's 1888 budget speech, outlining the extent of state provision to Victorian people. He was astonished, as he reported in the first of two articles in the *Atlantic Monthly*, by the range of services demanded and provided: bonuses for farmers' products, a proposition to establish a refrigerating depot, a new freight system for the purpose of bringing about new commercial relations for Victorian agriculturalists abroad.[4] He was also impressed by the collectivist approach to social welfare institutionalized by the government.

Whereas early American leaders, Royce noted, fearing the despotism of European tyrants, had emphasized individual liberty, Australian leaders focused on building "some new social tie" that would bind people together. Royce was impressed by this new direction in progressive politics. "After all," he pondered, were not "social ties the glory of rational human life?" Australian reformers were treading new paths. "At this rate," Royce concluded, in a third article on his "Impressions of Australia" written for *Scribner's* magazine, "before another century Australia will show us some of the most remarkable experiments in State Socialism that have ever yet been seen."[5]

The Harvard philosopher considered that Americans had much to learn from the experience of their "southern fellow-countrymen." For Australia—with its "relations to Asia, its important position in the Pacific, its vast resources, and its social progressiveness"—was assured "a significant place in the future tale of civilization."[6] Social progressiveness and empire building were not antithetical projects. An active state was an expansive state, and Royce and Deakin both considered Australian "progressiveness" the best qualification for its future role as a Pacific power. In extending settler colonial governance to dispersed groups of islanders, modern empire was understood as a progressive force.

This chapter begins with the conversations between the American philosopher and Australian political leader to explore the ways in which transpacific exchange built on shared settler colonial ambition as well as common political ideals. Deakin, "a young man, nervously active in temperament, cheerful, inquiring, speculative, [and] unprejudiced," was the sort of man, Royce observed fondly, who would "some day make Australia an empire."[7] He looked forward to the time when "our future sister republic" would become a "co-worker in the cause of free civilization" in a shared oceanic neighborhood.[8] Together, white progressives would govern an island empire.

Deakin's dreams as a colonial Liberal leader had long included an imperial role in the Pacific. He was especially pleased that the Australian constitution allocated power to the new federal government over "relations with the islands of the Pacific," despite the fact that Britain still retained authority over Australia's international relations more generally, laying the basis for future conflict, which would soon eventuate.[9] With the inauguration of a federated Australia, the nation would emerge, Deakin predicted, as "a great power, without peer or rival in the southern seas."[10] With its assertion of control over the former British colony of New Guinea, renamed Papua, the new Commonwealth of Australia would extend its reach as a colonizing state.[11]

Settler colonialism rested on and fired imperial ambition. As Theodore Roosevelt made clear, the white man's right to self-government also presumed a right to govern others, such as the peoples of the Philippines, "half-caste and native Christians, warlike Moslems and wild pagans." Most of these people he considered "utterly unfit for self-government, and show no signs of becoming fit. . . . Others may in time become fit, but at present can only take part in self-government under a wise supervision, at once firm and beneficent."[12] Progressive white men had to take up the burden of beneficent supervision through modern techniques of administration, training, education, and surveillance.[13]

Deakin's first voyage into the Pacific Ocean occurred at the age of twenty-two, when he traveled to Fiji as personal secretary to Sidney Watson, an elderly Victorian station owner with investments in the islands. By the late nineteenth century, a growing number of Australians saw new opportunities for trade, business investment, labor recruitment, and missionary work in Fiji.[14] The Melbourne Polynesia Company, casting itself as the "East India Company of the Pacific," investigated the possibility of new investments in sugar, coffee, and cotton, the last commodity in short supply since the American Civil War.

Private individuals began to settle in the islands. By 1871, the white population of Fiji had reached 2,760, and there was pressure on colonial governments to provide security for settlers. Perhaps Australians could assume this responsibility. "Since England can rule India," opined Melbourne's radical *Age* newspaper, "why should not Victoria make the experiment of trying to govern Fiji?"[15] Charles Pearson had often noted that Victoria liked to see itself as more progressive, energetic, and ambitious than other Australian colonies, more like New Englanders. Victoria was also the most "empire-minded" of the colonies. Victorian schoolchildren were routinely provided with maps that charted rival European imperial incursions into the Pacific Ocean to alert them to possible threats and future competitors.[16]

In the end, Britain established a Western Pacific High Commission in Fiji in 1877. Soon after, the Australian Colonial Sugar Refining Company (CSR) began operations there, at first employing locals but increasingly importing indentured Indian labor that made possible the rapid growth of a powerful monopoly. In the northern Australian colony of Queensland, the owners of sugar cane plantations also recruited (or kidnapped) contract workers from diverse Pacific island groups—including the New Hebrides, the Solomons, and New Guinea—in a violent trade that produced a high death rate among "Kanaka" workers.[17] This traffic in labor in northern Australia was roundly condemned by Liberal politicians and journalists in the south, especially in progressive Victoria. Charles Pearson, H. B. Higgins, Alfred Deakin, and G. E. Morrison—a doctor, journalist, and brother-in-law of Higgins, who investigated the labor trade for the southern press—were all vocal critics.

On their trip to Fiji, Deakin and Watson stayed in the old capital, Levuka, where the young adventurer wrote to his sister, Catherine, about the delights of the private members' club in which they were guests—balmy evenings spent relaxing on the verandah—and appraised the character of British officials. Governor Arthur Hamilton

Gordon was a man of "strong original autocratic character." The natives also made a favorable impression. A "remarkably fine race," Deakin reported.[18] He marveled at the lush vegetation—"fruits and flowers too numerous to recall"—and the rich productive soils. Although British officials prided themselves on "keeping their tables to the English style," Deakin was keen to taste local produce, sampling sweet potato, yam, breadfruit, bananas, and pineapples.[19]

Perhaps, he mused, his father should invest there. "I am half inclined to come myself," he told Catherine. "What is wanted is capital though large sums are needed to get quick returns—the climate is delicious the soil very rich and the natives very peaceful, but everything is unsettled at present owing to the land question."[20] Unlike in the settler colonies of Australasia, freehold access to land was restricted. Though a political autocrat, Gordon was a progressive colonialist, who determined that indigenous rights in land must be protected as much as possible. Purchase by foreigners was limited. Denied self-government, Fijians were governed through a system of indirect rule based on traditional indigenous rank. Most land obtained by the small minority of Europeans was held on a leasehold basis.

A few years later, Deakin journeyed into the Pacific again, crossing the ocean to California in his capacity as chairman of a royal commission appointed to investigate American irrigation schemes. First elected to parliament at just twenty-two years of age, Deakin was soon appointed minister for public works and water supply in the Victorian government. The "ideal" of irrigation, a technology that would enable agriculture to flourish in an arid country, was dear to his heart. In 1883, Deakin passed the Water Conservation Act, which copied "almost entirely" a "proposal for the creation of irrigation districts in California then pending before the state legislature in Sacramento."[21] In contrast with California, however, irrigation in Victoria would become a field for state enterprise and government investment—an idea that would quickly attract American attention, including, as we shall see, that of a young PhD student at the University of Wisconsin, working with economist Richard Ely on research into Australia's state economic experiments.

On his voyage to California, at the end of 1884, Deakin was accompanied by his wife, Pattie, and their young daughter, as well as by fellow member of the legislative assembly John L. Dow and engineer J. D. Derry. The ship's first port of call was Auckland, then the island of Tutuilla (where "crowds of natives swarmed around the ship in canoes loaded with fruit"), and on to Honolulu, in the still independent kingdom of Hawaii. Although their schedule permitted just a three-hour stopover, the young politician and his party managed a considerable amount of sightseeing in this exotic paradise, whose lush tropical vegetation stirred fond memories of Fiji.

Deakin's diaries suggest how formative were his travels and encounters with foreign peoples and places in consolidating his sense of self as a progressive Anglo-Saxon. Like Fiji, Hawaii comprised a number of islands, but there was a greater history of migration and mix of cultures and peoples. On arrival in the port of Honolulu, the party was keen to get ashore. Feeling "cabined, cribbed, confined and nauseated" by shipboard life, Deakin was first to jump onto the wharf, "crowded with people most of dusky skin." The local men and women, whom he described in terms of popular racial typologies, had "good eyes, but no especial beauty," at best "swarthy often flat-nosed Italian in type."[22] Flat noses were indicative for Deakin of racial "otherness."

His party hired a trap to take them up the "furrowed slopes" of the famous "pali," perhaps paying too much, Deakin reflected, for the convenience. They passed through the "European quarter," the "Chinese quarter," and then the "native quarter or suburbs," where gorgeous tropical vegetation—"cocoa-nut palms, and bananas, brilliant creepers and ferns"—grew over fine wooden villas and shops. "Sparkling streams of water cross the road—a plain stone chapel is the Mausoleum where lie the ashes of Hawaiian Kings." Deakin made an estimate of the racial composition of the population—Europeans "only about 2000," "Chinese (I should guess) 10,000," and "Hawaiians 6,000"—and noted the intense commercial activity of the Chinese, with buyers and sellers at every turn.[23]

Historians have estimated that in the mid-1880s, some eight thousand Chinese lived in Honolulu's Chinatown, largely a cluster of bachelor quarters together with a full range of restaurants, theaters, bars, tearooms, bakeries, pharmacies, slaughterhouses, warehouses, and factories, all open seven days a week. Men usually lived in the houses in which they worked, packed into second-floor attics or backyard sheds. The fortunate slept on verandahs.[24] Most of the structures were built out of timber, which fueled a terrifying fire a year after Deakin's visit that destroyed the original Chinatown. The chief lesson Deakin took from his stop in Honolulu was the commercial impact of dynamic Chinese populations settling across the Pacific.[25]

When they finally arrived in the "great city" of San Francisco, on a Sunday night in the middle of the northern winter, the Australian party saw a bustling metropolis lit up by gas and electric light. It seemed "busier and brighter than Melbourne," shops, hotels, and even grocers in "full living as usual," noted Deakin, and there were "second rate theatres to one of which we males went after dinner. I left after the first act."[26] Deakin was an avid theatergoer throughout his American tour, seeing shows in New York, Boston, Washington, and Nevada, and excellent performances by Edwin Booth, John Barrow, Wilson Barrett, and Ellen Terry. He was also a keen student of American men and women in daily life, attentive to their self-fashioning, bearing, girth, and dress. He thought the women in San Francisco were overdressed and overweight—and almost all were painted—but he was attracted by the men, fine types of American manhood. "The men dress well and nearly all shave," he noted. "Chief distinguishing feature the brightness of the eyes and quiet assurance which seem to say American."[27]

Everywhere modern architecture soared above the visitors. In San Francisco, they noted the omnipresence of two-story private residences, Swiss, Elizabethan, and Gothic in style, all timber built. "We have no idea in Melbourne what wood is capable of," Deakin observed of the building material that would again fuel an urban inferno after the earthquake in 1906. Like many visitors to San Francisco in the late nineteenth century, Deakin was astonished by the opulence of the hotels—"the finest buildings in the city"—all mirrors, carpets, chandeliers, and ornamented ceilings, their dining tables stacked with a fine variety of food. The Palace Hotel was seven stories high. The Baldwin, in which the Deakin family took up temporary residence, rose five stories. "Government House [in Melbourne] was small by comparison."[28]

Hotel guests were served by black waiters, whom Deakin considered "attentive but slow." San Francisco had the largest black population on the West Coast, and many found work in hotels and restaurants until the Cooks' and Waiters' Union pushed them out.[29] Of the nonwhite population, however, African Americans were vastly outnumbered by the Chinese, but Deakin appears not to have visited the famous Chinatown. He was, after all, on a business trip and had appointments with state officials in Sacramento.

There they were cordially received by Democratic governor George Stoneman, a former Union cavalry officer in the Civil War, who became an opponent of Radical Reconstruction in Virginia and an Indian fighter in Arizona. Stoneman introduced the Australian party to the state engineer, "a typical American," according to John Dow, "in his great courtesy and kindness to visitors."[30] Expert on every detail of irrigation works in India and Italy as well as in the United States, he supplied them with reams of information.

On February 6, Deakin and his male companions (Pattie and their daughter remained in San Francisco) journeyed south to Los Angeles to check out the legendary orange groves—"irrigated orange groves in every direction. Oranges! Everywhere oranges!"[31] In the settlement "colonies" of Pasadena and San Gabriel, Deakin noted, "the desert had been made to blossom like the rose." In Ontario, he met George Chaffey, a Canadian who, with his brother, W. B. Chaffey, had developed the famous irrigation settlement in the arid zone forty miles to the east. These meetings prepared the way for the Chaffeys to come to Victoria to establish state-subsidized irrigation systems on the Murray River.

In Los Angeles, Deakin was delighted to find a new city taking shape. California had been seized from Mexico by military "conquest," as Royce would note in his history of *California*. Nowhere else, he reflected, "were we Americans more affected than here, in our lives and conduct, by the feeling that we stood in the position of conquerors in a new land."[32] Royce referred to the conquest of Mexicans, not the defeat and massacre of local Indian tribes, who were all but absent from his history. In the new western state, Deakin encountered a mixed population, a "queer jumble of races and nationalities, English, American, French, German, Negroes, Mexicans, Chinese and half breeds," but was pleased to see a fine new Anglo-Saxon town with modern buildings, wide streets, and electric light "elbowing away the low adobe houses of the Mexicans."

In his report for the *Age,* Dow described Los Angeles as a mixture of modern American enterprise and ancient Mexican lassitude: "The shawl-draped, wide-sombreroed Mexican, as he slouches along, is elbowed by the bustling Yankee, while gorgeous blocks of business buildings are rising from among the 'doby' huts of the early settlers and of the Chinese, who here, as everywhere else in America 'hang out their shingle' proclaiming that 'Ah Sin washee well good.'"[33] In 1881, Australian colonies had introduced new immigration restrictions aimed at curbing the entry of Chinese. The following year, the United States government succumbed to Californian pressure by passing the Chinese Exclusion Act.

The Australian party traveled on to San Bernardino, a "Mexican settlement turned Yankee," but there were still "plenty of Mexicans" in view, "with their dark skins and strange dress." In Arizona, Deakin encountered Indian villages with "houses like caves and covered with earth. Only possible to crawl into them and not possible for me to stand in the centre." The men wore blue broad trousers and shirts that were often red. They looked exotic: "Long black hair. Copper skin and flat noses." The local Indians were impressive in their distinctive American way: "rough fellows but of the fine manly type." In Phoenix, the party inspected the Arizona Canal and collected more agricultural and statistical information. They took the train to El Paso, where they again surveyed irrigation works and changed money before entering Mexico on February 16.[34]

They crossed the Rio Grande ("not the great stream its name implies"—"no wider than the Yarra near its mouth") into Mexico. "By going so far south we have reached the East," Deakin mused in his diary. Mexico called up "Bible pictures" of the Middle East:

> The brilliant dress colours, the absence of head dress, the enveloping gaudy cloak. But for the cut of the clothing one could believe oneself in Palestine. The cloudless sky, the burned brown earth and treeless hills. The flat brown box buildings, the color of swallows nests. And of the same material. The wide stretching plain almost without verdure. . . . The wooden plough used in Egypt 2000 years ago and here as in Syria today.[35]

Even the church towers were like the minarets of a mosque.

In his Orientalist musings, Deakin saw in Mexico "the mystery of the East." Its history was elusive and seemed to confound the binaries of "civilized" and "savage":

> It has seen several civilizations but whence they rose and fell is an impenetrable mystery. The strange and startling character of its catastrophes together with the imperfection of its records render its appeals to the imagination constant and irresistible. . . . Its history is of peoples who were at once civilized and savage, amiable and bloody, it presents all the contrasts of all the zones of the physical world in immediate contiguity and . . . displays at every turn the 15th and 19th centuries side by side as are also side by side the splendour and squalor of the East. Its people today seem to live in a dream of a future that may prove to be baseless as a dream.[36]

Their dream of a future would surely prove to be baseless, because Mexico was "as entirely Spanish as Madrid or Seville and as utterly remote from everything Anglo-Saxon" as could be imagined. Its Spanish character couldn't last, because the social and political results were, to the progressive Australian mind, everywhere oppressive.

In this Spanish New World, there seemed to be little freedom, justice, or moral progress. To Deakin's mind, the Mexicans were not an advanced people. A visit to a bullfight disgusted him. "The whole exhibition was barbarous, brutal and bloody. . . . I have seen one bull fight. I never wish to see another. All this too on a Sunday under a cloudless sky and with women and children looking on. My faith in humanity was badly shaken that day. The dresses were brilliant but the moral atmosphere was black as hell."[37]

It was only Anglo-Saxons, in Deakin's view, who were blessed with the moral capacity for self-government, democracy, and equality.

> Mexico is a military despotism, its democracy is a farce. No-one votes and no-one is really elected. The poor are many and they are miserably poor, the few, the very few, have a feudal dominion over them such as exists in Russia. It is doubtful if the people will be able to do much for themselves until the Anglo-Saxon invasion comes. This may not be for a century but come it must.

The American conquest of California would surely be extended south, but when white men ruled the land, they would be confronted with a challenge in incorporating the Mexican population, who were untrained for democracy. "The problem of how to deal with the Mexican," Deakin observed, "will be something like the problem of what to do with the Negro was after the war—the Civil War."

The problem thought to be posed by millions of freed African Americans to American democracy would haunt Deakin and fellow Australian nation builders as it also troubled and confounded progressives in the United States, who endorsed policies of segregation, separate schooling, and voting restrictions. The chief lesson imbibed by Australian nation builders contemplating American history in the aftermath of the Civil War and Radical Reconstruction was the seeming impossibility of multiracial democracy. Deakin's encounter with Mexico—like Charles Norton's with the Vatican in Rome—confirmed his pride in his identity as a progressive New World democrat and deepened his disdain for foreigners.

From Mexico, the Australian party traveled east via Las Vegas, snug in a Pullman car while outside the January weather was biting cold. They inspected more irrigation works, visited Garden City, and went on to Kansas City. Deakin pondered the violence that accompanied the disappearance of local Indians, casting them, as had Pearson, not as the victims of colonial violence but as the perpetrators of atrocities on white men. "Fifteen years ago this was wild waste where massacres by the Indians were of regular occurrence. Since Las Vegas we have been keeping along the track of the old Santa Fey every mile of which has been reddened with blood."[38] But that was in the past. By 1885, "the reign of the Indian [was] over and . . . left no trace, but it was a reign of only yesterday." The narrative of the "vanishing Indian" was the ubiquitous corollary of the story of "American progress," on show in the new regional cities of Los Angeles, Cleveland, Buffalo, Denver, and Chicago.

In the older cities on the East Coast, the Australians saw "incalculable wealth and enormous population." Deakin, again like Pearson, was drawn to the literary and historic heritage of Boston in New England. He set out on a pilgrimage to Emerson's grave—"the main end of my visit." In his haste, he took the wrong train to the wrong Concord and ended up in New Hampshire. ("Only the thought of Emerson enables me to bear up against this blow, the first lost day of the whole trip.")

In Boston, he plotted his own freedom trail, visiting the sites of the revolution: the Bunker Hill monument; Faneuil Hall, "in which so many great speeches have been made" but only "the size of the Athenaeum squared"; the Liberty Tree on Boston Common; Christ Church in Salem Street. Boston impressed him as a "very handsome clean town of great extent[,] magnificent harbor & the same great buildings that decorate New York and Chicago." Women struck him as "more ladylike & being prettier than any" he had seen, and he liked the bookstores. Altogether, he concluded, it was "a very fine & remarkably interesting city of many historic memories."[39] With his detailed attention to colonial landmarks, it was clear that the Australian Liberal leader had made these historic memories his own.

Deakin rejoined his traveling party in New York and took the train to Washington, DC, where President Cleveland had recently delivered his presidential address, reaffirming the Monroe Doctrine, the equality of all freed men, and the desirability of Chinese exclusion.[40] Finally, the travelers returned to San Francisco, where Deakin was reunited with his wife and child.

Back in Melbourne in April 1885, he published his report, *Irrigation in Western America so far as it has relation to the circumstances in Victoria*, as a memorandum from the Royal Commission on Water Supply, which read, as Ian Tyrrell notes, as "a hymn of praise" to "the energy and self-reliance of American people." He stressed the racial, social, and geographical affinities between Australia and the United States. The "mainstay of our confidence," he argued, "must be experience in Western America—a new country like our own, with labor as dear as it is here, and markets in many places as difficult to reach."[41] As settler societies, Australia and the United States promoted land settlement and economic development as a basis for white men's wages and a high standard of living.

There were, nevertheless, important differences between the countries—historical, demographic, economic, and ideological—that led the state to play a more active and expansive role in Australia. Australian economic development in this period was fueled by government investment as states became major entrepreneurs and employers of labor.[42] Policies of "free selection" and "closer settlement" encouraged rapid farming on land only recently home to Aboriginal communities. During the 1880s, the area of land cultivated in Victoria grew by nearly one-half as local clans fought to retain control of their dwindling reserves.[43] Some Aboriginal men forced off reserves took up work on nearby properties as laborers or shearers, while a few who remained tried to farm on their own account. One Aboriginal resident of the Framlingham reserve told visiting Chief Secretary Deakin that "they only wanted enough land to live quietly and comfortably."[44]

In 1886, Deakin passed the Aborigines' Protection Act—to promote the merging of Aboriginal communities into the wider society, where they might become "useful citizens"—and the Water Supply and Irrigation Act, to facilitate white land settlement on lands once home to Aborigines. The two measures should be understood in the same analytical frame. The state was active on a number of fronts. To increase water supply for irrigation, legislation allocated a central role to the state in raising money for the construction of large-scale dams and reservoirs. It sometimes built on existing local initiatives, providing for "national" works undertaken by the government. The Act also asserted total ownership and control by the community of all natural waters and, unlike California, insisted on state planning of priorities.[45]

News of extensive state assistance to irrigation development in Australia soon traveled across the Pacific and became the focus of University of Wisconsin PhD student Helen Page Bates, who completed her doctoral dissertation under the supervision of progressive economist Richard Ely in 1896.[46] Later celebrated as the first woman in the United States to write a doctoral dissertation in economics, Bates was one of a cadre of young, socially committed economists gathered around Ely at Wisconsin, joined by a conviction that state regulation and public ownership were imperative to curb the concentration and cupidity of private capital.[47] Unlike many of her male fellow graduates, however, Bates was never able to win an academic job, having to make do with a series of part-time and casual jobs as teaching assistant, settlement worker, and librarian, denied the prestige and salary that would match her qualifications. She was also reduced in her mobility by her responsibility to care for and support her aging mother. "I feel dazed and brainless," she wrote in despair to Ely in 1902. "The last twelve years have been such a struggle. I am weary almost to death."[48]

Bates's academic work deserves recognition not just as a milestone in women's higher education but also as an example of transpacific intellectual exchange and policy advocacy that helped give currency in the United States to the idea of the active state as an instrument to promote social justice and equal opportunity. Assisted by US consuls in Melbourne and Sydney, Bates's doctoral research project drew general lessons about "Australian Experiments in Industry," which she laid out in the *Annals of the American Academy of Political and Social Science* in 1898. Throughout Australia, she observed, "the principle of state activity [was] well grounded and its efficacy unquestioned."[49] Her attempts to transform her dissertation into a book were discouraged, however, by Henry Demarest Lloyd, among others, keen to publicize his own investigations of Australasian state experiments in his upcoming volume, *Newest England*.[50]

Bates's PhD research was also significant as an early example of the kind of work that later characterized the "Wisconsin experiment"—encouraging university researchers to produce useful work focused on public policy challenges. "The university is the state research laboratory," wrote Frederic C. Howe in *Wisconsin: An Experiment in Democracy* in 1912. "Graduate students investigate pending questions, while the seminars in economics, politics and sociology are utilized for the exhaustive study of state problems." In the joint projects, undertaken by researchers in alliance with the state, "the political progress of the world" was recorded; from that came "a new chemical compound in the form of progressive legislation" that "made Wisconsin so widely known as a pioneer." The Wisconsin experiment "demonstrated," according to Howe in words that echo Deakin's, "the possibility of using the state as an instrument for the well-being of all the people."[51] Just as Australia and New Zealand were "types of industrial and social democracy," noted Howe, "so Wisconsin is building a commonwealth. . . . It is becoming an experiment station for America."[52]

Bates had alerted Wisconsin to Australian precedent in the 1890s in her PhD dissertation, supervised by Ely. Like Royce writing in *Atlantic Monthly* and *Scribner's*, Bates emphasized the novelty of political and economic developments in Australia. There governments "began to take to themselves many new and extensive functions never previously exercised by the state." Something unprecedented was happening in the burgeoning commonwealth of the South Seas. There was no "imitation of any other nation." It was doubtful if there were any other country "which they could have patterned themselves after at that time—any state that had taken to itself such powers as they had now assumed."[53] Roads, railroads, telegraph, and postal services were all under state control.

In addition to providing "general assistance to industry," Bates noted, "Australian governments [were] offering special aid to special industries": gold mining, fruit growing, sugar, wine, timber, and dairying. But there was a broader purpose. In her essay, on "Australian Experiments" the young Wisconsin scholar also praised the role of the state in securing "equality of opportunity":

> The munificent efforts of the state to socialize its public libraries and art treasures, to secure to each municipality large park reserves:—the liberal appropriations for the care of its state children, the public pawn shops,—the government life insurance,—the relief works for the unemployed,—the extreme activity of the state in labor legislation,—and the aggressive steps already taken in taxation reforms,—all measures aiming at a great equality of opportunity for the colonists.[54]

Howe made similar claims for the Wisconsin experiment in his later book: "Equal opportunity for all rather than special privileges for the few, became the motive of legislation."

Bates's surprise at the "munificent efforts of the state" in Australia echoed Royce's astonishment at Australian "state socialism" a few years earlier.[55] The elaborate "social organization of the colonies," Royce had written, "in view of their tender age, their complete independence of external political interference, and their purely democratic constitutions" was a "most remarkable fact."[56] But his curiosity about the burgeoning commonwealth—and its place in the world—ranged more broadly.

In his conversations with Deakin in 1888, Royce learned about the chief secretary's recent overseas trips to the United States and Britain, travel that had strengthened the Australian Liberal leader's commitment to shaping a new progressive nation "free of external political interference." On hearing of Deakin's trip to the United States and his personal pilgrimage to Emerson's grave, Royce urged his friend to reconsider his admiration for the American apostle of individualism, a creed he memorably critiqued as the "philosophy of the sacredness of broken ties." Individualism was surely inappropriate for an Australian dedicated to the cause of nation building. Rather, it was Deakin's historic task, Royce suggested in a letter the following year, to "increase the ties that bind."[57] Deakin agreed, resolving to devote himself to the "sacred cause" of federation, giving to it, he told Royce, "as much of my time as possible."[58]

Deakin's commitment to nation building had been given new focus and force when he traveled to London as Victorian representative to the first Colonial Conference in 1887. While there, he famously challenged the prime minister, Lord Salisbury, over Australia's interest in the future of the New Hebrides, threatened by French imperial claims. In later reports, Deakin cast this conflict as a defining episode in the Australian struggle against British imperial power. The prime minister, Deakin recalled, "breathed the aristocratic condescension of a Minister addressing a deputation of visitors from the antipodes whom it became his duty to instruct in current foreign politics for their own sakes."[59] While the New South Wales delegates responded, Deakin said, in "bated breath and whispering humbleness," vying with one another in "congratulations, felicitations and glorifications," the Victorian representative spoke, by his own account, like a man, "with unrestrained vigour and enthusiasm."[60]

Echoing the cadence and vocabulary of American revolutionary rhetoric, Deakin declared that "the people of Victoria would never consent to any cession of the islands on any terms and that the Australian-born who had made this question their own would forever resent the humiliation of a surrender which would immensely weaken their confidence in an Empire to which hitherto they had been proud to belong."[61] In his private notes, Deakin observed that "this was a question of sentiment with all the colonies & particularly with the native [born] Australians."[62] He considered his speech a triumph and was widely congratulated on it. ("Sir [Henry] Holland was pleased and [James] Service says he [Holland] has fallen in love with me as other elders have done.")[63] The main lesson Deakin took home was that the Australian colonies needed to speak as one. In union lay power.

Personal encounters with British aristocrats left Deakin unimpressed. Surrounded by dukes, duchesses, and liveried footmen, in a society fawning on rank, status, and "ridiculous" titles, Deakin's hostility echoed Charles Eliot Norton's strictures on British "flunkeyism" and Theodore Roosevelt's declared "anti-Anglomania."[64] Also visiting London in 1887, Roosevelt considered that it was only his attitude of "utter indifference and our standing sharply on our dignity," as he was pleased to tell his friend Henry Cabot Lodge, that made his British hosts so friendly.[65] English flattery and good manners didn't always win guests over, however. To a sensitive colonial subject, courtesy could seem like condescension.

Deakin found British intellectual and political leaders to be lacking in manhood. Charles Dilke had "less energy & force of character than I had hoped" (they would later become good friends); Lord Rosebery was "affected & selfish"; Sir Henry Holland was "very chatty and bright . . . but not a great power"; Sir George Trevelyan was "a light weight all round"; Lord Granville spoke with "an aristocratic lisp"; Balfour was "young foppish unprepossessing in appearance, egotistical & without oratorical grace"; Professor Seeley "a disappointing man to look at . . . pimply & florid with heavy features & expression & a shuffling walk." He filled his time complaining that his *Expansion of England* had sold poorly in the colonies.[66] Even the female monarch was disappointing: "shorter & stouter than I had supposed, no taller than Katie" (Deakin's sister).[67] Unlike some Australian delegates, Deakin refused all British titles and honors. Back home, the *Age* newspaper applauded his independent stance. "It is well that Downing-Street should know that there are politicians in the colony who cannot be bribed by a paltry decoration."[68]

Out on the English streets, Deakin observed ordinary people who lived impoverished lives. Young men were short, and young women bunchy. Old women were stout, and old men portly. Their children were rendered wretched by poverty, vulgarity, and darkness. Again his descriptions echoed Norton's denunciations of the "poverty of England." The Old World was dour and gloomy. Historic tradition was neither heroic nor uplifting. At Westminster Abbey, "the chair in which the English kings & queens have been crowned . . . [was] very broken & disreputable in appearance." The Tower of London was a "huge gloomy pile." The people lived in squalor. The city of Newcastle was "oppressive in its narrow streets, uniform houses & dense atmosphere in which one would think no natural joy or pure spiritual inspiration from nature could come." "The nobles of old I now know must have lived not only without luxury but without convenience, comfort or any sanitary precautions—the masses now thrust into their old abodes are stunted, dirty and plain." Edinburgh was "dismal & depressing."[69]

In the end, Deakin, like Roosevelt, allowed himself to enjoy London society—"here are all the wit & amusement wealth & fashion of the world at their best"—but he refused to be seduced by its charms. "I do not think the life good in itself or desirable." The contrast between wealth and poverty was too great and too visible: "wretchedness, want & famine, crime & despair" were but a step away from "incense, laughter, dissipation, fashion, folly and extravagance."[70] He departed for Australia via Europe on 11 May and was welcomed back as a local hero, the authentic voice of "Young Australia."[71] Describing the clash over the New Hebrides, Deakin told the Victorian parliament that it was imperative to pass legislation "to secure the islands of the Pacific."[72] The significance of his English visit was highlighted by Deakin in his book *The Federal Story*, but it can also be found in Royce's reports of their conversations in *Atlantic Monthly* and *Scribner's*. In jocular mood, Royce wrote privately to Deakin to express the hope that the publication of his articles would not "lead to your execution for treason against the Empire."[73]

Royce and Deakin's conversations and subsequent correspondence were formative for both philosopher and politician and progressive thinking more generally. Royce rehearsed ideas about "social organisation" and "the ties that bind" in his letters to Deakin, then copied passages into subsequent articles and developed his argument about the "ethical principle of loyalty" as the basis for community organization for his book *The Philosophy of Loyalty*, published in 1908. There he defined "loyalty" as "the willing and practical and thoroughgoing devotion of a person to a cause. A man is loyal when, first, he has some cause to which he is loyal; when, secondly, he willingly and thoroughly devotes himself to this cause; and, when, thirdly, he expresses his devotion in some sustained and practical way, by acting steadily in the service of his cause."[74] Deakin had dedicated himself to the "sacred cause" of federation, but he also worked, in a "sustained and practical way," for the related cause of "social justice."

Australian progressives were "radical for the State," Deakin explained in 1889 in a letter to English Liberal Charles Dilke, who was conducting research for his new book, *Problems of Greater Britain.* They were "against individuals save in the interest of the State." Australians combined "American and English characteristics—the opportunities and material wealth of the first with the constitution and constitutional caution of the second." Deakin hoped that an independent public service would prevent the growth of "party politicians of the American type" and protect Australians from "the machine." Australians, Deakin suggested confidently to Dilke, were making "a political type of our own."[75]

As a Liberal leader, Deakin deployed the agency of the state to extend land settlement and assist farmers, to enforce the assimilation of Aborigines and ameliorate labor exploitation, to abolish the sweating of outworkers and regulate the labor conditions of factory workers. A strike by the Tailoresses' Union in Melbourne in 1884 had drawn public attention to the exploitation of women workers and outworkers, leading to a royal commission that would investigate labor conditions more generally. Its report included thirty-nine recommendations for reform. Deakin's subsequent Factory and Shops Act of 1885—which he referred to proudly as the "first social legislation in the colonies"—set a new standard for working conditions in Australia.[76] Providing for the registration and inspection of factories, the enforcement of sanitary regulations, special limitations on the hours worked by women and children, and compensation for work injuries, it was, in the words of his biographer, "a pioneer act of social legislation."[77]

In the next decade, Deakin helped add to the significance of the Factory and Shops Act when he supported the introduction of an amending bill in 1895 that provided for the establishment of the first legal minimum wage in the world and associated wages boards.[78] He told the legislative assembly that it was politicians' duty to make "every possible effort to place people on the platform of justice." High wages and decent working conditions were an expression of respect for one's fellow citizens. "Let them at any rate see," declared Deakin in an uncharacteristically Marxist flourish, "that the clothes they wore and the bread they ate did not come to them stained with the blood from the martyrdom of the toiling masses." In supporting this historic legislation, Deakin characteristically appealed both to "patriotic sentiment" and "moral ideals."[79]

American reformers, including Florence Kelley, Justice Learned Hand, and Walter Lippman, would later praise this innovative Victorian legislation as a historic repudiation of "sweated" and "coolie" labor and the beginning of "economic democracy."[80] It was significant that this first minimum wage for adult male workers was introduced to protect "white men" from the competition posed by local Chinese furniture manufacturers and their employees. The parliamentary debate was explicit in elaborating on the idea of a white man's wage. "Our people were European in origins," explained H. B. Higgins, then member of the Victorian Legislative Assembly for Geelong, who, like Deakin, would be elected to the new federal parliament in 1901. They "did not want to have our workers degraded to the position of the people who lived in China. In China the people worked more hours and got less pay than the people here, and it was our policy to try to raise the standard of living and not to lower it."[81]

Members of parliament argued that a "high wage economy" was good for society as well as workers. It reinforced the equality of citizenship. Local Chinese employers would be compelled by law to adhere to the Australian tradition of the eight-hour day and pay the same high wages to their employees as other manufacturers. The state should adopt the principle, Deakin proposed, of "equality of wage for equality of work."[82]

When Royce had first sailed into Melbourne in June 1888, Deakin as chief secretary was preparing to attend the intercolonial conference in Sydney on Chinese immigration. He invited Royce to join him on his railway journey and to take a brief holiday in the Blue Mountains before conference proceedings began. He then took the opportunity to discuss the issue of Chinese immigration with his American visitor. Royce deplored vulgar "race prejudice" but considered that Australian wariness of the ambitions of the Chinese Empire—a rival in the Pacific—was justified. Australia had to resist "the growing influence of the Chinese Empire in the Pacific," Royce warned, "and above all . . . an unrestricted introduction of a Chinese population into her own territory." It was Australia's destiny to become "the first civilized power of the Pacific, and as such must always steadily strive to restrain the influence of China."[83] Conference delegates would have felt vindicated by Royce's warning and resolved to introduce new uniform Australian legislation, drafted in part by Deakin, to further curb Chinese immigration.

When the gathering dispersed, Deakin returned "solus to Mt Victoria," as he wrote to Royce, where the weather was finer than when they had walked there together a few days before. Still, he felt melancholy and (quoting Tennyson's poem of grief over the death of his friend Arthur Hallam) missed "the touch of a vanished hand and the sound of a voice that is still," forced to make do with long solitary strolls.[84] Royce also wrote to Deakin immediately upon leaving Sydney to tell him that he had decided to write about the lessons that progressive America might draw from Australian social and political experiments. To aid his research, he had detoured via New Zealand— rather than stopping over in Hawaii—to "get more ideas on your political life in the colonies in general by remaining in range of your newspapers."[85]

The inauguration of the Commonwealth of Australia in 1901 was framed by the "White Australia Policy." One of the first laws passed by the federal government was the Immigration Restriction Act, which employed a form of literacy test—a dictation test—to exclude unwanted "Asiatics." This was part of a transnational trend. From Mississippi to Natal to Melbourne, a literary or educational test was the preferred progressive device to enact different forms of racial exclusion.[86] In supporting the Immigration Restriction Act, Attorney General Deakin told the federal parliament: "We here find ourselves touching the profoundest instinct of individual or nation—the instinct of self-preservation—for it is nothing less than the national manhood, the national character and the national future that are at stake."[87]

Australian developments were closely watched by reformers in the United States. From Boston, Prescott Hall—secretary of the Immigration Restriction League, which had long advocated the introduction of a literacy test to restrict US immigration—wrote to Prime Minister

Edmund Barton in Melbourne to obtain a copy of the Australian Act, which he was pleased to note contained a "writing test."[88]

Progressive crusader and prolific publicist Frank Parsons elaborated on and commended the merits of "Australasian Methods of Dealing with Immigration" in the *Annals of the American Academy of Political and Social Science* in 1904. "The Yankees of the South Pacific," he explained, "are determined to prevent race fissures, babel cities and debased admixtures in their commonwealth." Bringing key progressive themes into one vision, Parsons declared: "They will not pollute the stream of life in the new world with the refuse of the old, nor dilute their civilization with inferior stock, nor lower the standard of comfort with low-grade labor, nor imperil their freedom and progress by the influx of immigrants unfit for self-government."[89] Parsons's exhaustively researched account of Australian political developments included a history of immigration restriction and a detailed account of the provisions of the 1901 Act, which also included bans on contract labor, paupers, prostitutes, diseased persons, and criminals, as well as those who couldn't write out at dictation a passage of fifty words in a nominated European language.

Parsons quoted Deakin's election speech of 1903 to demonstrate the "vigor" of Australian policy (also Roosevelt's term of praise) and its "progressive" orientation. "A white Australia does not by any means mean only the preservation of the complexion of the people of this country," Deakin told his audience, forgetting for the moment the continuing presence of Aboriginal peoples.

> It means the maintenance of conditions of life fit for white men and white women; it means equal laws and opportunities for all; it means protection against the underpaid labor of other lands; it means social justice so far as we can establish it, including just trading and the payment of fair wages. A white Australia means a civilization whose foundations are built upon healthy lives, lived in honest toil, under circumstances that imply no degradation.

Deakin linked immigration restriction and labor standards to tariff policy in a framework that came to be called "New Protection." "Fiscally a white Australia means protection." Refuting capitalist arguments favoring free trade and open markets, he declared: "We protect ourselves against armed aggression, why not against aggression by commercial means? We protect ourselves against undesirable aliens, why not against the products of undesirable alien labor? A white Australia is not mere sentiment; it is a reasoned policy which goes to the roots of national life, and by which the whole of our social, industrial and political organization is governed."[90]

Theodore Roosevelt replicated the idea of the social contract implicit in "New Protection"—tariff protection in return for the payment of high wages—when he spoke to the National Convention of the Progressive Party in Chicago of 1912. "The Progressive party is for honest protection; and honest protection is right and a condition for American prosperity . . . a tariff high enough to enable American producers to pay our workingmen American wages and so arranged that the workingmen will get such wages."[91]

The White Australia Policy strengthened national borders but also mandated colonial expansion. One of the first acts of the new federal government was to move to take control of British New Guinea, the large territory across the Torres Strait to the north of the continent, offering to relieve Britain of the burden of governing distant Pacific islands. White Australia was founded in dreams of empire—an "Island Empire" of the Pacific, as Prime Minister Barton told the British Colonial Office in 1901, reminding officials that the British government, in approving Australia's constitution, had endorsed Australia's statutory right to exercise the "power and influence of the Commonwealth in connection with the Islands of the South Seas."[92]

When Australia's proposal to govern the Cook Islands was rebuffed by Britain, Barton was moved to protest: "For many years past and throughout all the discussions which preceded the establishment of the Commonwealth, the hope was widely and sincerely held, that as time went on, the Federal Government would be able to exercise and direct a growing influence over the islands forming part of His Majesty's Dominions in the South Pacific. These islands have received the greater part of the civilization they possess from Australia."[93]

In the end, the British government preferred to give power over the Cook Islands to New Zealand, but Australia was pleased to acquire the "Possession" of British New Guinea. This was a large responsibility. They had to ensure, Attorney General Deakin told parliament, that "settlement shall take place on the lines of peace, order, and good government, so that great land monopolies and injustice to the natives may be prevented."[94] Theirs would be a self-consciously progressive colonial government, directed by a very modern Australian bureaucrat, Hubert Murray. All agreed that Australian white men needed to redeem their reputation as colonizers.

Like colonization, progressivism rested on the division of the world into advanced and backward peoples. The "backwardness" of Australia's colony of Papua became, significantly, a point of reference for Deakin when he introduced his government's signature policy of industrial arbitration.[95] The Conciliation and Arbitration Bill provided for the establishment of a new federal court, armed with full powers of compulsion, to settle industrial disputes through the regulation of wages, hours, and conditions of work. Parliamentary debate on the legislation became an occasion for federal legislators to define the progressive principles that governed their new nation.

In speaking to the bill, Deakin emphasized the "novel" nature of the role of "the State" in this proposed "legal tribunal": "It marks the beginning of a new era in industrial matters, not only because of its main object, the prohibition of strikes and lockouts, but because it brings into play a new force—the force of an impartial tribunal with the State behind it."[96] To be sure, colonial precedents for the Commonwealth Court of Conciliation and Arbitration existed in New Zealand and the former colonies of Western Australia and New South Wales.[97] Indeed, with an arbitration court established in 1894, New Zealand had gained a worldwide reputation as the very model of a progressive nation. From the 1890s, as we will see in Chapter 7, American visitors descended on the small nation and wrote in praise of the "country without strikes."[98]

The Commonwealth Court of Conciliation and Arbitration, Deakin insisted, represented a greater achievement, indeed nothing less than "the beginning of a new phase of civilization," because its aim was not simply to settle or prevent strikes but to inaugurate a new era of "social justice" by enlisting the power of the State to remove "inequalities" between classes and promote "the well being of the masses of the people." Deakin conceived the role of the Court of Conciliation and Arbitration in evolutionary terms. In pioneering the use of the state and the rule of law to inaugurate a new era of industrial harmony, the court ushered in a new phase of civilization.[99]

Progressivism was commonly represented as an evolutionary force. Deakin emphasized the advanced nature of compulsory arbitration in a narrative of evolutionary progress that contrasted "white government" with "the Papuan stage" of Australia's "new dependency":

> We are accustomed now-a-days to what we term, as regards society, the reign of law. Our own remote ancestors, before the historic period lived in a time in which private feuds and personal lawlessness prevented all possibility of social progress or political development. They were then in what may be termed the Papuan stage. They had reached the status of the natives living beyond the reach of white government, in our new dependency, where every little village is at war with every other village, and speaks its own dialect. In such conditions progress was impossible.[100]

His fellow Liberals agreed. The court marked a new era in their "social and economic history," indeed a new phase in the history of human progress. One legislator sketched their progress from old oppressions to new emancipations: "We have only to look back, as far as the light of history will enable us to see upon the line of human progress, to enable us to trace without much difficulty the steep and tortuous path by which the greater portion of mankind have sought emancipation, right upwards from slavery, through serfdom, until we find them today groping almost at haphazard through industrialism."[101]

The court was not only in the vanguard of progressive reform, however; it was essential to future material prosperity: "Permanent prosperity can only be based upon institutions which are cemented by social justice. . . . No measures ever submitted to any legislature offer greater prospects of the establishment of social justice and of the removal of inequalities than those which are based upon the principle of conciliation and arbitration."[102]

In response to those who still prioritized old notions of individual liberty and freedom of contract, Australian legislators insisted that "the advancement of the State" spelled the end of the reign of individualism. "Individual liberty, in the twentieth century," said Liberal Protectionist James Hume Cook, "is permissible only when it is consistent with the liberty of the people. When individual liberty interferes with the general well-being of the community it is time to interrupt its flow." Individualism denied the actual interdependence of communities. "We must not look to the interests of the individual," said G. B. Edwards. "Scientists and political economists agree that society is an organism, that each part is related to the whole, and that every part is inter-related. The only way in which we can promote the advancement of the State is by fully considering the relations of all its parts, and reconciling their differences upon the principle of justice." So-called economic laws that gave free reign to individual interests were the legacy of a barbaric past: the law of supply and demand was a "hideous and barbarous law."[103]

With the advent of the Commonwealth of Australia, people had been entrusted with the "full powers of self-government" so that they might seek "social justice by means of progressive measures," as Deakin put it in a 1906 election address. Their chosen method was "a free use of the agencies of the State."[104] In earlier times, Deakin explained, when government was in the "hands of an aristocracy," parliament had opposed "State intervention." Now that government had passed into the hands of the people, they had resolved to use the power of the state in the "interests of the whole community."[105]

In 1908, Deakin sought to further enhance "the well being of the masses of the people" through the introduction of invalid and old-age pensions. The authors of the Australian constitution had explicitly allocated this power to the federal parliament, and when the new government met, members were reminded of the government's obligation to "look after" old people: "It is the proper and legitimate function of the Commonwealth to look after its aged poor throughout the length and breadth of the Australian dominion." Old people deserved better than to be forced into asylums or treated as charity cases.[106] "In every enlightened community," Attorney General Littleton Groom told parliament, "the establishment of old-age pensions is regarded as an ideal whose attainment should be earnestly sought, it being felt to be a reproach to civilization that many persons whose lives have been spent working for the advancement of the country should in their old age, through no fault of their own, be compelled to end their days in charitable institutions." The aged poor should not be left to starve in the streets. "That is the spirit and feeling which is more and more animating the legislation of the times." The new federal pensions were established on a non-contributory basis, drawn from general revenue rather than individual insurance contributions.[107] And equal pay would prevail. Men and women would be paid pensions individually and at the same rate.

Even as the Old Age and Invalid Pensions Act was passed in Australia, strengthening the "social ties" that bound citizens together, Deakin was becoming increasingly preoccupied by developments in the wider world—especially the ascendancy of Japan as a naval power—and the need to foster "ties of kinship" across the ocean.[108] In a provocative gesture, Deakin invited Theodore Roosevelt to send his naval fleet, about to enter the Pacific Ocean, to Melbourne and Sydney. "No other Federation in the world," Deakin informed Whitelaw Reid, the American ambassador to Britain, when forwarding his invitation, "possesses so many features of likeness to the United States as the Commonwealth of Australia and I doubt whether any two peoples could be found who are nearer in touch with each other."[109]

Roosevelt was keen to oblige. "I particularly desire the fleet to visit Australia," he informed his secretary of the navy, asking whether it was feasible to keep the fleet in the Pacific longer than first planned to accommodate the Australians, even as he refused invitations for the fleet to visit Argentina, Uruguay, and Ecuador.[110] In his *Autobiography*, Roosevelt recalled, "It was not originally my intention that the fleet should visit Australia, but the Australian government sent a most cordial invitation, which I gladly accepted; for I have, as every American ought to have, a hearty admiration for, and fellow feeling with, Australia."[111]

As the Australian prime minister pondered the right note to strike in his welcome speech, he received an unexpected gift, a copy of Professor Royce's latest book, *The Philosophy of Loyalty*. "Our fleet is going to see you," Royce wrote in an accompanying letter. "I venture to send in advance of the fleet—vast and noisy as it is my very tiny and silent book . . . a word of greeting about our common ideals."[112] Twenty years had passed since their fateful meeting in Australia. Royce was now, he wrote to Deakin, "an oldish professor, who stoops a little, and carries too many books about, and plan many books that I do not write," whereas Deakin, he suggested, had become "a leader in his country's affairs."[113] Royce fondly recalled the pleasure of their time together: "Few memories stand out more clearly and encouragingly, and more pleasingly, in my life than our meeting in 1888, our days together in the wonderland of your mountains, our talks, and your kindness, and the gracious cheer of all your hospitality. What a place the meeting and your presence and personality have since occupied in my life, I can hardly tell you."[114] The Harvard professor felt he had little to give in return to his friend, who was now, as he had foretold, "an empire builder, and a man of affairs." "I hear of your long career with delight and admiration;—not indeed with envy, for I am a student, and love the life apart from affairs;—but I can fully appreciate the world's work; and I reverence the power that has made you so long a leader in your country's affairs. . . . Meanwhile as a sort of last expression of ideals, I put forth my book on 'Loyalty.'"[115]

Deakin was then serving his second term as prime minister. "I congratulate your country on having you," wrote Royce, "and you upon your career."[116] Royce's book arrived as the prime minister was writing drafts of a speech to welcome the US fleet to Australia. In the first version, he made reference to the shared necessity of immigration restriction, but after receiving the book on loyalty from "Prof Royce of Harvard," he changed his theme to the American motto, "e pluribus unum" and the spirit of community and unity immanent in the ideal of loyalty: "It is in this spirit, and in this hope, that Australia welcomes with open hand and heart the coming of your sailors, and of the flag, which, like our own, shelters a new world under the control of its vital union."[117] Deakin's speech and the Australian welcome to the American navy were suffused with deep emotion. In his *Autobiography*, Roosevelt noted that the reception accorded the fleet in Australia was "wonderful" and showed "the fundamental continuity of feeling between ourselves and the great commonwealth of the South Seas."[118]

Four years later, in 1912, Roosevelt put himself forward as the Progressive candidate for the American presidency. He surprised old friends and colleagues by his fervid embrace of a radical reform agenda that included workers' compensation, the eight-hour day, the minimum wage, old-age pensions, and "honest protection," later described as "one of the boldest visions in the history of mainstream American politics."[119] Speaking in Boston, Roosevelt explained his self-consciously New World vision. The United States was "foreordained through the ages to show the kings, the aristocracy, the powers of privilege in the Old World, that here in the New World we could have a true and real democracy."[120] Conservatives turned on his apparent radicalism but also charged him with mere imitation: a "flung-together program of so-called 'State Socialism,'" a mere rehash of Australasian policy. "Novel as the Roosevelt views may appear," wrote one critic, "they are neither new nor strange to any man informed of political currents throughout the world. In brief, they are a rehash of policies long in vogue in Australia and New Zealand."[121]

Former commissioner of Indian affairs Robert Valentine, Roosevelt's friend and political supporter, was more generous in his assessment of Roosevelt's conversion, suggesting in a letter to a puzzled mutual friend, Dr. Mumford, that "the Colonel" had "got a real grip on the social movement" and recognized the "fundamental importance [of] bringing about . . . true social democracy in this country." For it was "evolution," not "revolution," Valentine suggested, that now defined socialism, as progressives everywhere came to recognize that "the real function of Government in these days [was] social reform."[122]

CHAPTER THREE

Purifying Politics through Electoral Reform

ON 4 APRIL 1893, South Australian reformer Catherine Helen Spence embarked on a long voyage that would take her to Sydney and then across the Pacific to San Francisco, the first stop on her American speaking tour. Over the course of ten months she would present more than one hundred lectures, talks, and sermons on diverse subjects, including electoral reform, state education, the state's responsibility for child welfare, woman suffrage, and the "Democratic Ideal."

Spence was a novelist, journalist, Unitarian preacher, and social reformer, who had long been active in support of "State Children." Not only was she one of the leaders of the campaign to secure state payments to support the maintenance of dependent children in family homes, but she was instrumental in securing the world's first Children's Court in Adelaide in 1890, nine years before the establishment of the Juvenile Court in Chicago—since acclaimed as a "landmark event" in the history of child welfare.[1]

Spence was a self-styled pioneer and indefatigable proselytizer. Energetic and engaged, short of stature, but supremely self-confident, the sixty-seven-year-old Scottish-born activist was pleased to report a warm reception in the United States. From San Francisco to New York to Philadelphia, she found that the Australian colonies' reputation for democratic reform had prepared the way for her. "'You come from Australia, the home of the secret ballot?' was the greeting I often received and that really was my passport to the hearts of reformers all over America."[2]

Stepping off the boat in San Francisco, Spence was greeted by Alfred Cridge, son of a feminist writer and "the world's foremost advocate of proportional representation," according to his local admirers.[3] Spence and Cridge shared a passion for electoral reform, particularly proportional representation (PR), or "effective voting," as Spence called it. With her publication of *A Plea for Pure Democracy* three decades before,

Spence was internationally recognized as an advocate of PR, alongside Thomas Hare and John Stuart Mill in Britain. In their history of *Proportional Representation*, published in 1926, American writers Clarence Hoag and George Hallett considered that "Catherine Helen Spence of Adelaide, South Australia, deserves special mention." It was, they said, due to her educational work that PR, incorporating the single transferable vote and preferential voting, had become so widely known.[4]

Cridge was pleased to have this seasoned advocate at his side. "America needs the reform more than Australia," he told her. The tyranny of party politics had crushed the best elements in American political life. An independent candidate would have as much chance of getting elected as "a snowball would have in hell."[5] He arranged for Spence to address a meeting on PR at Berkeley, and they made plans to attend the foundational meeting of the American Proportional Representation League at the World's Fair together. There they would present papers alongside fellow advocates: social scientist John Commons; Massachusetts legislator William Gove; and Swiss-born, Boston-based reformer W. D. McCrackan. Cridge was excited at the prospect. For him, proportional representation was "the Golden Rule and the Declaration of Independence politically embodied."[6]

During her time in San Francisco, Spence was also invited to address a women's meeting. "To that celebrated journalist, poetess and economic writer, Charlotte Perkins Stetson [later Gilman], who was a cultured Bostonian," then living on the West Coast, she owed "one of the best women's meetings" she had ever addressed. The subject was "State Children and the compulsory clauses in our Education Act," and everywhere in the United States, Spence reported, "people were interested in the splendid work of our State Children's department and educational methods."[7] Compulsory schooling meant that all children could be educated for independent thinking and civic engagement. Spence had published a civics textbook, *The Laws We Live Under*, in 1880.

Charlotte Perkins Stetson had separated from her husband on the East Coast in 1888 and taken up residence in Pasadena. Her short story about a married woman's descent into madness, "The Yellow Wallpaper" was published in 1892. Her first collection of satirical verse, *In this Our World*, came out in 1893. (Spence carried a copy with her on her American tour and to England, where she helped find a British publisher.)[8] The two met up again in London.[9] Stetson became best known for her 1898 book, *Women and Economics*, in which she argued that women's subordination was the result of their dependence on men, and that they must strive to become economically independent. Spence was herself exemplary in this regard, a single woman supporting herself with pen and voice throughout her long life.

Charlotte Perkins Stetson was one of a number of progressive women with whom Spence became friends in the United States. Despite the age difference between them, the older "Miss Spence" and the young "Mrs. Stetson"—who was also developing a career as a lecturer, writer, and public intellectual—kept in contact.[10] Spence remarked more generally on the sense of kinship between Americans and Australians. They shared an English-speaking heritage, to be sure, but Americans looked on Australians "as nearer to them than the English themselves." Traveling through the country, she found people keen to learn about the new world coming into existence in the southwest Pacific. "Perhaps my travelling alone at my age made the curiosity a little more eager," she mused, "but there is the Australian ballot, which is now in most states an accomplished fact . . . hailed as a great advance towards security and purity of election."[11] Spence was impressed by the status of American women in public life but puzzled by their lack of political rights. Did they not need political as well as economic independence? Proportional representation, she believed, would make that possible.

Walking around San Francisco, the bustling "metropolis of the Pacific," the Australian reformer was struck, as Alfred Deakin had been eight years earlier, by the mix of nationalities—Chinese, Japanese, Italians, Spanish, and Negroes, as well as settlers of British descent. One group in particular caught her attention. "The Chinese number 25,000 and pervade the city."[12] Spence also noticed that "dark-eyed children" of different nationalities spoke English perfectly, a result, she surmised, of the excellent public school system. But the class differences and obvious disparity in wealth between citizens—the contrast between the mansions of millionaires and the hovels of the poor—shocked this exponent of the "Democratic Ideal."[13]

Spence might not have been young in years, but she considered herself a "New Woman," "awakened," as she put it, to "a sense of capacity and responsibility, not merely to the family and household, but to the State."[14] She earned her living as a writer and lecturer and achieved prominence as an advocate of electoral, social, and political reform. She was a well-known suffragist. When overseas, she was also conscious of her position as a representative of a new country, a pioneer "striking out new paths."[15] Her first biographer, Jeanne Young, celebrated Spence "not as a 'Woman Pioneer' of South Australia only, but as a 'Pioneer Woman' of the world."[16]

"Pioneer" was a favored trope in progressive discourse and an honor fondly bestowed by settler societies everywhere. The Harvard philosopher Josiah Royce had dedicated his history of California to his mother, "a Pioneer of 49," while Charles Pearson commended the hardy "pioneer men" of the West he encountered in his American travels.[17] Just as settlers pioneered the "untamed wilderness," so progressives were pioneers of the "great social movement"—as Robert Valentine named it—"pioneering" labor reforms, women's rights, and children's services. In 1918, the American jurist Felix Frankfurter thanked H. B. Higgins, Australian president of the Commonwealth Court of Conciliation and Arbitration, for his role as "a great and successful pioneer" in the "field of labor."[18] Catherine Spence told the International Congress of Charities, Correction and Philanthropy in Chicago that in the area of child welfare, the Australian government had forged "new paths."[19] In this discourse on "pioneers," progressivism was the political logic of settler colonialism.

It was well recognized that Australia had "pioneered" the use of a government-printed secret ballot, hence the popular designation as the "Australian ballot." Its rapid adoption across the United States was remarkable. First introduced in Massachusetts in 1888, the Australian ballot was adopted by more than 90 percent of states within just eight years.[20] In promising to lift the standard of elections and the qualifications of voters, who would henceforth be required to read, it was in many ways the quintessential progressive reform. But the reasons for its adoption in the United States were often markedly different from those advanced by its Australian supporters when it was introduced decades earlier to protect voters from subjection to improper external pressure—to secure, in Spence's words, "purity of election."

In American hands in the 1890s, the Australian ballot was often advocated as an exclusionary measure because, as a printed form, the technology enabled states to exclude illiterate and ill-educated voters—notably African Americans and many of the millions of newly arrived immigrants—from exercising the franchise.[21] In the South especially, the Australian ballot was promoted as a way to "discriminate against illiteracy" and "improve voting standards." Its adoption led to a dramatic drop in voter turnout. Progressive reforms could have profoundly antidemocratic outcomes.

The Australian ballot may have been Spence's "passport to the hearts of reformers" across the United States, but she was disappointed to find that her transpacific cousins were not equally enthusiastic about her favorite nostrum, proportional representation, which in replacing first-past-the-post / winner-take-all elections promised fairer political representation for minority views and small parties. In advocating electoral reform, American progressives were more likely to argue that it was the abstract category of "the people"—rather than "minorities"—that needed more effective representation to combat the power of "the interests" and "the parties." They usually proposed to enhance the power of "the people" through the reforms of initiative and referendum, direct legislation, and the direct election of senators, but in the 1890s—the decade of Spence's lecture tour—concern about corruption in city government brought proportional representation to the fore as a favored reform.[22]

But just as racial considerations had garnered American support for the secret ballot, so too were they important in mobilizing opposition to proportional representation. The category of "minority," in whose interests Spence spoke, usually carried racial connotations in the United States. "Minority" was often the term used to refer to African Americans and immigrant groups, such as the Irish, Italians, or Poles. Rather than deserving more effective representation, such groups were generally looked on with suspicion and deemed by many American progressives to pose a threat to good government.

In some American cities where PR was introduced, it was soon repealed when "minority candidates" increased their representation as a result. As Douglas Amy has observed, proportional representation, incorporating the single transferable vote, "encouraged fairer racial and ethnic representation. It produced the first Irish Catholics elected in Ashtabula, and the first Polish Americans elected in Toledo. In Cincinnati, Hamilton, and Toledo, African Americans had never been able to win city office until the coming of [PR]. Significantly, after these cities abandoned PR, African Americans again found it almost impossible to get elected."[23] Clearly, PR benefited the ethnic and racial minorities not favored by most American progressives.

As a way of giving an effective voice to minorities, PR had been first advocated in quite different historical circumstances, with different kinds of minorities in mind. With the advent of manhood suffrage in the Australian colonies in the 1850s, liberal reformers had been concerned with protecting the influence of the educated elite from the impact of "mob rule." Spence's "pioneering" pamphlet *A Plea for Pure Democracy*, published in 1861, was written in this context to allay fears about the coming of democracy. Like the English volume *Essays on Reform*, published in the same decade, in which Goldwin Smith had praised the "American Commonwealth" and Charles Pearson had defended the "Working of Australian Institutions," Spence wrote to reassure British readers that democracy need not be so radical or dangerous an experiment.[24]

"The opponents of the extension of the suffrage in England," Spence wrote, "can point triumphantly to the United States, and to Victoria, and ask if it is well to allow such floods of unwisdom to darken knowledge and to corrupt political virtue."[25] The reform of proportional representation, incorporating large multimember electorates and preferential voting, would serve as an antidote to these "floods of unwisdom" by ensuring that "the genius, the originality, the independence of the country," was still ensured a voice. Genius might be outvoted by the mob, but it would not be altogether silenced.[26]

By the time Spence proselytized for PR in the United States, her arguments had changed to emphasize its importance for independent-minded women voters and new, smaller parties, such as Single Taxers, Socialists, and Prohibitionists. Without proportional representation, she warned, women's votes and minority voices would be extinguished by the two-party system. Spence claimed suffragist Susan B. Anthony, whom she met at the Chicago World's Fair, as a convert to the cause: "[She] said publicly that I had taught her more of politics than she had learned before, and she apprehended that without effective voting the granting of suffrage to all women would be a delusion in regard to social reform as long as the present dual system between two parties continues. She is a shrewd old lady."[27] She was also a diplomatic one.

During her ten-month lecture tour in the United States, Spence found a country that shared a strong sense of English heritage and democratic political values, but she also discovered a political system that was more conservative, cautious, and prone to corruption, and a paradoxically elitist republic that was hostile to, or suspicious of, state intervention to improve ordinary people's lives and regulate working conditions. At the founding meeting of the American Proportional Representation League and the associated suffrage conference in Chicago in August 1893, Spence encountered a white political culture not well disposed to empowering racial minorities. She listened in admiration to the speeches by leading African Americans Frederick B. Douglass and Frances E. W. Harper, and agreed with them about the importance of educating, rather than excluding, voters.

Catherine Spence was a proud settler colonist. Migrating to South Australia from Scotland in 1839, at the age of fourteen, she fashioned a sense of herself as a pioneer and progressive in the light of her family's participation in the famous experiment of "systematic colonization," based on the ideas of British reformer E. G. Wakefield.[28] The scheme proposed selling land at a "sufficient price" to engender a social structure both hierarchical and mobile. Within it, all operations of the economy, government, worship, education, and culture would be free. No convicts would be sent to such a colony. Equal proportions of women and men, sponsored as migrants, would extend the refining influence of women throughout the settlement.[29]

Spence's father, David Spence, was pleased to obtain one hundred acres of land north of Adelaide, although in the end the family chose to settle in town, deterred by drought and possibly by Aboriginal resistance to the invasion of their country. Historians of South Australian settlement have documented the widespread violence between indigenous peoples and settlers near Adelaide in these early years of settlement. Even though often "covert and clothed in euphemism," white atrocities became so troubling to some colonists that local newspapers, surely read by the literate Spence family, were moved to carry a number of articles discussing—and justifying—the legitimacy of settlement.[30]

Settler colonialism rested on brutal violence. It required the systematic displacement and destruction of indigenous communities, but it also brought into being new social and political orders, as Josiah Royce emphasized in his history of California and Spence elaborated in her history of South Australia. Settler colonialism was a distinctive formation—distinctive from colonialism in general—as Lorenzo Veracini has noted: "Settlers are founders of political orders and carry their sovereignty with them."[31] In her later years, Spence fondly recalled the halcyon days, when "the community of labour and equality of the sexes" saw South Australia approach a Utopian condition, in which "there was very little difference in the actual circumstances of different classes."[32]

The innovative spirit of the settlement and the harmony said to characterize social relations in this "new community" constituted proud foundations for a new colony. In her "Autobiography," Spence reflected: "It is sometimes counted as a reproach that South Australia was founded by doctrinaires and that we retain traces of our origins; to me it is our glory. In the land laws and immigration laws it struck out a new path, and sought to found a new community where land, labour and capital should work harmoniously together."[33] The availability of and access to land in the New World, made possible by the dispossession of indigenous peoples, were central to realizing nineteenth-century dreams of economic independence and political equality in Australia and the United States. Only in these "unoccupied" lands might pioneers strike out new paths.

Settler colonialism promised new economic and social opportunities for colonists even as indigenous owners of the land were displaced from their country and their communities, their culture destroyed. The Spence family, whose prospects in Scotland were blighted by unwise investments on the part of Spence's father, sought, like many thousands of others—including Spence's friend Charles Pearson—to redeem their fortunes through migration to the colonies. As Goldwin Smith had written in "The Experience of the American Commonwealth," the success of equality in the New World depended on the availability of land.[34]

Recognizing the rapidly escalating property values in settler societies, many reformers were responsive to Henry George's call for a single tax on land. In her review of *Progress and Poverty* in the local newspaper, Spence pointed to the shared historical circumstances of the United States and Australia: "Fifty years ago the land on which San Francisco, Melbourne and Adelaide stood was valueless. The value has been conferred on this land by the population attracted to the country."[35] It was the rapid increase in population in settler societies—especially in California and Victoria, suddenly enriched by gold—that led to the steep increase in land prices. In a longer essay for the *Victorian Review*, Spence commended George as a theorist: "He strikes at private property in land, which is the only kind of wealth that has natural limits, and in the course of his argument he shows himself a forcible and an original thinker."[36] George returned the compliment, inviting Spence to stay with him and his wife in New York, where in 1894 she enjoyed a "delightful few days."[37]

Progressive colonists liked to think that the Old World could learn from their political and social experiments, especially as some reforms originated in radical ideas first enunciated, but thwarted, in the mother country. In 1867, Spence had traveled to England to publicize *Plea for Pure Democracy* and was thrilled by the attention paid to her booklet: "Mr Hare, John Stuart Mill and Professor Craik considered [it] the most powerful argument for equal or proportional representation from the popular side that had then appeared."[38] Mill had spoken in favor of proportional representation in the House of Commons, introducing a bill in 1872. Spence's *Plea for Pure Democracy* opened doors into reforming circles and made her a figure of interest: "It was the little pamphlet rather than the novels that procured me introductions into the best society, or what I call the best, the most intelligent in London."[39]

Spence also carried letters of introduction to British reformers Florence and Rosamund Hill, cousins of her South Australian friend Emily Clark, and to Clark's uncles, Rowland Hill, former secretary of the Colonizing Commission of South Australia, and Matthew Davenport Hill.[40] Through these connections, she came across the work of feminist social worker Frances Power Cobbe, who had investigated the care of destitute children in workhouses and recommended in a special report that these "institutions of pauperism" be replaced by the Scottish "boarding out" system.

In her essay "The Philosophy of the Poor-Laws and the Report of the Committee on Poor Relief," Cobbe introduced the concept of cit-

izen rights and proposed a child's right to be free of the "stigma of pauperism."[41] "As a matter of right, no child ought to bear the stigma of
pauperism; and, as a matter of public interest for the future of the community, every dependent child ought to be separated and removed as
far as by any means may be possible from pauper moral influences and
pauper physical and social degradation."[42]

Cobbe endorsed the emphasis on education in the Scottish system
and proposed "to send the children out first to be nursed, and then
boarded, by respectable poor families, under proper inspection." Families would be obliged to see that children were well educated alongside other children in the neighborhood. The families in charge of the
children should be obliged to send them to the school chosen by an inspector, and to produce certificates from the teacher of the child's attendance. Thus the desired end of education would be fully attained,
and with "the immense advantage of it being an education in common
with non-pauper children."[43] Spence became an enthusiastic convert
to the "boarding out" system and was pleased to find on her return to
Adelaide that Emily Clark had also read Cobbe's essay and begun im-
plementing a similar scheme on a voluntary basis.[44]

In 1872, Clark and Spence formed a Boarding Out Society and led a
deputation to persuade the South Australian government to adopt the
scheme as government policy. In these small democratic communities,
reformers had easier access to legislators and governments than they
were afforded in aristocratic Britain, and with manhood suffrage, some
reformers were elected to government. In 1885, South Australia established a State Children's Council, and its eleven members—the
majority of them women—included Clark and Spence. Further reforms
to "boarding-out" in South Australia included the introduction of li-
censes for foster mothers and closer state supervision by women
inspectors—initiatives that would attract interest in Britain and the
United States—although there was still strong resistance to the idea of
the state replacing private charity as the main agency in welfare work.

As chief secretary in Victoria in the late 1880s, Alfred Deakin was
proud of the child-welfare developments over which he presided, as he
reported to his English friend, Charles Dilke, who was collecting information for his forthcoming book *Problems of Greater Britain.* "Have
you noted our treatment of neglected and criminal children. I send also

a copy of the last report of this Branch of my Department," Deakin wrote. "I think the legislation is up to anything of the kind anywhere." He then described the path of emancipation children could take from jails, reformatories, and industrial schools "to the families with whom the children are boarded out. . . . In a few cases we pay mothers who have been deserted (and are of good character and industrious in their efforts) for taking care of their own children for a certain time until the family can be made self-supporting."[45] Thus did "boarding-out" schemes provide for the first mothers' pensions, with state agencies also acting in *loco parentis.*

Deakin pointed to individual examples of generous state support, with some "waifs" offered scholarships to high school and others apprenticed to "first class manufactories." Such cases indicated "State action in loco parentis," he told Dilke, "to an extent far beyond what appears to be practised elsewhere."[46] In New South Wales, where boarding out was introduced in 1881, "boarding-out" payments were extended to (mostly unmarried) mothers, as well as to foster mothers, offering recognition of the rights of working-class mothers to care for their own children. South Australia, as Spence was pleased to remind her audiences, had led the way in this regard.

As Spence prepared for her journey across the Pacific in April 1893, a journalist from the local newspaper called on her to inquire about her hopes and plans. He found her "seated before a pile of American letters and papers, for the San Francisco mail had arrived that day."[47] Spence had received encouraging letters and invitations from those who would be her hosts. "I may be a little Utopian," she confessed, "but as I am as willing and anxious to learn as to teach I am sure of spending a profitable time. I wish to understand the character of the social and political institutions of the United States thoroughly, and I want to aid by my voice and pen those who are working for electoral reform and the purification of politics."[48] In Australia, as in the United States, the "purification of politics" was deemed to be an especially appropriate, if elusive, goal for women reformers.[49]

Spence's main destination in the United States was Chicago, site of the World's Columbian Exposition, or World's Fair, where she was officially accredited by the State Children's Council of South Australia as a delegate to the International Congress of Charities, Correction and

Philanthropy—an organization on which Spence also served as international vice president. The International Congress of Charities was one of numerous conferences—professional, academic, and philanthropic—held in Chicago that year in conjunction with the World's Fair.

Commissioned by the US Congress to commemorate the four hundredth anniversary of Columbus's arrival in the Americas, the World's Columbian Exposition constituted an extended justification for European colonization and settlement, an "exhibition of the progress of civilization in the New World."[50] The exhibits covered more than six hundred acres, featured nearly two hundred new (but temporary) buildings of predominantly neoclassical design, and spotlighted the peoples and cultures of forty-six countries. Over six months, it attracted more than twenty-seven million visitors. One of the early arrivals, Theodore Roosevelt, considered it "the most beautiful architectural exhibit the world has ever seen," as he told his literary friend James Brander Matthews.[51] He was not alone in his admiration.

Catherine Spence, arriving later in June, was impressed by the sheer size and splendor of the buildings. She was especially intrigued by the preparation that went into the exhibitions mounted by the separate American states, and she was drawn to those that highlighted their common colonial heritage. The Massachusetts building displayed "priceless relics of old colonial days—of the revolutionary war, of social conditions now passed away, and, above all, autographs and portraits of the great men in history and in literature." The plain wooden furniture suggested the "plain living and high thinking which the early American New Englanders were proud of." Touring the displays with a new friend from Iowa, Spence was delighted to discover their shared literary interests. Her companion had "read the books which I had read in Australia," including American authors Prescott and Northey; Hawthorne and Emerson; and Longfellow, Bryant, Holmes, and Lowell.[52]

The World's Fair told proud stories about the evolution of humankind, American progress, and the advancement of women, but it also caught the ambiguities of progressive views with regard to the place of Native Americans in the United States. Just three years after the massacre at Wounded Knee, different displays presented contending narratives about American Indians. On the one hand, there were

"ethnographic" exhibits of primitive "vanishing races" and their
cultural artifacts, organized by Frederick Ward Putnam, director of
Harvard's Peabody Museum of Archaeology and Ethnology. In these,
different tribes engaged in traditional life. On the other hand, a display organized by the Bureau of Indian Affairs showcased modern
boarding schools, in which Indian youth were being prepared to take
their place as civilized members of the future nation.[53]

Visitors were also offered competing historical accounts of the
American frontier. In a formal address to the professional historical
congress, the academic historian Frederick Jackson Turner proclaimed
the closing of the frontier. Meanwhile, Buffalo Bill depicted savage
contests between cowboys and Indians in his "Wild West" show at
Sixty-Third Street, "opposite the World's Fair."[54] Although presenting
quite different histories of the American past—in Turner's version, the
"axe and the plow," the primary tools of civilization, enabled peaceful
settlement across a "free" land; in Buffalo Bill's version, "the rifle and
the bullet" were the means of violent conquest—both converged in
their conclusion that the era of the frontier had closed and white men
had made the country their own.[55] In their different ways, both pre-
sentations consigned Indians to the national past.

In reality, Indians were active participants in the World's Fair and
not just as actors in Buffalo Bill's "Wild West" or as ethnographic types.
They were also trenchant critics. On opening day, 1 May, Potawatomi
chief Simon Pokagon offered a "Red Man's Greeting," in which he reminded white Americans that their evident progress had been "at the
sacrifice of *our* homes and our once happy race." Born during the presidency of Andrew Jackson, the Indian leader had witnessed the forced
removal of most of his people from the Midwest.[56] Where visitors now
gathered in Chicago, the "red man's wigwams" had been swept away
in days of disease, death, and destruction that "tried our fathers' souls."
Their lands had been destroyed: "The cyclone of civilization rolled
westward; the forests of untold centuries were swept away; streams
dried up; lakes fell back from their ancient bounds; and all our fathers
once loved to gaze upon was destroyed, defaced or marred, except the
sun, moon and starry skies above, which the Great Spirit in his wisdom
hung beyond their reach."[57] In 1893, in the place where once the "red
man" had enjoyed a "contented and happy existence," tall buildings

defined the horizon as "great Columbian show-buildings stretched skyward."[58]

The status of Indians was also illuminated in a larger context. As Robert Rydell has observed, the organizers of the World's Fair divided the site into two racially defined areas: White City depicted the achievements of Western civilization, while the Midway Plaisance displayed a range of exotic and primitive races exhibited as objects of the white gaze.[59] These were also gendered spaces: "The seven huge buildings framing the Court of Honor represented seven aspects of civilization's highest scientific, artistic, and technological achievements— Manufactures, Mines, Agriculture, Art, Administrations, Machinery, and Electricity. All were presented as the domain of civilized white *men*."[60] Women were allocated their own Women's Building at the edge of the White City, specially designed by a young woman architect named Sophia Hayden, a "new woman," who enjoyed the honor of being the first female graduate in architecture from the Massachusetts Institute of Technology, although she would never practice architecture again.

At the World's Congress of Representative Women, held in the Women's Building in May, Australia was represented by a young delegate from New South Wales, Margaret Windeyer, who was invited to respond to May Wright Sewall's opening address to foreign delegates. Windeyer hailed delegates' "common interest" in working for "the advancement of women." The women's congress attracted an audience of some 200,000 visitors to hear papers on a broad range of subjects— literary, economic, social, political—by speakers from different countries. Although invited to speak at the congress, Catherine Spence was later discouraged from delivering her proposed paper on proportional representation, the Board of Lady Managers judging that the topic might not be of much interest to members of her sex. Spence was indignant but mollified by an invitation to present it on a later occasion, and she agreed to submit it for publication in the collected proceedings.

Spence's main commitment at the World's Fair, as a delegate from her government, was to attend and present a paper at the International Congress of Charities, where she spoke about "state children" and the role of Australian governments in securing children's welfare, drawing on a paper she had delivered in Melbourne at the Australasian Conference on Charity in 1890. At that conference, she had developed her argument that "Socialistic" action, widespread in Australia, was "the trend of modern thought, in spite of protests from individualists."[61] Socialistic principles meant "the right of the destitute to claim shelter and food from public funds."[62]

In Australia, Spence explained, the government understood that its duty was to provide support to the destitute, the unemployed, the aged and invalid, dependent mothers, and children, all from general revenue. These schemes were commonly called "socialistic" because they were not forms of social insurance (as prevailed in Germany) and they didn't require employees to pay contributions before they could access benefits. Rather, the agency of the state was employed to redistribute revenue to secure the people's social and economic well-being.

Boarding out had been promoted by Spence as the most advanced reform for children:

> In other English-speaking countries boarding-out in families is sometimes permitted; but here, under the Southern Cross, it is the law of the land that children shall not be brought up in institutions, but in homes; that the child whose parent is the State shall have as good schooling as the child who has parents and guardians; that every child shall have, not the discipline of routine and red tape, but free and cheerful environment of ordinary life, preferably in the country—going to school with other young fellow-citizens . . . guarded from injustice, neglect, and cruelty by effective and kindly supervision.[63]

Spence told the International Congress of Charities about South Australia's boarding-out scheme—taking "all the children of the State out of institutions [to] place them in [private] homes"—and she spoke, too, of the innovative work of South Australia's new Children's Court.

In her report home, Spence emphasized the international recognition accorded Australia's pioneering reforms:

> In the special department of which I am a delegate, the care of what is called here dependent children, Australia occupies a very high place indeed. "Many daughters have done virtuously, but thou excellest them all." In Australia alone has the State—the Government—grasped the cardinal principle that to such children it stands in *loco parentis*, and sees that this guardianship ought not to be merely official and regulative, but that for every waif thrown on its care

through poverty, orphanhood, parental sins, or juvenile delinquencies a natural home and a kindly respectable mother should be sought out, and the child's interests guarded by constant, efficient, but kindly supervision.[64]

If similar schemes had not as yet worked well in the United States, it was because there wasn't sufficient inspection of the homes to which children were sent or insistence that children attend school alongside other children. Boarding out, Spence emphasized, was not designed for the profit or the convenience of foster parents. Indeed, in Australia, it gradually became a means of paying children's own mothers to keep their children with them, freeing the mothers and their children from the need to go out to work. Such payments to mothers also signaled a policy shift from an exclusive focus on children's needs to new recognition of mothers' rights.

When Spence put her views before her audience at the International Congress of Charities, she met with spirited opposition from many delegates, who preferred the reign of voluntary benevolence and private philanthropy to what they perceived to be a "socialistic system." "We have provided charity for every deserving poor person that may ask for it," said Zilpha D. Smith, general secretary of Associated Charities in Boston, "as we do not live under a socialistic system, people, in order to save character, must provide for themselves."[65] A. O. Wright from the Wisconsin Veterans' Home similarly objected that "outdoor relief" was not charity but "a form of socialism." The one great evil of "outdoor relief," he believed, was that it destroyed the motive to private benevolence and replaced it with "a cold and mechanical arrangement on the part of the state."[66] J. R. Brackett from Baltimore said that taking money from the "public treasury" did not help in any way to bring the two classes—the prosperous and the poor—together, which was the aim of philanthropy.[67]

J. R. Walk, general secretary of the Society for Organizing Charity in Philadelphia, invoked the settler spirit of "independence" that had enabled Americans to build up the country, transforming the "great wilderness into a garden":

I would be extremely sorry if in my city widows and orphans were ever made to feel that the poor director's wagon would come around and back up to their door and cause the blush of shame to arise to their cheek. We do not want to undermine that idea of independence which is the very best thing among our people, and which has turned this great wilderness into a garden in the last one hundred years.[68]

When Robert Paine, president of Associated Charities of Boston, suggested that mothers and children who received assistance through a boarding-out scheme would be "marked as paupers," Spence responded sharply, "It is regarded as a right."[69]

Not all American delegates were hostile to state action, however, and transnational conversations and friendships could lead to a shift in their thinking. Spence became good friends with the president of the Children's Section at the conference, Reverend Anna Garlin Spencer, the first woman ordained in Rhode Island, who served as pastor of the Bell Street Chapel in Providence. The two were kindred spirits. Both were active in the cause of women's rights and served as Christian preachers. Spencer was president of the Rhode Island Equal Suffrage Association, while Spence was vice president of the Women's Suffrage League of South Australia. Spencer served in the Unitarian Bell Street Chapel, while Spence preached in the Adelaide Unitarian Church. Spence declared her American friend "the most interesting woman I met at the conference," an admiration evidently reciprocated. Spencer invited Spence to stay with her and her family and to speak at four meetings in Rhode Island when she toured the East Coast.[70]

As activist Christians, Spence and Spencer believed in the power of women's (individual and equal) souls as a political force, but whereas Spence looked to the state as the primary vehicle for achieving social justice, Spencer eulogized voluntary organization as the quintessential American expression of "woman's power."[71] According to Spencer, women who organized for "independent, or well-nigh independent action, so far as man's control is concerned," constituted the driving force of progressive reform in all areas of society. "We have the intellectual craving of women organized in clubs of women, in collegiate alumnae associations from women's colleges," she told the International Congress of Charities. "We have the desire for full freedom among women organized in woman suffrage associations and leagues, and in special combinations for securing juster laws. We have the protective power of women organized in friendly societies to succor young and exposed women seeking work in strange places, in associations which aim to guard those solitary children and women whom God has not set in families." When woman "found herself," she began to understand that she was a person and that "being a person as man is a person," she had both a right and a duty to "interpret her own nature and grow according to the law written in her own being."[72] For Spencer, the woman movement meant personal development and social organization, not political activism.

Spence and Spencer shared a Christian faith and feminist values, but they were divided by differences in political orientation. Spencer was a voluntarist, firmly believing in the role of private philanthropy and women's organizations in providing welfare for women and children and the less fortunate in the community. Women's organizations also provided a space in which middle-class women themselves might become more independent minded. Like most progressive Australians, Spence was more of a "state socialist," expecting the state to perform the main role in providing for people's welfare and lobbying and petitioning politicians to that end.

In her lecture on "the Democratic Ideal," which she presented in Rhode Island, Spence argued that when avowedly democratic countries, such as the United States, enshrined plutocratic values and focused solely on the goal of material prosperity, they lost sight of the ideals of equality and community that bound democratic citizens together in "oneness of spirit."[73] As democratic citizens, Australians and Americans should distinguish themselves, she urged, from "aristocratic," "monarchic," and "oligarchic societies."[74] Democracies brought different classes of citizens together.

This was her message regardless of the topic of her address—child welfare, education, woman suffrage, or proportional representation—and her audiences, she reported, were keen to listen. She promised, in particular, that if American reformers adopted proportional representation, they could "stop the political corruption that was checking all vital reform and discrediting the principles of democracy itself."[75] There was little point in self-government without fair and equal representation of all votes cast. Major political parties should not be allowed to stymie minority interests. Proportional representation,

Spence insisted, was both the precondition and the logical outcome of true democracy.[76]

At the Chicago World's Fair, Spence had been exhilarated by her encounters with "the best thought and the highest ideals of people from all over the United States."[77] She was later told that no one had participated more fully in the conferences: she managed to speak on ten separate occasions. She was also a regular visitor to Rev. Jenkin Lloyd Jones's Unitarian All Souls Church, a center of radical free thinking and ecumenicalism that welcomed women preachers. In 1905, Jones's nephew Frank Lloyd Wright would design the new Unity Chapel in Oak Park. Six years later, two of Wright's protégés, Walter Burley Griffin and Marion Mahony Griffin, would win the international competition to design Australia's new capital city of Canberra. The secretary to the competition was Andrew Inglis Clark's son, Conway Inglis Clark, named after radical Unitarian preacher Moncure Conway and trained as an architect in Boston.

In Chicago for an exhilarating four months, Spence met hundreds of public-spirited men and women. She addressed a conference on education in which she stressed the necessity of "the teaching of the social virtues and the duties of a citizen."[78] "I had a most attentive hearing," she reported, "and was frequently interrupted by applause, which is not such a common thing in America . . . as Mr Bryce points out in his American Commonwealth."[79] Audience members requested copies of her book, The Laws We Live Under, the first civics textbook written in Australia, but it was out of print. At the Labor Congress, reports of the effects of the economic depression in rising unemployment and widespread evictions left Spence feeling powerless. What could words do, she wondered, to fill hungry stomachs or house the homeless? Real political change was necessary, and to achieve that, electoral reforms were imperative.

With Alfred Cridge, she attended a demonstration of the unemployed. "They do not want to be violent," she reported. "They seek reform of conditions through the ballot, but at present working men in America are quite powerless."[80] Whatever palliatives were offered, she was in no doubt that "by improving the administration, by purifying politics," the "corrupt leakage of public money" could be stopped. Spence also addressed a gathering of working men and women at Hull

House, where her friend, Dr. Bayard Holmes, lectured on public health and treated the injuries and illnesses of children employed in local factories. Spence didn't report whether she met Jane Addams at Hull House, but they subsequently corresponded, and Spence ordered a copy of her 1902 book *Democracy and Social Ethics.*

As an Australian reformer, Spence found a ready audience among American progressives, and she addressed over one hundred meetings across the country in 1893 and 1894. Yet it was the "subject of electoral reform" that was her "main topic in America," as she "show[ed] by argument that it [was] just, and by the use of ballot papers that it [was] practicable."[81] "I have always got on well with my American audiences," she reported to Australian readers, "but never so well as when I was on my favourite and special subject of effective voting."[82] Her travels confirmed Cridge's observation that "reform elements" and "progressive ideas" were being "crushed between the upper and nether millstones of the two [party] machines."[83]

The progressive movement aimed to reform the political parties but also to transcend them. "Everywhere and always the 'politician' is the hindrance to all reform in America," wrote Spence from New York, "and therefore I preach electoral reform as the first step forward."[84] She arrived in the United States at a propitious moment, for, as Amy has noted, "Besides such issues as child labour laws, anti-monopoly legislation, and women's suffrage, Progressives were also interested in government reform." As he has noted, many reformers were particularly concerned about corruption in urban governments. "Large cities often were dominated by 'party machines,' of which Tammany Hall in New York City was the most infamous. Bribery, kickbacks, favouritism, and voting fraud were rampant in these cities. The progressives wanted to clean up these cities and blunt the power of party bosses."[85]

Spence's message was timely as well as insistent. Only when "each vote has equal weight" and "all minorities equitable representation" would party machines be defeated, politics be purified, and the democratic ideal realized. Spence had long been an advocate for women's enfranchisement, but unless "woman's suffrage and proportional representation . . . go together . . . the first will be a mere delusion." Without electoral reform, party politicians would simply use women's votes to augment their own "party victory."[86]

The foundational meeting of the American Proportional Representation Congress was held at the World's Fair on 10–12 August. "Of all the good things to be accomplished through the means of the Columbian Exposition, few, if any, are of more importance than the calling together of the friends of reform in representation," wrote Stoughton Cooley, who would become editor of *Proportional Representation Review* and the first secretary of the new American Proportional Representation League, the organization that would provide leadership of the electoral reform movement in the United States for almost four decades.[87] Spence spoke twice at the foundational meeting, on 10 August on "The Suffrage" and the next day on "Proportional Representation."

The opening address was delivered by John Commons, professor of social science at the University of Indiana, who declared that American legislative bodies were dominated by "an irresponsible oligarchy more dangerous than that that our fathers revolted against."[88] Commons, like Spence, believed that Christianity should be mobilized as a force for reform and that the church should play a role in promoting social justice. American political institutions were either corrupt or too conservative. In his book *Social Reform and the Church*, Commons claimed that "almost every reform you can name is today blocked at the doors of municipal, State, and Federal legislatures." This had occurred because of the power of the "party machine . . . the organized clique of spoilsmen who feed upon the public storehouse."[89] Changes in voting methods could challenge party machines and pave the way for progressive legislation.

Commons advocated the Swiss system of representation, which would abolish local residency in small districts as a qualification for voting, turning the entire state into a multiple member electorate. Another speaker at the conference, William Gove, advocated the form of representation that bore his name—combining the Hare and Swiss systems with a single transferable vote—familiar to the citizens of Massachusetts. Under his preferred model of PR, lists were prepared as in the Swiss system, but only one vote was allowed; if the candidate voted for didn't need the vote (for a quota), it would be transferred to the person on a list specified before the election.

In her paper at the conference, Spence similarly advocated a version of the Hare system that included a single transferable vote as the basis for the election of several members in large statewide electorates. At the conclusion of her address, she presided, as was her custom, over a practice session, the audience voting for six of the fourteen names presented on a ticket. "The result made a great impression upon all," reported Cooley, "especially upon members of the press."[90] But agreement on the best method of proportional representation remained elusive.

Conference discussions ranged over a number of topics, including qualifications for enfranchisement as well as the machinery of representation. In response to an address on the "Educational Limitations of the Suffrage," Spence argued against disqualification based on literacy tests. Progressives in the South often recommended such tests, first introduced in Mississippi in 1890, as a way to disqualify African Americans. Spence protested that it was not the votes of the ignorant or foreigner that posed a problem but the manipulation of their votes by machine men and political agents. Better to educate voters through the adoption of proportional representation than to disenfranchise them.

There was a dramatic clash over racial politics as, in Spence's words, a "Professor from the South" sought to justify Black disenfranchisement as "a necessity to securing dominancy to the white race, whereupon the aged, white-haired Frederick Douglass rose in his might and turned the argument inside out." Spence was impressed by Douglass's oratorical skills as well as the cogency of his arguments. She listened entranced. "I never heard more eloquence, more sarcasm, or more humour than was compressed into his twenty minutes' speech."[91]

And there was another black speaker, "a Mrs Harper, well to do, who also showed all the powers of the orator."[92] Frances E. W. Harper—novelist, lecturer, suffragist, Unitarian, and member of the Woman Christian Temperance Union—was, like Spence, sixty-seven years old and a supporter of a range of progressive causes, including education. She had earlier addressed the women's congress on the subject of "Woman's Political Future," in which she invoked the idea of women's "community of interests," but she also believed that black women had to campaign separately, in their own organizations, to secure racial uplift.[93] The following year, in 1894, Harper helped found the National Association of Colored Women, which held its first national conference in Washington in 1896. Spence was impressed by Harper's talk at the conference on electoral reform. Proud of her own capacity for public speaking, she was always observant of other women's platform performance and reported that Harper's "English was of the best and [her] accent very fine."[94]

The major outcome of the congress was the formation of the American Proportional Representation League to "promote the reform of legislative assemblies by abandoning the existing system of electing single representatives from limited territorial districts by a majority vote and substituting the following":

1. All representatives shall be elected at large, on a general ticket, either without district divisions or in districts as large as practicable.
2. The election shall be in such form that the respective parties, or political groups, shall secure representation in proportion to the number of votes cast by them, respectively.[95]

Spence was "gratified by hearing so many people asserting that of all the Congresses collected in Chicago this on proportional representation [was] the most vitally important."[96]

After leaving the World's Fair, Spence embarked on a speaking tour of the East Coast, beginning in Syracuse, where she was invited by Harriet May Mills, a leading New York suffragist from a family of prominent Abolitionists, to speak to the Political Equality Club. "The New York State women are slowly working for enfranchisement," reported Spence. "They have had the vote for School Directors for some years, and now have the vote for School Commissioners, but no other votes, municipal of political."[97] She was taken to a home for "wayward" children, where she was saddened to find so many girls institutionalized: "I was very sorry to see girls of ten and eleven in such a school."[98]

In Philadelphia, Spence's busy lecturing schedule was organized by another new friend from Chicago. Her topic for the university audience was proportional representation: "I have lectured before Reform Clubs, Liberal Leagues, and woman's suffragists, and had yesterday a very interesting morning with over sixty University students and three Professors of social and economic science in Pennsylvania University." In Philadelphia, she presented seven lectures on proportional representation titled "Effective Voting."[99]

As a guest in family homes, meeting reformers' daughters and their friends, Spence was impressed by the professional advancement of American women and their careers:

> Although American women are farther from the political vote than Australian they are industrially and professionally ahead of us. . . . In this Philadelphia home the eldest daughter is a physician—a specialist for throat, ear and nose diseases; the younger daughter learned wood engraving, and but for failing eyesight would have made a great success. She has plunged into social and economic questions, and has great mental energy. I meet here dentists and obstetric practitioners who are women. I met this week the first woman in the world who brought out a whole newspaper—printing, press work and all literary matter produced by female hands and brains.[100]

And, as in other American cities, the ethnic diversity of the population of Philadelphia caught her eye:

> There is a larger coloured population than in any other northern city. . . . Recently 25,000 Russian Jews have arrived. . . . They compete with the Italians, who are numerous, for street cleaning and other dirty and laborious work. . . . The [white] Native American is never a navvy. The Irish are policemen and railway employes and officials generally. The coloured women go out to wash. The Chinamen take washing to their homes. The Germans are more versatile. Germans and Irish are saloon keepers *par excellence*.[101]

Workingmen in general had a higher rate of home ownership in Philadelphia, she was told, than elsewhere in the United States.

Her speaking tour continued apace. In New York she spoke to a conference on delinquent and dependent children about "our Australian methods." "Of all matters accomplished in Australia there is none which excites such general interest in America as the method of dealing with dependent children, and I often get a hearing for a matter not yet accomplished in Australia or any English-speaking community—effective voting."[102] In Providence, Spence stayed with her friend Anna Garlin Spencer, who arranged four separate meetings: "two in connection with her own Church (Bell-street Unitarian), one before the Normal School of Rhode Island pupils and teachers, and one before Brown University."[103]

Spence presented "The Democratic Ideal" in both Philadelphia and Providence. When she spoke at Brown University, at the invitation of university president Alisha Benjamin Andrews, she lectured on "Present Aspects of Australia and New Zealand," at a meeting cohosted by Woodrow Wilson, chair of jurisprudence and political economy at Princeton University and future American president, who would introduce the first federal child labor laws in the United States. In 1885, Wilson had published *Congressional Government*, based on his PhD dissertation, in which he compared the American system of government unfavorably with the British parliamentary system of responsible government. In 1889, in a textbook called *The State*, he argued that government should be looked on as a positive force, an agent of social welfare—a view Spence also promoted in her speech at Brown with reference to the state experiments of Australasia.

In an informal conversation on the subject with her host, Spence learned that "'Mrs S' agrees with me as to the value of State action, but under present circumstances it is dangerous." Did Anna Garlin Spencer fear adding fuel to the fires of labor radicalism? The friends differed in their assessment of the necessity of state action, but they could agree on a more abstract ideal: "The purification of politics is the one thing needful for social reforms."[104] Spence not only had a "splendid time" in Philadelphia and Providence but also added considerably to her earnings, receiving payment for her lectures and journal articles, income that was essential in supporting her extensive travel.[105]

At this time, too, Spence met the ethnologist Alice Fletcher, who had presented a paper in Chicago on American Indian music to the Anthropological Congress. Like Spence, Fletcher supplemented her income with lecturing. She had played a key role in helping write, lobby for, and implement the Dawes Act, which provided for the individual allotment of Indian land, thinking that this would secure Indians' future in American society. In the early 1880s, Fletcher had met Susette La Flesche and Francis La Flesche, the daughter and son of Omaha chief Joseph La Flesche, a meeting that began a long association with the Omaha and a close relationship with Francis La Flesche, whom she adopted informally as her son. Together they would coauthor the massive ethnological study *The Omaha*. Fletcher had a long association with the Peabody Museum in Harvard and the Carlisle

Indian School. She encouraged the Omaha to send their children east to boarding schools.[106] Spence was clearly curious about this practice that seemed to diverge from her preferred policy. "She thinks it absolutely necessary," Spence recorded in her diary, "the young Indians should be separated from their parents and taught the English language."[107] The cause of progress mandated an exception to the rule. Indian children must be removed from their homes and families to be educated in boarding schools as a condition of their entry into white society.

In Boston, the home of New England's legendary literary culture, Spence was honored to meet the aging Oliver Wendell Holmes Sr. in what turned out to be the last year of his life. Spence recalled:

> He was the only survivor of a famous band of New England writers. Longfellow, Emerson, Hawthorne, Bryant, Lowell, Whittier, and Whitman were dead. His memory was failing, and he forgot some of his own characters; but Elsie Venner he remembered perfectly and he woke to full animation when I objected to the fatalism of heredity as being about as paralysing to effort as the fatalism of Calvinism. As a medical man (and we are apt to forget the physician in the author) he took strong views of heredity.

In her approach to reform, Spence was an environmentalist. Her efforts rested on a belief that a change of environment could change people for the better. "As a worker among our destitute children, I considered environment [a greater factor than heredity] and spoke of children of the most worthless parents who had turned out well when placed early in respectable and kindly homes." Before she parted from Holmes, she acquired a valuable memento, "an autograph copy of one of his books—a much prized gift."[108]

Books were prized currency, their acquisition, circulation, and consumption recorded assiduously in notebooks and diaries. In the same year that Holmes presented one of his books to Spence, his son, Oliver Wendell Holmes Jr., noted in his diary that he had read, among other works, the disturbing Australian prophecy penned by Spence's friend, Charles Pearson, *National Life and Character: A Forecast*.[109] Its troubling assessment of world forces was also a subject for discussion that year for Theodore Roosevelt and his circle in Washington: "All our men here . . . were greatly interested . . . in what you said," Roosevelt wrote to Pearson. "In fact I don't suppose that any book recently, unless it is Mahan's Influence of Sea Power has excited anything like as much interest."[110] Books created affinities across borders, but they also stirred new apprehensions.

In Brookline, Massachusetts, Spence stayed with another bookish family—that of William Lloyd Garrison, son of the famous Abolitionist. She was impressed by the modern amenities of their spacious home as well as their literary riches. And there were Australian connections:

> They lived in a beautiful house in Brookline, on a terrace built by an enterprising man who had made his money in New South Wales. Forty-two houses were perfectly and equally warmed by one great furnace, and all the public rooms of the ground floor, dining, and drawing rooms, library, and hall were connected by folding doors, nearly always open, which gave a feeling of space I never experienced elsewhere. Electric lighting and bells all over the house, hot and cold baths, lifts, the most complete laundry arrangements, and cupboards everywhere ensured the maximum of comfort with a minimum of labour.[111]

Conversations with the family confirmed her changing views about the color question. Chicago had introduced her to the powerful eloquence of African American leaders Frederick Douglass and Frances Harper. Now in the Boston household of legendary Abolitionists, Spence felt ashamed of "being so narrow in [her] views on the coloured question": "Mr Garrison, animated with the spirit of the brotherhood of man, was an advocate of the heathen Chinee, and was continually speaking of the goodness of the negro and coloured and yellow races, and of the injustice and rapacity of the white Caucasians."[112] Progressive opinion, Spence found, was deeply divided over the "colored question" and the possible future of the multiracial democracy. Most agreed that education provided the key to a solution, but what form should it take, and should it be integrated or segregated?

Spence encountered more reformers working against "race prejudice" when she attended the annual meeting of the National American Woman Suffrage Association (NAWSA) in Washington, DC. Her host in Washington, Emily Howland, had the "firmest faith in the future of the coloured race, and has expended a great part of her energy and as large part of her income for their education and elevation."[113] Spence was dismayed, however, at the extent of segregation in the United States. Even children with "a sixteenth part of African blood" were excluded from white schools. When she visited an institution for colored children, she was pleased to find that Mattie Lawrence, who had toured Adelaide with the Fisk Jubilee Singers, had been a teacher there before taking up her career as a singer. With a professional interest in civics and education, Spence was pleased to learn that the children were doing as well as white children of the same age. Most of their teachers, she noted, were women.

Spence left the United States on 3 April 1894, traveling home via her old home of Scotland. She told readers in Australia that she had been away 365 days, having spent much longer in the great republic than she had anticipated.[114] She had lived "the strenuous life to the utmost": "I had delivered over 100 lectures, travelled thousands of miles, and met the most interesting people in the world. I felt many regrets on parting with friends, comrades, sympathisers, and fellow workers." When she looked back on "the hundreds of people who had personally interested [her], it seemed as if there was some animal magnetism in the world, and that affinities were drawn together as if by magic."[115]

It was the political affinities between New World reformers— "friends, comrades, sympathisers, and fellow workers"—that encouraged Spence to feel as if they were all pursuing the same democratic ideal, even though they might espouse different methods and have different priorities. Most of her closest friends were women. Reflecting on her time in the United States, Spence pondered the paradox of American women's social and political position. These women made up the majority of her audiences. They were clearly at the heart of the movement for progressive reform and sustained a vibrant civic culture, yet they lacked political power, and the political parties were not likely to change this situation in the near future.

> I have repeatedly said the social force which women exercise in America is beyond anything they exercise elsewhere and one cannot go through the schools and Colleges without acknowledging that they are the educating and educated classes, but still neither party can see

any advantage likely to arise from their having even the municipal franchise, and the possibility of their sharing the offices, elective and appointive, which loom so large before the eyes of the American citizen is [to political parties] alarming.[116]

The apparent contradiction of American women's condition as confident, independent, outspoken individuals who yet lacked basic political rights perplexed Spence. It was also a source of considerable frustration because lacking political rights, they seemed less well informed about electoral systems and less responsive to her message about the urgency of reform.

In a long article in the radical Boston journal the *Arena*, titled "Effective Voting: The Only Effective Moralizer of Politics," published on the eve of her departure, Spence was pleased to claim that her lecture tour, happily coinciding with the founding conference of the American Proportional Representation League, had galvanized supporters to move beyond academic discourse toward an acceptance of the role of "active propagandism." Americans needed to be awakened to the necessity of proportional representation to subvert the power of the party machine.

Although the founding fathers had inaugurated a glorious republic, changing conditions in the late nineteenth century, the "greater accumulation of wealth, the greater disparity of conditions and the enormous influx of foreigners" required the introduction of a new electoral system to safeguard democracy. Traditions inherited from the Old World no longer sufficed.

> Local representation is an inheritance from our English fore-fathers, and it did good service in its day. The exclusively local representation of England was a counterpoise to the centralizing power of king and court; the plain men of English shires and boroughs opposed in parliament and in the field the aggressions of Charles I. . . . The exclusively local representation of the American republic [and] the sharp distinction of two parties . . . which results from . . . uninominal districts [was, however,] strengthening the power of King Capital and weakening the forces that fight against monopoly and injustice.[117]

The great republic was less democratic than Australia's self-governing colonies. Although the freedom of women was more marked in America,

Australia and New Zealand were more democratic in class relations and progressive politics: "the trend of legislation in Australia and New Zealand [was] more towards the equalization of opportunities, and is more favourable to labour than anywhere else in the world."[118]

Australia had a permanent and efficient civil service appointed on merit, voting by secret ballot was well established, and children had been removed from institutions and placed into well supervised family care. Major transportation and communication systems were in public hands. "In Australia railroads, telegraphs and waterworks are constructed by the government, while in America the ownership and control are in the hands of private corporations which are a standing menace to liberty."[119]

Soon after Spence left the United States, Alfred Cridge and John Commons—fellow reformers and foremost American advocates of proportional representation—published new books on the subject. Commons, then at Syracuse University, which would soon dismiss him as a dangerous radical, published *Proportional Representation* in 1896. Like Spence, Commons traced the long English history of legislative assemblies to show that in their present-day incarnations they were not truly representative assemblies. Like Spence, Commons condemned the despotic nature of the "party machine" in the United States, and he cited the practical demonstrations by "Miss Spence of South Australia," who, "in some 50 public meetings," showed how a system of proportional representation produced fairer and more democratic outcomes. "Proportional representation promises, above all, the independence of the voter and freedom from the rule of the party machine."[120]

Spence kept in touch with the larger international movement for proportional representation through correspondence. Cridge wrote regularly from San Francisco until his death in 1902. Commons reported on progress in the midwestern states. Eugene d'Alviella wrote to tell her about the triumph of the Belgian movement (proportional representation was introduced in 1899) and of its prospects in France, where, as reported in the *Revue des Deux Mondes*, the "Liberals," crushed between the Nationalists and the Socialists, were agitating for the reform.[121]

Toward the end of her life, Spence received a letter from Emily Parmely Collins of Connecticut, former president of the Hartford Equal

Rights Club, which Spence had addressed in 1893. Collins was a veteran abolitionist and suffragist, and a cofounder of the first women's rights society in New York in 1848, the year of Seneca Falls. In Hartford she had written on women's rights for the *Hartford Journal* under the pen name "Justitia." Though almost a decade had passed since they met, "I have no more forgotten you," wrote Collins, "than I have your system of Effective Voting with which your name is identified."[122]

Collins had become an ardent convert to PR and was confident of its ultimate triumph. "Since my first correspondence twenty years ago with the late lamented Alfred Cridge, who bought your system of Effective Voting to my notice," she wrote, "I have been astonished that people who believe in self government and the right of every voter to equal representation and his choice of representatives should hesitate to adopt a mode that would put an end to machine politics, ring rule, and all political corruption."

> You must be proud of your country, for Australia sets the pace for all civilized nations to follow. And with her recent almost complete enfranchisement of women she leads the world.
>
> I sincerely hope your efforts in the Parliament for Proportional Representation will be successful. But if not now, success will not long be delayed.[123]

Indeed, in the first decade of the twentieth century, support for proportional representation gathered pace in American cities—including West Hartford, Connecticut—and across Europe. Finland saw the introduction of full adult suffrage and proportional representation in 1906. Sweden followed in 1908, and Portugal in 1911.

In South Australia, with the federation of the colonies imminent, Spence continued to proselytize for proportional representation at the colonial and federal levels. As an enfranchised woman, she stood (unsuccessfully) as a candidate for the federal constitutional convention in 1897. The year before, the Hare system of proportional representation was introduced in Tasmania, made permanent in 1899 and named the Hare-Clark system in honor of its local champion, Attorney General Andrew Inglis Clark, who would achieve eminence as coauthor of the first draft of the Australian constitution.

In the United States, a number of cities and municipalities introduced forms of proportional representation. The cause received a boost when the National Municipal League included the single transferable vote in its model city charter. Soon after, a number of city governments adopted the electoral reform, including Boulder, Colorado; Sacramento, California; West Hartford, Connecticut; Cleveland and Cincinnati, Ohio; and, in 1936, New York City. Mostly, however, the major political parties opposed the introduction of PR, successfully containing a challenge that would have seen a significant reduction of their power.[124]

Although an ardent proselytizer for electoral reform, Spence's biggest impact in the United States was probably in the area of child welfare, where her advocacy of state funding, in particular for "boarding-out" schemes to remove children from institutions and the establishment of a separate Children's Court, had long-lasting influence. On her lecture tour across the United States, Spence helped popularize the concept of an active state with responsibility to provide for social justice despite the "protests of individualists." A pioneering settler colonist and progressive thinker, Spence was an ardent exponent of translating the "democratic ideal" into radical social and political reform, and she was gratified by the strong affinities she had found among American reformers.

Five years after Spence returned from the United States, a notable American reformer came from Chicago to Adelaide. Muckraking journalist Henry Demarest Lloyd arrived with a letter of introduction to Spence from her friend and fellow PR advocate John Commons. She was delighted to have "three long talks" with the author of *Wealth against Commonwealth*, as she reported to her friend Alice Henry, who would soon leave Australia and take up work with the National Women's Trade Union League in Chicago. "I found that he knew Hull House and Miss Jane Addams intimately," Spence wrote exuberantly, "and that my dear friend Dr Bayard Holmes was his closest friend."[125]

[CHAPTER FOUR]

Federal Idealism and Labor Realism

AT THE END of the nineteenth century, the United States was widely regarded as a model for the federal organization of government. In *National Ideals, Historically Traced*, the Harvard historian Albert Bushnell Hart described the history of American democracy and its constitutional achievement in terms of its distinctive guiding "ideals." He dedicated the book to Theodore Roosevelt, "practicer of American ideals," and a special chapter to the "ideal" of federal government: "The completest, most successful, and most world-inspiring American ideal of government is that, without danger to individual liberty, with-out sacrificing local self-government, and without weakening authority, a vigorous federal government may be created."[1] This "world-inspiring American ideal" became the key inspiration for the form of federalism adopted by the framers of the Australian constitution in the 1890s, but the barriers posed to social, political and specifically labor reform at the national level by the institutionalization of states' rights, the division of powers, the difficulty of constitutional amendment, and the vagaries of judicial interpretation were clear to progressive critics even as the Australian constitution came into being.

Vigorous debates over constitutional law and labor reform ensued among a transpacific network of intellectuals, jurists, and social reformers, including Albert Bushnell Hart, Andrew Inglis Clark, Oliver Wendell Holmes Jr., H. B. Higgins, Felix Frankfurter, Florence Kelley, Louis Brandeis, and Roscoe Pound. Viewed through the lens of the personal friendships of constitutional lawyers Clark and Holmes and labor law reformers Higgins and Frankfurter, their discussions illuminate American attempts to pass legislation to regulate wages and working conditions that would, in Frankfurter's words, better meet "the social and industrial needs of the time."[2] In Higgins, president of the Commonwealth Court of Conciliation and Arbitration, whom he first met in Boston in 1914, Frankfurter saw "a great and successful pioneer" in forging a "new branch of jurisprudence that must be scientifically studied and developed."[3]

In an influential article commissioned by the *Harvard Law Review*, Higgins outlined the ways in which industrial relations might constitute "a new province for law and order"—the "new province is that of the relations between employers and employees."[4] It was a timely intervention in American debates on "social legislation." In the US Constitution, Higgins saw not a perfect ideal but a formidable barrier to progressive reform. He initially forged his critique of the Constitution's inflexibility and restrictions in the context of Australian constitutional debate in the 1890s, when he tried to defeat his countrymen's "pedantic imitation" of the United States model of federalism.[5] He took his critique of the "Rigid Constitution" to the American public in an article in *Political Science Quarterly*, published in 1905.[6]

Meanwhile, in a series of commentaries on Australasian state experiments, American labor reformers commended their example of the legal regulation of hours and wages and working conditions. After spending a sabbatical year in Australia and New Zealand in 1911–1912, Matthew B. Hammond of Ohio State University penned a series of the most "trustworthy" reports (in Harvard economist F. W. Taussig's view) of the "Australian experiments."[7] Of Higgins's key role as theorist, Hammond wrote: "He has certainly expressed, at greater length and with greater clearness than has anyone else, the ideals which have animated the Australian people and the Australian lawmakers in placing on the statute books the body of social legislation which has drawn the eyes of all the world to Australasia, and which marks the most notable experiment yet made in social democracy."[8]

Australasian labor experiments attracted the attention of a wide range of American reformers—men and women—and drew many to visit these innovative democracies in the late nineteenth and early twentieth centuries. After reading reports by Henry Demarest Lloyd and Victor S. Clark, President Roosevelt became a prominent convert to the cause.

In 1912, the Progressive Party platform, taken to American voters by Roosevelt as presidential candidate, included not only Australian reforms, such as minimum wages, the eight-hour day, shorter working hours, workers' compensation, and old-age pensions, but pledges to "provide a more easy and expeditious method of amending the Federal Constitution," and it linked workers' living standards to tariff protection ("we declare that no industry deserves protection which is unfair to labor"), calling for the kind of social contract exemplified in Australia's progressive policy of "New Protection."

By 1918, eleven American states had enacted minimum-wage laws despite the judicial obstruction that characterized the Lochner era. "American statutes show the influence of Australasian legislation," noted one legal commentator, "but no state has yet attempted such a radical interference with the contracts of employer and employee as is common in the antipodes." The influence of Australian legislation and Higgins's insistence that legal judgments should be shaped on "the solid anvil of existing industrial facts" were hailed by American jurists who celebrated the "recent triumphs of realism in the field of constitutional law."[9] Labor realism was a progressive response to the barriers to reform constructed in the name of constitutional idealism.

Transpacific currents flowed both ways. In the drafting of the constitution of the Commonwealth of Australia, American precedents were formative, as Alfred Deakin was pleased to tell Josiah Royce.[10] According to Bernhard R. Wise, a federal convention delegate from New South Wales, "That our constitution so closely resembles that of the United States is due in a very large degree to the influence of Mr. A. I. Clark."[11] Recent legal scholarship has confirmed this assessment.[12]

Andrew Inglis Clark, Tasmanian attorney general and later Supreme Court judge, was a fervent admirer of the American republic and its institutions. He was also a states' rights man. As a progressive democrat from a small island colony, Clark believed strongly in a model of federalism that entrenched the power of smaller states. At the Australasian Federation Conference in Melbourne in 1890 and again at the first Constitutional Convention in Sydney in 1891, it was Clark who insisted that the Australian colonies follow the American model of federation, rather than the Canadian or Swiss examples, to create what he called "a truly federal government," one in which the states retained significant powers.[13]

In formulating a first draft of the Australian constitution, Clark had sought advice from Albert Bushnell Hart, the Harvard historian who taught courses on the constitutional and political history of the United States.[14] Hart sent Clark a copy of his reference work *An Introduction to the Study of Federal Government*—focused principally on the United States, Germany, Canada, and Switzerland—and asked if Clark would in turn supply him with documents from the Australian federal conventions to augment his teaching materials for "a University course on federal government."[15] "Your friends here are interested in the final result of the long labours of yourself and your colleagues," Hart wrote in 1899, "and we wish the new federation god-speed."[16]

In April 1900, Hart wrote again to thank Clark for copies of the debates, reports, and journals from the Adelaide, Sydney, and Melbourne conventions of 1897 and 1898 and advised that when he had finished teaching the course, the materials would be donated to the Harvard College Library. "The friends of good government throughout the world," he affirmed, "are rejoiced at the final accomplishment of your long task."[17] Clark duly received a certificate from the president and fellows of Harvard College acknowledging receipt of the volumes and pamphlets, "a gift to the Library of the University from A Inglis Clark of Hobart, Tasmania."[18]

Clark's American sympathies and local patriotism were shaped as he grew to adulthood in Tasmania, formerly Van Diemen's Land—a colony blighted by the civic shame of the convict stain. The transportation of convicts to Van Diemen's Land didn't end until 1852, when Clark was four years old. His parents had been active in the great anti-transportation movement, "the battle which stopped just short of violence against our slave system," as the historian John Reynolds told Mark de Wolfe Howe, biographer of Oliver Wendell Holmes Jr.[19] Clark and Holmes became friends and correspondents following Clark's first visit to the United States in 1890.

Tasmania's distinctive history shaped Clark's radical idealism. Despite the cessation of convict transportation, the shadow and shame lingered during Clark's boyhood. "Around him in the streets of Hobart," James Warden wrote, "were former convicts and their keepers. Every day of his life the young Clark passed amongst the broken bodies and lost souls of those who had outlasted but never really escaped the system."[20] In 1874, the violence of the convict system gained international notoriety with the publication of *For the Term of His Natural*

Life by Melbourne-based writer Marcus Clarke, who undertook research for his sensational novel at the Port Arthur penal settlement, which remained in operation until 1877.

For the young A. I. Clark, who had grown up with this oppressive legacy, his republicanism represented more than a break with the British monarchy. It was an uplifting ideal signifying the potential of a new era of freedom and equality and a redeemed manhood for colonial subjects. As he told the 1890 conference in Melbourne, federation would make possible a new "national type of manhood," as had already been achieved in North and South America.[21]

As a young man, Clark edited a progressive magazine called *Quadrilateral*, which dealt with eclectic matters "Moral, Social, Scientific and Artistic," including spiritualism and phrenology; the writings of John Stuart Mill, Walt Whitman, and Ralph Waldo Emerson; constitutional law; and electoral reform. In an essay advocating manhood suffrage, Clark decried "government founded on Privilege"; and in another on "Hare's System of Representation," he called for fairer representation in parliament of minority interests through proportional representation.[22] In 1896, Tasmania became one of the first states in the world to institutionalize PR and multimember electorates in what came to be called the Hare-Clark system.

As an admirer of the American republic, Clark had been among those who welcomed the crew of the USS *Swatara* when it arrived in the port of Hobart, bringing the scientific expedition charged with observing the transit of Venus. Stationed in Tasmania for several months, the ships' officers enjoyed generous hospitality from local residents, with the commander of the ship, Commodore Ralph Chandler, treated as something of a visiting celebrity. Clark became friendly with a number of the scientific men, including Captain William Harkness, who led the scientific expedition, and officers Charles Stockton and Lt. H. N. Stevenson, with whom he later corresponded.[23]

Clark sent his oldest son to study naval engineering with Stevenson, later a commodore and inspector of machinery for the US Navy. Harkness sent Clark a letter of congratulations on his appointment as judge on the Tasmanian Supreme Court in 1898. Stockton, later captain of the battleship USS *Monterey*, reported on political debate over the pros and cons of US imperialism in the Philippines.[24] Another naval friend,

George Dewey, recent commander of the American Asiatic Squadron and hero at the Battle of Manila Bay, suggested to Clark that one of the "pleasing results of the war between the United States and Spain" was the "strengthening of the bonds that [bound] the Anglo-Saxon peoples."[25] As historians have noted, the US war in the Philippines became for many a kind of Anglo-Saxon crusade.[26]

American naval visits to the Australian colonies strengthened Anglo-Saxon ties across the Pacific and added to scientific knowledge. The reports of the transit of Venus expedition—and some of the objects collected in the South Pacific—were on display at Philadelphia's Centennial International Exhibition in 1876, dubbed the first "World's Fair," at once a showcase of American industrial progress and the evolutionary assumptions underpinning settler colonialism. Tasmania contributed a distinctive collection of portraits to illustrate human evolution.[27] As the official report noted, "From Tasmania there was much to interest, prominent among the exhibits being some curious photographs of aboriginal women, one of them being the sole survivor of the Tasmanian aborigines. There was also a companion portrait of 'Billy Lanney,' the last Tasmanian aboriginal man." Coincidentally, just two days before the exhibition's opening on 8 May 1876, the so-called sole survivor of the Tasmanian Aborigines, Trugernanner (or Truganini), had died.

Following an official announcement of the "extinction of the Tasmanian Aboriginal race," the well-known local identity was buried on 10 May 1876, at midnight, in the grounds of the old convict Female Factory in South Hobart, but Trugernanner's remains were later exhumed and her skeleton exhibited in the Tasmanian Museum.[28] The apparent extinction of Tasmanian Aborigines, as Peter Hulme has written, "provided the indigenous *cause celebre* of the second half of the nineteenth century, and therefore a kind of template for reading other indigenous situations."[29]

The Tasmanian contribution to the Centennial Exhibition was sent to complement photographs of Native Americans, provided by the Office of Indian Affairs in Washington. The display of the portraits of Tasmanian Aborigines enabled close visual comparisons for purposes of ethnological study. In addition, over three hundred living Native Americans from fifty-three tribes were brought to the exhibition, to display "the original inhabitants" of the country and their mode of life, even as their "vanishing" was generally regretted. Then, on 6 July, news reached Philadelphia of the disaster in Montana Territory at Little Bighorn River, where General Custer's cavalry unit was destroyed and 268 soldiers (including Custer) were killed by the Lakota Sioux, led by Sitting Bull and Crazy Horse.

In Tasmania, the *Mercury* newspaper included a detailed report of the battle, together with the prediction that a "war of extermination against the Red Skins" would certainly follow. Meanwhile, celebrations of the centenary of the American revolution—the inauguration of the New World political order—took place across the Australian colonies as well as throughout the United States. On 4 July, Andrew Inglis Clark presided over a centennial dinner in Hobart hosted by the American Club, which he helped form, where he toasted the Declaration of Independence in cadences that echoed Lincoln's Gettysburg Address: "We have met tonight in the name of the principles which were proclaimed by the founders of the Anglo-American republic . . . and we do so because we believe those principles to be permanently applicable to the politics of the world."[30] By this time, the radical young lawyer had given up his parents' Baptist faith and embraced Unitarianism, a creed favored by progressive reformers on both sides of the Pacific, especially among those who identified Christianity with ethical and social activism.[31]

In 1878, Clark was elected to the Tasmanian parliament as a Liberal Democrat committed to legislative reform. In response to charges by the conservative press that he was a Communist, he asserted that to the contrary he believed in the theory of government propounded by "the late A Lincoln—'Government of the People, for the people, and by the people.'"[32] But unlike the mainland colonies of Victoria, New South Wales, and South Australia, Tasmania did not yet enjoy manhood suffrage. The conservative propertied interests that dominated both houses of parliament in the island colony resisted even the modest proposals for reform Clark introduced as attorney general, including bills to legalize trade unions, amend the Masters and Servants Act, restrict the immigration of Chinese, introduce manhood and womanhood suffrage, and abolish plural voting and all property qualifications for election to political office.[33]

Clark chose to remain a radical liberal even as the emergent Labor Party gained in political strength. When questioned by labor sympathizers about the extent of his support for their platform, he replied that though he might differ from labor men in "the best methods of realizing the true democratic and republican ideal, whether in regard to fixing the length of a day's labor for adult males by legislation, or as to the benefits of a protective or free trade fiscal policy, the leopard could as soon change his spots as I become a supporter of plutocracy and class privilege."[34] The hostility to privilege ran deep in this newly emancipated community, but Clark's labor sympathies never translated into a national vision of the kind that fired the imaginations of fellow Australian progressives, including Alfred Deakin and H. B. Higgins.

When Clark made his first trip to the United States in 1890, he carried a letter of introduction to Oliver Wendell Holmes Jr., former professor of law at Harvard and, from 1882, associate justice of the Massachusetts Supreme Court in Boston. In a series of lectures published as *The Common Law*, Holmes had famously declared that the "life of the law has not been logic; it has been experience." He elaborated on the kinds of experience he had in mind:

> The felt necessities of the time, the prevalent moral and political theories, intuitions of public policy, avowed or unconscious, and even the prejudices which judges share with their fellow-men, have had a good deal more to do than syllogism in determining the rules by which men should be governed. The law embodies the story of a nation's development through many centuries, and it cannot be dealt with as if it contained only the axioms and corollaries of a book of mathematics.

Clark, like many of his generation, was deeply influenced by this modern approach to legal interpretation. As a lawyer, politician, lecturer, and Supreme Court judge, he often quoted from *The Common Law*, cited it in legal judgments, and taught the text to his students at the University of Tasmania.

According to his first biographer, Clark found in Holmes "the most responsive spirit in his progressive intellectual world."[35] In their friendship and correspondence, Clark played the role of faithful disciple in espousing the spirit of legal progressivism, but the tension between reverence for the American Constitution as a sacred text and the conception of law as an instrument of political and social change was increasingly evident on both sides of the Pacific.[36]

On returning to Hobart, Clark prepared for the first Australian Constitutional Convention, in Sydney in 1891. A series of papers, lists of references, and two draft constitutions (one drawn up by Clark, the other by Charles Kingston from South Australia) were presented to convention delegates, who were expected to undertake extensive preliminary reading. Legal historian Nicholas Aroney has noted that the framers of the draft Australian constitution drew heavily on the opinions and commentaries concerning the American Constitution, especially the *Federalist Papers* by John Jay, Alexander Hamilton, and James Madison. They also referred to the work of a range of later writers, including George Bancroft, John Fiske, Albert Venn Dicey, Alexis de Tocqueville, John Marshall, John C. Calhoun, Daniel Webster, John W. Burgess, and Woodrow Wilson, and, above all, Englishman James Bryce's *The American Commonwealth*, published in 1888 and adopted as the "bible" of convention delegates.[37]

Besides Bryce, the most frequently referenced authority on federal constitutions was Bryce's university mentor (and Charles Pearson's old enemy) E. A. Freeman, the English historian and proponent of Anglo-Saxonism. Clark introduced Freeman's publications to the assembled delegates at the Sydney convention as the work of a writer who had "studied the most closely, and written the most exhaustively on federal government." Freeman, like Clark, was also an admirer of the great republic, to which he had gone on a family and academic visit in 1881. Like Herbert Baxter Adams, his host at Johns Hopkins, Freeman regarded the United States as the culmination of centuries of English constitutional development. Freeman gave a course of lectures, later published as *Greater Greece and Greater Britain; and George Washington, the Expander of England*.[38] In 1884, he was appointed Regius Professor in History at Oxford.

Clark began his speech at the Sydney Constitutional Convention by quoting Freeman's classic study of the *History of Federal Government*, emphasizing federal government as an "ideal" that, "in its highest and most elaborate development, is the most finished and the most artificial production of political ingenuity. It is hardly possible that federal government can attain its perfect form except in a highly refined age, and among a people whose political education has already stretched over many generations."[39] Freeman enjoyed a high reputation among liberal-minded Australians and Americans who were encouraged to think that as fellow Anglo-Saxons, they shared a long and venerable "race history" and genius for self-government.[40]

As a resident of the small island colony of Tasmania, Clark was keen to ensure that the Australian self-governing federation did not become a simple "amalgamation," a unitary state, extinguishing the life and interests of its smaller federal components. He insisted that "each State [was] a separately organised community which [had] a distinct collective and corporate life and distinct interests" requiring separate representation in the federal parliament—through equal representation in the Senate—and an effective veto in the constitutional amendment procedure.[41] The American model was useful, according to Clark, in providing an example of how the "corporate life and distinct interests" of former self-governing British colonies could be maintained in a new "Federated Australia."

The decision to name the new nation the Commonwealth of Australia was taken at the Sydney convention. In the sometimes heated debate, Clark joined Deakin in supporting the name "commonwealth" against those who condemned its dangerous "republican ring," as Deakin characterized their objections in his article on the "Federation of Australia," written for *Scribner's*.[42] The motion to adopt the name "commonwealth" was passed 26 votes to 13. In the American journal *Forum*, English Liberal Charles Dilke also worried about its antimonarchical implications, noting the absence of "all effusive expressions of loyalty . . . from the gathering" in Sydney "except as regards the speeches of Sir Henry Parkes."[43]

The name "commonwealth" had Cromwellian associations, but just as important for Deakin and Clark were its American usages. Two of the oldest American colonies were the Commonwealths of Virginia and Massachusetts. Goldwin Smith had written on "the Experience of the American Commonwealth" for the 1867 English collection *Essays on Reform*, a volume to which, as we have seen, both Bryce and Pearson also contributed. Bryce subsequently appropriated Smith's title for his large survey work *The American Commonwealth,* in which he characterized the United States as a "Commonwealth of commonwealths, a Republic of republics, a state which, while one, is nevertheless composed of other states even more essential to its existence than it is to theirs."[44]

With the conclusion of the Sydney Constitutional Convention, delegates returned home to deal with pressing political concerns, as the Australian colonies—like the United States—were engulfed by economic depression and industrial conflict. Banks crashed and unemployment rose. It was in this context that the first branches of the Labor Party were formed in Queensland and New South Wales. While Labor leaders and nationalist journals, such as the *Bulletin,* opposed the proposed federation as undemocratic—with voters of tiny Tasmania given equal representation in the Senate with voters from populous New South Wales—supporters of the cause, including members of the nationalist Australian Natives' Association and the Sydney Federation League, began to talk of a people's movement and called for a new convention of representatives elected directly by the people.[45] It was also agreed that the draft constitution would be submitted to a series of referenda to secure popular approval.

The first session of the second series of Constitutional Conventions in 1897 met in Adelaide, presided over by the premier of South Australia, Charles Kingston, but led by New South Wales political leader Edmund Barton, who would become the first Australian prime minister. Deakin played the key roles of orator, conciliator, and negotiator. He spoke of the virtue of sacrifice in pursuit of the ideal but also of the delegates' responsibility to posterity: "The Constitution we seek to prepare is worthy of any and every personal sacrifice, for it is no ordinary measure, and must exercise no short-lived influence, since it preludes the advent of a nation."

The provisions of the constitution were debated clause by clause at convention sessions in Adelaide, Sydney, and Melbourne until the delegates' work was finally done. It was then sent to a meeting of colonial premiers, who made further small changes, before placing it before the people of each colony to vote in favor or against. Once approved, the

Bill to Constitute the Commonwealth of Australia, which, crucially, included provisions for the federal enactment of woman suffrage, the direct election of senators, the establishment of an industrial court to settle interstate labor disputes, and the exclusion of indigenous Australians from the national census (so their numbers wouldn't affect the allocation of seats for the House of Representatives) was sent to the imperial parliament for enactment into law in 1900.

Sacrifice and compromise were necessary on all sides, because the draft constitution could not please everyone. Delegates from smaller colonies were determined to retain full self-governing powers, but Clark's urging of the American federal ideal on Australian convention delegates met considerable opposition—especially from residents of the larger colonies—to the undemocratic provision that all states would enjoy equal representation and status in the Senate. In the view of critics, democracy meant majority rule. Perhaps the most severe critic of Clark's "pedantic imitation" of the US model was progressive Victorian delegate, lawyer, and member of the Victorian Legislative Assembly, H. B. Higgins, who castigated the draft Australian constitution, in its deference to the interests of small states and the barriers erected to later amendment, as profoundly retrogressive in character. He was supported in his campaign by the institutions of organized labor, including the Victorian Trades Hall Council.

Higgins was a passionate, if austere, reformer, strongly committed to the potential of the law as an instrument for social and political reform. Migrating from Northern Ireland with his parents at the age of eighteen, Higgins had enrolled in law at the University of Melbourne, where, like Deakin, he joined Charles Pearson's Debating Society. He worked as a lawyer before winning election, in 1894, to the Victorian Legislative Assembly as the Liberal member for Geelong. In debate on the path-breaking 1896 Factory Act, which introduced the first legal minimum wage in the world, Higgins became known for his outspoken support for the interests of white workingmen and social justice more broadly.

As a delegate to the Australian Constitutional Conventions of 1897–1899, Higgins expressed dismay at the prospect of Australia adopting an inflexible and undemocratic constitution at the moment of its inauguration as a modern progressive nation. He made clear his opposition to the privileging of states' rights and the proposal that all states, from the smallest to the largest, should have equal representation in the Senate. Such provisions, he argued, ran directly counter to the progressive aspirations of the new commonwealth.

The American model, adopted under pressure in the late eighteenth century, was, he insisted, ill conceived. "The question is what are we to do?" he asked fellow delegates as he outlined an ideal of federation that respected plural (but not indigenous) sovereignties:

> I submit that the true tendency of the federal systems . . . the true ideal of federation is that the people shall rule on subjects of common interest, and that within separate organisations they shall rule as to matters which come within those separate organisations. That would be a true ideal of federation; but here, unfortunately, we are going back to the ruck; we are going back to retrogressive legislation. We are going to try and adopt the system which was adopted under pressure in America, and which they would never adopt if they had to start again.[46]

Higgins's strong opposition to key aspects of the draft Australian constitution was stated at a series of public meetings and in newspapers and reviews, and led him finally to advocate a no vote in the final referendum.[47]

Higgins argued that the "states-house theory" was, in reality, "out-and-out provincialism" under a softer name. "I have rejoiced to watch, in the course of our discussions, the steady growth of the true federal idea," he wrote, "but still the narrow provincial spirit is too much for us. My objection to this bill is, not that it is federal, but that it is provincial. I have come to the conclusion that it ought to be called a 'bill to perpetuate provincialism.'"[48] The undemocratic basis of the Senate was clear for all to see: Tasmania, with its 170,000 people, would have the same voting power as New South Wales, with its 1.32 million, a discrepancy bound to grow with time. The equal representation of all states in the Senate violated "the principle of the rule of the majority," the key principle of democracy. "We liberals," Higgins insisted, "uphold the rule of the majority in order to attain peace—to make particular interests, special interests, subordinate to the general interest; to make the laws of a nation a true reflection of current opinions and cur-rent culture." The constitution would thwart the national will—the will of the people—erecting a barrier to reform for all time.

Higgins also condemned the constitutional amendment procedure that required an artificial majority—four of the six states (later amended to three) as well as a majority of the total population—to agree to any proposed amendment, including in relation to the composition of the Senate itself. Delegates "voted that this provision should be unchange-able, no matter how much Tasmania may dwindle or New South Wales increase." The constitution, he warned, would prove to be a straight-jacket for future generations. Furthermore, in years to come, Higgins predicted, when the people of Australia realized that law courts could sit in judgment on the legislature and treat a law as invalid because of its being beyond the powers of the legislature, "the funda-mental importance of the flexibility and plasticity in the written con-stitution will be even more apparent than it is now."[49]

"Federation is a grand ideal," Higgins declared, "towards which we are making rapid strides. We are one people—we have one destiny. . . . We have the same origin, the same habits, the same ideals." But the constitution as proposed by the convention of 1898 didn't ex-press that ideal, and he couldn't support it. "The time had arrived, but the fruit was not yet ready to be consumed. . . . I think this glorious ideal of federation as of a noble and perfect fruit, rounding to ripeness, but as yet green and crude and acrid."[50]

Not so, according to Andrew Inglis Clark, who in a series of news-paper articles rebutted Higgins's critique and returned to his advocacy of states' rights: "each State is a separately organised community, which has a distinct, collective, and corporate life and distinct interests which may be more or less affected by federal laws." Furthermore, "each colony has had a separate local history, out of which a distinct body of senti-ments and opinions on many matters has grown up."[51] The residents of small states shouldn't have had to submit to laws they didn't like. Clark invoked authorities such as Freeman, Hart, Burgess, and Wilson to insist that the federal ideal, with its equal representation of the states and preservation of their distinctive corporate life, was, indeed, perfect.

Higgins was moved by a different vision. In an essay on "Austra-lian Ideals," he suggested that his country was torn by "a struggle between two conflicting principles . . . the commercial or bourgeois principle and the principle of solidarity—the principle of the special or private interest against the principle of the common interest."[52] Newly elected to the first federal parliament in 1901, Higgins became a champion of the common interest, as expressed in the ideal of a national "commonwealth" as a global beacon for progressive labor and advanced social legislation.

In the year of the inauguration of the Commonwealth of Australia, Clark published his reflections on the constitution in a volume called *Studies in Australian Constitutional Law* (reprinted in 1905) and sent copies of both editions to his American interlocutors, Hart and Holmes. A reflection on the character of Australian federalism, the text was also a tribute to Holmes, expressing Clark's expectation that the constitution would remain relevant to the "social conditions and the political exigencies of the succeeding generations." The law was not "a dead letter," he wrote, but a "living force," responsive to society's changing needs. Interpretation of the constitution, he emphasized, should proceed on the basis that it was "not made to serve a temporary or restricted purpose, but was framed and adopted as a permanent and comprehensive code of law," useful for future generations.

Times change and new challenges arise. Inevitably, the social conditions and the political demands of the succeeding generations of every progressive community would produce new governmental problems to which the language of the constitution must be applied. Hence,

> it must be read and construed, not as containing a declaration of the will and intentions of men long since dead, and who cannot have anticipated the problems that would arise for solution by future generations, but as declaring the will and intentions of the present inheritors and possessors of sovereign power, who maintain the Constitution and have the power to alter it, and who are in the immediate presence of the problems to be solved. It is they who enforce the provisions of the Constitution and make a living force of that which would otherwise be a silent and lifeless document.[53]

In explaining the differences between federal constitutions, Clark noted that there were, in general, two types of federation: one model vested most political power and authority in the central government, as had occurred in Canada; the second type allotted a limited number of powers to the larger community, leaving its component parts in possession of all residual political power and authority, as exemplified by the United States and Australia.

In the same year, Clark wrote to Holmes of his longing to be in America:

> I suppose that you had a good time in England. I often wish that Australia was as near to California as Massachusetts is to England. I should then see Boston every three of four years, and would probably be preparing now for a journey there early next year. But I must bow to the geographical configuration of the earth and all its consequences and wait in patience until my time to cross the Pacific Ocean again arrives.[54]

Holmes replied with a letter calculated to thrill his Tasmanian friend, with its warm depiction of Civil War manhood. He reported that he lately had staying with him "an ex-Confederate officer who was doing his best to kill me 40 years ago." He had made a party of the occasion by inviting the Virginia classicist Basil Gildersleeve, "a distinguished scholar and another ex-Confederate, who was badly wounded," and Holmes's kinsman, Henry Higginson, who had "a beautiful sabre cut on his face," to meet his southern houseguest. And there they were—"two from each side of the old war—hobnobbing as cheerfully as possible." In fact, Holmes reflected, "the opposite soldiers got on very well in the intervals of fighting," fondly invoking the conceit of manly solidarity across the battle lines that underpinned reconciliation between North and South.[55]

Holmes was a thrice-wounded hero of the Civil War. His father was Oliver Wendell Holmes Sr., medical man and author of *The Autocrat of the Breakfast Table*, whom Catherine Spence had been pleased to meet in 1894. Holmes's mother, born Amelia Lee Jackson, was an abolitionist. Holmes Jr. was a charismatic figure: a tall, lanky, and self-assured New Englander, whose legal authority and patrician bearing attracted numerous protégés, including Louis Brandeis and Felix Frankfurter. Dining in a Boston hotel together, he and his Tasmanian friend must have looked and sounded like incongruous companions. Clark was tiny, less than five feet tall. Eager and excitable, he had a nervous disposition and a frail constitution, often succumbing to illness. Holmes, though wounded in the Civil War, lived a long and vigorous life, not retiring from the Supreme Court until he was ninety-one years of age. In his Tasmanian visitor, the loquacious Holmes found an avid listener.

Holmes reported to Clark on his recent court cases and also his reading, recommending E. A. Ross's book *Social Control* as "a mighty sharp little popular work."[56] Ross was one of the new breed of Midwest academics, who would prove influential in the development of socio-logical jurisprudence, demanding that law keep up with and respond to the changing industrial, social and political order.[57] *Social Control* was published in 1901; his *Sin and Society*, with a preface by Theodore Roosevelt, in 1907. Ross's works anticipated the "realism and ame-liorism" of the sociological school of law later associated with Roscoe Pound, who taught with Ross at the University of Nebraska. Pound credited his colleague with setting him on "the path the world [was] moving in." "It is recognized," Pound wrote to Ross, "that in the sepa-ration of jurisprudence from sociology there is stagnation and that law has been greatly deficient in the past by virtue of its divorcement from social ends."[58] Before arriving in Nebraska, Ross had taught at that cradle of progressive thought, the University of Wisconsin. After leaving Nebraska, Pound moved to Harvard, where he was appointed dean of law in 1916.

Progressives agreed that the law should be "a living force," as Clark had written in *Studies of Australian Constitutional Law* in 1901, but it was increasingly clear that the US Constitution and higher courts, so revered by Clark, were serious obstacles to reform. As the Tasma-nian jurist prepared to cross the Pacific again, he read that Theodore Roosevelt had appointed Holmes to the bench of the Supreme Court. His congratulatory note had a wistful tone: "Boston will never seem quite the same again to me when I think of it without you."

Holmes took up his position in Washington in December 1902 in a period of "legislative exuberance," as his protégé, Felix Frankfurter noted in a later appreciation: "To an extent unparalleled in the coun-try's and Court's history, the Supreme Court became the arbiter of po-litical controversies."[59] Many of those centered on the legitimacy of labor law, Frankfurter's (and Higgins's) special field of interest. In his

Mr. Justice Holmes and the Constitution, Frankfurter argued, in the spirit of Holmes, that it was not legal texts but judges who gave meaning to the law and the Constitution. In interpreting constitutional law, "each Justice is impelled to depend upon his own controlling conceptions, which are in turn bound by his experience and imagination, his hopes and fears, his faith and doubts."[60]

This was the realist view of constitutional interpretation, but the judicial activism of conservative judges troubled progressives, who counseled restraint, believing that elected legislatures were the proper bodies to make laws.[61] In 1905, in the landmark case of *Lochner v. New York,* Holmes, in his dissenting opinion, castigated the activism of the majority who struck down a New York law, the Bakeshop Act of 1895, that limited bakers' working hours to a ten-hour day and a sixty-hour week. Following appeal to the Supreme Court, the majority declared the law unconstitutional, as violating the Fourteenth Amendment's guarantee: "nor shall any State deprive any person of life, liberty or property without due process of law."

The limit on working hours was held to infringe the right of freedom of contract. In his dissenting judgment, Holmes declared that "a constitution is not intended to embody a particular economic theory, whether of paternalism and the organic relation of the citizen to the State or of laissez faire." The majority had decided the case "upon an economic theory which a large part of the country does not entertain." In a democracy, the law should reflect public opinion, not defy it.

H. B. Higgins also worried about judge-made law. In the same year as *Lochner,* he noted in his article on the "Rigid Constitution" that because it was virtually impossible to amend the Constitution, "men who have had to work under it have been forced to very critical and ingenious discussions as to its meaning."[62] But judges were not, in his opinion, the right people to amend the Constitution or make law: "Their function is to interpret and apply the law, not to make it or change it." Was it not better in a democracy "to leave the task of improvement to the action of public opinion, inspired by public needs, and speaking through its appropriate organs of Congress and the polling-booth?"[63]

But how might the Constitution be amended to make it easier to legislate for reform? The "Rigid Constitution" was a major obstacle to

progressive initiatives. It was an injustice that "the men of one generation" were able "to bind, by inflexible governmental arrangements, the
generations which succeed."[64] Higgins deplored the fact that the Australian constitution had followed so closely the American example,
making it, too, practically "unalterable."[65] Only when the draft Constitution had been put to popular referenda in the larger states had
opponents secured some concessions—such as curbing the role of the
Senate in money bills—but even so, "the Australian Constitution still
bears the traces of the United States system of curbing and restriction
and minority rule; it still requires the concurrence of artificial majori-
ties for amendment; but it [was] less hopeless to look for amendment
in Australia than in the United States."[66]

Higgins pointed to the high rate of failure of proposed amendments
to the US Constitution, on subjects ranging from woman suffrage, to
hours of labor, to uniform marriage and divorce laws, to the method of
electing the Senate. The Australian constitution had specified that
marriage and divorce law be defined as a federal matter. "It is surely
not presumptuous to hold that uniform legislation on a subject which
lies at the very root of all civilized society would be better than the
present conflict between the marriage law and practice of the strict
states and that of the lax states."[67] Attempts to amend the constitution to have senators elected by the people, rather than by state legislatures, had also been defeated in the United States. "That the people
as a whole would probably approve of the change, is shown by the fact
that the House of Representatives has endorsed it by the requisite two-
thirds majority. But the Senate will not have it. Senators will not
abandon the ladder by which they have attained to power."[68] Not until
the passage of the Seventeenth Amendment in 1913 were direct elections for Senators introduced in the United States.

The difficulty in amending the US Constitution, Higgins observed,
had led to some very creative judicial interpretation, "expansions of the
constitution by judicial decision," and the identification of "implied
powers":

From the short clause enabling Congress "to regulate commerce with
foreign nations and among the several states and with the Indian
tribes," the court has deduced an implied power to legislate for the

control of all navigable waters (even a state river such as the Penob-
scot), for the construction of wharves and other works, for the prohibition of immigration, for laying an embargo on shipping, for the establishment of an interstate commission with power to interfere
with railway companies and with transportation rates.[69]

Yet the United States now faced new social and political problems for
which their Constitution was ill adapted. These included the operation
of corporations, trusts, and combines; government of overseas colonies and dependencies; and widespread labor problems. Surely labor
relations—wages, conditions, and hours—had to be regulated at the federal level. "When there is one common tariff for imports, there is one
economic area; and if the national legislature deals with tariffs it should
be free to deal with labor problems."[70] This was the conceptual link at
the basis of the Australian policy of "New Protection," whereby manufacturers were granted tariff protection in return for paying workers
a "living wage," whose meaning would be defined by Higgins as president of the Commonwealth Court of Conciliation and Arbitration in
his landmark *Harvester* judgment of 1907.

In the Australian constitution, Higgins advised American readers,
"We have managed to confer on the federal Parliament power to legislate for 'conciliation and arbitration for the prevention and settlement
of industrial disputes extending beyond the limits of any one state.'"
This federal power had been written into the constitution by Higgins,
Charles Kingston from South Australia, and others at the final Melbourne Constitutional Convention. Since then, a bill providing for the
exercise of this far-reaching power by a new court had become law.[71]

Alfred Deakin's legislation of 1904 had created the Commonwealth
Court of Conciliation and Arbitration to prevent and settle disputes
extending beyond one state. It was a tribunal, moreover, that required
workers and employers to be represented by their industrial organizations, encouraging and facilitating the growth of trade unions and
thereby according them a new status and legitimacy in civil and
political society. In case of a dispute, the two parties would be required
to submit their respective cases, based on facts, to a legal tribunal, presided over by an impartial judicial authority—a member of the High
Court.

In 1906, Prime Minister Deakin appointed Higgins to the High Court, with the expectation that he would assume duties as president of the Court of Conciliation and Arbitration in 1907. In that year, it became his historic task to determine whether agricultural machinery manufacturer Sunshine Harvester paid a "living wage" that was "fair and reasonable" to its employees. What was a "living wage"? Higgins decided that such a wage should be sufficient, as he put it in his careful formulation, to meet "the normal needs of the average employee, regarded as a human being, living in a civilised community."

Crucially, Higgins's humanist advocacy rested on the key progressive distinction between civilized communities and others, a distinction that had been invoked in 1896, when he supported the introduction of the legal minimum wage and wages boards in Victoria. In Australia, progressive labor laws were designed in the context of a global labor market, to uphold white men's standards, in ways that also served to differentiate men's work from women's work. In Melbourne, Higgins's 1907 *Harvester* judgment was applauded as a "swashing blow" against capitalists, "a really magnificent statement of the case of the poor man."[72]

To ascertain human needs in a civilized society (and inspired by an essay by feminist leader Vida Goldstein), Higgins suggested that the relevant trade union should obtain the details of the cost of living from working people's household budgets.[73] Higgins initiated his own sociological research project. He arranged to interview a number of workers' wives and, on the basis of their testimony, the evidence of their budgets, and that of tradesmen and real estate proprietors, arrived at the estimate that a weekly wage of two pounds two shillings per week was necessary to support "the normal needs of the average employee, regarded as a human being, living in a civilised community." In treating working-class women as expert witnesses and calibrating their actual household expenses, Higgins pioneered a form of sociological jurisprudence that anticipated the famous Brandeis brief prepared by National Consumers League advocate Josephine Goldmark the following year in *Muller v. Oregon*.

Although the Australian High Court (ironically, given Higgins's objections to the "Rigid Constitution") struck down the Excise Tariff Act, which had framed the *Harvester* case, as unconstitutional, Higgins's historic definition of that wage as sufficient to meet the needs of workers, defined as human beings, living in a civilized society, would prove influential not only across Australia, as M. B. Hammond told American readers, but also, as historian Lawrence Glickman has noted, in the United States.[74] Workers were not mere units of production. Workers, Higgins told a meeting of businessmen in Sydney, were "human beings with . . . human wants . . . not machines or automata," but "beings with their lives to live."[75]

In *Muller v. Oregon*, Brandeis successfully argued that the ten-hour law in the state of Oregon was constitutional.[76] The compilation of evidence for the brief was wide ranging and comparative and included reports of the benefits of shorter working hours long established in Australia. "From the whole sordid, miserable record of exploited workers under unregulated hours there stood out," Goldmark later wrote, "clear and luminous the regeneration that followed a more decent limitation of hours."[77] For the first time, argument in a Supreme Court case was based not on legal precedent but on "the living facts of industrial America."[78] The *Muller* case was "epoch-making" according to Frankfurter, not because of its decision but because of the authoritative recognition given by the Supreme Court to his method of argument.[79]

Sociological evidence was crucial to the outcome of this path-breaking argument and seemed to turn the tide in favor of worker protection. "One of the great theorists of sociological jurisprudence, Oliver Wendell Holmes Jr had declared that the life of law is experience, not logic," noted legal scholar Melvin Urofsky. "Louis Brandeis became the great practitioner of that school of thought."[80] It was Brandeis's "craving for authentic facts," said an admirer in the *New Republic*, that led him to "create practically a new technique in the presentation of constitutional questions":

> Until his famous argument on the Oregon ten-hour law for women, social legislation was argued before our courts practically *in vacuo*, as an abstract question unrelated to a world of factories and child labour and trade unions and steel trusts. In the Oregon case for the first time there were marshalled before the Supreme Court the facts of modern industry which called for legislating limited hours of labor. This marked an epoch in the argument and decision of constitutional cases and resulted not only in reversal of prior decisions, but in giving to the courts a wholly new approach to this most important class of present-day constitutional issues.[81]

It was not, in fact, a wholly new approach. Such assessments ignore the transpacific precedents that shaped the new sociological or realist approach to labor law. In Higgins's insistence the previous year on attending to actual experience and researching "existing industrial facts" in the *Harvester* judgment, his jurisprudence—as many contemporary American jurists recognized—anticipated this new American approach.

In 1912, the platform announced by the new Progressive Party included a number of reforms already on the statute books in Australia, including the eight-hour day, minimum wage, workers' compensation, and old-age pensions. The time had come to bring common problems resulting from changes in the industrial system under national jurisdiction: "It is as grotesque as it is intolerable that the several States should by unequal laws in matter of common concern become competing commercial agencies, barter the lives of their children, the health of their women and the safety and well being of their working people for the benefit of their financial interests." It was time for traditional investments in "States' rights" to give way to the imperative of securing "social and industrial justice" to meet the contemporary needs of Americans, who by the twentieth century were surely no longer a collection of disparate communities but "one people."[82]

When Higgins visited the United States in mid-1914 in response to an invitation by "industrial counselor" Robert Valentine (a friend of Frankfurter and Roosevelt and the former commissioner for Indian affairs), he was warmly welcomed into a lively network of progressive reformers centered on Valentine's Washington, DC, home, fondly dubbed by Oliver Wendell Holmes Jr, a frequent visitor, as "the House of Truth."[83] In Cambridge, Boston, New York, and Washington, Higgins met Louis Brandeis; Roscoe Pound; F. W. Taussig; Richard Dana; Albert Bushnell Hart; Elizabeth Glendower Evans; Florence Kelley; Mary Chamberlain and Christina Merriman from the *Survey*; Irene and John Andrews of the American Association for Labor Legislation; manufacturer Stanley King and his wife, Gertrude, a graduate of Vassar; and judges Learned Hand and Felix Frankfurter.[84]

Recently appointed to Harvard Law School, Frankfurter soon became one of Higgins's close friends and confidants, sharing a long correspondence preserved in Frankfurter's papers. An Austrian-born Jewish immigrant, Frankfurter was naturalized in New York in 1898.

An outsider determined to achieve high national office, he was, in the recollection of a friend, "small of stature, long of stride, strident of voice, putting a steely grip on one's elbow." He was an enjoyable companion "from whom came a cascade of talk—challenging, contentious talk—and an explosive laugh."[85] He was "barely five feet five inches tall," another friend recalled, but broad shouldered, with a round, bird-like face accented by fine, bluish-gray eyes framed by spectacles.[86]

A graduate of Harvard Law School, in 1910 Frankfurter went to work as a legal adviser to Henry L. Stimson in the Bureau of Insular Affairs in the War Department. The government of American dependencies in the Caribbean and the Pacific called for progressive administration and programmatic training. In his paper "Government and Administration of the Philippine Islands," Frankfurter noted the expectation that American rule would gradually extend to Filipinos, and "as they shall show themselves fit to exercise it, a greater and greater measure of popular self-government."[87] Filipinos would come into their right to self-government under progressive tutelage.

In mid-1914, Frankfurter was lured back to Harvard. "I do feel very deeply the need of organized scientific thinking in the modern state," he wrote to Stimson as he accepted the academic appointment, "and particularly in a legalistic democracy like ours, the need of a definitely conceived jurisprudence coordinating sociology and economics."[88] He was an intellectual who wanted to shape public policy. To Oliver Wendell Holmes, he wrote:

> What challenges me is to bring public life, the elements of reality, in touch with the university and, conversely, to help harness the law school to the needs of the fight outside. You know better than the rest of us how empirical, how inadequate the foundation of our legislative output, how unthought out much of reform legislation is. . . . It's up to the Law Schools to deal with theories of legislation (I know it's a tough job) and in turn help shape the course.[89]

Frankfurter courted senior men such as Stimson, Holmes, and Brandeis. In the Australian jurist Higgins, an esteemed authority, learned and reserved, he found a like-minded ambition, if markedly dissimilar temperament. Frankfurter became Higgins's host in Cambridge and Boston.

In Washington, Higgins was visited at his hotel by Theodore Roosevelt. "He had been urged by his 'progressive' friends in Boston and

New York to meet me," Higgins wrote in his diary.[90] He was also introduced to members of Woodrow Wilson's administration (W. B. Wilson, secretary of labor, and Louis Post, assistant secretary of labor), he witnessed a woman suffrage deputation, and caught up again with Brandeis, who took him to a memorable luncheon meeting of the Common Council, mainly heads of federal government departments.[91] While there, he joined a discussion about the regulation of competition between railroads by the Interstate Commerce Commission.

The Interstate Commerce Act of 1887—the first federal law to regulate private industry in the United States—required that railroad rates be "reasonable and just" but did not empower the government to fix specific rates. Higgins was asked about his experience in the *Harvester* case, when he had to rule on unfair competition in the manufacturing industry. He spoke about his difficulty in arriving at the principles on which to determine a "fair and reasonable" wage.[92] He explained to the men in Washington how he arrived at his determination. As he later wrote to Frankfurter: "They told us that labour disputes were nonjusticiable as there were no principles of right to guide us; but we found principles—invented principles if you like—[based] on justice and humanity."[93]

Higgins was greatly inspired by the public-spirited men and women he met in Chicago, Boston, Cambridge, New York, and Washington, but the contradictions of this vibrant yet conservative democracy bothered him. "It is to America that we must look for the humanizing of our civilization," he wrote to Frankfurter. Yet it was in America that "the danger of dehumanizing is greatest. . . . [You are] horribly shackled by your constitution." He was, however, encouraged that Brandeis not only had great faith in "the enlargement of horizon of [the US] Supreme Court" but was "sustained by his experience in the Oregon case." But others shared Higgins's concerns. He noticed that English Fabian and social psychologist Graham Wallas had written to the same effect in the *New Republic*. "If you have time," Higgins suggested to Frankfurter, "you might care to look up an article of mine on the subject of 'The Rigid Constitution' in the *Political Science Quarterly*."[94]

At Frankfurter's urging, Higgins would write for more American journals. In early 1915, he was invited by Gerard C. Henderson, editor in chief at the *Harvard Law Review*, to make a contribution. "We are making an effort," Henderson wrote in April 1915, to secure articles from "foreign jurists of note."

> I feel that one from you would be ideal for our purposes especially on such a topic as Labor Law. We in America have much to learn from foreigners. Your realistic and sensible treatment of this branch of law in your conduct of arbitration proceedings in Australia contrasts so favourably with the artificial and fruitless discussions of natural rights and liberty of contract in which American lawyers indulge, that a discussion of it from a lawyer's point of view from your pen would be a real service to the Bench and the Bar of this country.[95]

Higgins obliged and wrote "A New Province for Law and Order: Industrial Peace through the Minimum Wage and Arbitration" over his vacation. Henderson was delighted. "I do not know how I can adequately thank you." And he observed: "Many lawyers here will say that it doesn't deal with a legal topic. To me the principles and precedents that you have worked out seem to be of the essence of law—a new branch of jurisprudence that must be scientifically studied and developed. PS Prof Frankfurter asks to be especially remembered to you."[96]

Frankfurter was also pleased with Higgins's contribution, commending it immediately to Holmes: "I wonder if you thought as well as I did of Justice Higgins' article in this month's Harvard Law Review? It seemed to me to have all the romance of bending theories to the test of life—of trying to adjust conflicting demands to larger common interests, or at least making men know their demands through disinterested expert guidance."[97]

In the *Harvard Law Review* article, Higgins described the aims of the Commonwealth Court of Conciliation and Arbitration and explained how it worked. "The arbitration is compulsory in the sense that an award, if made, binds the parties." It was progressive in that it substituted reason for barbarism.

> The Act makes a strike or a lockout an offence if the dispute lies within the ambit of the Act—if the dispute is one that extends beyond the limits of one State. In other words the process of conciliation, with arbitration in the background, is substituted for the rude and barbarous process of lockout and strike. Reason is to displace force; the might of the State is to enforce peace between industrial combatants as well as between other combatants; and all in the interests of the public.[98]

But as his subtitle made clear, Higgins wanted to highlight for Americans the role of a legally recognized minimum wage (defined as a "living wage") in establishing industrial peace.

The legislation that framed his decision gave no guidance to the principles on which to determine a living wage, so Higgins adopted a standard based on "the normal needs of the average employee, regarded as a human being living in a civilized community." He set out an expansive list of normal needs. Besides rent, food, and fuel, there were other costs entailed in living as a human being in a civilized community: "light, clothes, boots, furniture, utensils, rates, life insurance, savings, accident or benefit societies, loss of employment, union pay, books and newspapers, tram or train fares, sewing machine, mangle, school requisites, amusements and holidays, liquors, tobacco, sickness or death, religion [and] charity."[99] Men were also obliged to support their families. Based on his calculations, Higgins decided that a living wage for an unskilled laborer must be at least forty-two shillings a week. "No employer was entitled to purchase by wages the right to endanger life or treat men as pigs."[100]

In the new industrial relations system created in Australia, workers were represented in the legal process by trade unions, as only registered organizations could use the arbitration court, and each organization had exclusive coverage of that occupation. As Higgins wrote, the system was "based on unionism." It followed, therefore, that the court would not assist an employer in "devices to stamp out unionism." The court would also direct that preference be given to unionists in employment, other things being equal. Finally, Higgins argued that the imposition of a minimum wage was based on an explicit recognition that "freedom of contract" was "a misnomer as applied to the contract between an employer and an ordinary individual employee." These were not equal parties. The position of the employer was so much more powerful than that of the individual employee. The court should play a vital role, he suggested, in exposing such antiquated theories to "the light of day."[101]

Judge Learned Hand spelled out the implications of Higgins's jurisprudence for understandings of "full citizenship" in an article on "The Hope of the Minimum Wage" in the *New Republic* and offered his endorsement. "We must insist upon the reasonable expectation of those who view it hopefully," he wrote, "and we must seek to advance it, at least until it has been demonstrated to be false."[102] The next year, *New Republic* editor Herbert Croly echoed Higgins's views in an article on "Unionism and Anti-Unionism":

> It should be the policy of the American nation to discriminate in favour of unionism, to recognize its merits, to define its functions, and to make it an essential part of the national industrial system. . . . [There should be no] popular or official discouragement of any attempt by employers to outlaw unionism. . . . The law has declared that labor is not a commodity; but despite the law it must remain a commodity unless wage-earners possess the power to participate effectively in the negotiations whereby their work is bought and sold.[103]

In a letter to Frankfurter, Higgins summarized Croly's views: "Labor unions must be frankly recognized and must have preference in the giving of work. He has caught the fundamental ideas of the minimum wage and collective bargaining (which in Australia we aid by 'arbitration')."[104]

Higgins was elated at the *New Republic*'s repudiation of individualism and apparent turn to collectivism. "It is economic individualism," wrote Higgins to Frankfurter, "which most injures American individuality." He welcomed Croly's recognition of the federal constitution as a "distraction to democratic progress" but was dismayed by his militarism: "Of course war does often help nationality; so would the eating of babies satisfy hunger."[105]

The outbreak of war in August 1914, just after Higgins had left the United States for England, was a catastrophe, leading to a massive loss of life on far-flung battlefields. It also proved deeply destructive to family and community life on the home front, fostering division, despair, and political disenchantment. In Australia, the advent of war brought progressive experiments to a sudden halt. For Higgins, the war proved a double calamity: his only son was killed in battle, and political attacks, including intervention in the arbitration process by jingoistic prime minister W. M. Hughes, led to Higgins's resignation from the presidency of the Commonwealth Court Conciliation and Arbitration. A "clever little fellow of no physique," as Higgins described Hughes to Frankfurter, he had "recklessly ruined a most promising experiment."[106] Letters of consolation arrived from friends in the United

States, but their own country's entry into war, although opposed by peace activists such as Jane Addams, proved paradoxically productive for some progressive reformers, such as Frankfurter, who returned to Washington to work with the Wilson administration.

Frankfurter joined Secretary of War Newton Baker as chairman of the War Labor Policies Board, invoking the exigencies of war to settle industrial disputes by laying down a new labor code that recognized workers' rights to a living wage, an eight-hour day, and collective bargaining. He publicly extolled the example of the "experiments and legislation" of "progressive countries," such as Australia.[107] He also worked with Assistant Secretary of the Navy Franklin D. Roosevelt, who as president in the 1930s would call on Frankfurter to help draft New Deal legislation.

The wartime administration seemed to herald new opportunities for progressive labor reform, but the postwar period saw a concerted backlash and new repression. In 1922, conservative columnist Samuel Crowther wrote a much-quoted article for *Collier's* magazine, titled "Who Wants a Living Wage?," about the expectations unleashed by the movement for a minimum wage: "The American workman having enjoyed high wages during the war now wants a 'living wage' not only defined by law, but granted by law." He referred to Australian experience to illustrate the perils of such developments. There, "the living wage [was] based, not on the value of a man's work but on his requirements as a man in a civilized society." The results, he said, were disastrous: wages very high, prices very high, and taxation ruinous.[108]

Still, Higgins's legacy lived on. In *Adkins v. Children's Hospital*, the 1923 case that challenged the constitutionality of the Washington, DC, minimum wage law, Holmes, in minority, quoted Higgins's *Harvard Law Review* article to rebut the doctrine of "freedom of contract." The majority declared the minimum wage unconstitutional and in violation of "economic law." In his dissenting judgment, Holmes quoted Higgins to say that freedom of contract was "a misnomer" when used to describe the contract between an employer and an employee:

> In Australia the power to fix a minimum for wages in the case of industrial disputes extending beyond the limits of any one State was given to a Court, and its President wrote a most interesting account

of its operation. If a legislature should adopt what he thinks the doctrine of modern economists of all schools, that "freedom of contract is a misnomer as applied to a contract between an employer and an ordinary individual employee," I could not pronounce an opinion with which I agree impossible to be entertained by reasonable men. If the same legislature should accept his further opinion that industrial peace was best attained by the device of a Court having the above powers, I should not feel myself able to contradict it.[109]

For labor law to gain national traction in the United States, new ways would need to be found to circumvent the "Rigid Constitution" and the "misnomer" of "freedom of contract." Higgins wrote to thank Holmes for his generous citation and congratulated him for his ongoing labors. "I have been encouraged to keep on," replied Holmes. "It seems to me legitimate to gratify one's desire to produce as much as one can. To put out their best forever as fully and as long as one can is both the duty and joy of life."[110]

Not until 1938, following a long campaign by the National Consumers League, former member and now secretary of labor Frances Perkins, and Amalgamated Clothing Workers of America leader Sidney Hillman, working with Frankfurter's assistance as unofficial adviser to FDR, did the Fair Labor Standards Act introduce a federal minimum wage, justified in constitutional terms with reference to the federal government's power to regulate commerce "among the several states," just as the Commonwealth Court of Conciliation and Arbitration could set wages and hours based on its constitutional power to deal with industrial disputes "extending beyond the limits of any one state."[111] Transpacific precedent proved persuasive in identifying a path and rationale for legislative reform at the federal level to meet the social and industrial needs of the time, as labor realism sought to enshrine a new humanist idealism.

CHAPTER FIVE

Woman Suffrage as an Object Lesson

In February 1902, woman suffragists from around the world assembled in Washington, DC, for the first International Woman Suffrage Conference. It had been organized by the National American Woman Suffrage Association (NAWSA), whose secretary, Alice Stone Blackwell, serenaded the Australian delegate, thirty-two-year-old Vida Goldstein, in verse composed for her "Autograph Book":

> Australia, infant Commonwealth,
> Is full of vigour, vim and health;
> Youngest of nations gathered here,
> In some respects she has no peer.

Goldstein was a "sister in language and in blood," who had traveled to this historic meeting from the new commonwealth across the Pacific.[1]

Goldstein's story—and that of her friendships with Alice Stone Blackwell, Carrie Chapman Catt, Catharine Waugh McCulloch, and Maud Wood Park—offers a new perspective on woman suffrage as a transnational movement in which Australian women's precocious political success set an example, both in their maternalist platform and their nonparty, post-suffrage organization, which American women would follow with the founding of the National League of Women Voters in Chicago in 1920. Maud Wood Park would serve that organization as its inaugural president.

Settler colonizing states forged a distinctive women's movement that espoused "women's values" and championed "women's votes" in the name of their broader civilizing mission. Nonparty, post-suffrage women's organizing, pioneered in Victoria and New South Wales, brought that civilizing mission to electoral politics in defining a distinctive role for women citizens. Goldstein met Maud Wood Park in Boston in 1902, when the Australian visitor addressed six meetings—including the Boston Equal Suffrage Association for Good Government, which sponsored Park to visit Australia in 1909. As Goldstein's guest in Melbourne, Park was introduced to the leader of the Australian Labor Party, Andrew Fisher, and several federal politicians. She also met a range of post-suffrage women's groups in Melbourne and Sydney, from whom she gained "a pretty definite idea of what 'women's causes'" were.[2]

At the international conference in Washington, DC, in 1902, American conference delegates vied with one another in hailing Australia's "new world's promise" and path of "experiment": "safer ballots, wiser laws." Goldstein was heralded as a "light bringer from the Southern Seas." The delegate from Rochester offered greetings "to the other new country," while the representative of Colorado women, enfranchised in 1893, hoped that "the Australian and American women [would] progress spiritually side by side on the upward path of our common race."[3] Harriet May Mills, who had hosted Catherine Spence's visit to New York in the previous decade, welcomed Goldstein as one who brought "bright and inspiring messages from far away Australia."[4] It was a heady moment for the young Australian, which presaged, she hoped, greater things to come. Women, it seemed, were entering a new political era.

Carrie Chapman Catt, the forty-two-year-old president of NAWSA ("a beautiful young woman," according to Goldstein, with "pretty, wavy, prematurely grey hair" and "great personal charm"), inscribed her message of solidarity more soberly in prose. "It is our hope," she wrote, "that the bond of sympathy and good fellowship forged between the Australian Woman Suffrage movement and that in the US through the presence among us of 'Little Australia,' as we have learned to call her in affection, will bind us continually closer until every woman in both countries has gained the right to self-government."[5] The use of the diminutive signaled not just affection, perhaps, but a reminder of the status of the American suffragists as the true "pioneers," if not of women's rights then of the great women's movement itself. Catt spoke for a glorious tradition, of which she was a part, having been present at the landmark convention that saw the formation of NAWSA in 1890.

In some ways, the conference in Washington in 1902 seemed as much a celebration of the American women's movement itself as the beginning of a more international orientation. The youthful representative of Australian women, the first women in the world to gain full political rights, would not be allowed to upstage American women in their national capital. In welcoming foreign delegates, Clara Barton, president of the American Red Cross, reminded them: "It was here that the first hard blows were struck. It was here the paths were marked out that have been trodden with bleeding feet for half a century." Of all the "pioneers," veteran suffragist Susan B. Anthony, elected amid great applause to chair the conference, was the "great prototype."[6]

Certainly the American women's movement had much to be proud of. In her report on the progress of women in the United States, Catt stated that they were "unquestionably . . . less bound by legal and social restrictions than the women of any other country, unless we except progressive Australia and New Zealand."[7] Mindful of their shared history as British colonies, Catt often expressed frustration that women from the "younger" Australian colonies had been able to win the right of "self-government" before women of the great republic were able to enter into their rightful heritage. "The little band of Americans who initiated the modern [suffrage] movement would never have predicted," Catt told the conference, "that the island continent of Australia, then unexplored wilderness, would become a great democracy, where self-government would be carried on with such enthusiasm, fervour and wisdom that they would give lessons in methods and principles to all the rest of the world."[8]

The United States was proud of its history of self-government. "The American people were the first to formulate those fundamental principles of self-government upon which has been based the movement towards universal suffrage during the last century," Catt told NAWSA. "However, by a curious inconsistency, we must turn for the broadest application of those immortal principles to a dependency of the government, which denied by force of arms the truth expressed in the American maxim 'governments derive their just powers from the consent of the governed.'"[9]

An ardent patriot, Catt was embarrassed that her country continued to deny women due recognition and respect as citizens well into the twentieth century, while "progressive Australia and New Zealand" became the trailblazers in securing actual political rights. And as white women, the authors of NAWSA's Declaration of Principles were even more indignant that American women suffered "the degradation of being held not so competent to exercise the suffrage as a Filipino, a Hawaiian, or a Porto Rican [sic] man."[10] To Catt's mind, civilized women should surely take precedence over the men of the republic's own newly acquired dependencies.

In 1902, white women in the Commonwealth of Australia became the first in the world to win both the right to vote and the right to stand for election to the national parliament. New Zealand women, enfranchised in 1893, had not yet won the right to stand for election. "It is well known that new countries are far more free from the mandates of custom and conventionality than old ones," Catt told the international conference, "and that dissenters from established usage are far more willing to adopt new ideas and extend new liberties than those bound by traditional belief."[11] She was speaking about her compatriots, but it was Australian women who became the New World's exemplary progressives, winning, in American suffragist Josephine Henry's words, "the greatest victory ever won for women."[12]

As Vida Goldstein and Carrie Catt both explained to the international conference, the progress of woman suffrage in their two countries—or lack of it—owed much to their respective federal constitutions, which, during conventions held more than one hundred years apart, forged groups of British colonies into new federal nation-states. "Were it possible to secure suffrage for women in the United States by congressional or legislative enactment, as in most foreign countries," observed Catt, somewhat testily, "the women of the United States would have been enfranchised long years ago."[13] The problem was, she recognized, "Constitutional Law." For, as H. B. Higgins— jurist and delegate to the Australian constitutional conventions in the 1890s—had warned, the "Rigid Constitution" framed by American founding fathers posed significant barriers to progressive reform, including the enactment of woman suffrage.[14]

The Australian constitution, by contrast, as a result of women's campaigns in the 1890s, explicitly enabled the national enfranchisement of women.[15] As American historian Ida Husted Harper explained in a history lesson for readers of the *Washington Post*, one of the pledges made to the Australian people during their constitutional conventions was that "franchise and official privileges should be given to all equal to those possessed in the most liberal of the divisions."[16] At that time, all women in South Australia had the full franchise and the right to a seat in the legislature. In 1902, the national parliament granted the same rights to all (white) women of the new commonwealth (indigenous women had also been enfranchised in South Australia but were more generally classified as wards of the state). In the United States, Congress did not have the power to enfranchise women by a "single enactment." Rather, a proposed amendment to the constitution had to be submitted for ratification by three-quarters of the states, and there was a "very strong sentiment against any further amending of that document," Harper advised. There was "no other nation in the world," she lamented, "which [made] it so hard for women to secure the franchise."[17]

Campaigns for woman suffrage had a long history in both the United States and Australia, where self-government was based, from the mid-nineteenth century, on manhood suffrage, a defining feature of modern representative democracies. In these new worlds, the qualification for participation in government was no longer property or status, class, education, or religion but the fact of men's manhood.[18] It was an age, in the words of New South Wales republican poet Daniel Denehy, when "glorious manhood" asserted "its elevation" over rank, status, and title—and over women.[19] In the Australian colonies, manhood suffrage in the 1850s also extended to Aboriginal and Chinese men.

Women were excluded from these modern polities on the basis of their sex. Thus, leaders of the women's movement in both countries—and in the transnational American Woman Christian Temperance Union (WCTU), which put down deep roots in settler societies but not in Britain—spoke perforce of women's rights, women's needs, and women's values. As Nancy Cott has observed, the long tradition of manhood suffrage acted as a point of departure for woman suffragists in democratic countries by "differentiating all women from all men."[20]

In Australia, demands for woman suffrage followed the introduction of manhood suffrage and reflected the democratic culture fostered by the gold rushes in the southeastern colonies in the 1850s.[21] Early advocates tended to argue, based on men's and women's shared status as settlers and taxpayers, that they should have equal rights to political representation. Radical liberal reformer Henry Higinbotham, for example, introduced a motion to the Victorian parliament in the 1870s in support of votes for women on an equal basis with men. By the time woman suffrage organizations became active in the 1880s, however, the ideology of separate spheres was entrenched and the idea of motherhood as a civic vocation was in the ascendancy. Suffragists increasingly argued that women's distinctive interests and special talents as spiritual mothers were needed in public life to purify politics and protect women and girls from men's cruelty and selfishness.[22]

In these settler societies—but not, significantly, in Finland, the first European nation to enfranchise women, in 1906—the women's movement became increasingly maternalist and separatist in orientation. In Finland, suffragists argued for their rights as part of a broader nationalist independence movement that soon saw, as also in Norway, women elected to the national parliament.[23] In contrast, Australian, New Zealand, and American suffragists declared themselves to be mothers of a new progressive world, with special responsibilities for children's welfare and the protection of women.[24]

In 1884, Henrietta Dugdale and Annie Lowe formed the Victorian Women's Suffrage Society, in part a response to a series of sexual assaults on women and girls. A year later, Mary Leavitt, the American "world missionary," established the Melbourne branch of the WCTU. A second world missionary, the dynamic Jessie Ackerman, arrived in Melbourne in 1889 and set about organizing a national convention ("the first inter-colonial assembly of women ever held in Australia") that defined woman suffrage as an official part of the WCTU platform. Ackerman would spend six years in Australia and return on a number of later visits. She was an indefatigable organizer, writing hundreds of newspaper articles and letters and founding local branches. She also delivered innumerable speeches. The WCTU found especially receptive audiences among women in masculinist frontier societies.[25]

In advocating the value of "mother-heartedness," the WCTU characteristically linked the welfare of women in the home to the "highest national welfare": "what is good for the home is also good for the

State."[26] Branch secretaries excelled at grassroots organization, and membership proliferated. In 1891, members of the Victorian Women's Suffrage Society joined forces with the WCTU to organize what came to be called a "monster petition," containing thirty thousand signatures to demonstrate that Victorian women demanded the vote. Hundreds of supporters canvassed door to door across city suburbs and country towns to collect signatures. One of the youngest workers in the cause was twenty-two-year-old Vida Goldstein, whose mother, Isabella, also a confirmed suffragist, encouraged her daughter to become active in politics. Vida later recalled that canvassers met with little opposition: "Wherever the workers went they found the great majority of women in favour of the vote, and of being on a footing of equality with men in every respect."[27]

As a woman in her twenties, Goldstein was mentored by older and more experienced women, including family friend Annette Bear-Crawford, who moved in 1894 to bring all the different organizations—including the fourteen suburban Women's Progressive Leagues—under the umbrella of the United Council for Woman Suffrage. Bear-Crawford trained younger women, including Goldstein, in meeting procedure, political lobbying, and public speaking, showing them how to handle hecklers and answer difficult questions. By the time Goldstein left for the United States in 1902, she was an eloquent and effective lecturer, ready to take to the international platform.

The United Council for Woman Suffrage had been successful in securing a number of reforms, including the appointment of women as factory inspectors and legislation to raise the age of consent to sixteen, a reform considered a key victory for working-class girls, who otherwise might be seduced into prostitution or forced into an early marriage. Perhaps Bear-Crawford's major achievement was the foundation of the Queen Victoria Hospital for Women, which grew out of her concern for the welfare of unmarried mothers and their children. She initiated the Queen's Willing Shilling fund in 1897 to launch the scheme, but didn't live to see the hospital open, dying suddenly from pneumonia in 1899, at age forty-six.

Bear-Crawford's young protégé Goldstein, who earned her living running a school with her sister, assisted in raising money for the hospital. She also worked for the Anti-Sweating League on behalf of women workers. By 1900, she had become the leading figure in the Victorian campaign for woman suffrage. She established a monthly publication, the *Australian Woman's Sphere*, in which she advocated an independent path in politics: "Women should carry on the fight and the campaign by means of their own organisations, and not by means of any existing ones controlled and directed by men. If they do the latter they must adopt men's methods and men's aims, and simply help in perpetuating the old order of things. The right of the franchise will have been bestowed on them for no purpose."[28] Like many reformers of the time, Goldstein had also been exploring new religious faiths and become a convert, along with friends Lilian Locke, Ina Higgins, and Miles Franklin, to the American-based Christian Science movement, founded by Mary Baker Eddy.[29]

In neighboring South Australia, woman suffragists also worked with the local branch of the WCTU and, as in Victoria, organized a monster petition to demonstrate South Australian women's demand for the vote. Suffragists there also supported efforts by local working women to improve their wages and conditions. When the Trades and Labour Council formed a Working Women's Trades Union, fifty-eight-year-old Irish immigrant and widowed mother Mary Lee was appointed secretary, and German immigrant Augusta Zadow became president. Campaigners for political rights in South Australia, as in Victoria, enjoyed the influential support of liberal-minded men, one of whom, Edward Stirling—a disciple of John Stuart Mill and a professor of medicine at the University of Adelaide—introduced a motion into parliament in favor of woman suffrage, albeit on a property basis, in 1885.

At the same time, reformers in the South Australian Society for the Promotion of Social Purity were successful in urging the government to pass legislation to raise the age of consent, again to sixteen years. Mary Lee, active in campaigns for both the age of consent and economic justice for working women, persuaded supporters to bring the causes together in a separate Women's Suffrage League (WSL), formed in 1888. Prominent reformer and journalist Catherine Spence accepted the office of vice president of the WSL in 1891 and led a number of deputations to government. Campaigning for woman suffrage—with no property qualification—became more focused and insistent. Their petition, with more than 11,600 signatures, was presented to parliament in 1894, and at the end of that year, woman suffrage was finally legislated.

News of the advent of woman suffrage in New Zealand in 1893—where local suffrage societies, the WCTU, and petition campaigns also played a major role—had given added momentum to the campaign in South Australia.[30] Fresh elections saw the recently established Labor Party return new members of parliament, who supported the Liberal administration led by Premier Charles Kingston and the cause of woman suffrage. Previously an opponent of woman suffrage, when he thought it a conservative force, Kingston changed his mind and introduced the bill as a government measure. The efforts of suffragists combined with the growing support of the labor and reform movements persuaded him that woman suffrage would strengthen support for his government.[31]

One of the most important factors in the introduction of woman suffrage in South Australia in 1894—which established the crucial precedent that shaped the enabling provisions of the Australian federal constitution—was the increase in power of Labor and Liberal forces following the 1893 elections.[32] South Australia had consolidated its reputation as a laboratory of advanced democracy, with manhood suffrage and the secret ballot in place from 1856, compulsory schooling from 1875, payment to members of parliament from 1887, and woman suffrage introduced in 1894.

At the end of that year, Catherine Spence arrived back in Adelaide from her American lecture tour to an atmosphere of nervous anticipation. After attending a welcome-home party, local women returned en masse to the parliamentary galleries to "await the ultimate decision." The local newspaper described their late-night invasion of this gentlemen's domain: "Ladies poured into the cushioned benches to the left of the Speaker, and relentlessly usurped the seats of gentlemen who had been comfortably seated there before. They filled the aisles and overflowed into the gallery to the right, while some of the bolder spirits climbed the stairs and invaded the rougher forms behind the clock."[33] But still they had to wait until the next morning for the final vote. Immediately plans were made to woo the woman voter. The Labor Party invited Catherine Spence and Mary Lee to stand as endorsed candidates in the next election, but they declined.

The determination to organize and consolidate the women's vote, irrespective of party allegiances, anticipated post-suffrage organizations in the Australian Commonwealth, including Goldstein's Women's (Federal) Political Association in Victoria, Rose Scott's Women's Political Educational League in New South Wales, Bessie Rischbieth's Australian Federation of Women Voters, and the South Australia Women's Non-Party Association, as well as the National League of Women Voters in the United States, formed in 1920.

In 1902, after consultation with local women's groups, Goldstein was selected to represent the women of Australia and New Zealand at the International Woman Suffrage Conference in Washington. Spence offered her the benefit of her travel experience, international networks, and letters of introduction. She also told her of her budget: "It cost me 200 pounds and what I earned." She described how women without private means might manage international travel:

> I found people always ready to show me where to live and board cheaply—I did not spend so much at Chicago as I expected because I got into a place where I paid so much for my room 15 shillings a week and for meals as I had them—At New York I was in the Margaret Louise Home far more comfortable for the same money. But I had a great deal of hospitality. Of the ten months I spent in the States I was with friends five months—I earned by writing for *Harper's Magazine* 15 pound, *Christian Advocate* 8 pound six and six pence, *Arena* 4 pound 3 and 4 pence, *Voice* 1 pound and 7 shillings. I earned by fourteen paid lectures. fee varied from ten pound up to 50 pound in Boston— . . . I earned nothing in England or Scotland at all—nothing in Canada.[34]

As Vida Goldstein would also discover, American women were the most attentive and generous of hosts.

Goldstein's trip was supported in part by a travel fund established by her journal, the *Australian Woman's Sphere*. Like Spence, she intended to research American policy on neglected children and report on industrial conditions and the workings of penal institutions. It was nevertheless difficult to raise travel money in competition with other good causes. Spence told Alice Henry: "10 shillings is all I can spare and that not very well as I have gone in for helping a Co-operative

Clothing Factory to the extent of 5 pound to get electric power applied to their machines, so as to be able to compete with workers in big factories."[35] Subscribers to the fund included leading Liberal politicians Alfred Deakin and H. B. Higgins; local member of the legislative assembly Dr. Maloney; labor women Clara Weekes and Lilian Locke; and women's organizations, such as the Victorian Lady Teachers' Association, the Stawell branch of the WCTU, and the Victorian Women's Public Servants' Association. A farewell meeting chaired by the Reverend Charles Strong of the Australian Church included a "capital programme of music and recitations," which served to augment the travel fund.[36]

The Australasian delegate traveled to the United States via Sydney, where she stayed a few days with her friend, esteemed New South Wales suffragist Rose Scott, president of the Womanhood Suffrage League. Scott was also a founding member of the New South Wales branch of the National Council of Women, whose members asked Goldstein to act as their delegate to the International Council of Women meeting, scheduled to follow the suffrage conference. To send off her friend, Scott hosted an evening gathering of "ladies who have interested themselves in the suffrage" to wish Goldstein "God-speed." The ladies reassembled the next morning on the wharf to see her step aboard the SS *Sierra* on the first phase of the long journey across sea and land to Washington, DC.[37]

In their Pacific crossings, travelers usually encountered for the first time a range of Islander peoples, as ships stopped to load coal, deliver and collect mail, or take on supplies. Some Islanders worked at the ports, others wished to trade, while others provided entertainments. As Goldstein's ship approached Samoa, even before it had anchored "the ship was surrounded by ever so many boats, filled with natives, some carrying goods for sale." Determined to go ashore, Goldstein was immediately struck by the Samoan men's physique: "Tall and beautifully formed, they bear themselves like kings." Yet despite their regal bearing, the men could suddenly resemble creatures of the jungle when they climbed coconut trees. "We asked a native to climb one," reported Goldstein. "'Money' he said. We gave him some and he ran up the bare stem like a monkey, and threw coconuts down to us—also just like a monkey. All the time we were surrounded by natives offering their wares." Back on board, passengers compared their souvenirs as the ship steamed on to Hawaii, but heavy rain and rough seas made the voyage very unpleasant. "I don't know who was the master of irony who named this the Pacific Ocean," wrote Goldstein. "A more unpacific expanse of water it would be difficult to find."[38] Oceanic crossings were not for the squeamish or fainthearted.

On arrival in San Francisco in the cold of late January, Goldstein was pleased to find that Carrie Chapman Catt had made arrangements for her accommodation and onward travel. "When I got on to the wharf, I found Miss Whelan, Miss Fairbrother and Miss Schlingheyde waiting for me, and bringing three letters from Mrs Catt, giving me directions as to my travelling east." Catt had arranged for Goldstein to rest for three nights with Mrs. Speddy in San Francisco, but her onward trip across the continent via Salt Lake City and Chicago had to be speeded up. After a "hurried rush across America," she arrived in the capital just in time for the conference opening.[39]

While there, she attended church services, prayers, "a spirited rendition of The Battle Hymn of the Republic", congregational singing, and greetings to foreign guests by May Wright Sewall, president of the International Council of Women; Clara Barton, president of the American Red Cross; Susan B. Anthony, honorary president of NAWSA; and the Reverend Anna B. Shaw, vice president of NAWSA, who together provided an imposing demonstration of the longevity of the American women's movement. The opening night was dedicated to the "pioneers": Elizabeth Cady Stanton, Susan B. Anthony, Mary A. Livermore, Julia Ward Howe, Isabella Beecher Hooker, and Carolina Hallowell Miller.

Foreign delegates to the conference constituted a diverse set of "representatives," as Goldstein noted. Only a minority represented democracies. Florence Fensham, who spoke for Turkey, was dean of the American College for Girls at Constantinople. The report by the Chilean delegate, Carolina Huidobro, was "a revelation to most of the audience, who had no idea that the women of the South American republics were so advanced." The German delegate was Antonie Stolle, a tiny woman, whose qualifications included expertise in art history. The Russian delegate, Sofja Friedland, was conversant with developments in the United States because she divided her time equally between

America and her Russian estate. English delegate Florence Fenwick Miller was an excellent speaker with great stage presence. Emmy Evald's "proud boast" was that her country, Sweden, was the first to enfranchise women taxpayers. Norway was represented by Gudrun Drewsen, an activist and migrant bride married to a Danish American chemist.[40]

There were numerous delegates from the United States. The organizers had hoped that all countries would send an equal number of representatives, but the cost of travel meant that foreign women's organizations could manage to send just one delegate, if any at all. Some "foreign delegates" were already based in the United States. Conference greetings were followed by an evening with "the New Woman," at which a number of professional women spoke of their pioneering work as doctors, lawyers, and accountants. Addresses by state presidents of NAWSA and reports from the enfranchised women of the states of Wyoming, Utah, Colorado, and Idaho concluded the day's program.

On Saturday, 14 February, there was "An Evening with England and her Colonies"—so-called despite the inauguration of the Commonwealth of Australia in 1901—at which Florence Fenwick Miller, Vida Goldstein, and the Honorable James Hughes—a public school inspector from Toronto—each spoke. On Sunday, Catherine Spence's old friend, the Reverend Anna Garlin Spencer, assisted by Rev. Olympia Brown of Wisconsin and Rev. Anna B Shaw from Philadelphia, conducted services at the Presbyterian Church. Spencer delivered her sermon on the Ecclesiastes text: "Accept not the person of any against the soul, and reverence no man unto thy falling; be steadfast in thy understanding and let thy word be one." As she had long argued, the advancement of women required them to assert their individuality and freedom.[41]

Reports on the condition of women around the world, compiled in response to a questionnaire distributed by NAWSA, were presented on behalf of twenty countries. Carrie Chapman Catt emphasized the social and educational advancement of American women and the constitutional difficulties in the way of their political enfranchisement. "The suffrage rights of women in the United States are surprisingly few when the strength of sentiment in favor of woman suffrage is taken into account," she said. "This fact is due to the exceeding difficulty with which the constitutional law of the country is changed. Minor suffrage, which may be obtained by legislative enactment alone, has been largely extended to women. In twenty-five States women have the privilege of voting in school elections."[42]

American women had struggled for decades to achieve political rights at the state and national levels. Wyoming had granted women the right to vote in 1869, Utah in 1870, Colorado in 1893, and Idaho in 1896. From 1875, when the Supreme Court ruled that the American Constitution did not confer the right of suffrage on women, the movement led by Susan B. Anthony and Elizabeth Cady Stanton resolved to bring about a constitutional amendment. This was an especially onerous path in the United States because of the hurdles to constitutional amendment written into the American Constitution. An amendment would need to be passed by a two-thirds majority of both Houses of Congress and ratified by three-quarters of the states. In some cases, the drawn-out amendment and ratification process not only made change difficult to achieve and wearied campaigners but also provoked fresh opposition and the mobilization of forces opposed to the reform in question.

In Australia, by contrast, the "New Woman" became—in constitutional terms—a foundational element of the "New Nation," as legal scholar Helen Irving has noted.[43] As a result of lobbying by women's organizations in the 1890s, combined with the active support of progressive male delegates to the federal conventions, the Australian constitution made it easier for woman suffragists to secure their rights in the new nation-state.[44] A large meeting in Melbourne, for example, had "unanimously [resolved] that this meeting strongly urges the Federal Convention to embody the principle of woman suffrage in the Federal Constitution Bill."[45] It was a live issue. Similar resolutions were carried across the country and petitions sent to the constitutional conventions in Adelaide, Sydney, and Melbourne.

In her paper to the Washington conference on "the Australian Woman in Politics," Goldstein explained how the constitution enabled Australian women's political progress: "The Federal Constitution Bill provides that the Federal Parliament cannot take away from the electors in any state the franchise rights they already possess; also that when it regulates its own franchise, it must make it the same for each state."[46] The fact that the Commonwealth of Australia came into existence at the beginning of the twentieth century, when the suffrage movement was at its peak, rather than at the end of the eighteenth century, as did the American republic, had significant ramifications for the timing and enactment of women's political rights in the two countries.

Goldstein embarked on her trip to the United States just four months prior to the passage of Australia's historic franchise legislation in June 1902. In anticipation of success, she became a triumphant ambassador: "This will be the greatest step in the direction of political equality that we have yet seen, and must be a splendid object-lesson to every civilized country in the world."[47] She bestowed her good wishes on American women, expressing the hope that Australian success would "hasten the day when you American women will stand before the world as the political equals of your men folk."[48] It was taken for granted that only white women—"civilized women"—were enfranchised at the national level in Australia. Indigenous women were eligible to vote in South Australia alongside white women from 1894, although it was reported that "only one or two who have been civilized and are settled on the land" had their names on the roll.[49] Aboriginal men had been eligible to vote at the state level in Tasmania, New South Wales, and Victoria, but not in Queensland and Western Australia, the states in which most indigenous Australians lived and where special laws excluded them from enfranchisement and other citizen rights. Even as the new federal parliament enfranchised white women, indigenous Australians were denied federal voting rights.

The status of white women as New World civilizers and citizens in Australia and the United States was predicated on indigenous loss of sovereignty and lack of citizenship. Australia and the United States had offered indigenous peoples—conceptualized as "dying races"—dubious "protection" as "wards of the state," rather than the rights of citizenship and nationality. In the United States, attainment of citizenship rights depended on Native Americans' proven competency to assimilate into "civilization." Woman suffragists' approaches to "the Native problem" in both countries varied, with many invoking their maternal responsibilities to protect indigenous girls and women, even as they advanced their own status within the binary categories of "civilized" and "savage."[50]

Theodore Roosevelt, author of *The Winning of the West* and president of the United States at the time of the International Woman Suffrage Conference in Washington, was a great admirer of the advanced democracy exemplified by settler societies. "Nineteenth century democracy needs no more complete vindication for its existence than the fact that it has kept for the white race the best portions of the new world's surface, temperate America and Australia," he wrote in a review of Charles Pearson's *National Life and Character*.[51] In letters to British diplomat Arthur Cecil Spring Rice, written around the same time, Roosevelt counseled against his friend's end-of-the-century pessimism with regard to the future of the British Empire by pointing to the great "vigor" of Australia's "giant Commonwealth."[52]

Roosevelt invited Goldstein to a private meeting in the White House. He greeted the young Australian with enthusiasm, and she was charmed by his evident interest in meeting her. He "looked such a young man to be the ruler of 80 millions of people," wrote Goldstein, "yet his face disclosed strength of character and resolution." She found him to be cordial, loquacious, and very interested in Australia.[53] "I was introduced to him," she reported in a lecture on her return to Australia, "and he said, gripping my hand in a vice, "I am delighted to meet you."

> All Americans say that, and you often feel that it is a mere *façon de parler*, but there was no doubting the cordiality or Mr Roosevelt's greeting. "And you're from Australia: I'm delighted to hear that. Do you know I'm very interested in your country, and in New Zealand, which seems to be making great progress. Of course you know I had a number of Australians in my regiment?"
> "Yes" I replied, and you found them good men and true?"
> "Excellent, excellent."
> General conversation followed about social and political conditions [in Australia], and then he said he hoped that some day he might visit.[54]

Indeed, wild enthusiasm had been expressed in Australia in support of the American role in the Spanish-American War, and many young men had determined to enlist despite Britain's official position of neutrality.[55]

Roosevelt never made it to Australia, but he did make a personal decision, six years later, to detour the Great White Fleet to visit the new commonwealth in response to a special request from Prime Minister Alfred Deakin. "I have, as every American ought to have, a hearty admiration for and fellow feeling with Australia," Roosevelt explained.[56] At his meeting with Goldstein in 1902, he had also confided that he was personally in favor of woman suffrage.[57] His public pronouncements were rather more cautious, but in 1912, as leader of the new Progressive Party, Roosevelt became the first presidential candidate to officially support votes for women.

The main outcome of the International Woman Suffrage Conference in Washington was the proposed constitution and Declaration of Principles for the new international body, the International Woman Suffrage Alliance, which reflected the political traditions of its mainly American authors. The first principle was an assertion of equality and liberty: "That men and women are born equally free and independent members of the human race; equally endowed with talents and intelligence, and equally entitled to the free exercise of their individual rights and liberty."

Principles 4 and 5 emphasized a right to self-government "in the home and the State" as an "inalienable right":

4. That self-government in the home and the State should be the inalienable right of every normal adult, and in consequence no individual woman can "owe obedience" to an individual man, as prescribed by old marriage forms, nor can women as a whole owe obedience to men as a whole as required by modern government.

5. That the refusal to recognize women as individual members of society, entitled to the right of self-government, has resulted in social, legal, and economic injustice to them, and has intensified the existing economic disturbances throughout the world.

Principle 6 called for recognition of women's "right of consent," while Principle 7 argued that the ballot was the only means to defend the rights to "life, liberty, and pursuit of happiness" inscribed in the American Declaration of Independence and "accepted as inalienable by all civilized nations." Principle 8 called for support for woman suffrage from all the nations of the world.[58]

The Declaration of Principles was a quintessentially New World postcolonial document, asserting women's status as "equally free and independent members of the human race" and enshrining the principle of "self-government" in the home and the state. Women did not owe obedience to men either individually or collectively. Vida Goldstein, thrilled to be elected secretary of the conference, was a member of the drafting group and appointed to the committee to organize the next international conference of the International Woman Suffrage Alliance, planned for Berlin in 1904.

After the "fortnight's really hard work" in Washington, the young Australian was in need of a rest. In March, she took time off to relax and enjoy the entertainments and sights of New York, courtesy of her host, Carrie Chapman Catt, before embarking on a series of public talks across the country. Like Catherine Spence before her, Goldstein extended her stay in the United States in response to the many invitations she received to speak. She decided she must help the cause. As the *Australian Woman's Sphere* reported, "Everywhere in America, where she has been, she has received unbounded kindness and splendid hospitality from the leaders of the suffrage movement and she now feels bound to do what she can for a time by working or speaking to help the cause they have at heart."[59] Newspaper reports of Goldstein's lecture tour served to focus fresh attention on woman suffrage across the United States at a time when the campaign had lost some momentum. The press announced her arrival in their towns and cities, sent reporters to interview her, published a large number of photographs, and printed her views about the role women might play in politics.

When Goldstein arrived in New York, she went straight to the headquarters of NAWSA, where she found a reporter from the *New York Herald*, waiting to interview her. He came with a photographer who took four likenesses, including "one by flashlight." The journalist dismayed her, however, by saying that he was "most bitterly opposed to Woman Suffrage." Furthermore, his conversation and his questions "betrayed a lamentable ignorance of politics, not only those of the rest of the world, but also of those of his own city—New York."[60] The subsequent report in the *Herald* featured Goldstein's photograph over the headline: "Comes from Australia to Plead the Cause of Woman Suffrage." During the interview, the young visitor had been courteous but insistent with the reporter: "America can teach us a whole lot, but we feel we can show some things to you that you would profit by adopting and one of these is women's suffrage."[61] Afterward, she repaired to the home of Carrie Chapman Catt, who over the next several days showed Goldstein around the city.

Entertainment was interspersed with lecturing. The young visitor spoke at six meetings in Manhattan and its neighborhoods and addressed a senate committee of the state legislature. Goldstein was also eager to learn. Here was a society that shared an English-speaking heritage and culture but one shaped by a very different history of race relations, including slavery, the Civil War, emancipation, and segregation. She was particularly interested, as Spence had been, in the position of the "coloured people" ("they are always spoken of as 'coloured persons' by those who respect their sensitiveness," she explained, "as they do not like to be called 'niggers' or 'black'"). The conference in Washington had coincided with Frederick Douglass's birthday, celebrated at a concert at the local colored high school, where his grandson Joseph Douglass, a violinist who had played at the Chicago World's Fair, performed for the Washington schoolchildren. Susan B. Anthony had been invited to speak and invited Goldstein to accompany her.[62]

In New York, Goldstein took the opportunity to attend a lecture by Booker T. Washington, "the negro lecturer," considered "one of the finest platform speakers in America." She was impressed by his evident achievements "in spite of every obstacle that [was] put in the way of the advance of the coloured men in the South." She reported:

> He has compelled the respect of the white man, but he remains true to his own race, and has devoted his life to an organised movement for elevating them by means of industrial education. He spoke of his own early life as a slave, and told how, when working in a coal mine, he heard of the Hampton Institute, where negroes could get a free education. He left the coal mine and tramped to Hampton. He reminded the audience that the "negroes were in America to stay, and were an ever-in-creasing force to be reckoned with." "You must remember," he said, "we came here by very express invitation, and we're about the only people who ever did. You whites, if I remember rightly, came here in face of the strongest opposition of the native population of this country."[63]

Perhaps Goldstein was moved to reflect on the position of the native population of her own country. She was increasingly ashamed of the appalling treatment of Aborigines meted out by colonial settlers and would later question the qualification of white Australians to rule the mandated territory of New Guinea after World War I.

From New York, Goldstein traveled to Boston, a city whose historic and literary associations she, like her compatriots Pearson, Deakin, and Spence relished. Like Deakin, Goldstein also experienced frustration and delays in getting to Concord to see Emerson's grave, but in her case, it was not the wrong train but the "automobile fiends on the road," which meant she never made it at all and had to be content with Lexington. She was visiting the Garrison family:

> We intended going to Concord to see the houses where Emerson, Hawthorne and Louisa Alcott lived, but the crowd was so great, the automobile fiends whizzed along at such a rate, that our horses became frightened, and we had to turn off the main road and give up our trip to Concord. I was, of course, very much disappointed, but there was compensation, as we went to Lexington instead, saw the monument there to the Minute Men, and the house in which Adams and Hancock were sleeping, when Paul Revere arrived with the news of the approach of the British troops. . . . Mr. Garrison's house is full of interesting relics of anti-slavery days. I saw the complete file of "The Liberator," the desk at which Garrison wrote his famous editorials, the table on which was written the anti-slavery Declaration of Sentiments.[64]

Goldstein enjoyed the warm American hospitality. She was staying at Dorchester as a guest of Henry Blackwell and his daughter, Alice Stone Blackwell, editor of the *Woman's Journal*, who had penned such gracious verse in Goldstein's "Autograph Book." While in Cambridge, she also met Deakin's friend Josiah Royce.

Boston, according to Goldstein, was "a queer-looking, old-fashioned city, with narrow winding streets, but every inch of it is hallowed ground on account of its historical associations." She was disappointed that she couldn't visit all the old landmarks, "but this American trip of mine means work first."[65] A large number of associations and women's clubs beckoned, and press publicity followed. When the

Boston *Advertiser* sent a reporter to meet her, he seemed relieved that "Miss Goldstein's appearance" was in "direct contradiction to images of the women who demanded equal rights as depicted by caricaturists and comic papers."[66] The youthful and photogenic Goldstein was often praised as an attractive representative of the advanced woman.

She addressed the Massachusetts Woman Suffrage Association (MWSA), the Brighton and Allston Woman Suffrage Club, the Wollaston Equal Suffrage Club, the Cambridge Political Equality Club, the Brookline Political Equality Club, and the Boston Equal Suffrage Association for Good Government (BESAGG), formed the previous year by Pauline Agassiz Shaw, Mary Hutcheson Page, and Maud Wood Park. Shaw, the daughter of renowned scientist Louis Agassiz, had married the wealthy businessman Quincy Adams Shaw and become an influential patron of child care, settlement houses, education, and reform and the first president of BESAGG. (Her husband was first cousin to the historian Francis Parkman, who dedicated *The Oregon Trail* to him.) Taking up the invitation to speak to BESAGG, Goldstein warmed to the subject of how woman suffrage led to better government, a more moral community, and the purification of politics.

In 1909, it was Pauline Agassiz Shaw who financed Maud Wood Park's trip to Australia, when, accompanied by fellow suffragist Mabel Willard, Park was hosted by Goldstein in Melbourne and learned about the work of her post-suffrage organization, the Women's Political Association, and its insistence on a nonparty political strategy. Park would later become the key Washington lobbyist in the final years of the campaign for the constitutional amendment, activity documented in her book *Front Door Lobbyists*. One historian of the Massachusetts women's movement has suggested that in their focus on a "few personalities," historians of woman suffrage have tended to overlook the activism of lesser-known women and their crucial links with "foreign counterparts."[67] Goldstein's friendship with Maud Wood Park offers important insights into the transpacific dynamics of the suffrage movement and the development of post-suffrage feminist strategy.

In the United States, Goldstein realized that although American women had not yet achieved political rights, the great women's movement, in its very longevity, had become an object of veneration and commemoration, already producing its own national mythologies and multivolume history. Goldstein was particularly impressed by the reverence accorded the "pioneers":

> Wherever I go, I find that Miss Susan B. Anthony is simply revered by everyone. . . . Her name is reverenced from one end of the States to the other. If she is seen to enter a public hall, the crowd rises and cheers her wildly, and showers roses on her. . . . Another of the pioneers whom I have met is Mrs. Elizabeth Cady Stanton; she is eighty-six years of age, and, though un-able to get about much, her intellect is as bright as ever, and she is at work every day. . . . She gave me a copy of her "Reminiscences."[68]

Goldstein felt honored to be invited to Susan B. Anthony's home in Rochester, which had become a kind of memorial. "Everything about her is reminiscent of the life of fifty years ago—no up-to-date fashionable furniture, no thick Axminster carpets or frilled eider-down cushions—nothing but plain, simple, substantial furniture. There was no shoddy about the homes of two generations ago. The walls of her study are simply covered with addresses, breathing sympathy and admiration, from noted women workers in America and abroad."[69] A special treat was an invitation to the attic to see the "records of suffrage work for fifty years, an amazing collection of reports and letters, all docketed, all arranged chronologically. I saw the fourth volume of the history of the women suffrage movement in manuscript—the first three volumes written by Miss Anthony and Miss E. Cady Stanton brought the history up of 1884." The fourth volume was being completed with the assistance of Ida Husted Harper.

The elderly suffragist presented her young visitor with copies of the *History of Woman Suffrage* and her *Biography*, which together inscribed a proud feminist narrative of American exceptionalism. From Goldstein's perspective, however, Americans had much catching up to do, a view she shared with her fellow British subject, the Indian lawyer Cornelia Sorabji, whom she met when she returned to Manhattan. Goldstein reported that the "Parsee lady, one of the famous Sorabji family, who have done so much for the education of women and children in India," was "much impressed with the smartness and rapidity of Americans" but "astonished [and] delighted when she heard me say that I considered America was very far behind the times in its political institutions." She seemed amused that "anyone regarded this exceedingly vivacious country as being behindhand in any respect, especially when that one came from the other side of the world, from a far-away country, such as Australia."[70] In New York, Goldstein also met the investigative journalist Jacob Riis, a migrant from Denmark whom President Roosevelt had recommended as "one of the finest citizens of the United States."[71]

On her return journey to the West Coast, Goldstein stopped in Indianapolis, where she conferred with May Wright Sewall, the president of the International Council of Women. They discussed the progress of the National Council of Women in Australia—where state-based branches jealously guarded their separate identities—and talked about the difficulties thus posed to forming stronger international ties. Goldstein traveled on to Chicago, where her arrival was heralded, as had become customary, by newspaper headlines. "She Votes in Australia," declared the *Chicago Daily Tribune* in a report of her talk to the Political Equality Club.[72]

The meeting in Chicago was marked by "spirited debate." Conflict erupted, not over feminist strategy but over the injustice of imperialist wars and suspicion of foreign immigrants. Tired of hearing about how progressive Australians were, Dr. Anna Blount of Oak Park asked about their participation in the Boer War, "If the Australians are so intelligent and of such high political morality, why did you send soldiers to crush out a sister republic in South Africa?" Goldstein's host, the leading local suffragist and lawyer Catherine Waugh McCulloch, rushed to her visitor's defense. "I am an American woman and I'll answer that question," she said. "I don't think that we who are trying to crush out the poor Filipinos are in a position to throw stones at England or Australia." For her part, Goldstein explained that regrettably voters in Australia had no say in the Australian government's decision to send troops to South Africa, but in the last six months, popular feeling against the Boer War had grown: "I believe the people now would vote in opposition to sending any soldiers if they had a say about it."[73]

There was another controversial intervention when Cordelia Kirkland rose to suggest that the reason the United States had not been able to introduce woman suffrage was the predominance of foreign immigrants. "This country has been inundated by an influx of immigrants who are almost brutes and they bring their almost animal wives with them," she said. "These men are influenced by low motives and their wives will do as the men command." Again McCulloch took the floor to say that foreign women were not all ignorant, and in any case the intelligent vote outnumbered the ignorant vote. She was supported in her stance by Sarah Parker Willis, who stated her disagreement with Kirkland's view, asserting that America had nothing to fear from foreign immigration.[74]

Goldstein enjoyed the "animated discussion," but she also remembered the antipathy to foreigners. She was more impressed, however, by her host's ability to combine a profession as a partner in a law firm with political activism and raising three children. As legislative superintendent of the Illinois Equal Suffrage Association, McCulloch, who had been successful in winning equal rights for women to the guardianship of their children (1901), would also be instrumental in securing an increase in the age of consent for girls from fourteen to sixteen (1905) and later winning support for mothers' pensions in Illinois (1911). She also served a term as vice president of NAWSA.

Goldstein's next stops were Minneapolis–Saint Paul and Denver, and finally she returned to San Francisco, where she was again interviewed and photographed by local newspapers. She presented several talks and attended a reception in her honor organized by her old friend Mrs. Speddy, who had provided her accommodation when she had first stepped off the boat back in January. Goldstein visited the Fabiola Hospital, run entirely by women, then visited the University of California. "In the library at Berkeley University I saw the original manuscript of Bret Harte's 'Heathen Chinee.'" She toured Stanford University and was shown around the library, chapel, and mausoleum. "Stanford is the most richly endowed University in the States," she told her readers, "built by Senator and Mrs. Stanford, in memory of their son, Leland, who died at the age of 15."[75] And there were Australian connections: T. W. Stanford of Melbourne, who had been a generous subscriber to Victorian suffrage funds, was a brother of Senator Stanford. The university president, Dr. David Starr Jordon, was also a good suffragist. In 1907 and again in 1914, he visited Melbourne to deliver a course of lectures for the University Extension Board.

Goldstein counted her visit to the United States a great success. "Here I am back in San Francisco, after a triumphal progress through the States," she reported happily. "America is a truly wonderful country." Still, it had been "real hard work."[76] Traveling on trains, living out of trunks, engaging in discussion and meeting new people, conducting research into social and industrial conditions—all were tiring activities. She returned to Australia full of admiration for the achievements and inquiring minds of American women: "the most interesting and interested audiences I ever saw . . . the American women are delightful—I can't help repeating it. They are so receptive and so intelligent that it is a pleasure to speak to them."[77] But like Spence before her, Goldstein was puzzled by their lack of political progress. From an Australian perspective, the United States was in many ways a deeply conservative country, a democratic republic constrained by political institutions founded in the eighteenth century and political parties that proved strongly resistant to change. Goldstein's advice to American women was that they should build coalitions with the labor movement, as had been done in Australia.

Back in Melbourne, however, the growing electoral strength of the Labor Party and its appeal to enfranchised women would prove an obstacle to her own political ambition. Goldstein determined to build on her countrywomen's political status by standing for election to the federal parliament, but her independence from the established political parties would prove a barrier to her success. Although Goldstein counted herself a socialist and was sympathetic to the labor movement, she was strongly committed to women's nonparty cause and stood for election five times as an independent woman candidate. Nonparty principles for Goldstein meant a belief that "all civic action should be prompted by conscience and principle rather than by party interest and tradition."[78] As a woman candidate, Goldstein put the interests of women and the protection of children at the top of her agenda.

Goldstein's trip to the United States confirmed her belief that women reformers should avoid party machines. At the same time, her lectures and the story of political success she conveyed gave American suffragists useful material for propagandizing. Women had their own interests, values, priorities, and responsibilities, most notably the welfare and nurture of children. Australian suffrage leaders pointed regularly to the success of women voters in achieving a range of maternalist reforms, including juvenile courts, boarding-out schemes, mothers' pensions, the appointment of women to public office, shorter hours of labor, the equal guardianship of children, and raising the age of consent. And they suggested that women's participation in political life had lifted its moral tone.

In campaigning for woman suffrage, Carrie Chapman Catt and others invoked Australasian precedent. "The great Commonwealth of Australia and the progressive British colony of New Zealand have granted full suffrage rights to their women."[79] Australasian women's political rights could also be invoked to provoke American men, with the national executive of NAWSA declaring: "We believe the women of America are not inferior to those of Australia in intelligence and patriotism and we call upon American men to emulate the legislators of Australia in justice and chivalry."[80]

In a congratulatory letter to Australian women, published in the *Australian Woman's Sphere*, Carrie Chapman Catt, in her capacity as president of NAWSA, hailed Australians as leaders of the progressive world and settler societies more generally: "Verily it is the young nations, untrammelled by tradition and custom, which make the great strides forward! Where will the world turn for courageous and advanced action when there are no more young countries?" The United States had led the way in democracy, she reminded her readers, but Australia had led the way in extending suffrage to women. "All honour to her. The hearts of all reformers, all lovers of the truth, all believers in a better order of things, have already learned to love the word Australia." Catt again pointed to the constitutional hurdles in the way of suffrage reform in the United States and, like Cordelia Kirkland in Chicago, named foreign immigrants as enemies of women's struggle: "herds of foreigners are constantly arriving," and within five years, no matter how ignorant, they are permitted to vote on the enfranchisement of American women. US suffragists were "not envious" of Australians, she insisted, though they did grow weary. But truth would conquer in the end.[81]

American newspapers reported on the results of women's enfranchisement in Australia. "Labor Gains," reported the *New York Times*; "Women Voters Support the Labor Party."[82] In a 1907 article titled

"What the New Suffrage Movement Has Done for Australia," the *New York Times* reported on the impressions of "Rev WA Hobson, a Congregational minister, who had just returned from a journey through Australia." In supporting the eight-hour day, early closing of shops, and measures against gambling, women voters had insisted, he said, on elevating "national and civic morality" above financial considerations.[83] Another visitor applauded the extent of "socialistic" measures: "I have seen in Australia socialistic kindergartens, theatres, stores, gas and water companies, schools, churches and homes."[84] However, reports linking woman suffrage to "state socialism" could also serve to strengthen opposition to the movement and reinforce conservative suspicions.

It was often suggested that the exercise of women's vote augured well in Australia for the emergent Labor Party. The steady increase in the nationwide vote for Labor, which led to the formation of the first Labor government in the world in 1910, was attributed to the impact of enfranchised women.[85] *Harper's Weekly* suggested, not altogether sympathetically, that Australia had fallen under "the domination of the working-man and the voting woman."[86] Alice Henry, newly arrived in the United States in 1906 and speaking to the annual convention of NAWSA, also attributed Australia's spirit of progressivism—its advanced social legislation—to the fact of women voting.[87]

Women's equal political rights were understood to be both a reflection and a cause of Australia's progressive legislation. "To those who are familiar with the trend of affairs in Australia and New Zealand," wrote an "American sociologist" in the *Independent*, "the successful experiments in land nationalization, compulsory arbitration between between capital and labor, equal suffrage for men and women, direct legislation, and, in general a thoroughgoing governmental control of public utilities—the Australian people seem to have gone far beyond us in equalizing opportunity." Old-age pensions also indicated how the state was deployed to promote social justice, which the writer judged to be "a more radical activity of the state than we are ready for."[88] The example of Australian women's political power could be seen as a warning as well as an object lesson and might well have augmented conservative opposition to American women's enfranchisement.

Maud Wood Park decided to learn about the Australian experience firsthand. A member of the MWSA and BESAGG and a graduate of Radcliffe, Park had also formed a younger women's organization, the College Equal Suffrage League (CESL), to attract students and alumni to suffrage work. Her first NAWSA meeting in Washington as a twenty-nine-year-old had convinced her that younger women should be recruited to spread the message. First in Massachusetts, then in New York, and then across the country, Park helped establish local branches of CESL as well as a national association with an executive council headed by M. Carey Thomas, president of Bryn Mawr. Park was elected vice president.

Accompanied by her friend and fellow suffragist Mabel Willard, Park traveled to Asia—Japan, Korea, Siam, Singapore, and India—and Australia, where she concentrated her time in the two more progressive states of New South Wales and Victoria, the latter home to the new federal government in the temporary national capital of Melbourne. Just four years later, young American architects Walter Burley Griffin and Marion Mahony Griffin would win the international competition to design a new capital in Canberra, trouncing their British rivals. The secretary of the international design committee was the son of Andrew Inglis Clark, Conway Inglis Clark, who lived next door to Royce in Cambridge and studied architecture in Boston.

In investigating how women were using their newfound political power in Australia, Park was interested not only in the reforms they had secured but in how women activists were organizing post-suffrage to achieve their aims. As she wrote, "The question is often asked: 'After woman suffrage, what?' Sometimes the asker means what methods of organization will women employ; sometimes, what ends will they seek; sometimes, what results will they obtain."[89] While American suffragists still campaigned for suffrage, Australia women citizens were theorizing the meaning of women's citizenship and experimenting with the possibilities and potential of women's political power in the public domain.

From Sydney and Melbourne, Park reported in detail on the new post-suffrage organizations, noting the political differences that divided women—their existing party affiliations as well as the establishment of nonparty women's organizations determined to transcend party divisions. In New South Wales, she noted the existence of the Women's Liberal League, the Women's Branch of the People's Reform League, and the Labor-oriented Women's Progressive Association. Like Catherine Spence and Vida Goldstein, Rose Scott, veteran leader of the New South Wales suffrage movement, had declined an invitation to join the Labor Party. She grieved, she said, to see women locked into party politics. "They cannot serve two masters—the spirit of the ideal . . . and the spirit of a party faction: the spirit of the motherhood of women, which is to protect and care for *all*, and the spirit of a fighting faction, which, alas, too frequently cares more for itself than for the real interests of the country and the people."[90]

In this spirit, Scott formed the Women's Political and Education League, which listed the following measures as among those they wished implemented: the Girls' Protection Bill; the Family Maintenance Act; registration of nurses; hours of hospital nurses to be limited; equal pay for equal work; equal ownership and guardianship of children by both parents; economic independence of married women; and appointment of women sanitary inspectors, boarding-out inspectors, school inspectors, and truant officers. The final objective of the twenty-six listed was the settlement of international disputes by peace and arbitration.

Park noted that there were two national political organizations of women headquartered in Melbourne. The larger body, the Australian Women's National League, was anti-socialist and affiliated with the Women's Liberal League of New South Wales. The other organization that aimed for national status was Goldstein's Women's (Federal) Political Association (WPA), whose platform included uniform marriage and divorce laws and joint guardianship of children. Its other goals included equal pay for equal work; protection of boys and girls to the age of twenty-one; reforms in methods for dealing with neglected and delinquent children; and the appointment of women as police matrons, sanitary inspectors, inspectors of neglected and boarded-out children, inspectors of state schools and truant officers, inspectors of all state institutions in charge of women and children, and members of municipal and shire councils. To educate its members in the practice of good government, the WPA held a women's parliament every month.

The WPA proposed, Maud Wood Park noted, to "remain non-partisan, permitting its members to affiliate with either party on general questions, but urging them to vote only for candidates who will promise to support measures deemed . . . necessary for the protection of women and children." This would be the formula later adopted by Park as president of the National League of Women Voters in the United States.

Park and Willard were invited to afternoon tea at parliament house by Andrew Fisher, leader of the federal Labor Party, and his wife, Margaret Fisher. They were joined by Vida Goldstein and a group of Labor women and also met a large contingent of male politicians. The local press reported that "much satisfaction was expressed by the visitors with the leading position in politics of women in Australia." In responding to the hosts' words of welcome, Mabel Willard commented that

> whilst advocating the claims of the Equal Franchise League in America, she had often been advised to go away for 500 years and then return to America, by which time she might expect to see the reforms she advocated established. Since visiting Australia she would be able to advise those who assailed her with such remarks to visit the Commonwealth and, not in 500 years, but at the present moment, see the system of equal adult suffrage in operation.[91]

Goldstein also invited Park to speak at a meeting of women electors in the suburb of Brighton, organized by the WPA to thank local women for the record number of votes they cast at the recent federal election.[92]

The American suffragists were delighted with their warm reception and impressed at the respect with which they were greeted by male political leaders. There was "no more illuminating incident," Park wrote, "than the interest which men in public life took in discussing public questions with 'mere women.'"

> The presentation of our letters of introduction, by no means pressing in their nature, to the leaders of the opposing parties in the Federal Parliament, brought us travellers as we were, several pleasant opportunities to visit the House and Senate; and two Parliamentary tea parties were given for us in the visitors' room of Parliament House, one

by a member of the Ministerial Party, one by a leader of the Labor
Party, to each of which busy representatives and senators came quite
as a matter of course to have a cup of tea with two women and in
some cases to make speeches of welcome or of explanation of public
affairs.

Park was impressed that "the sense of the political equality of women
in a country where they are enfranchised was a deep-rooted conviction."[93] She noted in particular "women's equal standing in the industrial and political organization of the Labor party." She suggested that
because the Labor Party had adopted many women's objectives in its
party platform, women's aims would soon be achieved.

The broader effects of women's enfranchisement were difficult to determine, but Park summarized the "changes" evident in Australia as
the gains specifically for women in laws and increased business or professional opportunities; increased protection of children and greater attention to public education; increased legislation on the subject of public
morals; increased legislation for social betterment, particularly in the
care of the dependent and delinquent classes; improvement in personal
character of candidates for public office; greater orderliness at elections
and public meetings; and an increase in general interest in political
questions. She concluded, importantly, that despite party differences,
the similarities in women's platforms were such as to give "a pretty definite idea of what 'women's causes'" were.[94] On all sides, they agreed on
the desirability of protecting maternity, infancy, and the home.

When Park and Willard returned to the United States, American
women were still many years away from winning political rights at
the national level. Park resumed her lecturing role, drawing on her experience in Australia to promote the role of women in politics. In the
next four years, Washington State, California, Oregon, Arizona, Kansas,
Nevada, and Montana would grant women suffrage. In 1916, Democratic president Woodrow Wilson declared himself in favor of woman
suffrage, and Carrie Chapman Catt announced NAWSA's "winning
plan" of lobbying simultaneously at the federal and state levels. She
brought Park to Washington to direct the crucial lobbying effort in the
capital. Finally, on 4 June 1919, the US Congress approved the Nineteenth Amendment, which was ratified on 18 August 1920.

Immediately the new National League of Women Voters (NLWV) was formed in Washington, but from the beginning, there was tension and uncertainty about its role in politics and its relationship to established political parties. Catt declined a leadership position in the organization but urged Park to accept the role of president. Catt was clearly ambivalent about the way forward and also urged women to become more active in the political parties: "The only way to get things in this country is to find them on the inside of the political party. More and more the political parties become the power through which things are accomplished."[95]

As president of the NLWV, Park played a key role in finalizing the aims and platform of the first women's nonparty post-suffrage organization. Its focus, echoing that of nonparty, post-suffrage women's groups in Australia, such as the Women's Political Association and the Women's Political Educational League, was "education in citizenship and the interests of women as voting citizens," and "to come together as women and consider the measures women want."[96] Women voters would be urged to support and encourage sympathetic male legislators, and would be inspired to "support . . . what the man himself is trying to do."[97]

The first plank of the NLWV was

Child Welfare. Realizing that the hope of the nation lies in the children of today, the citizens of tomorrow we pledge ourselves to support:
    Adequate appropriation for the Children's Bureau;
    The prohibition of child labor throughout the United States;
    The protection of infant life through a Federal program for maternity and infancy care.[98]

The first legislation for which the NLWV, working with the Women's Joint Congressional Committee, claimed credit was the Sheppard-Towner Maternity and Infancy Act, passed in 1920, the first major legislation relating to women following their enfranchisement and an expression of the maternalist politics of child protection accorded priority by the post-suffrage transpacific women's movement. It was one of the first measures in the United States that extended federal funding to social welfare, supporting the establishment of child and maternal health centers that contributed materially to the decline in infant mortality.

Although the National Woman's Party, formed in 1916, diverged radically from the maternalist priorities of the NLWV, with its focus on the achievement of "equal rights" for women, it reinforced the idea that women shared common interests. Post-suffrage politics focused on maximizing women's power as a bloc of voters rather than on advancing their success as political candidates for the legislature. The achievement of woman suffrage was thus paradoxical. Though the vote could be acclaimed as the emblem of women's equality, the strategy of nonparty politics had the effect of marginalizing women as aspiring politicians. In this regard, Vida Goldstein's political career could itself be seen as the object lesson. She was a prominent public figure. She edited the feminist journals *Australian Woman's Sphere* and later the *Woman Voter*, founded the Women's (Federal) Political Association, played a key role in mobilizing women voters to secure greater protection for women and children and in securing the appointment of women to public office, but when she stood five times as an independent woman candidate for election to the federal parliament, she was defeated in each case by male candidates endorsed by the major political parties. What should women citizens do?

Carrie Chapman Catt felt "deep concern" with the NLWV's interpretation of "women's issues."[99] In a forthright letter, she confessed to her friend Maud Wood Park that she didn't like the way the League of Women Voters was "drifting"—child welfare, social hygiene, pure food—these should not, she thought, be women citizens' main concerns. The maternity bill, she said, had "no more to do with good citizenship than diamond tiaras."[100] Catt's misgivings were soundly based, but in the progressive new world of Australia and the United States, maternal citizenship ruled. "Of all the activities in which I have shared during more than forty years of striving," Florence Kelley of the National Consumers League later recalled, "none is, I am convinced, of such fundamental importance as the Sheppard-Towner Act."[101] Suffragists tended to measure their success in terms of achieving maternal and infant welfare reform rather than with reference to building careers as politicians. Not for many decades would significant numbers of women be elected to the national legislatures of Australia and the United States, and they gained success, for the most part, as endorsed party candidates.

CHAPTER SIX

Mothers of the Nation

WHEN CATHERINE SPENCE addressed the International Congress of Charities, Philanthropy and Corrections at the Chicago World's Fair in 1893, calling for dependent or neglected children to be removed from institutions, and advocated the Australian scheme of state assistance (or "boarding-out") to support children nurtured in family homes—increasingly their own homes—many in the audience were aghast. Disapproving of the "socialistic" nature of such state expenditure, they espoused instead the uplifting virtues of private philanthropy, individual benevolence, and manly independence.

Zilpha D. Smith, general secretary of Associated Charities in Boston, reminded the gathering that the United States did not live under "a socialistic system." To "save character" and preserve their "independence," families in need should provide for themselves or accept private charity. According to A. O. Wright of Madison, Wisconsin, public assistance was not proper "charity" but "a form of socialism."[1] Charitable agencies dominated the 1893 congress, and many participants ran their own institutions or were well-known philanthropists.

Spence was indignant. In the new democratic world, she insisted, people had a "right" not to be "pauperized" in workhouses, orphanages, reformatories, or other institutions. The destitute had a right to financial assistance from the state; children had a right to family life and a proper education. "Socialistic" action to realize these democratic ideals was, Spence believed, "the trend of modern thought, in spite of protests from individualists."[2]

By 1909, when American reformers gathered at the White House for the Conference on the Care of Dependent Children, called the year before by President Theodore Roosevelt, it was clear that a marked shift in orientation had occurred among those interested in child welfare. In his opening address, Roosevelt expressed his earnest hope that "members of this conference will take a progressive stand. . . . In other words, I earnestly hope that each of you will consider not only the interests of his own immediate locality, but the interests of the nation as a whole."[3] National interest now demanded that state financial assistance be provided to enable dependent children to be cared for in private homes, preferably by their own mothers. The "keynote of the conference" declared that "home life is the highest and finest product of civilization. Children should not be deprived of it except for urgent and compelling reasons."[4]

One of the delegates to the White House conference was A. W. Clark, superintendent of the Child Saving Institute in Omaha, Nebraska. Clark had heard Spence speak at the International Congress of Charities in 1893 and confessed to a change of mind regarding "socialistic measures" afterward. Several years ago, he told the Washington audience, after some very great mistakes, he had realized the necessity of "keeping parent and children together."[5] State funding to assist mothers would facilitate this important goal.

Max Mitchell, superintendent of Federated Jewish Charities in Boston, explained how "boarding out" worked:

> The placing of children in private families is an expense, and, if the original home lacks desirability, the tone of the home can be raised by giving the mother the same payment for the board of the children as is incurred through placing them in a private family or maintaining them in an institution. . . . Let the amount involved be paid to the mother in the exercise of her own trade, which she already knows—a mother's trade—the bringing up of her children, the highest and noblest calling, the making of good men and women.[6]

Catherine Spence would have been thrilled that her argument was now being promulgated at the highest level in American politics.

Established in the late nineteenth century, Australian "boarding-out schemes" anticipated by several years what would be called mothers' or widows' pensions in the United States, first introduced in Illinois in 1911, two years after the White House conference. In that state, Henry Neil, the self-described "father of mothers' pensions," conceived of the Funds to Parents Act, inspired, he explained, by the New Zealand example.[7] In this matter, New Zealand had followed the Australian example.[8] Neil gave his bill to Senator Carl Lundberg to introduce in the state legislature, where it passed with little opposition. That would come later, when charitable agencies and orphanages mobilized opposition to the initiative, again citing the dangers of "state socialism" but to little avail.[9]

The mothers' pension movement swept the country, with some forty states legislating in the next decade to provide state assistance to enable widowed or deserted mothers to care for their children at home. Women's clubs, progressive journalists and judges, and labor and child welfare reformers all offered support, variously arguing that state payments would prevent the separation of families, alleviate poverty, put an end to child labor, and recognize the social service performed by mothers. Increasingly drawn to the idea of an activist state, women reformers and researchers, including Julia Lathrop, Sophonisba Breckinridge, Edith Abbott, and Florence Kelley, played a key role in transforming American "social thought" in this area and thus securing widespread support of new social policy.[10] At the federal level, the nationalization of mothers' pensions through Title IV of the Social Security Act in 1935 confirmed assistance to mothers as a cornerstone of the American welfare state.[11]

During the same years, however, the spread of Indian "boarding schools" and the implementation of "outing programs" pointed to a quite different fate for indigenous families. Indian children, it was believed, should be removed from their homes and placed with white families and in white institutions so that they might learn English, adopt civilized manners, and be better assimilated into the national culture. Spence had encountered this view on her American lecture tour, when she heard Alice Fletcher, the leading ethnologist and advocate of the Dawes Act, speak in Providence, Rhode Island. "She thinks it is absolutely necessary," Spence had noted in her diary, "the young Indians should be separated from their parents and taught the English language."[12]

Roosevelt's paean to "home life" as the highest product of "civilization" was telling. Central to progressive thinking in settler societies was the assumption that white civilization marked the zenith of global evolutionary progress. In this framework, indigenous peoples were expected to advance toward civilization and citizenship through processes variously named "assimilation," "absorption," and "protection." The education of children was thought to be key to their advancement, even at the cost of their lives. Diseases ran rampant through the Indian boarding schools, and the high mortality rates necessitated the construction of special cemeteries adjacent to the classrooms. At Haskell Indian School, children from thirty-seven different tribes were buried in the cemetery. One hundred children were interred between 1885 and 1913. Most were teenagers, but some were as young as six and seven. Brenda Child has commented on the irony of schools whose aim was to remove all vestiges of tribalism choosing to engrave the children's tribal identities on their tombstones. Ojibwes were buried next to Hopis, and Seminoles alongside Cheyennes. Many more bodies were transported home by train for traditional funerals.[13]

With the focus on the ideals of civilization and citizenship and the ascendancy of global "whiteness," progressive thinking became more pessimistic about the future place of American Indians in the nation, as well as that of African Americans, Asian Americans, and the migrant groups ("primitive people" with "untrained minds," in Jane Addams's formulation) who were also targeted by advocates of assimilation through education and disenfranchised by electoral reform.[14] Literacy tests were implemented by the states to disenfranchise African Americans, beginning with Mississippi in 1890; lynchings peaked in 1892; and four years later, Plessy v. Ferguson affirmed the legal basis of segregation. There was also a revival of deportationist thinking in the United States, initiating a debate over whether African Americans—"an alien element, unabsorbed and unabsorbable"—could be transported "back" to Africa. At the same time, pressure increased for the enactment of further immigration restrictions.[15]

In this context, Native Americans posed a distinct challenge to policy makers. The territory of the United States comprised their ancestral homelands. They were the first Americans. As survivors of dispossession, disease, and the dislocation wrought by settler colonialism, their future inevitably lay in absorption or assimilation by the nation. "In dealing with the Indians," Roosevelt told Congress in 1902, "our aim should be their ultimate absorption into the body of our people. But in many cases this absorption must and should be very slow."[16]

Roosevelt's appointment first of Francis Leupp—a champion of civil service reform, economy, and efficiency—and then progressive crusader

Robert Valentine as commissioners of Indian Affairs reflected this approach. The aim of federal policy in Indian affairs, Leupp announced, was "improvement, not transformation." Indians should not be expected to become white men's equals overnight. Education should focus on vocational training, practical training for low-skilled jobs, and domestic work for girls. Improvement in medical services was also crucial to stem infant mortality rates and the deadly toll of infectious diseases—tuberculosis, pneumonia, influenza, measles, meningitis—in boarding schools and on reservations.

Robert Valentine, appointed commissioner in 1909, was an idealist who believed it was necessary to "vitalize" the different services offered by the Bureau of Indian Affairs into "a single great progressive force."[17] Failure in this regard would lead to a bleak future. In an address to the nation, Valentine declared portentously: "It is possible to do only two things with the Indians—to exterminate them or to make them into citizens."[18] While many Indians believed that assimilation was itself a form of "extermination," progressive reformers were convinced that advancement required the immersion of Indian children in the white man's culture and economy.[19]

But there were particular challenges in the case of Indians, Valentine advised,

> more than would be demanded in the case of the backward among our own people or in the case of the immigrant. We are dealing with a people without generations back of them trained more or less in the ways of civilization. Within the next few decades we must foreshorten the road which is really centuries long, and while leading the Indian along it we must of necessity try to do in months what nature should do in years.[20]

Indian schools; industrial training; "outing" of Indian youth on white farms, in white homes, and in white businesses; and other coercive methods of instruction were considered necessary to expediting this goal. Valentine also ordered the building of school sanatoriums for Indian children.

Thus, even as progressive reformers argued for the desirability of removing neglected and dependent white children from institutions so that they might grow and prosper in a salubrious home environment, indigenous children in both Australia and the United States were systematically removed from their families and communities and sent away to institutions. For progressive reformers, the goal was the conversion of "savage" tendencies to mainstream "civilized" values, the transformation of "primitive natives" into "useful members of society."[21] As the critical Meriam report on Indian administration later noted, "Education for the Indian in the past has proceeded largely on the theory that it is necessary to remove the Indian child as far as possible from his home environment; whereas the modern point of view in education and social work lays stress on upbringing in the natural setting of home and family life."[22]

In both Australia and the United States, reformers "routinely asserted that the removal of indigenous children from their families would 'save' the children from lives of backwardness and poverty . . . civilize them and make them useful in Australian and American societies."[23] The White House conference had declared that children should not be deprived of home life except for "urgent and compelling reasons." Clearly the imperative of inculcating natives with civilized values and destroying their own cultures and languages was thought to supply such reasons, even though the trauma of family separation, for both children and parents, was clear and long lasting.

Many families resisted the removal of their children and sought to bring them home, especially if family members were ill. Parents wrote letters pleading for the release of their children. The father of one child at Flandreau explained that his wife, the child's mother, was dying of tuberculosis: "My wife would like to have her home while she is alive. . . . Mattie has been away to school all her life and has never been home for any length of time. . . . Her mother wants her home very much right now." As was mostly the case, the school declined the request.[24]

Understanding progressivism in the framework of settler colonialism helps explain its constitutive contradictions, its simultaneous emancipatory and coercive, uplifting and repressive, character. It also highlights the centrality of children—white and indigenous—to the vision of progressive reform as a project with national import. In the name of the child, progressive reformers demanded national action at the federal level in the key areas of Indian policy, child welfare, and industrial life. To that end, Florence Kelley and like-minded reformers established the National Child Labor Committee to win federal laws to curtail and protect child labor. "The noblest duty of the Republic," declared Kelley in 1905, was "so cherishing all its children that they . . . may become self-governing citizens. . . . The care and nurture of childhood is thus a vital concern of the nation."[25] Realizing the aim of turning all children into self-governing citizens in a settler society that defined Indians as backward and barbaric was a deeply racialized process. With limited funding, Indian boarding schools exploited child labor to carry out their basic operations. Children worked in gardens and on farms, in laundries and in kitchens; they milked cows, erected buildings, and did carpentry. Instead of engaging in the normal classroom work of public schools, Indian students spent long hours at work.[26]

In Australia, enfranchised Labor women considered new forms of state assistance to white mothers—including payments to enable mothers to care for their children at home—a proud achievement of the new Commonwealth. Lilian Locke-Burns, Vida Goldstein's erstwhile suffragist coworker and later an organizer for the Political Labor Council and member of the Trades Hall Council in Melbourne, celebrated their success in characteristically evolutionary and nationalist terms as an advancement beyond the "barbaric stage":

> In no other part of the world, as far as one can ascertain, is so much being done by the State in the way of providing for mothers and children as in the Australian Commonwealth. . . .
>
> In Great Britain and some other countries which lay claim to some share in democratic reforms, the mothers are only protected (if protection it may be called) under some form of social insurance. In the American States also very little has been done so far in this direction beyond some attention to delinquent children, and the usual institutional efforts that we find in most countries which have evolved beyond the barbaric stage.[27]

As indicators of progress, Locke-Burns referred specifically to the Australian reforms of "boarding children out, either to their own mothers or to foster-mothers," and the federal Labor government's 1912 Maternity Allowance Act, which introduced a generous payment from the federal state to mothers on the birth of a child, including, controversially, unmarried mothers—those "who became mothers in a dishonorable way," in the words of one critic—but not to nonwhite mothers.[28]

White women reformers were central to fashioning new kinds of maternalist welfare states, heralding in the words of New South Wales suffragist Rose Scott: "the advent of the mother-woman's world with loving heart and sheltering arms."[29] The enfranchisement of Australian women at the national level in 1902, one year after the inauguration of the new Australian Commonwealth, gave voice, as Scott put it, to the "National Motherhood of Women."[30] But not all mothers were deemed eligible to be citizen mothers or to nurture young people and train them to exercise the rights and responsibilities of citizenship. "Asiatic," Aboriginal, and Islander mothers were excluded. Payments were made to women in their capacity as citizens, and in settler societies, citizenship was a racialized condition. Among the few voices that strongly objected to the racial exclusions was Vida Goldstein's paper, the *Woman Voter*, which denounced the denial of payments to nonwhite mothers as "the White Australia policy gone mad," for surely "maternity [was] maternity whatever the race."[31] Motherhood, she insisted, was a universal condition.

In both countries, child welfare and the civilizing of children (though under state jurisdiction) came to be considered crucial to the larger project of nation building. Motherhood now entailed more than physical nurture, as one delegate to the White House conference pointed out. Mothers did more than "bring up animals of the human kind. . . . We demand that they shall educate their offspring; that they shall train them to be good citizens."[32] But when it came to thinking about maternal rights as well as duties and conceptualizing mothers as rights-bearing subjects, the Australian and American welfare states diverged, in part because of the prominent role of organized labor and socialist women as enfranchised citizens in shaping policy in the Commonwealth of Australia.

Old-age and invalid pensions, legislated by the Australian government in 1908, also recognized women's equal and independent citizenship. Introduced by the Deakin Liberal government and supported by Labor, they provided for equal and individual payments for men and women upon retirement, men at the age of sixty-five and women at sixty. Explicitly "granted as a right and not as a charity," old-age pensions were not work-based social insurance schemes, as in Germany, but paid directly from government revenue. First introduced in New Zealand in 1898 and in Victoria and New South Wales in 1900, Australian old-age pensions represented an explicit repudiation of the Old World order, with its workhouses and asylums, a desire to deinstitutionalize the indigent and de-pauperize the lives of the aged and destitute.[33]

Yet because they were considered an entitlement of citizenship, pensions in white Australia were denied to nonwhite residents, to "Asiatics . . . aboriginal natives of Australia, Africa, the islands of the Pacific, or New Zealand," although a later amendment granted eligibility to people of Asian descent born in Australia. The exclusion of indigenous peoples was contested in parliament as especially egregious. Why, asked Senator Gould, "should an aboriginal native of this country in which we are practically intruders, be denied an old-age pension?" Equally, why should Aborigines who were farmers and good citizens be excluded? In response, concessions were made. If Aborigines were "half-castes," advised the minister—in other words, on the path to assimilation—they would not be excluded from the old-age pension.[34]

The Australian Maternity Allowance followed suit in its articulation of the rights of citizenship. Also to be paid from general revenue, it was promoted by Labor prime minister Andrew Fisher not as a "baby bonus," as his conservative critics dubbed it, but as a citizen's right. Introduced in response to lobbying by Labor Party women, it was duly celebrated as the first "instalment of the mothers' maternal rights."[35] Once enfranchised, Australian women of all classes had mobilized as voters, as American visitors Maud Wood Park and Jessie Ackerman had noted, establishing both party-based and women's nonparty organizations to achieve their goals at the state and federal levels.

For progressive reformers, the state payment to mothers was a key achievement. Conservatives, however, were outraged at this overreach of "government maternalism," citing the recent critique by the Adelaide University professor W. Jethro Brown, whose book *The Underlying Principles of Modern Legislation* was published the same year.[36] American commentators were astonished in particular at the legislation's "non-discriminatory" character—that the payment extended to mothers "irrespective of [the circumstances] of their birth," regardless

of whether the mother was married or unmarried, deserving or un-
deserving, rich or poor.[37]

The politics of maternalism could be deployed to serve a range of
political causes. Conservative women invoked motherhood as a special vocation, but only worthy women were deemed eligible for support. Many Labor women advocated a regular state income to mothers
to secure their right of economic independence from men.[38] Economic
support from the state was a citizen's right and would alleviate mothers'
demeaning dependence on husbands or fathers. Some Australian
women activists with more radical views, such as Vida Goldstein, Ada
Bromham, and Mary Bennett, began to argue that all mothers had
rights as mothers—to the custody of their children, the sanctity of their
bodies, and economic independence—regardless of their class or race.[39]

In introducing a payment to mothers from federal revenue, the
Maternity Allowance set an international precedent, as an inquiry
commissioned by the US Children's Bureau testified.[40] Reporting on
maternity benefit systems in fourteen countries, its author noted that
Australia was "the first country to institute a system of national aid to
relieve the financial burdens of childbirth without requiring some direct contribution on the part of the wage earner."[41] In circulating the
findings, Bureau Chief Julia Lathrop commented that the report had
been compiled "in the hope that the information might prove useful to
the people of one of the few great countries which as yet have no system
of State or national assistance in maternity—the United States."[42]

In place of financial assistance, American women were granted the
Children's Bureau, the major outcome of the White House conference,
established, like the Australian Maternity Allowance, in 1912. As a
number of historians have pointed out, its creation represented a major
achievement on the part of American progressive reformers—"the arrival of progressive reform at the federal doorway"—although progressives like Valentine and others working at the Indian Bureau might
have disputed this claim to precedence.[43] The establishment of the
Children's Bureau as an advisory and research institution reflected,
moreover, the dominance of middle-class professional women in the
ranks of progressive reformers in the United States.

Central to the vision of a maternal welfare state in both Australia
and the United States was the appointment of white women to a

range of supervisory positions—as police, prison matrons, doctors, lawyers, magistrates, school inspectors, factory inspectors, boarding-out inspectors—and as protectors: teachers and employers of indigenous mothers and children. One of the major goals of Australian women campaigning for the welfare of Aboriginal women and children in the early decades of the twentieth century was to have white women appointed to official positions as state "protectors."[44] They were unsuccessful. Most white women reformers were not remunerated for their efforts; "mother work" usually went unpaid. In the United States, the Women's National Indian Association (WNIA) argued for the centrality of domesticity to civilization and were active in promoting the role of model homes as a transformative influence on reservations. As Jane Simonsen has suggested, the WNIA characteristically answered a national question with a woman-centered solution.[45]

In this mother-woman's world, new employment opportunities gradually opened up for women as once-voluntary positions were professionalized.[46] As Catherine Spence explained to readers of *Woman Voter*, the South Australian "boarding out" scheme preferred to use women—rather than police—as inspectors of licensed foster homes: "The police are very good in their way. Both in the Destitute Board and in the State Children's Department their services are most valuable, but the supervision of homes and food and care for babies is women's work, and cannot be done rightly by men."[47] Similarly, the Women's Political Association explained how its goal of "protection" would be realized with the appointment of women to positions of "supervision": "Wherever women and children are in subjection, supervision by women is necessary and women should vote to secure the appointment of women as inspectors of asylums, boarded out children, hospitals, schools and gaols."[48] In New South Wales, Rose Scott was pleased to report on the successful lobbying efforts of the Women's Political Educational League, which led to the appointment of police matrons, factory inspectors, doctors, social workers, and more: "Gladly did we welcome the appointment of Miss Duncan as our Lady Factory Inspector; or Miss Ferguson as a Sanitary Inspector; and we have to thank the late Government for appointing Dr Mary Booth as a Lecturer on Hygiene to the Public Schools, and Dr Agnes Bennett to care for poor women lunatics."[49] As Alice Henry, the Australian labor journalist working with Margaret Dreier Robins at the National Women's Trade Union League in Chicago, saw it, women's entry into public life restored them to their "true position of maternal supervision," which they had lost as individual mothers with industrialization and the introduction of compulsory schooling: "But because the mother can no longer oversee her own child all the time, the mothers of all the city should be able to do so. This they can do only through the vote and through their being placed in administrative positions in the legislature, on boards of schools, recreation parks, and as police women and matrons."[50] In this new "mother-world," all children would come under the supervision of the national motherhood of white women.

In the United States, even as Alice Henry outlined her vision, women remained unenfranchised. As Linda Gordon has pointed out, however, organized women were nevertheless "influential disproportionately to their formal political power in the creation of a modern child-welfare consciousness and movement."[51] But it was middle-class women (and men) who were most influential in shaping American maternalist reforms, more oriented to children's needs than to securing mothers' rights. Led by Jane Addams and Lillian Wald from Chicago's Hull House and Florence Kelley of the National Consumers League, child welfare advocates were supported by the National Child Labor Committee, the National Conference of Charities and Corrections, and the General Federation of Women's Clubs.

Crucially, their cause was espoused in turn by Roosevelt, an admirer of Australian political developments, as he had confided to Vida Goldstein in Washington in 1902. Six years later, when he invited over two hundred delegates to the first White House Conference on the Care of Dependent Children, his "Call for the Conference" suggested that "nothing ought to interest our people more than the care of the children who are destitute and neglected but not delinquent. . . . I very earnestly believe that the best way in which to care for dependent children is in the family home."[52]

In an accompanying memorandum, Roosevelt listed nine propositions that might guide conference deliberations. The first suggested the establishment of a children's bureau. The fourth pointed to a scheme of "boarding out," or mothers' pensions, asking, "Should children of parents of worthy character, but suffering from temporary misfortune,

and the children of widows of worthy character and reasonable efficiency, be kept with their parents, aid being given to the parents to
enable them to maintain suitable homes for the rearing of the
children."[53] By the conclusion of the conference, most participants had
endorsed this proposal, but there was still some disagreement on the
best source of such aid.

The main challenges to Roosevelt's child-oriented agenda, however,
were posed by social critics Judge Ben Lindsey and Jane Addams, who
asked the conference to consider the basic causes of poverty and family
misfortune and discuss possible legislative remedies, including workers'
compensation, improvements in wages and conditions of work, and
greater regulation of factories. Family destitution and distress called
for national reforms. "We can not, then, fairly consider the problem of
the dependent child," said Lindsey, "unless we consider its relation to
the great industrial, social and political questions which concern us
as a nation. The child is the state and the state is the child." It was the
responsibility of politicians and courts, he advised in characteristic
evolutionary terms, to enact laws that were more than "relics of feudalism and barbarism." Legislatures confronted different realities than
had existed "when precedents were made to protect property rather
than human life." New legislation was now needed to achieve justice
for laboring people. "Industrial barbarism" and "social injustice" were
the main causes of child dependency, and these should be addressed at
their source.[54]

Jane Addams also focused on the "harshness of modern industry"
as the cause of the accidents, illness, premature death, poverty, over-
work, and unemployment that were the underlying causes of child dependency. Addressing the conference on the topic of "modern devices
for minimizing dependency," she, too, referred to the necessity of legislative reforms, including employers' liability, restrictions on working
hours, and regulation of modern industry, wondering why Americans
were apparently so reluctant to embrace financial assistance from the
state.[55]

"Are we afraid of 'paternalism' or of some other hard words which
we so readily apply to such undertakings in America?" she asked. "If
we insist on being so much more Anglo-Saxon than England itself,
if we contend that each man must take his own risk of life and limb

and must care for his own family, possibly a remedy could be found if we approached the whole situation from the point of view of the little child." For, Addams observed, "the child has always appealed to America."[56] In the name of the child, progressivism became a national crusade. Three years later, Addams would chair the Chicago convention that launched the Progressive Party on the national stage, with Roosevelt as presidential candidate. Its platform included child labor laws, old-age pensions, workers' compensation, and a living wage.

In the settler states of Australia and the United States, child welfare was central to a shared vision of national reform, but the Maternity Allowance and Children's Bureau reflected divergences in political orientation and expectation. Whereas Australian Labor women spoke of maternal rights and ways to achieve economic independence for working-class mothers, the Children's Bureau was established to "investigate and report upon all matters pertaining to the welfare of children and child life among all classes of our people," providing advice to mothers and careers for a new and expanding college-educated professional class.[57]

The Children's Bureau was located in the Department of Commerce and Labor. The first women to be appointed to positions as professional "mothers of the nation," including Julia Lathrop, came from backgrounds in progressive reform and social work. Emma O. Lundberg, head of the Social Service Division, was a graduate of the University of Wisconsin and a researcher for the Wisconsin Industrial Commission. Her friend, Katharine Lendroot, had also matriculated at the University of Wisconsin, where she studied social science with Richard Ely and John Commons and wrote a research paper supporting Wisconsin's minimum wage law. Lendroot met Lundberg while working on the Wisconsin Industrial Commission.

Robin Muncy has observed that the Children's Bureau carried "the settlement ethos into the federal government and with it the culture of female professionalism created in the settlements."[58] She doesn't mention that it also carried the culture of settler colonialism. Histories of American maternalist reform movements have not, in general, conceptualized the United States as a settler state built on the dispossession and displacement of indigenous peoples. Conversely, studies of white women's role in the "protection" and "uplift" of Indian women, as "white mothers to a dark race," have rarely located these efforts in the larger framework of progressive reform. But clearly the removal of indigenous children to boarding schools and the training of mothers and girls as domestic citizens was a key, if bureaucratically separate, progressive project.

In Australia, the state-based laws that provided for the separation of Aboriginal children from their parents were initially cast as acts "to provide for the protection and care of aborigines" in the tradition of earlier protectionist legislation aimed at other groups of "neglected" or "dependent" children.[59] Gradually the legislation was amended to become more targeted and coercive, with authorities relieved of the need to prove that Aboriginal children were actually neglected. In both Australia and the United States, the acclaimed vocation of "national motherhood" was racialized in conception. Neither Aboriginal nor Indian mothers were seen as qualified to perform the civilizational, educational, and national work that was the responsibility of modern motherhood.

In *A Final Promise*, Frederick Hoxie identified the different components of national assimilation—allotment of reservation land, education, and citizenship—and important shifts in emphasis between 1880 and 1920, as progressive investments in economy and efficiency, together with the increasing dominance of policy making by "frontier" settler interests, came into play.[60] From the late nineteenth century, Indian educators aimed, in Hoxie's words, at "the complete absorption of Indian children into white society."[61] There was a general consensus that the old reservation system should be abolished. "If every Indian child could be in school for five years," urged the *Journal of Education*, "savagery would cease and the government support of Indians would be a thing of the past."[62]

Children were the main target of these educational efforts, taught in a national Indian school system that combined day schools with an extensive system of boarding schools. Increasingly, the teaching of "civilization" came to mean preparation for a life of manual labor, mainly farm work for boys and domestic work for girls. The new type of progressive bureaucrat entrusted with Indian education was exemplified by Estelle Reel, a Republican from Wyoming, appointed as national superintendent of Indian schools in 1898. Like her contemporary,

Australian reformer Catherine Spence, Reed was a single professional woman who traveled alone for her work. Both were also journalists and had worked for the reform of asylums. Both stood for election to political office, but unlike Spence, Reel stood as an endorsed party candidate (Republican) and won. The first female candidate elected to state office in Wyoming, Reel became, with her appointment to head the Indian schools by the McKinley administration, the first American woman confirmed for high federal office.

As superintendent of Indian schools, Reel defined her mission as the defeat of savagery and barbarism: "The Indian child must be placed in school before the habits of barbarous life have become fixed, and there he must be kept until contact with our life has taught him to abandon his savage ways."[63] But it was girls' education that was deemed especially important to the future of the nation, as Reel told the *Woman's Journal:* "I wish to emphasize the vital importance of teaching . . . every Indian girl. If anything it is of more importance than industrial education for boys. Through the girls in the schools is almost our only way of reaching the home, and as they are to be the future wives and mothers, the fate of coming generations will be, in a large measure, in their keeping."[64] As "advanced women," these reformers claimed a special role in progressive programs focused on the welfare of children, public education, the protection of the home, and the care of "dependent" natives.[65]

Yet it was men who dominated the formulation and implementation of indigenous policy in both the government and bureaucracies. Women usually worked as field and "outing matrons," teachers, clerical assistants, and advocates. Hampton Institute, one of the first Indian boarding schools, was initially established to educate "freedmen" after the Civil War, but it opened its doors to Indian prisoners of war in 1878. Its leader, former Civil War captain Richard Henry Pratt, then applied for permission from the federal government to open the new coeducational Carlisle Indian Industrial School in Pennsylvania.

The aim of education, according to Pratt's famous axiom, was to "kill the Indian and save the man." Military drills ordered daily life. Boys were taught agricultural and mechanical skills; girls were trained in sewing, cooking, laundry, and general housework. The language of instruction was English—the "white man's language." Speaking native languages was forbidden, and students' names were changed. Many came to be embarrassed by their tribal identities. Students were discouraged from returning to their families. During the summer months, most would be boarded with neighboring white Christian families. Although Pratt was the "original architect of the outing program," it soon extended to Phoenix Indian School—the second major base for outing in the first two decades of the twentieth century—and spread to encompass domestic service in a number of urban areas, where "outing matrons" supervised young Indian women's work and their social relationships.[66]

Pratt had initially managed to persuade a number of prominent Indian families to send their children to Carlisle. When traveling west in 1879, he enlisted the support of Sioux chief Spotted Tail, whom Charles Pearson had earlier encountered in Cheyenne and dismissed as a murderous savage. Enticed by Pratt, the Sioux leader agreed to send his children to boarding school, and other Sioux followed his example. Soon after, more children joined them from Indian Territory. Alice Fletcher also helped Pratt recruit children to Carlisle. By 1900, the school had educated more than 1,200 students from seventy-nine tribes, but there was increasing resistance on the part of communities to let their children travel so far from their homes.

Indian boarding schools proliferated in the last decades of the nineteenth century, enrollments accelerated, and federal funding duly increased. The task of educating the Indian, "to train him and fit him for the white man's civilization," was pursued with particular zeal by Thomas Jefferson Morgan, commissioner of Indian affairs from 1893 to 1897.[67] "The Indian youth," he stated, "should be instructed in their rights, privileges, and duties as American citizens; should be taught to love the American flag; should be imbued with genuine patriotism, and made to feel that the United States, and not some paltry reservation is their home."[68] Indian children should be removed from their families so that they might better learn to love the nation. It was Morgan's idea to exhibit a model boarding school at the Chicago World's Fair in 1893, and he was pleased with the result. Considered a fair representation of a small boarding school, able to accommodate thirty pupils, even its lack of conveniences and space he considered "an added realistic touch."[69]

By the turn of the century, twenty-five boarding schools had been established in fifteen states, educating twenty thousand students. Most took in students from a diversity of tribes, though reservation schools, such as Riverside in Oklahoma and Keams Canyon in Arizona, served local populations. Despite modest funding increases, however, Indian students' experience at boarding schools continued to be blighted by poor and inadequate food, malnutrition, long hours of unpaid labor, the spread of infectious diseases, and terrible homesickness. Countless children also became physically ill.

Many parents resisted the efforts of Indian agents and their roving police to send their children away to boarding schools. Some Hopi parents played games of "hide and seek" with their children when police arrived.[70] Commissioner Morgan initially denied that parents had any rights in this regard, but with increasing opposition, he modified his approach somewhat. Although remaining convinced that an education at an off-reservation boarding school was in the best interests of the child and the nation, it was counterproductive, he realized, to engender distrust and antagonism. The "forcible taking of children a long distance from their homes against the will of their parents," Morgan wrote in his 1893 annual report, was a "matter of very doubtful expediency. Even ignorant and superstitious parents have rights."[71] Moral suasion was advocated in place of force. Many parents submitted to the pressure but later tried to rescue their children. One mother complained to a superintendent at the Flandreau School in South Dakota about the difficulty in getting her daughter home: "It seems it would be much easier to get her out of prison than out of your school."[72] The father of another student explained his refusal to let his boy go away to school by saying that he "preferred to have a live cowboy than a dead scholar."[73]

Indigenous parents in Australia also offered strong resistance to the efforts of state authorities to remove their children to state institutions, mission schools, apprenticeships with white families, and work on cattle stations. They, too, played "hide and seek." They tried to hide children in the bush or in rivers or to otherwise keep them out of sight.

"In New South Wales," Ann McGrath wrote, "mothers swam across the Murray [the state border with Victoria] . . . in order to keep and rear their own children."[74] In South Australia, Aboriginal parents gave evidence to a Royal Commission that although they wanted their children educated, they didn't want them "to go too far away." When new legislation gave further power to the chief protector to forcibly remove children, a spokesperson for the Aboriginal parents at the Point McLeay and Point Pearce Missions wrote that "the army of motherhood has taken up their position in opposition to the bill."[75]

In northern Australia, the exploitation of Aboriginal children in the workforce was especially rife, leading to considerable conflict between wealthy employers and governments trying to regulate the use of Aboriginal labor. Some white residents tried to intercede on Aborigines' behalf. William Craig, a local shire clerk in Cardwell, protested about employers dragging young children away from Aboriginal camps. Writing to the police commissioner, he observed that "family affection is their strongest feeling. . . . [They grieve] and wail for months if [the child] dies or is taken away from them."[76] And from the town of Bloomfield in north Queensland, a distressed father wrote that his wife had died brokenhearted, "killed on that unlucky day when [our daughter] was arrested by [police] . . . dragged by animal force from her family and weeping mother on a false charge of being neglected."[77] In both the United States and Australia, archives of letters testify to indigenous parents' anguish and grief.

Aboriginal activist Margaret Tucker wrote a moving memoir, *If Everyone Cared*, that described the fear of children and the profound distress of mothers who saw their children taken by police. As one of the children removed, she had hoped at first that it couldn't happen: "I didn't believe for a moment that my mother would let us go. She would put a stop to it!" But her protests were to no avail as the children were loaded into the car to be taken to the Cootamundra Domestic Training Home for Aboriginal Girls. Tucker heard years later about her mother's broken heart, "how after watching us go out of her life, she wandered away from the police station three miles along the road," where she finally collapsed. Many days later, family members "found our mother still moaning and crying. They heard the sounds and thought it was an animal in pain." She lived in dread of an approaching police car forever after.[78]

Margaret Tucker's family lived in New South Wales. Aboriginal policy in Australia remained under the jurisdiction of the states until 1967. Until the passage of a constitutional referendum that year, Aborigines were subjected to a variety of laws and regulations passed separately by the colonies—after 1901 by the states—empowering authorities, usually through Aborigines' Protection Boards and police, to remove Aboriginal children to work in white homes and institutions in order to separate them from "primitive" and "barbaric" influences and assimilate them into the lowest rungs of the workforce. As in the United States, landless indigenous peoples were prepared for wage labor in rural and industrial economies.

The rationale for the removal of Aboriginal children from their homes and families was usually stated in Australia as "the interest of the moral or physical welfare of the child."[79] In reality, institutional training meant preparation for a life of menial servitude at the bottom of the social hierarchy, either in white homes or in other state-arranged employment. With little pretense that they were civilizing Aborigines or preparing them for equal citizenship, state governments ensured that Aboriginal communities "provided a cheap and reliable state-regulated labour pool for agricultural and pastoral industries and a regular supply of domestic servants."[80] Although their stated objectives might differ in emphasis, in both Australia and the United States, the ultimate goal of progressive administrations was the absorption and thus disappearance of indigenous groups as distinct peoples.

Assimilationism could sometimes assume a more genuinely progressive aspect, as H. B. Higgins, president of the Commonwealth Court of Conciliation and Arbitration, demonstrated when he was asked to determine award wages for rural workers in southern Australia. When asked by the Australian Workers' Union, representing white workers, if Aborigines would be paid the same wage—so as not to undercut white wages—Higgins replied: "There will be no need of this 'Black labor to be paid the same as white labor'. I do not put in my award, black, white or anything. If he is a member of your organisation and an employee it is quite enough." Unionists were accorded preference, but Higgins was not simply protecting white workers' wages.[81]

In response to the employers' case that they should not have to pay Aborigines a living wage because they were already provided with rations and accommodation, Higgins responded sharply:

> It is argued that this is a patriarchal industry, unfit for the hard lines of rights; but I have yet to learn that in patriarchal times those who did labor were reduced to the condition of these men, without any right in respect of land or stock. . . . The truth is that these employees on stations have the normal needs of a human being as much as employees in the cities.

Aboriginal workers were human beings with normal needs, and Higgins assumed that those needs included their obligations as male breadwinners.[82] As American jurists Louis Brandeis, Felix Frankfurter, and Learned Hand understood, Higgins's jurisprudence was trailblazing in conceptualizing labor rights as human rights. It also broke new ground in insisting that Aboriginal employees should be paid the same award wages as white workers.

Feminist activists in Australia also began to advance universalist arguments in support of the maternal rights of Aboriginal mothers. Just as Goldstein had declared that "maternity was maternity whatever the race" in response to the racial exclusions of the Maternity Allowance Act, so, too, women activists working with Aboriginal women demanded recognition of their rights as mothers. The political possibilities of "maternalism" were thus rather more politically ambiguous than has sometimes been suggested. Australian reformers such as Ada Bromham, Edith Jones, and Mary Bennett invoked the "common status of motherhood" (in Bromham's phrase) to demand recognition of Aboriginal women's rights as mothers.[83]

Mary Bennett, an indefatigable and imperial-minded activist, was eloquent in her account of the destruction of Aboriginal lives caused by colonization and linked the plight of mothers to their dispossession:

> These women suffered an agony of fear, and the effects may still be seen in their children. . . . They endure all the untold sufferings of serfdom because we have deprived them of land to live on and refused them education, with all the other rights that are founded on education—medical services, wages . . . and a political standing by which they might obtain other rights due to them.

In fierce opposition to the policy of Aboriginal child removal, Bennett asserted to a Western Australian Royal Commission: "No Department in the world can take the place of a child's mother."[84]

Similarly, American women who, like Bennett, worked with indigenous families began to criticize policies of child removal and family separation in terms of the impact on mothers as well as children. Like Bennett, Constance Goddard DuBois, who worked with the "Mission Indians" of southern California, explained the plight of Indian mothers in the larger context of colonial dispossession: "We have robbed the Indians, persistently, systematically, under process of law and without law; but never has there been such bitter robbery as this. They have been driven by force, like herds of cattle from the lands the white man coveted; yet even then the Indian mother might keep her child if only to see it die within her arms."[85]

Estelle Aubrey, a schoolteacher who worked with the Navajo, also became a fierce critic of the government's "kidnapping" of Indian children. In her memoir, she was moved to ask, "What right have we to take these children from their parents? What right have we to break up Indian homes? Why do we deny Indians the rights we claim for ourselves?"[86]

In the Indian Bureau, there was increasing recognition of Native American mothers as key to the welfare of Indian communities and thus the future of the nation. Commissioners of Indian Affairs Leupp and Valentine became persuaded of the superiority of day schools over boarding schools for Indian children, not just because separating families might be wrong but because day schools allowed parents to learn from their children in the interests of the nation.

If living at home, the children could instruct their parents—and crucially their mothers—in modern manners and civilized culture. Simple day schools, with one teacher and one housekeeper, were encouraged "where Indian families were thickly settled enough to support a school of even fifteen children," and they could do the work "which the elaborate Indian school system should have done in the first place." Commissioner Leupp reported his surprise at finding in a Hopi village a "table set and the house kept in a way that would have done credit to the cleanliness and methods of many good white housekeepers." The mother explained that her little daughters, who were going to school at the foot of the mesa, had taught her. "There each day," Leupp enthused, "they had learned washing and cooking and every night had taught their mother about it."[87]

Whether day schools or boarding schools, "distinctively Indian schools" began to be regarded as "a temporary expedient." It must never be forgotten, said Commissioner Valentine, that the "tendency must be unceasing toward Indians in white schools and whites in Indian schools." Complete assimilation must be the basis for the modern nation. For Valentine, reform in Indian affairs was part of the great modern social movement. "Making some progress in the Indian business," he told a friend, was "part of the general social movement" led by his progressive friends Felix Frankfurter, Learned Hand, Walter Lippman, and Theodore Roosevelt.[88] When Roosevelt was endorsed as the Progressive candidate in the 1912 presidential election, Valentine resigned from his position as commissioner of Indian affairs to become an active worker in the cause, believing that unless "the Colonel" became president, there was "little hope on the horizon for social work in governmental activities."[89]

But some "social work in governmental activities" could be badly misguided, as the Meriam report on Indian administration noted in 1928. Sending children away to boarding schools could be deeply damaging to their health, self-esteem, and family life. "Many children are in Indian schools as the result of coercion of one kind or another and they suffer under a sense of separation from home and parents." Home and family were, after all, essential social institutions.[90] But although there was growing concern for the well-being of the child, there was little thought given more generally to the anguish or rights of Indian mothers, who had been told they were not fit to rear their own children or perform the role of mothers of the nation.

There was little recognition of the decades of harm done to "the Indian woman," who was, according to Marie Baldwin, "above all a mother—fond, loving, careful, religious," as she stated in her paper at the founding conference of the Society of American Indians in Columbus, Ohio, in 1911.[91] Baldwin, a Chippewa woman, worked as a clerk for the Bureau of Indian Affairs, appointed in 1904 by Roosevelt and subsequently trained at the Washington College of Law as an attorney.[92] She was one of the "small but vibrant urban Indian community" in

the national capital, "a little band of Redskins," as they called themselves, and an active member of the local suffragist community, who
marched for the vote. She was a generous host to visitors and a mentor
to young Native American women living in the city. She served, in the
words of one, as "a mother to all Indians here."[93]

In her proud identification as both a daughter of the great Chippewa
nation and a cosmopolitan career woman, Baldwin modeled a future
for Indian women not confined, or defined, by the binaries of civilized
or primitive, advanced or backward, and traditional or modern. She enjoyed her mobility ("I have travelled by airplane, and I find it is wonderful") and independence.[94] As an emerging pan-Indian political
activist, Baldwin took the opportunity in 1911 to respond to the
decades-long denigration of Indian women, which had accompanied the
removal of Indian children, to advance an alternative maternalist vision for the nation. Insisting on Indian women's power in traditional
society—she was the equal of her brothers and sons—Baldwin also emphasized the Indian mother's "tireless devotion and self-sacrifice to
home, husband and dependent children," which yield "the first place
to that of no other woman."[95]

It was the Indian woman, Baldwin suggested in maternalist vein,
who qualified above all others to serve as mother of the modern American nation. The politics of maternalism could be put to diverse political purposes. The reality of most Indian mothers' lives in the first
decades of the twentieth century was, however, far removed from
Baldwin's romantic vision. At a time when reservation life became a
deepening struggle with poverty, unemployment, illness, and premature
death, Indian mothers, sometimes forced away from the reservation in
search of work, were beset by hardship, anxiety, heartbreak, and grief.
Often ambivalent about whether to send their children away to boarding
schools, perhaps to gain new training and skills, "the lonesomeness of
parents for their children," as Brenda Child has written, "sometimes even
exceeded the homesickness of their children."[96] Many mothers sickened
and died. Grandparents and older siblings stepped into the breach.[97] As
the ranks of the poor, sick, and orphaned in Native American communities grew, so motherless children became increasingly common among
boarding-school enrollments.

CHAPTER SEVEN

Labor Investigators Cross the Pacific

"THE PEOPLE OF New Zealand," Henry Demarest Lloyd declared in 1899, "were the happiest people in the world . . . the most fortunate, most contented, most prosperous people in the world."[1] In these remote islands of the southwest Pacific, the people of New Zealand, it seemed, had created a settler colonial paradise. There colonists had found "the last piece of virgin soil on earth where the white race can spend its governing genius, unhampered by climate, slavery, monarchy, vested rights and vested ruts, immigration or the enervating seductions of power over subject races." There were no "subject races," according to Lloyd, because the Maori had disappeared, happily reclassified by nineteenth-century ethnologists as "Aryan."[2] "It was," Lloyd concluded cheerfully, "a white man's country if ever there was one."[3]

In this endorsement, the Chicago visitor captured the animating vision of Australasian nation builders, for perhaps the primary and most consequential of all their state experiments, underpinning the rest, was race-based immigration restriction. Such laws, first inscribed in legislation in the 1850s in Victoria, then repealed and reinstated across most Australasian colonies, were designed to exclude "Asiatics"—"utterly unfit," according to W. Pember Reeves in *State Experiments in Australia and New Zealand*, "to use political rights in a democracy."[4] Just as Alfred Deakin and H. B. Higgins were key architects of White Australia as a progressive project, so John Ballance, Richard Seddon, and W. Pember Reeves performed a similar role in New Zealand. It was "the wish of colonial Progressives," Reeves explained, "that their reformers should not be afraid to lead the way."[5]

Lloyd planned his trip, with his son as his companion, in 1898. "I am going to study this democratic efflorescence," he wrote to William Mather in England, "to rouse Americans from their pessimism about the possibility of progress in self-government."[6] Assessing possibilities for "progress in self-government" was a comparative international project. He was visiting Australia and New Zealand, he told the press, "to study the questions of land, labour and taxation," especially the effect of "the new experiments in advanced democracy" on "the distribution of wealth and the welfare of the people."[7] Along the way, he became convinced that in these newest countries of the New World he was witnessing a "renaissance of democracy."[8]

Lloyd spent several months in New Zealand and the eastern Australian states, undertaking research that included discussions with politicians, trade unionists, businesspeople, and public servants. In New Zealand, he was materially aided in his research by Edward Tregear, the long-serving secretary of labor and "the leading publicist and theoretician of New Zealand labor reform."[9] Tregear was a willing research assistant. After Lloyd's arrival back in the United States in September 1899, Tregear wrote, "I will make enquiries about the Westport Co-operative Coal Mine. I send the documents (you asked the Premier for) by this mail. I have not been able to get the photos yet." And he added, "Please write "Department of Labour" instead of "Labour Bureau."[10]

The Chicago journalist published two books based on his investigations. The first, *A Country without Strikes*, was a study of New Zealand's innovative Industrial Conciliation and Arbitration Act of 1894, which introduced state-regulated compulsory conciliation and arbitration to settle disputes between unions and employers. Its main architect was then labor minister Reeves, who had departed New Zealand in 1896 to take up the position of New Zealand agent general in London, where he worked as a tireless publicist abroad. Described by Lloyd in glowing terms as one who stood "in the front ranks of the geniuses who have proved themselves able to affect human destiny for good, by carrying constitutional and political development a step farther," Reeves had improved social relations—"the life of man with man"—"by bringing new evils under the dominion of the old principles of social justice and mercy."[11]

Lloyd's claim regarding Reeves's originating genius has since been brought into question. Compulsory arbitration was a shared Australasian project with diverse authors, including Charles Kingston, Liberal leader in South Australia, whose "founding document" Reeves seems to have copied.[12] Reeves was also crucially assisted in drafting the New

Zealand Industrial Conciliation and Arbitration Act and related labor legislation by Tregear, who also served as chief inspector of factories and registrar of industrial awards. In 1894, the New Zealand Factories Act, which outlawed child labor and specified maximum hours for women and children, had also been passed.

Nine years later, Tregear would host Victor Selden Clark's investigative mission on behalf of the US Labor Bureau when he eventually persuaded Clark to revise his initially skeptical opinion of compulsory arbitration. Tregear was not just an able bureaucrat but, like Minister Reeves, an indefatigable promoter of New Zealand's "humanistic legislation," writing for a global readership as well as a regional one. His audience included the readers of American progressive periodicals and trade union journals.[13]

The extravagance of Lloyd's praise of Labor Minister Reeves extended into a glowing account of the working of the arbitration and conciliation system, "one of the most original pieces of work done in modern times."[14] Its "special and primary object" had been, in Reeves's words, "to bring about industrial peace," and he was pleased to report that there had been no strikes in New Zealand since its inception. (This would soon change.) Not surprisingly, Reeves, who would later publish his own work on the "state experiments" of Australia and New Zealand, was pleased to write the introduction to Lloyd's glowing account of his legislative handiwork, unblushingly commending the factual accuracy and "impartial opinion of an able American observer."[15]

Elaborating on a theme common to Australasian advocates of "state socialism," Reeves wrote in Lloyd's introduction: "The state, in New Zealand, is the people, and the people being vitally interested in labour battles, has surely the right to say to the parties that their disputes shall be adjusted in such a manner as not to damage the community of which they are members, and for the benefit of which in the end their industry is carried on."[16] Strikes caused deep suffering, and were socially disruptive, economically damaging, and sometimes fatal in their consequences. Lloyd noted that he had personally witnessed the effects of the Pullman strike and lockout in Chicago in 1894.

In Lloyd's second book about Australia and New Zealand, *Newest England*, he sounded the common theme: "In a democracy, in self-government, state-help is self-help."[17] The main focus of his discussion was the work of the state insurance office, the public ownership of roads and railways, telegraphs and telephones, old-age pensions, and industrial arbitration. He saw the "democratic efflorescence of Australasia" as having world-historic import, a progressive development that paralleled and extended the American rebellion against the "Mother Country" in the eighteenth century.

"The old ideas and institutions, given a new chance in a new country, gain a new vigor," wrote Lloyd. "It is their new world." Just as the American Revolution performed the historic task of saving "English constitutional liberty," Lloyd mused, so it was to be hoped that Australasians, "in their extension and acceleration of reforms that are in the air everywhere, are saving the commonwealth of the whole world."[18]

Lloyd's effusive accounts of progressive democracy in Australasia appeared in his books and reviews, in newspapers and journal articles, in interviews and public talks. He also reported on his investigations in correspondence with other reformers. In Boston at the end of 1899 to present some lectures, he responded to an inquiry from Florence Kelley, who was hoping to enlist his support for the National Consumers League. In reply, Lloyd outlined his own plans. First, it was important "to get the wealth that was made honestly according to the rules of the game (even though the game be a bad one ultimately) to help us smoke out and exterminate the bad wealth, which was made in violation of the rules of the game." Second, he hoped "to make known to the people, so far as I can, the constructive things that are being done by nations that have got a little farther along than we have got." At the time, he was writing up his report on his investigations in Australia and New Zealand, countries that provided "free democratic illumination."[19]

Newest England was published in 1900. Lloyd wrote to Professor Richard Ely at Wisconsin to complain about what he considered to be the poor promotional efforts of his publisher. "It seems to me they don't advertise enough—in fact I don't see that they do so at all. . . . My book Newest England seems to me to have just the story to tell American people need now to hear."[20] Ely replied to say that he didn't think Lloyd had any cause for complaint. "I have seen advertisements of both your books, as well as many reviews. . . . I have, indeed, felt encouraged to see the favor with which your books are being received. It seems to me that they must be having a fair sale." Lest Lloyd had doubts, Ely added his own endorsement: "It is needless for me to say that I have done and am doing what I can to bring your books forward and secure favorable notice of them. I am much pleased with them and think they ought to do a great deal of good."[21]

Lloyd need not have worried. His ideas reached hundreds of thousands of people, general readers as well as academics, journalists, reformers, politicians, and the president. According to Lloyd, Roosevelt told a New Zealand official that he had been moved to take action to end the 1902 anthracite coal strike because of "the inspiration derived from the laws of your country."[22] Roosevelt was probably alerted to the relevance of the "Australasian Cures for Coal Wars" by Lloyd's article on the subject in *Atlantic Monthly* in which he described "arbitration" as a "right" that saw the substitution of the calm and reason of the courtroom for the violence of labor war.[23] Roosevelt appointed a presidential commission that secured the agreement of both sides of the "coal wars" to binding arbitration.

In the context of the industrial turmoil of the 1890s and early 1900s, Lloyd's writings and those of other investigators led to new curiosity about the labor experiments across the Pacific that promised to settle disputes peacefully and end strikes for all time. Confronted with "the most severe of capitalism's crises to that time," as Leon Fink has noted, American policy makers located themselves as never before in "a larger international spectrum" of economic experience and policy development. Although there was some interest in European developments, reformers were increasingly drawn down the "Australasian road."[24]

Of particular interest was compulsory arbitration in New Zealand, New South Wales, and Western Australia; the legal minimum wage and wages boards established in Victoria in 1896; and the new Commonwealth Court of Conciliation and Arbitration created in Australia in 1904. As a result of the efforts of H. B. Higgins, Charles Kingston, and other delegates to the constitutional conventions of the 1890s, the Australian federal government had been expressly granted constitutional power to settle industrial disputes extending beyond the borders of one state. As the first attorney general, Alfred Deakin introduced the required legislation in the House of Representatives in 1903.

Proclaiming that the Act represented nothing less than "the beginning of a new phase of civilization," Deakin suggested that it would inaugurate a new era of "social justice" by enlisting the power of the state to remove "inequalities" between classes and promote "the well being of the masses of the people."[25]

That same year, Carroll Wright, commissioner of the US Labor Bureau, dispatched Victor Selden Clark, then working as president of the insular board of education, across the Pacific to investigate labor conditions in "advanced countries" as well as in the Philippines and the Dutch colony of Java. The role of the Labor Bureau, which Roosevelt had moved into the Department of Labor and Commerce, was to investigate and provide detailed statistical and other reports on industrial conditions across the United States and the world. The bureau's directive to undertake comparative international research was of particular interest to the peripatetic Clark. His subsequent publications on Australasian labor conditions—especially his articles for the Labor Bureau's *Bulletin* and his book *The Labor Movement in Australasia: A Study in Social Democracy*—were widely circulated and reviewed, and commonly praised as objective, informative, and reliable—by implication less gushing than Lloyd's reports. The *New York Sun* enthused, "No other writer—in America at least—has brought back from that economic wonderland so reliable a report of the alleged marvels wrought in the name of 'progress.'"[26] The *New York Times* agreed that "the general conditions, racial, political, social and industrial," in these southern Anglo-Saxon lands were "enough like our own to make comparisons . . . instructive."[27]

The common conditions arose from shared experience as English-speaking settler colonizing states. Clark's life and career illuminate the continuities of settler colonialism in shaping the culture of progressive reform. In many ways, the labor investigator was an exemplary progressive technocrat, deeply committed to education, training, and progress. Settler colonialism framed his childhood and understanding of the world. Its logic also shaped the thinking of the Washington bureaucracy that employed him as well as the administration of the new American dependencies (where he also worked) in Puerto Rico, Cuba, Hawaii, and the Philippines.

His father, Major Selden N. Clark, described in a biographical note as the "direct descendant of two Wyoming County pioneers," was appointed Indian agent for the Chippewa of Lake Superior in 1870, on the recommendation of the American Missionary Association. His son, Victor, born in 1868, spent some of his childhood with an uncle, J. A. Davis, in Portageville, Missouri, who described the boy as "just one of the nicest, most manly little fellows in the world." The adult Victor would later write poems and short stories about manliness in its many phases and guises.

Many of these works—with titles such as "Red River Valley," "Chippeway Country," and "High-Tide Wilson"—focused on pioneer settlers and disappearing Indians and explored the relations between "white men," "Indians," and "half-breeds." In "Chippeway Country," the protagonist, Tom, not "just a frontiersman" but "a pioneer," is visited by a "Chippeway half-breed—one of those in whom the Indian blood predominated." The Indian was devoted to Tom, who felt only frustration in return: "Confound those Indians. They don't look at these things like a white man."[28] In another story, "High-Tide Wilson," we learn that "the Indians themselves had disappeared, but down in the heavy timber of the bottoms, on land belonging to my claim, there was a little clearing on a point, with a single room log cabin, where a halfbreed woman lived. . . . She lived as much in another world from the rest of us as did the foxes and muskrats in her vicinity."[29]

Except that we later find that "High-Tide Wilson" shared her world, intimately connected to the "halfbreed woman" through sexual relations. She had borne his child. Interestingly, Clark himself remained a lifelong bachelor, a condition that perhaps encouraged his cosmopolitan mobility and later fed nostalgia for "tinkling ukuleles" and "dusky maidens," "Hawaiian skies" and "brows crowned with leis," as recalled in his poem "Unmonopolized; or, Reply to a Bachelor's Lament."[30]

Clark's father's patron in Indian affairs was the prominent Methodist missionary Clinton B. Fisk, founder of Fisk University and a member of the Board of Indian Commissioners, who wrote to Major Clark about the "radical reforms" they were hoping would solve the "Indian problem." "I am having considerable correspondence with agents in the field," he advised in 1880, "nothing short of Indian manhood—citizenship—lands in severalty—protection and restraint of law will ever solve the problem."[31] Quoting Bigelow, Fisk added the lines,

> This is the one great American idea
> To make a man a man and let him be.[32]

But when it came to providing the necessary education that would transform Indians into "men" and "citizens," there was considerable competition between boarding schools and religious sects, such as Methodists and Catholics, which sought government aid in support of their own "contract schools."

Captain Richard Henry Pratt, principal of Carlisle Boarding School, complained to Major Clark about attempts by Catholics to segregate Indian pupils and the role of Congressman William S. Holman, Democrat from Indiana and member of the Indian Affairs Committee, in supporting them. His sarcasm made clear his assimilationist assumptions and implied Clark's agreement:

> Holman is going to civilize the Indians by keeping them out of civilization and break up the tribes by compacting them. He will make them citizens, by keeping them away from citizens, get them into the US by keeping them out, make them industrious by keeping them in idleness. Teach them the English language by keeping them away from it and do other equally miraculous things for and with them, even if he has to import more Catholic priests and nuns to help.[33]

Just four years later, thirty-two-year-old Victor Clark would also embark on the challenge of educating the newly colonized, enlisted by Theodore Roosevelt's administration to serve as president of the Insular Board of Education and head up the New Model and Training School in Puerto Rico.

A letter of recommendation addressed to Roosevelt in support of Clark's appointment suggested that it would offer welcome "recognition of high scholarship and character in politics."[34] Clark held a bachelor's degree from the University of Minnesota and a PhD in classical history from Columbia University. He had worked briefly as superintendent of schools in Lake City, Minnesota, before being invited by

Roosevelt to take up the position with the Insular Board of Education. In Puerto Rico, recently wrested from the Spanish Empire, Clark saw his task as a complete overhaul of the school system in anticipation of the territory's "full local autonomy."[35]

To that end, he prepared a manual—"to give to the teachers a brief account of the system of school organization which prevails in the United States and also of American educational literature and theory"—and a school textbook.[36] It was to be a model school in fact as well as in name: "The ventilation and sanitary arrangements are to be of the best character similar to those of like schools in the United States."[37] It was also to be a modern coeducational school (unlike the denigrated Spanish schools), aiming to recruit teachers from the ranks of women graduates of American universities. The settler colonizing state offered "new women" new career opportunities and travel abroad.

Clark's own employment opportunities also broadened. While president of the Board of Insular Education, he was commissioned to investigate labor conditions in Cuba, on which he reported in the Labor Bureau's *Bulletin* in 1902.[38] The next year, he was asked to extend his investigations across the Pacific and made arrangements to travel to Hawaii en route to New Zealand, Australia, and the Philippines. He contacted New Zealand secretary of labor Edward Tregear, who instructed his officers to show the young researcher "every attention and courtesy" and provide him with all the information he required. The two became personal friends and confidants. Clark kept Tregear's very long and intimate personal letters, now preserved in his papers in the Library of Congress.

The fifty-seven-year-old Tregear was more than twenty years older than Clark when they met, but they liked each other and had much in common. They shared postcolonial sensibilities, intellectual interests, and masculine sexual jokes. The experience of living and working alongside the indigenous peoples of their countries informed their conversations, stories, literary endeavors, and professional ambitions. In mid-1903, the two men entered into a rousing correspondence that combined a frank exchange of political views, much provocative teasing on Tregear's part, and considerable sexual innuendo.

Clark had reported on his first impressions of the native Maori. "Your studies in anthropology at Rotorua were I am sure of interest,"

Tregear replied, "if you could only have related the un-Bowdlerized facts—as the old adage says 'there are only 30 real original jokes in the world and 29 of these must not be related to ladies.'" His own jokes continued. "You must acknowledge that Maori evening dress has one merit—it is not expensive; just as their habit of cannibalism precluded wasteful display at funerals; the ambulating tomb requires no costly marble monument."[39] Tregear's jests also carried serious import. As a self-proclaimed socialist, he abhorred displays of wealth and he had a professional interest in Clark's "anthropological" account of Rotorua.

Tregear was an internationally respected authority on Maori culture. As soldier and surveyor, he had lived and worked with Maori communities, learning their customs and language, which he controversially claimed to be "Aryan" in derivation. In 1891, Tregear published the massive *Maori-Polynesian Comparative Dictionary*, which was favorably received across the world. His intellectual curiosity was voracious, and his literary output prodigious. He wrote for scholarly journals and popular magazines, for local audiences and British and American ones; he addressed the general public as well as specialists; he received fellowships from the Royal Geographical Society and the Royal Historical Society; and he was a member of both the Anthropological Institute of Great Britain and Ireland and the Philological Society in London.

By the 1890s, as his biographer has noted, Tregear was "among the country's most prominent, prolific and controversial intellectuals."[40] When he met Clark in 1903 and began corresponding with him, the Maori were on his mind, as he was preparing to publish his large work of ethnography, *The Maori Race*.[41] "I am now in the throes of literary parturition," he told the American investigator, "hoping that my baby will be well received."[42]

Tregear's other passion was economic justice. He detested labor exploitation and economic inequality. He abhorred the greed of the rich—"their eyes blind with fatness"—and was shocked, as Charles Pearson had been, by their lack of manly fellow feeling. Proud of New Zealand labor reforms, Tregear waited anxiously in the second half of 1903 for Clark's report to the US Labor Bureau. "I hope the report is filling out solidly and well, and that you don't press too hard on points where Compulsory Arbitration is unfit for Americans." Surely simple

prudence required Americans to adopt some form of industrial arbitration. "If you don't help it along there you will see, before you die,
the bloodiest struggle of the ages, because the rich, with eyes blind with
fatness, will dam back the flood and think they have stopped it." But
when the dam burst it would wash all before it.[43]

When the New Zealand parliament resumed in mid-1903, Tregear
complained that it was his lot to "dabble in the sewers of legislation
while you are basking in the smiles of the fair ladies of Manila."[44] Clark
had left New Zealand for Australia and the Philippines and was also
visiting other "isles of palm" in the adjacent island groups of New
Britain, New Guinea, and the Dutch East Indies. When he sent an advance draft of his report to Tregear, the secretary of labor was disappointed and annoyed at the suggestion that compulsory arbitration
would not be acceptable to Americans. "So you have finished the Report," he wrote testily, "and that scathing document will come back
like a boomerang to behead our poor little Arbitration Act. Or at all
events to clip its pinions so that it can never fly in the air of the USA.
You are afraid of your big Eagle if another bird soars there—that's the
fact."[45]

Clark had suggested to Tregear that radical ideas would not be acceptable in the United States because there the "hayseed" element
ruled. Was he thinking of his compatriots in Minnesota, Missouri, and
Wisconsin? "I had forgotten how vast your great country is," Tregear
replied to this self-styled "child of the Bald eagle of the Rockies," "how
multitudinous its rural occupations." But what of all the rural wage-
earners? Surely they would soon increase in number and demand wage
justice?[46]

Perhaps, however, it was really Clark himself who wasn't sympathetic to oppressed workers and "the desperate straits to which some
of them are reduced by merciless exploiters." Perhaps, Tregear fanta-
sized, Clark was really a millionaire, who had come as a spy:

> You are a young Vanderbilt or Rockefeller in disguise and you just
> came across to find out the weak joints in our New Zealand armour.
> Doubtless in your country-house at Newport or at Saratoga Springs
> you will jest as you pour out the ruby red wine among your brother
> millionaires and say "I have these Compulsory Arbitration lunatics
> on the point of my fork"—and Colonel Wright—doubtless also a
> conspirator—will chuckle as he drinks "the Victor's health."[47]

Clark had suggested to Tregear that each country must find its own method of social salvation, and as an American progressive, he placed his faith in education.

Tregear acknowledged that Americans seemed to have different priorities: "the idea of individualism seems stronger in Americans than in us colonials or the Old Country. If you can get what you want by education (moral & economic) so much the better; then you keep the initiative. How long you do so is another matter." Clark had said that he preferred liberty to socialism. But, Tregear objected, American "liberty" was a sham, a ruse to justify wage theft. "No one can be quite so patient under tyranny as the American *vide* the rule of a bullying conductor of a New York street tram. You do not mind giving up liberty in pocket-picking—there is a court for that. Nor for civil debt, there is a court for that, also. But there must not be a court to say that Brown is cheating Smith of a fair proportion of his wages."[48]

In any case, Tregear observed, there were other pressures. Modern societies also had to deal with the race question. "Race questions" and "physiological developments" posed distinct challenges to "economic arrangements." Because, among advanced peoples, the father of one advised, "brains exhaust bodies, especially sexually." Progressives had to deal with "the fecundity of lower and barbarous elements" in populations, whether they be "Asiatic swarms" or the "Huns of great cities." How could they be fed, especially as land had been "divided and subdivided *ad infinitum*"? Were they to become mere fodder for capitalists? "Are they to be run through the Chicago sausage machine & emerge as 'tinned beef'?" Both the United States and Australasia had dealt with the "Asiatic" threat by restricting immigration, but what if, like Japan (with "mental training & Mausers"), Asian countries acquired Western weapons?[49]

Although Tregear was pleased to learn from Clark that workers' wages in New Zealand were on average as high as those in the United States, he insisted that material reward wasn't the only measure of well-being. "I do not want to see the N.Z worker get more earnings if they are to be obtained only by running at top speed for long hours." There was more to life than money-making.

As in Deakin and Royce's conversations in the Blue Mountains, Tregear's exchanges with Clark about the merits of "state experiments" extended into philosophical musings on the ideal society. "I consider humanity's sole purpose is not as food for commercial & industrial enterprise," insisted Tregear, "and I think the man who all his life has toiled from daylight to dusk, spent his daylight hours in labour & his nights in weaving schemes for money getting is an immeasurable ass." Shakespeare, rather than Jay Gould, should be the model for humanity. Certainly not everyone could be either a Shakespeare or a Gould, but "the tendency, the ideal—is it to be towards the world of Shakespeare or of Jay Gould? To the semi-divine or the law of the wolf?" Reflecting on his own life, Tregear considered it a life well lived. "I have had the society of women, the delight of flowers & music & poetry and (ahem!) dictionaries."[50]

But Tregear did fret about money and regretted that his relative poverty prevented him from traveling abroad as much as he would have liked. "Sometimes," he confessed to Clark, "I wish I cared more for the making of money than I do—then I should be able to take my womenfolk to see the world instead of being cooped up in this one-horse place." Then in mock (and perhaps mocking) self-flagellation for this apostasy, he exclaimed, "Good Heavens! I have written blasphemy! I meant 'cooped up in the Paradise of the Working Man and Foremost of Progressive Democracies'—what curious mistakes one makes."[51]

While Tregear attended to his duties as a public servant in Wellington, Clark continued to visit the islands of the southwest Pacific. "What a wanderer you are!" said Tregear. "If you marry & settle down you will find your heart yearning for "the Long Trail," for the windswept seas & the palm beaches, over & over, again & again." With Clark always on the move, Tregear wasn't sure where to address letters, but then the American investigator announced he was back in Melbourne. He had visited Australia briefly the year before. "I'm glad you've dined with Mr Deakin," Tregear had written to Clark in November 1903. "It is possible that I may go across to see him—when the Commonwealth Arbitration Bill gets through."[52] Clark returned to Australia in 1904 to continue research for his next *Bulletin* article, "Labor Conditions in Australia," published in early 1905.[53]

"I am glad to hear from you again among civilized men and as one who has escaped from the 'great unwashed' of the isles of palm what ethnological pangs you evoke in my breast!" Tregear envied Clark his freedom to roam. "You can go to New Guinea, to New Britain, to Java, to all the haunts of my dreams and where I could get innumerable matter for 'papers' while I have to stay here registering trade unions & things—*Vae mihi!* But then if it had not been for trade unions etc I should not have had the pleasure of knowing you so there are compensations here as everywhere." Tregear was sorry, however, that Clark had not been able to get him some Philippines lace: "I wanted it badly because I fell in love with a specimen years ago & wished therewith to adorn the person of the *cara sposa.*" Mrs. Tregear was well, he was pleased to tell Clark, although their daughter, Vera, had had to break off an unfortunate engagement.[54]

For all his banter, Tregear was seriously annoyed at what he considered Clark's patronizing dismissal of industrial arbitration as fine for antipodeans but not for his fellow citizens, his implication that "full bellies & good laws may be good for colonials but are not worthy of the American citizen."[55] He set out his criticisms in fresh articles for US progressive journals, the *Independent* and *Arena.*[56] He wanted Americans to know that he did not feel "squashed" and remained steadfast in his belief that "regulated industry" was "better for the majority & the public than the wild article." Could not rational Americans see where their country was heading if they didn't adopt a scheme of impartial conciliation, mediation, and arbitration between capital and labor?

"I knew you and Carroll Wright, too, believe with Gompers in unrestricted freedom," wrote Tregear, "but see how you are evolving. In Chicago, you who scorn the compulsion of an impartial Court, have to sweat beneath the burdens laid on you by the unholy alliance between the trade unions and employers. In San Francisco you are under the thumb of the Labour Boss entirely—the employer, like the general public, has 'no say' in his business."

Tregear's assessment of Sam Gompers, president of the American Federation of Labor (AFL), as a major obstacle to American support for industrial arbitration was well founded. Gompers later confirmed his hostility to state regulation in a letter to H. B. Higgins and in strenuous attacks on the Kansas arbitration court. As Fink has noted, the "macho braggadochio" of the AFL "high command" resulted in a persistent representation of state intervention in industrial relations as a "negation of liberty" that would lead to a "demoralised, degraded and debased manhood."[57] For Gompers, "the call to voluntarism was as its core an admonition to manly independence."[58] Australasian reformers, by contrast, consistently advocated state protection and regulation to uphold the equality and dignity of (white) manhood.

Still, Tregear didn't want his political differences with Clark to affect their friendship. "Now dear boy," he wrote in avuncular mode, passing on his family's "kind & loving remembrances," "any difference of intellectual opinion is not to dull our friendship. You did your work, I am trying to do mine." Clark reassured him of his enduring affection and sent as testament a recent photo of himself. Tregear hoped it promised his return in the flesh. "It is a good likeness and brings back thoughts of many pleasant anecdotes."[59]

Clark's investigations led to the publication of a series of long and detailed reports on labor conditions and the operation of compulsory arbitration in Australasia in successive *Bulletin* articles. As a writer, he was at once a geographer, historian, statistician, political analyst, and tourist. He applauded the humanistic sympathies that shaped the experiments in the state regulation of industry, wages, and conditions of work, but doubted if they would be acceptable to individualistic, freedom-loving Americans.

Clark found the divergence of ideals between conformist New Zealanders and ambitious Americans especially marked. "To sum up the relative labor conditions of New Zealand and the United States," Clark wrote in his 1903 report, "the former country is marked by uniformity, the latter by diversity; the first is socialistic, the second individualistic in its tendencies and sympathies; while the working classes of both are looking ultimately towards economic betterment, those of the colony seek this primarily through legislative and social reform, those of the Union through individual and self-help and the improvement of industrial processes."[60]

Yet as Clark spent more time thinking about the issues involved, and when he studied Australian conditions more closely for his next report, he was becoming persuaded that Australasia did indeed provide an admirable example of ethical thinking, practical policy, and legislative reform that American progressives would do well to emulate.

Progressivism meant curtailing individual ambition and embracing social reform in the interests of the whole community. In their preference for "legislative and social reform" over individualistic "self-help," Australia and New Zealand modeled progressivism as practical policy. As numerous commentators remarked, the United States, Australia, and New Zealand were similar in racial and political heritage, "a race so akin to our own," in Clark's words, sharing a historical commitment to democratic ideals. Clark became a convert. "An American feels very much at home in the Commonwealth," he concluded in his report on Australia. "He is apt to view its ultimate future almost as enthusiastically as a native citizen. And he is certain to regard with the most cordial sympathy and satisfaction the growing power and prosperity of this kindred Federation of the South Pacific."[61]

Although Labor Secretary Tregear had detected hostility toward industrial arbitration on Clark's part in 1903, by the time the American investigator returned to Washington, he had begun to assume the role of advocate. His book *The Labor Movement in Australasia*, published in New York in 1906, was well received as "a sympathetic account of the rise, policy and results of the political labor movement in Australasia." The *Nation* noted that the "frankly socialistic" nature of the movement was acknowledged at the outset. But Americans had no reason for hostility, because it was "a vigorous popular demand for concrete reforms which are immediately brought into the demand of popular politics."[62]

Even the British *Bankers' Magazine* was well disposed to Clark's book, which showed the results of "the adoption of the labor programme" in the Commonwealth of Australia and "what might be expected . . . were a similar programme [to be] carried out" in the United States. "The eight-hour day, old-age pensions, industrial arbitration, a minimum wage, State-owned railways etc etc are some of the things the Australians already have and which many people in America are evidently longing for. A study of the experience of the Antipodes in the struggle for industrial and social betterment will at least afford Americans an opportunity to look before they leap."[63]

The *Boston Times* commended Australasian idealists as progressive evolutionists. "They see in the labor movement a phase of a worldwide progress towards socialism, economic equality, the abolition of poverty by collective action and have a conscious theory of social justice that denies the validity of the present industrial system."[64] As many reviewers noted, Australasian progressives weren't dogmatic Marxist theorists of the European kind, but new-style social democratic, humanistic, practical politicians. Americans were encouraged to follow suit. As the London *Athenaeum* noted, "Dr Clark thinks there will soon come change in the Socialist direction among his fellow-countrymen in the United States and that it will follow the Australian line of development."[65]

In 1908, industrial arbitration was again brought to Clark's attention when he was contacted by Theodore Roosevelt with an invitation to undertake a new investigation in Canada. While employed to "promote original research" as head of the Manufacturing Department at the Carnegie Trust, Clark was asked by the president if he would take leave to report on the new Canadian Industrial Disputes Investigation Act. Roosevelt had been in discussion with William Lyon Mackenzie King of the Canadian Department of Labor when he was in Washington to discuss common concerns about Asian immigration and the riots in Vancouver.[66] As head of the department under Minister Rodolphe Lemieux, King had played a major role in drafting the legislation, parallel to the role of Tregear in New Zealand.

Following Australasian precedent, Roosevelt was keen on introducing some form of arbitration in the United States, but he was persuaded that the Canadian Act might be a more appropriate model for the United States because it adopted voluntarism, rather than compulsion, in its dealings with employers and workers. The president commissioned Clark to investigate and report on public attitudes to the legislation and the operation of the boards of conciliation and investigation.

"President Roosevelt," Clark told Canadians, "is much interested in it personally." Furthermore, he advised, perhaps prematurely, "the Government has decided to pass legislation of a conciliatory nature which will have the effect of settling trade disputes by a board of arbitration along the lines of the Canadian Disputes Act."[67] He didn't foresee any constitutional difficulties: "I have no doubt the constitution would prove to be sufficiently elastic to allow us to apply such a measure as the Canadian Act to railways and telegraphs and even to other industries if it should prove to be for the general welfare of the country."[68]

In his eighty-three-page report to the Labor Bureau, Clark recommended the voluntary Canadian legislation as "much more acceptable to the people of the United States than the compulsory arbitration of New Zealand and some parts of Australia."[69] The aim in Canada was not to prohibit but to prevent strikes and lockouts, nor did the government seek to impose a minimum wage or maximum working hours. There was no compulsion, and neither employers nor workers would be forced to return to work against their will. Investigation by an impartial board of three and efforts at conciliation would publicize the issues and thus put public pressure on the parties to the dispute to resume work on agreed conditions.[70]

While in Canada, Clark was based in Ottawa, but he attended conciliation proceedings before two boards of conciliation and investigation. In one case, the proceedings involved the claims of an international railway union against Grand Trunk Railway for advances in wages, overtime, and changes in conditions of employment. The session occupied one day and reached an agreement. The second board hearing was at Glace Bay, Cape Breton, and involved a settlement of labor conditions among seven thousand coal miners. After one week, a settlement was reached. "So far as appeared to an outside observer," he wrote in his report for the Labor Bureau, "the effect of the proceedings was to promote good feeling between the parties as well as to bring them to a business understanding."[71] Clark was determinedly upbeat about the Canadian experience and clearly wanted the United States to follow suit.

The Australian and New Zealand legislation provided the point of reference for Clark's report, which concluded with forty pages of detailed clause-by-clause comparisons of the different Acts. Specific differences included that "the closed shop has not been urged as it has been in New Zealand and Australia, because the unions assume no responsibility under the Act"; and the appointment of separate boards for different disputes made "the coat fit the individual wearer, so to speak, much better than the arbitration courts of Australasia."[72] The Canadian Industrial Disputes Act was "much more applicable to American conditions than compulsory arbitration laws, like those of New Zealand and Australia, because its settlements are based on the agreement of the parties and do not prescribe an artificial wage, often illy [*sic*] adjusted to economic conditions."[73]

For Clark, now a convert to industrial regulation through courts of conciliation, the Australasian legislation was useful in supplying a radical extreme that made the Canadian model look eminently moderate. It provided a middle way, but possibly, one journalist opined, it would please neither labor nor capital. "Mr Clark will perhaps disappoint alike the extreme radicals who regard Australasia as a workmen's paradise and grow enthusiastic over the progress made there by socialism," commented one newspaper, "and those other extremists who like to be told that Australasia is doomed to bankruptcy and famine and demoralization as the result of socialism and the violation of the 'natural law.'"[74]

Ultimately it was Roosevelt and Clark who were disappointed. Americans were resistant. Despite seriously debating the proposal, on a number of occasions and at a number of industrial commissions, they weren't ready for industrial arbitration, voluntary or compulsory, at the federal level. Different schemes were implemented at the local level in Illinois, Colorado, and Kansas—where Governor Henry J. Allen copied Australia's model of a unitary judicial authority—and in the garment industries in New York and Chicago. In these feminized workforces, as Fink has observed, the manliness of the workers was not at stake.[75]

In an appraisal of the new Kansas Court of Industrial Relations, established in 1920—"the latest, boldest and most interesting experiment in the adjudication of labor disputes"—William R. Vance, professor of law at Yale, provided a history of the struggle for the "extension of the rule of law in place of the chaos of violence."[76] He noted the significance of New Zealand and Australian precedents ("the most extended and valuable experiments in compulsory arbitration") and that, by 1920, "most of the American states [had] statutory provisions for the settlement of labor disputes by mediation, conciliation, and arbitration" and that one state, Wyoming, had included such a provision in its constitution.[77]

However, the state laws had been little used. Perhaps Kansas spelled a new departure. In his *Yale Law Review* article, Vance hailed the new body of what he termed "labor law," which was beginning to take shape in Australasia and the United States, and insisted that fair hearings, fair rules, and fair determinations must prevail.[78] Still, President Wilson's recommendation to Congress in 1916 for legislation to provide for compulsory arbitration at the federal level was never acted on. And in 1925, after the Supreme Court declared a number of the rulings of the Kansas Court of Industrial Relations invalid, the Kansas legislature abolished it.

As Americans sought remedies to industrial conflict in legislative reform, it was not, in the end, industrial arbitration that proved the most influential of Australasian labor experiments. Rather, it was shorter working hours (the eight-hour day was introduced in Victoria in 1856) and the legal minimum wage (implemented in Victoria from 1896) that proved most persuasive. Another important element, arising out of the *Harvester* judgment in 1907, was H. B. Higgins's definition of the minimum wage as a living wage—a wage sufficient to meet the needs of workers defined as human beings living in a civilized society. Reviews of Clark's *Labor Movement of Australasia* had highlighted the legislation "to establish minimum wages through government boards as a means of insuring all a decent standard of living" and noted that in Australia, the "minimum wage doctrine [had] found embodiment in law."[79]

By 1908, American reformers were learning about these transpacific developments through a range of networks and publications. In September of that year, at an international conference of consumers' leagues in Geneva, Florence Kelley—feminist, socialist, and founding general secretary of the National Consumers League—first learned from English delegates about the Victorian legal minimum wage and associated wages boards. Soon after this meeting, the NCL resolved to change its strategy from using the consumer boycott to lobbying for legislative reform to secure a legal basis for minimum wages and shorter hours.[80]

Founded in 1898 by bringing together several local consumers' leagues, the NCL initially worked to improve working conditions for women and children by attaching labels, "the White Label," to clothes made in factories with good conditions, hours, and wages, thus certifying their value to the buying public. The certification read: "Made under Clean and Healthful Conditions. Use of Label Authorised after

Investigation." Goods bearing the label had to be manufactured in factories that met four conditions: the state factory law was obeyed; all goods were made on the premises; overtime was not worked; and children under sixteen were not employed.[81]

At the tenth annual session of the Council of the National Consumers League, held in Providence, Rhode Island, in March 1909, Kelley reported that the current method of dealing with the sweating system had proved wholly insufficient and proposed that "more radical measures must be considered." Legislation was required to introduce the coercion of the law to prohibit sweating. She and others reported on the international conference in Switzerland, where delegates had spoken about Victorian wages boards and the legislated minimum wage. There they agreed that it was "the duty of everyone to go home and agitate for the creation of official minimum wage boards until such legislation should be successfully enforced throughout the civilized world." The American delegates agreed that this should become part of the ten year program of the NCL.[82]

Maud Nathan, the New York–based vice president of the NCL, suggested that minimum wage boards should be established in the United States. The meeting resolved: "That the National Consumers' League recommends that state and local leagues study the subject of minimum wage boards with a view to a legislative campaign . . . and that the President be authorized to appoint a special committee . . . to further this object."[83] To guide members in this direction, a list of references was provided, which included Victor S. Clark's "Labor Conditions in Australia," described as "a careful account of the Victorian system, based on investigation on the ground," and his book *The Labor Movement in Australasia*.[84]

Also on the list were Henry W. Macrosty's "State Arbitration and the Minimum Wage in Australasia," in John Commons's collection *Trade Unionism and Labor Problems* ("another good account of the system in Victoria by an impartial writer"), first published in *Political Science Quarterly* in 1903, and A. F. Weber's "The Report of the Victorian Industrial Commission," in the *Quarterly Journal of Economics*, recommended as "a summary (both of facts and conclusions) of the report of a commission appointed in Victoria to investigate the operation of the Factories and Shops Law in Victoria, the bulk of the report being devoted to the *wages boards*" (emphasis in original). In Victoria, members of the NCL were informed that "the legal determination of wages [was] posited as part of the established order of things."[85]

In Australia, importantly, legal minimum wages were designed to protect men as well as women. They were introduced in the historical context of the global mobility of Chinese manufacturers and workers to uphold "high wages" and compel Chinese factory owners to comply with Victorian standards. H. B. Higgins, then member of the Victorian Legislative Assembly for the seat of Geelong, defended this unprecedented extension of "protection" to working men: "It was by no means extraordinary or extravagant for us . . . to pass exceptional legislation for the protection of our workmen." The original bill had proposed a minimum wage solely for women and children. Higgins and other progressives thought it should be extended to adult men. "Our people were European in origin," he explained, "and we did not want to have our workers degraded to the position of the people who lived in China. In China the people worked more hours and got less pay than the people here, and it was our policy to try to raise the standard of living and not to lower it."[86]

The international context for this policy innovation was important, as Walter Lippman saw clearly when discussing the Victorian legislation in an article in the *New Republic.* In rendering the low wages of "coolie," indentured, sweated labor illegal, a compulsory minimum wage represented a development of historic significance that in his view the United States should follow. Foreign immigrant labor must be required to adhere to American standards. "We are against sweating. That means we are against cheap labor and for the economy of high wages. . . . What we are struggling for is a minimum that shall be a living wage."[87]

Lippman also noted that in Victoria, the minimum wage and wages boards had been good for business. "Employers are always threatening a migration to less civilized nations. . . . [But] in Victoria when the law was first passed in 1896 there were 3,370 factories employing 40,814 people; after fifteen years' experience of the law there were 5,638 factories employing 88,694 people." Wages boards, he enthused, in inviting workers to participate in setting their own wages and conditions, was the "beginning of economic democracy . . . a school of democracy in which people have a chance to learn how to govern the conditions of their work."[88]

Boston labor reformer and Massachusetts Consumers' League member Elizabeth Glendower Evans also researched the pioneering Victorian legislation. A dedicated suffragist and friend of Florence Kelley, whom she met in 1903, Evans worked with the local Women's Trade Union League to lobby for legislation to establish a minimum wage and wages boards in her state. She was appointed to the Massachusetts Commission on Minimum Wage Boards with fellow NCL activist Mary Dewson, who served as secretary. Their efforts contributed to the enactment in 1912 of the first minimum wage law in the United States.

At the Massachusetts commission, evidence was presented about the experience of other countries, including Australia and the United Kingdom. Britain had introduced trade boards in 1910, following an investigative visit to Australia by Ernest Aves, who actually recommended against their introduction. The commission reported in detail on the operation of the "Victorian system," drawing on the investigations of Victor Clark, "who had visited Victoria in 1903 and 1904."

> At the instance of either employers or employees, or of the minister of labor, the Legislature may authorize the creation of a special board, which is empowered to fix a minimum wage for a given trade. Employers and employees are equally represented upon such a board, and a nonpartisan chairman is selected by the two parties at interest, or, if they fail to agree, is then appointed by the minister of labor. The chairman has a casting vote. Determinations, as the decisions of the special boards are called, if accepted by the minister of labor, are published in the Government Gazette and become law for that trade.

The commission was also told, again drawing on Clark's assessment, that employers in Victoria were generally supportive of the system. "Propertied interests were not opposed to a statutory minimum wage. . . . The better employers rather courted some provision that freed them from the competition of the less scrupulous men of their own class."[89]

The Massachusetts wages boards followed the Victorian example in setting minimum wages based on the cost of living, as ascertained by the board, rather than by statute, as would happen in some other American jurisdictions. The law also allowed for subminimum wages for learners and children and, like Victoria, granted exemptions for "slow" workers. Unlike Victoria, however, there was no legal compulsion; the penalty for noncompliance was adverse publicity.

Members of the commission publicized the new minimum wage legislation in public meetings around the country. In Philadelphia in May 1913, at a City Club meeting held in the "Ladies Restaurant" at the classy Hotel Walton, hundreds of women reformers gathered to hear Evans and H. La Rue Brown speak about the new developments. A period of adjustment would be necessary, Evans explained. "In Australia more than fifteen years ago . . . wages boards were organized by the state" to prevent exploitation. It was now illegal to hire a person at a lower wage. They had been so successful that they existed in virtually every branch of industry. "The Australian experiment was later adopted in England," she told her audience, "and last spring a similar law was enacted in Massachusetts."[90]

The Massachusetts reformers were hopeful about the outcome but cautious. "Wages boards as a method of fixing a minimum wage are not advocated as a panacea," Evans told her audience. "They will not bring in the kingdom of heaven. . . . But where they have been tried it has been found that they do tend to correct certain flagrant abuses. They tend to bring the standard of the worst employer up to the best."[91] The following year, Evans was proud to show visiting president of the Commonwealth Court of Conciliation and Arbitration H. B. Higgins, accompanied by Felix Frankfurter, the operation of one of the first boards, the Candy Makers' Board, during which Higgins was, as he reported, "closely questioned."[92]

On his visit to the United States in June 1914, following "a thoughtful and earnest letter of enquiry" from Robert Valentine, Higgins was welcomed as an international authority on labor law and feted as a celebrity, sought out for interviews in Chicago, Boston, Cambridge (where he met Roscoe Pound, R. H. Dana, and Albert Bushnell Hart), New York (where he met Florence Kelley and John Andrews), and

Washington (where Roosevelt called at his hotel).[93] By then, the Australian innovation of the legal minimum wage, defined as a "living wage," had been widely publicized in progressive circles. Higgins's compatriot, Alice Henry, the editor of the Women's Trade Union League journal, *Life and Labor*, had written an editorial on the living wage in 1913, in which she emphasized its humanitarian basis and revolutionary character. The idea of the living wage, she suggested, marked a new phase in the history of human rights.[94]

There was something in the air, she wrote, "different from anything that has gone before." A "living wage" was much more than the slave-owners' idea of a "minimum wage," more than a subsistence wage. It meant "food wholesome and appetizing, clothes comfortable and graceful, and education broad and adequate, not forgetting the primal need for recreation." In fact a "living wage" was "more than humanity ever asked for before. It is a noble, a dignified demand, something at least worthy of humanity. For it means more than life, it means the right at last for all to be human, to be their best selves, to develop who knows what capacities, what unguessed-of powers."[95]

Also in 1913, M. B. Hammond, professor of economics and sociology at Ohio State University and vice chairman of the Industrial Commission of Ohio, who had taken sabbatical leave in Australia and New Zealand, published the first of a series of articles on Australasian labor legislation, in which he sought to identify the theory or philosophy underpinning the new labor experiments. The minimum wage in Australia, he emphasized, had long ceased to be a subsistence wage. Like Henry, Hammond emphasized that the new "living wage" marked a new era in the history of human rights, representing a response to the "growing sense of the value of human life."[96]

As Hammond had prepared to embark on his trip to Australia and New Zealand, he wrote to John Andrews at the American Association for Labor Legislation (AALL) to ask if he should gather materials for their library collection.

> I have a year's leave of absence from the University and am planning to spend most of it in New Zealand and Australia in studying the experimental legislation of those lands rather than go to the old world countries.

> I . . . shall be very glad if later my observations can assist in any
> way the Association for Labor Legislation. Since the subject of
> Minimum Wage laws is in the air in this country, perhaps I can get
> material of interest.[97]

It was a timely offer, as the AALL had been asking the British branch
for "special information and publications on the subject of the minimum wage" in Australia. "I hope you may be able to send us something in the near future," Andrews reminded British secretary Sophy
Singer, "as this question is becoming more important week by week."[98]

The experience of the Old World in this field was limited, as Hammond understood: "English experience with the minimum wage has
been too brief and too limited in its industrial range to afford much
information for constructive purposes or to enable us to judge as to the
general acceptability of the principle. Throughout Australasia, on the
other hand, the principle of the minimum wage has now found general acceptance."[99]

The AALL was grateful for the offer:

> We are receiving many inquiries for information on the subject of
> minimum wage boards from members of state commissions and our
> members, and we wish you would consider yourself specially dele-
> gated to represent our Association on your trip . . . and collect and
> mail to us from time to time, such documents and news on this sub-
> ject as you think we ought to have in our little office library.[100]

On his return, Hammond published several lengthy and detailed articles on his Australian investigations and discussions with judges,
wages board chairs, public officials, and trade union and employer
representatives.[101]

Hammond's account of Australian labor law in *American Economic
Review* emphasized the humanist values that underpinned the "most
notable experiment yet made in social democracy." In explaining his
role on the Court of Conciliation and Arbitration, Higgins had emphasized that it was not his function to tell captains of industry how do
their business. Rather, it was his job to secure industrial peace and, to
that end, ensure that the employee enjoyed "a reasonable return for his
labor," sufficient to meet the primary wants of human life, including
rest and recreation. Hammond quoted Higgins's reflection: "A growing

sense of the value of human life seems to be at the back of all these methods of regulating labor, a growing conviction that human life is too valuable to be the shuttlecock in the game of money-making and competition."[102]

When Higgins read Hammond's article in *American Economic Review* in July 1913, he wrote to thank him for his careful study of the text of his judgments and his close attention to their reasoning. "Do you know that I have deliberately stated my reasons for awards so elaborately in order to attract examination and criticism? I was not bound to give reasons. I wanted the public for whom I hold a grave trust to see, all along, the course which I was [following]."[103] Increasingly subject to conservative political attacks at home, Higgins found such intellectual engagement—more common, he had found, in the United States than in Australia—deeply gratifying.

Like Henry Demarest Lloyd and Victor S. Clark before him, Hammond became a convert to Australasian labor regulation and urged that his own country follow their example. "Of course we are not obliged to follow Australasian precedents, but in this matter we have no other precedents to follow and it seems both natural and proper that we should profit by the experience of a people who are of the same race, have inherited the same juridical and ethical ideas [and] have the same spirit of progress."[104] Hammond thought Sam Gompers badly misguided in his "opposition to the legislative route," as he told Gompers's successor, William Green. Gompers was "out of harmony with the tendencies of the times." Labor could gain some things, Hammond insisted, "which it cannot secure by collective bargaining."[105]

Despite American critiques that labor legislation was "paternalistic" or "socialistic," and despite the obstruction of Sam Gompers and other trade union bosses, the National Consumers League led the way in lobbying for the introduction of minimum wage laws across the country. Higgins's visit in 1914 lent the cause added momentum. Goldmark and Kelley reprinted his seminal *Harvard Law Review* article as a special issue of their Minimum Wage Series. Learned Hand recommended it in the *New Republic* as an intimation of the idea of "full citizenship."[106] In 1915, Florence Kelley edited *The Case for a Minimum Wage*, a special issue of the *Survey* that included articles by Brandeis and Hammond, who had, wrote Kelley, following the example of Henry

Demarest Lloyd, "journeyed to those distant lands in order to study on the spot their contribution to the theory and practice of industrial life."[107]

Kelley identified three ways in which the American approach to minimum wages differed from those in Australia and England: "The first is the omission of men; the second is its reference to the welfare of the people as a whole" (necessary under "the police power"); the third is "its subordination to the courts on the grounds of constitutionality." She was particularly scathing about the obstructive role played by Gompers and other male trade union leaders, particularly their opposition to wages boards for men. "The attitude of these leaders towards minimum wage laws for men appears to be a part of the same reactionary disposition which led their American predecessors to oppose the presence of women in unions." Another source of their hostility, she speculated, was that the women's NCL campaign was achieving results.[108]

In his article "The Constitution and the Minimum Wage," Louis Brandeis explained the path adopted in Oregon in 1913, where legislation established an Industrial Welfare Commission to set maximum hours and minimum wages for women workers. The legislators "looked about the world" and found a remedy to wage exploitation that looked more promising than American methods of education, trade unionism, or adverse publicity. Oregon considered "the system which had been in force for eighteen years in Victoria, which had gradually been adopted by the other Australian colonies and by New Zealand, and which had been applied there with such extraordinary success that is was adopted in Great Britain in 1909." The Victorian legislation of 1896 "undertook to prohibit by law under threat of fine or imprisonment, the employment of persons at less than living wages."[109]

Brandeis emphasized the common heritage of settler colonialism that linked the states of Oregon and Victoria—"lands newly settled by men and women with the Anglo-Saxon inheritances and traditions of liberty and freedom." As new communities, they were bound to experiment. Victoria had "entered upon the experiment of dealing with the evil of inadequate wages in this particular way; and no people could have been more intelligently conscious of the fact that what they were proposing was an experiment." Oregon, too, wished to embark on this experiment and were determined to "follow the lead of a commonwealth of English speaking free people who had made the experiment, entering on it with much trepidation and with as much doubt as some now feel . . . today."[110]

In introducing minimum wage legislation for women, Massachusetts was followed within a year by eight more states: Oregon, California, Colorado, Minnesota, Nebraska, Utah, Washington, and Wisconsin. The majority followed Victoria in employing wage commissions to determine an adequate living wage. In 1917, Josephine Goldmark of the NCL was pleased to report to Higgins, "We have moved fast in the last few months," and she sent "warm greetings" from Mr. and Mrs. Brandeis.[111] By 1923, minimum wage laws had been passed in fifteen states, the District of Columbia, and Puerto Rico, but they applied only to women, who were consistently characterized, as American feminist historians have shown, as biologically weaker and in greater need of protection by law than men.[112]

Australia institutionalized gendered labor standards in a different way. With minimum and award wages prescribed for men and women, men's wages were set at a higher level in recognition of their traditional responsibilities as breadwinners, a principle that also entrenched the sexual division of labor in the workforce. As a radical humanitarian, Higgins had defined workers as human beings—they were not "coolies" or "pigs," he insisted—and put human needs, rather than productivity or profit or output, at the center of his jurisprudence, but the human being he envisaged was a man.

It was Higgins's humanism that led him to define the worker ("a human being in a civilized society") as central to his determination of a living wage. This worker's human needs included, in Higgins's view, the need to support a family. The employee was a worker with "normal wants." When feminist labor activist and writer Mary Gilmore objected to this logic, suggesting that the "individual," not the "family," should be the basis for the living wage, Higgins replied that he was simply administering the law. While Gilmore was full of praise for his "amazing" *Harvester* judgment, which prioritized human need, she asked why the living wage could not be paid to every worker as an individual. Higgins clearly missed the point of her objection. He had been asked, he said, to identify "normal wants," and these included "food, shelter, clothing—and family life. This family life cannot be had under existing conditions without money wherewith to maintain a wife and children." The merits of any "larger schemes for social betterment" were not his business.[113]

Higgins's definition of workers as human beings living in a civilized society rested on the binary evolutionary distinctions dear to progressives, between civilized and primitive societies and white men and Asiatics, distinctions that he had first invoked when supporting the original minimum wage legislation in the Victorian Legislative Assembly in 1896. In civilized families, women were not drudges or beasts of burden. Men went out to work to support their wives and families at home. As "civilized human beings," breadwinners, in Higgins's view, had particular needs as men.

In the United States, the campaign for minimum wages, inspired, in part, by the Victorian precedent of 1896 and Higgins's promulgation of the idea of a "living wage" in 1907, was given energy by feminists in the NCL, who continued to campaign in the years of political backlash in the 1920s. Led by women such as Frances Perkins and Molly Dewson, during the Depression years reformers moved to introduce, as part of the New Deal, a federal minimum wage for both sexes, with an equal wage for men and women. In the Fair Labor Standards Act of 1938, approved by the Supreme Court in 1942, decades of activism on the part of the NCL, progressive trade unionists, and jurists such as Felix Frankfurter culminated in legislation to secure a federal minimum wage at the same rate for men and women. More generally, however, equal pay for equal work would continue to prove elusive in the United States and Australia and proves elusive still.

In 1938 in Australia, women labor activists initiated a new phase in their campaign for equal pay—styled as "the rate for the job" (not the sex)—and mobilized to defeat the distinctions Higgins drew, not between white men and others but between men and women, men's jobs and women's jobs. In 1938, Victorian labor activist Muriel Heagney established the Council for Action for Equal Pay. The contradictions of and challenges posed by progressive reform enacted in the name of civilized humanist values ran deep.

This was also clear to indigenous peoples, who were usually assumed to be not yet ready to participate as equals in modern civilization. In the first decades of the twentieth century, they too began to mobilize in response to the provocations of a progressive movement shaped not just by the white man's civilization but more profoundly by the logic of settler colonialism—the dispossession and displacement that underpinned the promise of equal opportunity in the white men's democracies of Australasia and America.

CHAPTER EIGHT

Indigenous Progressivism Calls Settler Colonialism to Account

In July 1911, Dr. Charles Eastman (Ohiyesa), Santee Sioux physician, lecturer, writer, and witness of the Plains Indian wars, who had attended survivors of the Wounded Knee massacre in 1890, presented a paper to the Universal Races Congress in London on "the North American Indian." Later that year, Eastman—described by his contemporary, the sociologist Fayette A. McKenzie, as "the best known Indian in the country" and by historian Hazel Hertzberg as "the dean of progressive American Indians"—would play an inspirational role in the founding of the Society of American Indians (SAI), sometimes dubbed the "Red Progressives," in Columbus, Ohio.[1]

Eastman planned his paper for the Universal Races Congress, in the spirit of the gathering, as a presentation about the truth of his people as a "race," who, although once governed by a "primitive," "non-progressive philosophy," were now "capable of receiving a higher civilization" and progressing toward "the fuller development of the twentieth century."[2] The paper began with a survey of the "aboriginal nations of North America" at the time of its "discovery" and "invasion," moved on to an examination of the misery and demoralization of the "transition" and "reservation" periods under settler colonialism, and concluded with his hopes for the future of the "new Indian," who would be educated and successful in the white man's world while remaining a bearer of his people's "genius . . . in art, eloquence [and] mechanics."[3] Eastman was himself an eloquent interpreter of the beliefs and ideals of traditional Sioux culture.[4]

Participation in the London event called up a sense of "race pride" and strengthened Eastman's commitment to creating a national pan-Indian organization on his return to the United States. The Universal Races Congress brought together over a thousand delegates from around the globe—political leaders, academics, clergy, reformers, and writers—representing more than fifty "races" and "nationalities," to discuss, "in the light of science and the modern conscience, the general relations subsisting between the peoples of the West and those of the East, between so-called white and so-called coloured peoples, with a view to encouraging between them a fuller understanding, the most friendly feelings, and a heartier cooperation."[5] Eastman shared these aspirations for mutual understanding and friendly cooperation and, like his compatriot W. E. B. Du Bois—also a US delegate—was impressed by the spirit of racial equality that pervaded the gathering. "What impressed me most," said Eastman, "was the perfect equality of the races."[6]

Delegates included a number of the "new cosmopolitans," who constituted an emerging globally oriented nonwhite elite. Dr. Wu Tingfang, Chinese revolutionary and ambassador to the United States, presented a paper condemning "the white policy" adopted by settler societies such as the United States and Australia. General Francois Denys Legitime spoke on "Some general considerations on the people and government of Haiti," while G. K. Gokhale, former president of the Indian National Congress, called for recognition of India's right to self-government.[7] Du Bois was particularly pleased with "the infiltration of Negro blood": "The two Egyptian Feys were evidently negroid, the Portuguese was without doubt a mulatto, and the Persian was dark enough to have trouble in the South."[8]

Still, Western delegates predominated. The congress was chaired by Lord Weardale, former UK Liberal politician and president of the International Parliamentary Union, and attended by numerous current and former politicians. Self-styled "white men's countries" were represented by former New Zealand labor minister William Pember Reeves, then serving as director of the London School of Economics. Former Australian prime minister Alfred Deakin was listed as one of the "Premiers" who offered his endorsement but was not able to attend in person. Academics, including anthropologists, were prominent. Felix von Lushan, first chair in anthropology at Berlin's Frederick William University, argued provocatively that "race antagonisms" were inevitable: "Nations would come and go but racial and national antagonism would remain."[9] However, in a paper on "the Instability of Human

Types," the American anthropologist Franz Boas suggested that "culture" was a more useful concept than "race" and played a more formative role in the development of human societies.[10]

Several delegates—from Africa, Asia, and America—spoke of the destructive political effects of white man's rule. Eastman and Du Bois spoke of the ways in which segregation, discrimination, and prejudice had destroyed their people's "manhood." "Whether at last the Negro will gain full recognition as a man," Du Bois declared, "is the present Negro problem of America."[11] "The sooner all restrictions can be removed," stated Eastman, "all specializing institutions discontinued, and all trust funds divided per capita, the better for the manhood and full independence of the Indian citizen."[12] Delegates from India, campaigning against British imperial rule, agreed. Independence and freedom were essential to their people regaining a sense of national manhood.[13]

In the United States, it was during the "miserable prison existence" of the reservation period, following Native Americans' "complete subjugation," Eastman told his audience, that "the manhood of the Indian suffered its final eclipse." In his "beggarly apathy," the Indian came to resemble "a wild animal confined in a zoological garden."[14] Salvation could be found in education and civilization. Quoting educator Richard Pratt's "unanswerable logic," Eastman affirmed: "To civilize the Indian get him into civilization." In his paper, he offered special praise to Pratt, the founder of the Carlisle Indian Industrial School, as a "thinker and administrator of the first rank," especially for his work in "bringing the young Indian into direct contact and competition with Caucasian youth."[15] In preparing his address, Eastman had written to Pratt seeking references on the place of the Indian in the United States and, in particular, on Indian education.[16]

The Dakota Sioux writer had been schooled in Canada and the United States, completing his education at Dartmouth College (courtesy of an Indian scholarship) and graduating with a medical degree from Boston University in 1889. Many of those active in founding the SAI in 1911—the first national Indian organization in the United States—were similarly college educated. Some had attended the same Indian boarding schools. Of eighteen members of the Temporary Executive Committee, eight had graduated from Carlisle. Outspoken member Carlos Montezuma (Yavapai-Apache) had served as resident physician at Carlisle, remained a champion of Pratt, and always remembered the boarding school fondly. Montezuma would become one of the fiercest critics of reservations and the paternalism of the federal Bureau of Indian Affairs.

Boarding schools offered very diverse and mixed experiences to their students. Often a source of misery and disease, they could also forge solidarities and foster leadership skills.[17] School friendships became the basis of enduring ties between students from different tribal, cultural, and religious backgrounds. Established with the purpose of "Americanizing" Indian students, Carlisle, Haskell, Sherman, Chilocco, and other boarding schools also had the effect of "nationalizing the Indian."[18] But so, too, did the federal bureaucracy and the laws under which Native Americans lived and international gatherings, such as the Universal Races Congress, that required delegates to speak not on behalf of their "tribe" but on behalf of their "race."

The Society of American Indians was the first organization in the United States whose membership was restricted to indigenous Americans: "Persons of Indian Blood Only." Non-Indian sympathizers were invited to become associate members. Du Bois, who played a key role in establishing the National Association for the Advancement of Colored People just two years earlier, was one who accepted this invitation. Robert Valentine, the progressive reformer appointed commissioner of Indian affairs in 1911, also became an associate member, as did Fayette McKenzie, professor of sociology at Ohio State University, where the first conference of the Red Progressives was held, on 12–15 October 1911.

There had been much preparatory work. In 1903, McKenzie met Rev. Sherman Coolidge (Arapaho) at the Wind River Reservation Boarding School, where McKenzie taught as part of his postgraduate training, and discussed the possibility of establishing a national association run by Indians for Indians. Coolidge, an Episcopal minister, would become the second president of the SAI. In 1904, McKenzie wrote to Du Bois, sounding him out about the prospects of an Indian association committed to "unity and solidarity," "intelligence and progress."[19] The next year, McKenzie was recruited to the faculty at Ohio State, joining labor economist M. B. Hammond, recruited to the Department of Economics and Sociology the same year. (Hammond, committed to the other progressive cause of labor reform, would be on sabbatical leave in Australia in 1911.)

In 1908, the year in which McKenzie's doctoral dissertation was published as the book *The Indian in Relation to the White Population*, he had invited Coolidge, Eastman, and Montezuma to present a series of lectures at Ohio State on "the several phases of the Indian problem" in a course he was teaching on "the Indian." Their addresses to the university, local churches, and a range of civic organizations were featured prominently in the local press and elicited support for the idea of a future national conference.[20]

McKenzie was keen for "educated and progressive Indians" to take the lead in organizing the conference, which would introduce the "new Indian" to the Ohio capital: "Even as the navigator Columbus discovered the old Indian in 1492, may we not hope that the city of Columbus shall discover the 'new Indian.'" In a preliminary meeting, six leading Indian intellectuals met at the university in April 1911: Dr. Charles Eastman (Santee Sioux), Dr. Carlos Montezuma (Yavapai-Apache), attorney Thomas Sloan (Omaha), Bureau of Indian Affairs supervisor of employment Charles Dagenett (Peoria), and educators Laura Cornelius Kellogg (Oneida) and Henry Standing Bear (Oglala Lakota). The anthropologist, Arthur C. Parker (Seneca) was invited but unable to attend. The Temporary Executive Committee declared that "the time has come when the American Indian race should contribute, in a more united way, its influence and exertion with the rest of the citizens of the United States in all lines of progress and reform, for the welfare of the Indian race in particular, and humanity in general."[21]

The civic, political, and university leaders of Columbus invited the Temporary Executive Committee to hold its first conference at Ohio State later in the year. The conference call set out the reasons for such an event:

1. The highest ethical forces of America have been endeavoring on a large scale and in a systematic way to bring the native American into the modern life. It is well to see whether these efforts have brought results.
2. The time has come when the Indians should be encouraged to develop self-help. This can be achieved only with the attainment

of a race consciousness and a race leadership. We cannot predict the race leader, but a gathering of the educated, progressive members of all the tribes is a prerequisite to his discovery.

3. The Indian has certain contributions of value to offer to our government and our people. These contributions will be made more efficiently if made in an authorized and collective way. They will, at least they may, save us immense losses from mistaken policies which we might otherwise follow.

4. The white man is somewhat uncomfortable under a conviction that "a century of dishonor" has not been redeemed. If in any degree he can convince himself and his red brother that he is willing to do what he can for the race whose lands he has occupied, a new step toward social justice will have been taken.[22]

Thus did the conference call combine a demand that the white man acknowledge his occupation of Indian land and record of past injustice—the "century of dishonor"—with an assertion of Indians' right to participate in modern life and national government. Helen Hunt Jackson had sent copies of her book *A Century of Dishonor*, published in 1881, to all members of Congress, asking them to redeem the name of the United States from the stain of a "century of dishonor."[23]

Progressive Indians demanded that white men acknowledge the oppressive legacies of settler colonialism, while asserting their right as a race to shape its future in a more inclusive direction. Most focused their hostility to the rule of white men on the Bureau of Indian Affairs, but as many active members of the Society of American Indians also worked for the bureau—for instance, Charles Dagenett and Marie Baldwin—the ambivalence and tensions inherent in the Red Progressive project were evident from the beginning. For the moment, however, founding members were determined on unity and solidarity, keen to participate in the government of the nation.

The Temporary Executive Committee met again in June at the Wisconsin home of well-traveled Oneida woman Laura Cornelius Kellogg. Charles Dagenett, from Oklahoma, was in the chair. McKenzie, now listed as "local representative" at Ohio State, was also present. As Philip Deloria has observed of this "think tank for Indians," three of the organizers of this crucial meeting were women—Laura Cornelius Kellogg;

Emma Johnson, a teacher in the Indian Service and a skilled stenographer; and Rosa La Flesche, a Chippewa, who did the majority of the office work—and more women became active members of the SAI.[24]

At the Wisconsin meeting, committee members decided on the wording of the letters of invitation to the October conference: one, an "Indian letter"; the other addressed to associate members. The "Indian letter," sent to "about 4000 Indians," began by asking, "What is to be the future of the American Indian?" The organizers appealed to every "progressive Indian" to become an active member by helping to organize across tribal lines, insisting: "Personal freedom and personal advancement are dependent upon racial rights and racial advancement."[25] The time had come "when the American Indian should take the initiative in the struggle for his race betterment, and to answer in his own way some of the vital questions that confront him."[26] Caught in the logic of settler colonialism, the Society of American Indians asserted a proud racial identity, at the same time denouncing the use of race as a ground for discrimination. It called for the necessity of racial advancement while asserting the fact of Indians' inherent equality as human beings; it invoked the value of civilization while inciting members to perform a new kind of "Indianness," completely removed from the stereotypes of Wild West shows.[27]

In the end, forty-three Indians attended the founding conference over the Columbus Day long weekend in October, aware of the irony and significance of the date in the context of their desire to inaugurate a new social, political, and economic order for Indians in the New World of the United States.[28] The site was also saturated with the historical significance of settler colonialism for their peoples: in the eighteenth century, Ohio had witnessed mass violence; and in the nineteenth century, mass removals.[29] By the early twentieth century, with "the Native presence all but erased from campus, city and state," civic and political leaders were keen to offer their full support for the conference, which heralded a new beginning in the relationship between Indians and other Americans, with an era of conflict hopefully giving way to cooperation.[30]

The conference elected Thomas Sloan as president and Charles Dagenett as secretary-treasurer of the SAI. The provisional platform included six planks that began and ended with citizenship:

First. To promote the good citizenship of the Indians of this country, to help in all progressive movements to this end, and to emulate the sturdy characteristics of the North American Indian, especially his honesty and patriotism.

Second. To promote all efforts looking to the advancement of the Indian in enlightenment which leave him free, as a man, to develop according to the natural laws of social evolution.

Third. To exercise the right to oppose any movement which appears detrimental to the race.

Fourth. In all conferences and meetings of the Association, there shall be broad, free discussion of all subjects bearing upon the welfare of the race.

Fifth. This association will direct its energies exclusively to general principles and universal interests, and will not allow itself to be used for any personal or private interests. The honor of the race and the good of the country will always be paramount.

Sixth. It is the sense of this committee that every member of the association should exert his influence in every legitimate way to bring before each member of the race the necessity of promoting good citizenship.

These aims received warm support from Valentine, the commissioner of Indian affairs, who was pleased to attend, if only briefly. Valentine prided himself on his progressive thinking and commitment to the progressive social movement. In his opening address, he told his audience that when he first heard about the event, he felt that "a new day had come in Indian affairs." He expressed his hope that the society, in becoming truly representative, would have a real impact on the public opinion of the country: "I hope that this organization will continue to broaden its membership till it includes every critic of the Government, every class and shade of opinion. . . . We need an All-Indian public opinion. This meeting is epochal."[31]

The next month, Valentine promoted the aims of the SAI in an address to the Sherman Institute boarding school in California, where he told students that they should strive to assist one another in moving forward and dealing with white people on equal terms: "your ultimate hold on your lands, and your ultimate provision for yourselves and your children in the years to come, [depends on this]." National representation was needed as a step toward self-government: the white

paternalism of the past had been a mistake. "I have no doubt whatever in my mind that the time has now come when your fate rests
with yourselves. . . . The day has come when the Indian Bureau at
Washington makes a mistake if it seeks to take a single step forward
in connection with your affairs without consulting you Indians yourselves about it."[32]

A possible mode of self-government, incorporating local economic
development based on the resources of the reservation, was proposed
to the conference by Laura Cornelius Kellogg: industrial villages combining "the foreign Garden City with the Mormon idea of communistic
cooperation," organized along Rochdale lines and with a provision preventing any individual from obtaining 51 percent of the voting stock.
Kellogg suggested that because various Indian groups were at different
stages of development, the type of industry selected would depend on
local skills and needs but be adapted to the market economy. Indians
could thus make a future for themselves on their own lands and provide employment for students returning from boarding schools. It was
a collectivist, tribal, land-based, visionary plan that anticipated the
ideas of self-determination promulgated in the 1930s.

In promoting this proposal, Kellogg urged that Indians could adopt
the most useful features of white society while rejecting the evils of
the factory system and urban crowding. "I have not berated white
institutions because they are white," she stated, "but because all economists have already agreed that they are not as economic nor as equitable as they hope to be." Social justice rested on relations of equality
and principles of cooperation. "Let us take the natural advantages the
race already has in its possessions and make for ourselves Gardens and
teach the white man that we believe the greatest economy in the world
is to be just to all men."[33]

Although Kellogg's ideas anticipated the kinds of craft industries
developed by the Pueblo and the principle of self-management later proposed under the Indian New Deal, they were largely ignored at the
conference in 1911. This was probably, as Hertzberg has observed,
because they envisaged reservations as a permanent, rather than a
"transitional" stage in Indian development, as Eastman had depicted
them in his paper on "the North American Indian" in London, a paper
he also presented to the Columbus conference. Carlos Montezuma, an-

other critic of reservations, was insistent that they were barriers to Indian progress and should be dismantled.[34]

Kellogg was also at odds with her male delegates in their heralding of the "new Indian." This figure was a "fake," she retorted: "I am not the new Indian, I am the old Indian adjusted to new conditions."[35] Perhaps women were less compelled by the new Indian's promise of redeemed manhood, freed from the domination of the federal government and the dependency of reservations. As Christina Stanciu has written, Kellogg had never attended an Indian boarding school, as had some of the more prominent male Indian intellectuals. She was, nevertheless, an elegant and eloquent orator, a writer and woman of the world, who had attended a number of colleges in the United States, including Stanford and Barnard; spoke several languages; and lived for a time in Germany and England, where she was hailed as an "Indian Princess."[36]

Kellogg's main passions were education, self-determination, and land rights for the Oneida. At a later meeting of the SAI, she delivered a scathing critique of the European instruction offered to Indians at boarding schools and suggested that the "old" traditional education could be superior:

> There are old Indians who have never seen the inside of a classroom whom I consider far more educated than the young Indian with his knowledge of Latin and Algebra. There is something behind the superb dignity and composure of the old bringing up; there is something in the discipline of the Red Man which has given him a place in the literature and art of his country, there to remain separate and distinct in his proud active bearing against all time, all change.[37]

Kellogg insisted on the value of Indian culture and the intelligence of Indians. "Dr Franz Boas of Columbia University, the greatest anthropologist in America, claims that so far as his investigations have gone, there is no difference between the brain of a Caucasian and that of an Indian, in actual weight and grey matter."[38] In the end, Kellogg's work with the SAI was short-lived. Dissension over accusations of embezzlement and charges of nude dancing led her to resign in 1913. However, she would later speak before the League of Nations.

Marie Baldwin, a suffragist and lawyer employed by the Indian Bureau, was another prominent woman member of the SAI in its foundational years, serving on the Executive Planning Committee and, from 1912, the General Committee. But she, too, felt increasingly marginalized by the continuing attacks by Montezuma and others on the "race disloyalty" of those who worked for the bureau. In many ways, Baldwin was the consummate modern Indian woman, secure in her Chippewa tribal identity and at home in the nation's capital. Baldwin lived in Washington for almost fifty years, after moving there with her father to help defend the treaty rights of the Turtle Mountain Chippewa nation.

Baldwin worked for the Bureau of Indian Affairs for twenty-eight years, appointed by the executive order of President Roosevelt in 1904 as a clerk on a salary of $900, then one of only two Indian employees and the only Indian woman in the Washington office.[39] In her paper to the Columbus conference in 1911, "Modern Home-Making and the Indian Woman," Baldwin emphasized native women's equality in the context of the high value accorded traditional Indian motherhood. As a feminist, Baldwin also believed in the importance of women's economic independence, and although paid less than white and male employees, her bureau work as clerk, auditor, and later attorney was essential to securing her a position of influence in Washington as well as her being able to support herself. As Cahill has noted, the so-called radicals, such as Montezuma, relentlessly criticized her choice to work for the Indian office, even as she used her position as an advocate for Native Americans in the capital, all the while living a modern mobile life as a progressive woman.[40]

In 1912, anthropologist Arthur C. Parker became secretary of the SAI, replacing Dagenett, who had also been criticized for his employment at the Indian office, while Rev. Coolidge replaced Thomas Sloan as president.[41] The SAI became increasingly successful during these years, aided by the considerable unpaid labor of a number of women and men, especially La Flesche, Parker, and Baldwin, working in and for the Washington office. In addition to his work as secretary-treasurer, Parker assumed the role of editor of the new *Quarterly Journal of the Society of American Indians*, "a new departure in the history of the race," providing a national voice for Indian writers by publishing a record of their people's oral history and discussions of policy positions on contemporary issues. In its first issue, the publication declared that the SAI afforded "both the native American and the American who has become so, because he has found on these shores a land of freedom, the means for cooperation."[42]

The 1913 conference in Denver, Colorado, was perhaps the most successful and harmonious in the SAI's history. It drew on a broader base, with large groups of delegates from Nebraska and Oklahoma. While still dominated by educated middle-class Indians, a large number of reservation-based Indians also participated.[43] Some signaled their identity in Indian dress, others wore the modified Indian dress common on reservations. They straddled two or more worlds. Policy discussion focused on the goal of citizenship, the right of Indian access to the US Court of Claims, and support of the Carter Bill on citizenship (passed in 1924).

Efforts to claim compensation for land wrongly alienated or to retrieve tribal lands unlawfully occupied by settlers became a major preoccupation among Native Americans in the early twentieth century, as high immigration fueled population pressures, railway companies claimed rights of way across Indian reservation lands, and white settlement spread across the continent. The competition for land became more acute as settler territories acquired the status and representation of new states of the Union. In 1903, Indians experienced a major setback to their efforts to retain a hold on their land in *Lone Wolf v. Hitchcock*.

When Kiowa chief Lone Wolf and others charged that they had been defrauded of their land in violation of the Medicine Lodge Treaty, the Supreme Court ruled that the Indian office was not required to follow treaty procedures when negotiating for the sale of "surplus" tribal lands without the consent of the tribes involved. In a significant challenge to the traditional authority and autonomy of Native Americans, the court maintained that Congress had held "plenary authority" in Indian affairs from the founding of the United States. In delivering the ruling, Justice White observed that Indians were wards of the state, dependent "remnants of a race," who needed congressional "protection." Shortly after the decision, the federal government opened up Kiowa land to white settlers, and over fifty thousand arrived to occupy these "surplus" lands.

The Society of American Indians prioritized the right of Indian tribes to sue over loss of land in the US Court of Claims without the need to first obtain congressional approval, which was an inefficient process, causing endless delays and loss of hope. Surely, the SAI suggested, Congress would pass the legislation, authorizing "any nation, tribe or band of Indians to submit claims against the United States to the Court of Claims with the right of either party to appeal to the Supreme Court of the United States." In "An Appeal to the Nation," the Legal Aid Committee of the SAI wrote: "Surely a great nation of one hundred million people can afford to do justice to the remnant of that race which once ruled our domain from shore to shore. Surely such a nation can trust the settlement of claims against itself in its own high courts."[44] Failure to right the wrongs of the past posed an obstacle to future progress. "While the nation delays, the Indian suffers, oft times in estate, always in mind. The rankling sense of injustice is a bar to progress."[45]

The SAI made its case on the grounds of justice, but the campaign also highlighted the assumption that tribal reservations had a future, an assumption disputed by the assimilationism of federal policy and the so-called SAI radicals, such as Montezuma. As Fred Hoxie put it, "How could the Indian Office spend countless dollars 'civilizing' the Lakota, officials might reason, trying to transform them from hunters to farmers, while allowing a lawsuit that might return ownership of the Black Hills to them?"[46] Moreover, in an age when reservation superintendents were working hard to undermine the authority of traditional chiefs, tribal lawsuits promised to give new status and voice to indigenous leaders.

The mobilization of Indian activists and writers, supported by the Society of American Indians, led to a new articulation of Indian history, interests, priorities, and rights in the public domain. Increasingly, one of those rights was imagined as a right to self-government or self-determination. At the same time, the progressive insistence that modern citizenship meant leaving traditional customs behind began to be challenged by a modern indigenous insistence that the old ways, people's traditions, and governing ideals were of intrinsic value and should be protected and preserved and enhanced, not relegated to a shameful past.

Indigenous progressivism was both a product of and reaction against the settler colonial assumptions that informed the larger progressive project. Central to the challenge posed by indigenous activists was a contest over the meaning of history. The Society of American Indians effectively recast the past. Members insisted on speaking the truth about the costs of settler colonialism to better explicate their needs in the present and hopes for the future. They remembered, in Secretary Parker's words, "the awful wars against Indian women and children, the treacherous onslaughts on sleeping villages, the murders of the old and the helpless, broken promises, the stolen lands, the robbed orphans and widow, done by men professing civilization and religion." Even more terrible than "the robbery of lands, more hideous than the scalping and burning of Indian women and babies, more harrowing than tortures at the stake . . . [was] the crushing of a noble people's spirit and the usurpation of its right to be responsible, self supporting and self governing."[47]

Parker called for "the Restitution of the Seven Stolen Rights," the rights to an intellectual life, social organization, economic independence, freedom, a knowledge of his Maker, an assured status, and "a good name." American Indians had been shamefully misrepresented and maligned as savage, treacherous, cruel, and immoral. Indian women had been denigrated as slovenly drudges and incompetent mothers. Yet a "great nation like the United States needs not to vilify the history of its Aborigines." Rather, the federal government should direct every effort to securing their rights. Indigenous men, in particular, "must be made to feel the thrill of manhood, the joy of having a part in the making of their country."[48]

Australian Aborigines were also under increased pressure in these years, as government promotion of various schemes of white settlement led to further loss of land. At the same time, "protection" authorities increasingly threatened the removal of Aboriginal children. Persecuted by white settler bureaucracies, Aborigines were also excluded from the rights of citizenship. They, too, began to demand justice and reform in the name of progressivism in state-based political organizations. As a result of the federal division of powers in the Australian constitution, Aboriginal affairs remained under state jurisdiction until a referendum in 1967 extended federal power and enabled new national policy.

With foundational federal jurisdiction in Indian affairs, the US government led the way in progressive reform at the national level.

The position of Native Americans was always already a national matter—thus the insistence in the first decade of the twentieth century on the necessity of a pan-Indian organization to give voice to an "all Indian public opinion" at the national level and the call for federal government action to grant citizenship rights to Indians and access to the US Court of Claims, so that they might more expeditiously challenge the ongoing theft of their land.

Land theft was a major focus for indigenous activists in the early twentieth century on both sides of the Pacific. The Australian Aboriginal Progressive Association (AAPA)—"progressive and [aiming] to lift the Aboriginal people in every way"—was formed in New South Wales in 1924, announcing a "progressive policy" of "drastic reforms in matters of Aboriginal interest."[49] But the AAPA was also inspired by a larger transnational vision of black freedom. The leading historian of the association, John Maynard—a grandson of one of its founders, Fred Maynard—has documented the influence of Marcus Garvey's Universal Negro Improvement Association (UNIA) as an inspiration for the AAPA, shaping its platform and clarion call of "One God! One Aim! One Destiny!"[50]

Jamaican-born Garvey brought the UNIA to New York in 1916. Four years later, the organization had 1,100 chapters in forty countries, including Australia. Little is known of the Australian chapter, but it is clear that some Aboriginal activists were members and sent news of Australian developments back to New York. The Coloured Progressive Association—an earlier organization based on the Sydney waterfront, with a membership drawn mainly from African Americans and West Indians and a small number of Aboriginal men—had organized social events to mark heavyweight boxer Jack Johnson's triumphant first visit in 1907. Some of its members probably became members of the Sydney branch of the UNIA, which sent delegates to the international convention in New York in 1920. Robert Usher, an Aboriginal man, wrote to the UNIA paper, *Negro World*, in 1923 to say that Garvey's message was "resounding through out the length and breadth of this small continent."[51]

The following year, Tom Lacey, who had been a member of the UNIA since 1920 and an organizer since 1924, wrote to Amy Jacques Garvey to pledge the support of ten thousand Aboriginal people in New

South Wales and sixty thousand nationally. Lacey's sister, Mrs. Hassen, was treasurer of the Sydney branch and supplied Australian papers to the writers of *Negro World*, which reported regularly on the oppressed position of Aborigines, whom "so-called civilized man" was helping to become one of "the extinct types." The parallel with Native Americans was made clear: "It is hardly believable that the white rulers of Australia, who have taken the country by force from the blacks, as they took the North American continent from the Red Men, have dealt with the black natives in a spirit of exterminating them root and branch, and with no regard whatsoever for the humanities."[52]

By that time, Australia's "black natives" had decided to form their own Aboriginal organization, with Tom Lacey appointed as treasurer and Fred Maynard as president. In his poem "Africa for the Africans," Garvey had declared momentously:

Europe Cried to Europeans, Ho!
Asiatics Claim Asia, so
Australia for Australians
And Africa for Africans.

"Australia for Australians" was borrowed for the AAPA logo.[53] The influence of Garvey's organization was also evident in AAPA goals. The UNIA manifesto declared "we are organized for the absolute purpose of bettering our condition, industrially, commercially, socially, religiously and politically." Maynard's declaration of aims at the inaugural conference of the AAPA omitted only the "commercial" dimension of Garvey's project (there would be no Black Star Line in Australia). "We aim at the spiritual, political, industrial and social," said Maynard. "We want to work out our own destiny."[54]

Aboriginal activists identified with black ideals of self-determination and international solidarity even as they defined their demands as indigenous peoples, the original owners of the land, robbed by settler colonialism of their country, culture, language, and children. They demanded the full rights and privileges of citizenship—they had caught "the progressive spirit of the day"—even as they took pride in "age old tribal customs," "old time native displays," and the performance of "corroboree."[55] Again indigenous peoples recast the past in order to progress in the future. The old people of their communities were revered as the custodians of language, culture, and wisdom. While demanding equal citizenship rights and recognition of racial equality in modern Australia, the AAPA insisted on their status as the original owners of the country and the value of their traditional culture.

The Aboriginal leaders of the AAPA—like the founders of the Society of American Indians—were assisted by key white supporters. In New South Wales, former missionary and reformer Elizabeth McKenzie Hatton, who had worked with South Sea Islanders in Queensland before being jolted into awareness of the injustices meted out to Aboriginal people—particularly the vulnerability of "half-caste girls"—had established an Aboriginal girls' home in Sydney, which, she was pleased to tell authorities, had become "the centre of the 'Australian Aboriginal Progressive Association.'"[56] The AAPA was also supported by John Moloney, a widely traveled Newcastle journalist, who declared in his newspaper, the *Voice of the North:* "The treatment of the native people of Australia is a black blot upon our national history."[57]

The membership of the AAPA expanded as new branches were formed across the state of New South Wales. The first conference in Sydney in 1925 attracted more than two hundred supporters. In the words of the local newspaper, "the old and young were there. The well dressed matronly woman and the shingled girl of 19. The old man of 60 and the young man of athletic build. All are fighting for the preservation of the rights of aborigines for self-determination."[58] Press reports highlighted the significance of the event with promising headlines: "On Aborigines' Aspirations—First Australians to Help Themselves—Self Determination" and "Aborigines in Conference—Self Determination is their Aim—to Help a People."[59] The demand for "self-determination" was the dominant theme, both reflecting the international promise given currency by American president Woodrow Wilson and anticipating by many decades indigenous political mobilizations of the 1970s.

In a letter addressed to the editors of several newspapers, AAPA president Fred Maynard insisted that the position of Aboriginal peoples was a "National subject." Although state based, the Australian Aboriginal Progressive Association—as its name suggested—thought of itself as a national organization, seeking national recognition and redress for indigenous people. Its international connections with the UNIA had encouraged this national orientation. Activists were hopeful that a federal Royal Commission would lead to reform in Aboriginal policy at the national level. "Our requests are few," Maynard wrote to his fellow citizens, "and their equity cannot be denied. We confidently anticipate your kindly endorsement of this just request, feeling sure that it is your desire to give our people and their children every reasonable opportunity in their own land. We are only asking to be given the same privileges regarding our family life as are being freely offered to people from other countries."[60]

Settler societies were immigrant nations, and in Australia, as in the United States, immigration fueled the settler hunger for land and economic opportunity. Like immigrants, indigenous peoples were expected to assimilate but were denied equality of status and resources as citizens. "Conditions for Greeks and Italians are far better," observed one AAPA member, "than those applying to our own people."[61] Land set aside as reserves or allocated to indigenous men as farmers and fishermen was taken from them at an accelerating rate in the years before and after World War I, and to provide for the settlement of Australian and British soldiers returned from the war.

The advent of World War I and President Wilson's soaring rhetoric about oppressed people's right to self-determination also inspired Native Americans to think that the time had come when they, too, might be afforded the right to rule their own lives. Charles Eastman, the "dean of Progressive American Indians," wrote a "Plea for Freedom" in 1919, in which he argued for this self-determination as a matter of right and in response to their contribution to the war effort. The just demands of Native Americans, he stated, should now at last be recognized. "Their request is not hard to grant, since it involves no separate government or territory. All we ask is full citizenship."[62]

The younger Crow leader, Robert Yellowtail, also linked the Wilsonian promise of self-determination to his stand in support of his people's land rights. Removed from his family at the age of four and placed in the local agency boarding school, Yellowtail extended his education at the Sherman Institute, in California, where he excelled. When he returned to the reservation, tribal elders employed his talents as a translator and adviser.[63] Challenged by white settlers and their political representatives, who wanted to change the boundaries of the Crow reservation in order to open up more land to homesteaders, Yellowtail spoke before the Senate Committee on Indian Affairs in 1919 in defense of traditional Crow borders but more generally in support of "the inherent right of . . . self-determination."[64] He noted that the president "but yesterday" "assured the people of this great country, and also the people of the whole world, that the right of self-determination shall not be denied to any people, no matter where they live, nor how small or weak they may be, nor what their previous conditions of servitude may have been."[65]

But then it had occurred to the Crow leader that "perhaps the case of the North American Indian may never have entered the mind of our great President when he uttered those solemn words." Indeed, probably not. Wilson's lofty rhetoric was directed at minorities living in Europe. As historians have since noted, when Wilson promised self-determination, he didn't have colonized peoples in mind.[66] However, Yellowtail's delegation to the national capital, where he presented his people's land claims, had some success, when the Crow Act passed in 1920. During the next two decades, he continued to forge a remarkable career as a tribal politician.

In many ways, however, the postwar decade would prove to be a reactionary, repressive period in both Australian and American political history. In the United States, much progressive legislation—especially in labor reform—was challenged and overturned by the courts, but there were some advances in recognition of Native American rights, with their citizenship (but not voting rights) confirmed by federal law in 1924. Local Indian activism focused on land claims, particularly attempts to reclaim land leased during World War I to grow food in support of the war effort. Despite deepening poverty and disease on the reservations and because of it, many Indian tribes expressed new determination to maintain control over reservation land and resources.

The case of the Pueblo communities of New Mexico, faced with the Bursum Bill, which threatened further settler encroachment on their traditional lands, attracted national attention, largely through the efforts of the Californian branch of the General Federation of Women's Clubs (GFWC), which had been urged by founding SAI member Gertrude Bonnin (Zitkala-Sa) to establish an Indian Welfare Committee.

The first chair of the committee was Stella Atwood, who grew up in Saint Cloud, Minnesota, among Chippewa and Sioux and later, like so many, read Helen Jackson Hunt's influential *Century of Dishonor*. Settled in Southern California, Atwood committed to progressive causes: she organized the Riverside Community Settlement, the first Parent-Teachers' Association, the Juvenile Industrial Training Camp, and literacy programs for immigrants. She also became active among Indians in the Riverside area in 1917, seeking remedies for the problems of the Morongo, Cahuilla, and Soboba.[67]

Atwood's activism led her to the founding meeting of the Mission Indian Federation (MIF), a radical Southern Californian group that asserted rights to self-government ("home rule") and an end to government by the Bureau of Indian Affairs. Attended by seventy-five Indian leaders, representing more than two thousand of their people, and assisted by white supporter Jonathon Tebbutt, who lent his home for the meeting, the organization appointed Adam Castillo, a Cahuilla of the Soboba Band, as president, and two graduates of Sherman as MIF officers. The following year, Tebbutt traveled to Saint Louis to urge the SAI to take up the cause of "home rule" for Native Americans.[68]

As chair of the Indian Welfare Committee of the GFWC, Atwood invited New York social worker John Collier, who was visiting California, to work with them as an investigator, a position funded by wealthy philanthropist and clubwoman Kate Vosburg, who had donated thousands of dollars to the cause of Indian reform.[69] The new alliance, dedicated to remedying the plight of "our landless Indians," launched a nationwide publicity campaign to defeat the Bursum Bill. "For the great public sentiment which has been stirred up on the question we are especially indebted to the Women's Federation of Clubs under the able leadership of Mrs Atwood, of Riverside, California," Herbert Welsh, secretary of the Indian Rights Association, wrote to Herbert Croly at the *New Republic*.[70] Claiming that she brought with her the "2,000,000 strong voting women of the GFWC," Atwood played a pivotal role in mobilizing a national campaign in support of Indian land rights.[71]

The Pueblo were encouraged to put their own case through an All Pueblo Council, formed in November 1922 when a gathering of 121 delegates from the nineteen Pueblo communities met to discuss the

Bursum Bill, with members of the GFWC and Collier in attendance. The Pueblo rejected the idea that they had been consulted by government and denied that they had approved the proposed legislation. In fact, they were bitterly opposed to its basic provisions. A statement of their position was published on the front page of the *Santa Fe New Mexican*, which highlighted the longevity of their traditional form of government and demanded the protection of their "pueblo life." Pueblo Indians, they said, had always been self-supporting. Yet now, with white settler encroachment, they faced further loss of land.

> We have lived in peace with our fellow Americans even while we have watched the gradual taking away of our lands and waters. Today, many of our pueblos have the use of less than one acre per capita of irrigated land, whereas in New Mexico twelve acres of irrigated land are considered necessary for a white man to live on. We have reached a point where we must either live or die.[72]

When Australian Liberal leader and self-styled champion of the "white man" Alfred Deakin had visited Pueblo communities in 1885 during his investigation of irrigation settlements, he had assumed that as a primitive people the Pueblo, like other American Indians, were doomed to extinction as the Anglo-Saxon conquest rolled onwards.

But the Pueblo resisted this fate. In 1922, they appealed to the American public to prevent the destruction of their way of life. They insisted, moreover, that white men recognize the long record of Pueblo civilization:

> The Pueblo, as is well known, existed in a civilized condition before the white man came to America. We have kept our old customs and lived in harmony with each other and with our fellow Americans.
>
> This bill will destroy our common life and will rob us of everything which we hold dear, our lands, our customs, our traditions.[73]

The idea that indigenous communities were not backward peoples, destined for assimilation or extermination, but citizens with their own lands, distinctive culture, and valuable traditions began to challenge fundamental settler colonial and progressivist assumptions. The Pueblo protest proved successful. New legislation drafted in 1924, with their support, created a Pueblo Lands Board to adjudicate claims. The law also stipulated that there could be no decision against the Pueblo community without a unanimous decision of the board.

The new national interest in the Pueblo, their ancient culture, collectivist way of life, and dynamic craft traditions—especially in pottery—also attracted numerous American artists, writers, anthropologists, and tourists to sympathize and indeed identify with their cause. Franz Boas and his distinguished woman counterpart, Elsie Clews Parsons, were both drawn to the Southwest for fieldwork, Parsons believing that the Pueblo were a sexually egalitarian society, a "land of women's rights." As Margaret Jacobs has noted, in the 1920s, "the Pueblos found that they had become the 'representative Indian' in the American imagination, temporarily displacing Plains Indians." For romantic primitivists, they offered a model of a different kind of future, an alternative to industrializing, exploitative, and individualistic America. These new admirers of the Pueblo also rallied to defend their dances against official charges that they were lewd and immoral.[74]

When the Society of American Indians wound up its affairs in 1923, some of its remaining members joined John Collier and Stella Atwood in the American Indian Defense Association, established to provide legal and other support to the Pueblo and other Indian communities. They were invited in turn by Secretary of the Interior Hubert Work to join the Committee of One Hundred to review and offer advice on the future direction of Indian policy. This diverse group of eminent persons included Robert Yellowtail, David Starr Jordan, William Jennings Bryan, William Allen White, Rev. Sherman Coolidge, Arthur C. Parker, Charles Eastman, Henry Roe Cloud, and Fayette McKenzie.

On their recommendation, the Coolidge administration commissioned Lewis M. Meriam of the Brookings Institution to conduct a two-year study of the overall condition of Native Americans. The report, *The Problem of Indian Administration*, was highly critical of many aspects of assimilationist practice, including the removal of children to boarding schools and the neglect of Indian health, employment, and welfare. Published in 1928, the Meriam Report, as it became known, finally prompted a shift in government policy and informed the "Indian New Deal" promulgated under the leadership of John Collier, as commissioner of Indian affairs.

The story of John Collier's role in forging a new kind of indigenous progressive policy in the 1930s begins not with his move to California in 1919 and romantic embrace of the Pueblo of New Mexico but with his work among immigrants in New York and his investigation of the "Wisconsin experiment" in state socialism in Milwaukee while serving as civic secretary of the People's Institute of New York in 1911. The origins of both FDR's New Deal and the Indian New Deal might thus be located in the same historical framework. Collier's first published article, written for *Harper's Weekly*, reported on the Milwaukee socialist government, and he proclaimed it successful: "All Americans interested in good government and in progressive democracy, will congratulate the Milwaukee socialists." This was not a doctrinaire project, he was pleased to note. Rather, its main achievement had been to show Americans that while socialism subordinated business considerations to human welfare, it did not subordinate human welfare to economic theory.[75]

Concern for the human welfare of the Pueblo of New Mexico and sympathy with their communal, collectivist, and ceremonial way of life drew Collier into the cause he would make his own. While in New York, Collier had sat in on classes at Columbia University, where anthropologist Franz Boas advocated the primacy of culture over race in the formation of human difference. Working with immigrant communities, Collier also came to believe that a people's culture was profoundly important to their sense of self and well-being. He became a critic of assimilationism and accepted an offer by Mary Gibson to work as director of community organization for the California State Housing and Immigration Commission. Gibson introduced him to Atwood, and in his work for the Pueblo in the Southwest, this passionate reformer determined to reverse the allotment policy initiated by the Dawes Act.

Collier served on the American Indian Defense Association from 1923 until 1933, when he was appointed commissioner of the Bureau of Indian Affairs by FDR. His moment had arrived. In Washington, he organized a conference with a range of interested parties to discuss the future of Indian policy and announce his intention to replace the Dawes Act with a program of "Indian self-government." Chaired by Lewis Meriam, the meeting recommended, with the criticisms of the Meriam Report in mind, repeal of the allotment laws, consolidation of trust lands under tribal ownership, change in inheritance laws, organization of the Indian communities, and transfer of power from the federal government to Indian tribes. Collier enthusiastically circulated his proposals for "Indian Self-Government" to Indian tribes and individuals across the country, but he must have been disconcerted, as Francis Pucha has suggested, at "the negative tone of most of the replies."[76]

Although the Pueblo had come to serve as the "representative Indian" in the American imagination, it soon became clear to Collier that there was great diversity in the situation and desires of indigenous Americans, whose aspirations were shaped by their different historical experiences of settler colonialism and geographical locations. And there was irony in Collier's determination to impose the settler colonial concept of "self-government" on the diversity of Indians, many of whom already enjoyed their own form of tribal government. "We object most strenuously to taking away of our independence to control our own affairs and transact our own business," wrote the Nez Perce. "We want our children's future to be preserved and our people kept in safe ground. We do not want them to be turned back to forty years to take up the old communal life which never made for progress. After forty years of advancement we object to going back to the status of the Navajoes and Pueblos which you mention in your letter."[77]

Some said that they didn't have enough educated Indians on their reservations to manage self-government, while others claimed that there was little traditional tribal organization left. Others commented that they were used to living with white man's laws and working with their white neighbors. Some feared that Collier's proposal would perpetuate segregation under the guise of self-government. A series of referenda among the tribes eventually returned a majority vote in favor of the Indian Reorganization Act, but there was also considerable dissent and outright opposition on the part of the Navajo. The new law would not apply to Native communities in Oklahoma or Alaska.

The Indian Reorganization Act was passed after months of negotiation and compromise with congressional and other critics. The law marked the beginning of a new understanding of the meaning of progressivism in Indian affairs. It ended allotment, fostered the establishment of autonomy and tribal government, and encouraged tribal economic activity. Fred Hoxie has rightly cautioned that accounts of these political transformations should not focus on "one man," John Collier. Indeed, Margaret Jacobs, Karin Huebner, and others have alerted us to the key role played by "unsung GFWC women" in creating nation-wide support for the cause of the Pueblo and the rights of and respect due to Native Americans more generally.[78]

Most importantly, we should recall the diverse campaigns of Indians themselves, including those of the Pueblo and the earlier activism exemplified by the Society of American Indians, notably the proposal by Oneida activist and author Laura Cornelius Kellogg for Indian self-determination put to the foundation meeting of the SAI, more than two decades before the Indian New Deal. In her vision of the transformation of reservations into self-managed industrial communities, Kellogg recognized the importance of transforming Indian reservations into cooperative, self-governing land-based communities, achieving autonomy through economic and political sovereignty. Kellogg's proposal anticipated campaigns to come.

The Oneida activist spoke many languages and worked on many fronts. Her struggle for land rights took her back to Wisconsin, while her international plea for justice led her, like Charles Eastman, to speak on the international stage on behalf of her "oppressed people." At the League of Nations in 1919, Kellogg located the plight of her people in the world context of oppressed peoples everywhere. Kellogg was also a suffragist. The *Washington Post* acclaimed her as one of a number of "New Indian Women." And she was a political analyst. In 1920, she published *Our Democracy and the American Indian: A Presentation of the Indian Situation as It Is Today*. Like many progressive Indians, Kellogg saw education as essential to the future of her people, but an education that was conducive to self-respect: "We want education, yes, we want to know all the educated Caucasian knows but we want our self-respect while we are getting his knowledge."[79]

Laura Cornelius Kellogg's critique of the oppression of her people spoke to the ways in which progressivism worked as the political logic of settler colonialism, a New World reform project that encoded a racial order based on distinctions between advanced societies and primitive ones, whose vision of advancement rested on an understanding of indigenous communities as backward peoples destined to extinction or absorption. As a white man's project, progressivism was constituted in a series of contradictions that generated new demands.

Kellogg wanted progressive education and equal citizenship rights to be available to her people, but not at the expense of their self-respect. "I would not be anything but an Indian," she declared to a Los Angeles journalist. "I am not weaned from my people and never will be. More schooling than usually falls to the lot of an Indian woman and more contact with Caucasian artificiality and insincerity have graduated me into what might be called a polite Indian and the process I think has taken a lot out of me."[80]

The progressive education of white men was empowering to its subjects but also demeaning and diminishing for indigenous Americans. As a product of settler colonialism, progressivism entrenched racial hierarchies and a binary way of thinking about the world that was deeply oppressive. As the Society of American Indians recognized, there could be no "personal freedom and advancement" without "racial rights and racial advancement."[81] In calling progressivism to account, in challenging its colonizing conceits and civilizational collusions, indigenous thinkers and activists would also transform progressive thought itself.

Abbreviations

AAPA	Australian Aboriginal Progressive Association
AFL	American Federation of Labor
BESAGG	Boston Equal Suffrage Association for Good Government
CESL	College Equal Suffrage Leagues
GFWC	General Federation of Women's Clubs
IWSA	International Woman Suffrage Alliance
NAWSA	National American Woman Suffrage Association
NCL	National Consumers League
NLA	National Library of Australia
NLWV	National League of Women Voters
PR	Proportional Representation
SAI	Society of American Indians
WPA	Women's Political Association

Notes

INTRODUCTION

1. Josiah Royce, "Reflections after a Wandering Life in Australasia," first paper, *Atlantic Monthly* 63 (May 1889): 676.

2. Deakin's letters were preserved by Royce and can be found with Royce's papers in the Harvard University Archives, HUG 1755.3.3, box 1; Royce's letters were preserved by Deakin and can be found, along with copies of some of Deakin's letters to Royce, in the Deakin papers, MS 1540 / 1, NLA.

3. Frank M. Oppenheim, *Royce's Voyage Down Under: A Journey of the Mind* (Lexington: University Press of Kentucky, 1980); Josiah Royce, *The Philosophy of Loyalty* (1908; repr., Nashville: Vanderbilt University Press, 1995). Royce sent a copy to Deakin when, as prime minister, he was preparing to welcome the US naval fleet, sent into the Pacific by President Roosevelt.

4. "Words of Professor Royce at Walton Hotel at Philadelphia, December 29, 1915," in *The Basic Writings of Josiah Royce*, vol. 1, *Culture, Philosophy and Religion*, ed. James McDermott (New York: Fordham University Press, 2005), 31.

5. Deakin notebooks, Deakin papers, MS 1540 / 3 / 1-2, NLA.

6. Patrick Wolfe, *Traces of History: Elementary Structures of Race* (London: Verso, 2016), 31–32.

7. Stuart Macintyre, *A Colonial Liberalism: The Lost World of Three Victorian Visionaries* (Melbourne: Oxford University Press, 1991), 15–16; Alan Atkinson, *The Europeans in Australia: A History*, vol. 2, *Democracy* (Melbourne: Oxford University Press, 2004); Terry Irving, *The Southern Tree of Liberty: The Democratic Movement in New South Wales before 1856* (Sydney: Federation Press, 2006).

8. Royce, "Reflections after a Wandering Life in Australasia," second paper, *Atlantic Monthly* 63 (June 1889): 814.

9. Josiah Royce, *California: From the Conquest in 1846 to the Second Vigilance Committee in San Francisco: A Study of American Character*, American Commonwealths Series, ed. Horace E. Scudder (Boston: Houghton Mifflin, 1886).

10. Ibid., vii.

11. Benjamin Madley, *An American Genocide: The United States and the Californian Indian Catastrophe* (New Haven, CT: Yale University Press, 2016).

12. Royce, "Reflections after a Wandering Life in Australasia," first paper, 681.

13. Ibid., 684.

14. Josiah Royce, "Impressions of Australia," *Scribner's Magazine* 9, no. 1 (January 1891): 86.

15. Josephine K. Henry, "800,000 Women Are Enfranchised: The Great Victory for Woman Suffrage Which Was Recently Won in Australia Discussed by a Woman," *Bluegrass Blade* (Lexington, KY), 20 July 1902, 4, repr. in *Commercial Tribune* (Cincinnati, OH), 20 July 1902, 8. Henry was a suffragist

and prohibitionist from Kentucky, who worked with Elizabeth Cady Stanton to create the *Woman's Bible*.

16. Ida Husted Harper, "Franchise for Women," *Washington Post*, 17 January 1904, 10.

17. Ibid.

18. Vida Goldstein, "Autograph Book," cited in Marilyn Lake, "'Stirring Tales': Australian Feminism and National Identity, 1900–40," in *The Politics of Identity in Australia*, ed. Geoffrey Stokes (Melbourne: Cambridge University Press, 1997), 82–83.

19. Lake, "'Stirring Tales,'" 82–83. On the Colorado campaign, see Carolyn Stefanco, "Networking on the Frontier: The Colorado Women's Suffrage Movement, 1876–1893," in *The Women's West*, ed. Susan Armitage and Elizabeth Jameson (Norman: University of Oklahoma Press, 1987), 265–276; and Patricia Grimshaw, "Reading the Silences: Suffrage Activists and Race in Nineteenth-Century Settler Societies," in *Women's Rights and Human Rights: International Feminist Perspectives*, ed. Patricia Grimshaw, Katie Holmes, and Marilyn Lake (London: Palgrave, 2001), 36–40.

20. Marilyn Lake, "Between Old Worlds and New: Feminist Citizenship, Nation and Race, the Destabilisation of Identity," in *Suffrage and Beyond: International Feminist Perspectives*, ed. Caroline Daley and Melanie Nolan (Auckland: Auckland University Press / Pluto Press, 1994), 277–294; Louise Newman, *White Women's Rights: The Racial Origins of Feminism in the United States* (New York: Oxford University Press, 1999).

21. *Report of the First International Woman Suffrage Conference*, Washington, DC, 12–18 February 1902 (Washington, DC: NAWSA, 1902), 39.

22. On historians' diverse and shifting accounts of Progressivism, see Robert D. Johnston, "Re-Democratizing the Progressive Era: The Politics of Progressive Era Political Historiography," *Journal of the Gilded Age and Progressive Era* 1, no. 1 (January 2002): 68–92. Key works include Richard Hofstadter, *The Age of Reform: From Bryan to FDR* (New York: Knopf, 1955); Hofstadter, *The Progressive Movement, 1900–1915* (Englewood Cliffs, NJ: Prentice-Hall, 1963); Robert H. Wiebe, *Businessmen and Reform: A Study of the Progressive Movement* (Cambridge, MA: Harvard University Press, 1962); Arthur S. Link and Richard L. McCormick, *Progressivism* (Arlington Heights, IL: Harlan Davidson, 1983); Michael Roe, *Nine Australian Progressives: Vitalism in Bourgeois Social Thought, 1890–1960* (St. Lucia: University of Queensland Press, 1984); Gwendolyn Mink, "The Lady and the Tramp: Gender, Race and the Origins of the American Welfare State," in *Women, the State and Welfare*, ed. Linda Gordon (Madison: University of Wisconsin Press, 1990), 93–114; Daniel T. Rodgers, *Atlantic Crossings: Social Politics in a Progressive Age* (Cambridge, MA: Belknap Press of Harvard University Press, 1998); Sidney M. Milkis and Jerome M. Mileur, eds., *Progressivism and the New Democracy* (Amherst: University of Massachusetts Press, 1999); Glenda Gilmore, ed., *Who Were the Progressives?* (New York: Palgrave, 2002); Michael McGerr, *A Fierce Discontent: The Rise and Fall of the Progressive Movement in America, 1870–1920* (New York: Free Press, 2003); Shelton Stromquist, *Re-*

inventing "The People": The Progressive Movement, the Class Problem and the Origins of Modern Liberalism (Urbana: University of Illinois Press, 2006); Leon Fink, *The Long Gilded Age: American Capitalism and the Lessons of a New World Order* (Philadelphia: University of Pennsylvania Press, 2015).

23. Wolfe, *Traces of History*, 18–19; Katherine Ellinghaus, *Blood Will Tell: Native Americans and Assimilation Policy* (Lincoln: University of Nebraska Press, 2017). On the global politics of whiteness, see Marilyn Lake and Henry Reynolds, *Drawing the Global Colour Line: White Men's Countries and the International Challenge of Racial Equality* (Cambridge: Cambridge University Press, 2008), 1–12.

24. Lionel Fredman, *The Australian Ballot: The Story of an American reform* (East Lansing: Michigan State University Press, 1968), 46; Macintyre, *Colonial Liberalism*, 29.

25. Peter Brent, "The Australian Ballot: Not the Secret Ballot," *Australian Journal of Political Science* 41, no. 1 (2006): 39–50.

26. Richard H. Dana, "The Practical Working of the Australian Voting System in Massachusetts," *Annals of the Academy of Political and Social Science* 2 (May 1892).

27. J. Morgan Kousser, *The Shaping of Southern Politics: Suffrage Restriction and the Establishment of the One-Party South, 1880–1910* (New Haven, CT: Yale University Press, 1974), 52–53.

28. Ibid., 53–54.

29. Jerrold G. Rusk "The Effect of the Australian-Ballot Reform on Split Ticket Voting," *American Political Science Review* 64, no. 4 (1970): 1221.

30. African Americans were also disenfranchised through the application of a range of literacy tests beginning in Mississippi in 1890.

31. Patrick Wolfe, *Settler Colonialism and the Transformation of Anthropology: The Politics and Poetics of an Ethnographic Event* (London: Cassell, 1999), 163; Wolfe, "Settler Colonialism and the Elimination of the Native," *Journal of Genocide Research* 8, no. 4 (2006): 387–409. See also related work on colonial genocides, for example, A. Dirk Moses, ed., *Genocide and Settler Society: Frontier Violence and Stolen Indigenous Children in Australian History* (Oxford: Berghahn Books, 2004). For a recent review of such work, see Stephen Howe, "British Worlds, Settler Worlds, World Systems, and Killing Fields," *Journal of Imperial and Commonwealth History* 40, no. 4 (2012): 691–725.

32. On "facsimiles," see Duncan Bell, *Reordering the World: Essays on Liberalism and Empire* (Princeton, NJ: Princeton University Press, 2016), 39.

33. Lorenzo Veracini, *Settler Colonialism: A Theoretical Overview* (London: Palgrave, 2010), 3.

34. Henry Reynolds, *Aboriginal Sovereignty: Reflections on Race, State and Nation* (Sydney: Allen and Unwin, 1996); Wolfe, *Traces of History* 32, 34–37. The situation was more complicated in the United States, where the former sovereignty of Indian tribes was initially recognized through a series of treaties that were later ignored or repudiated. White sovereign power superseded older sovereignties. Wolfe, *Traces of History*, 35; Nicholas Guyatt,

Bind Us Apart: How Enlightened Americans Invented Racial Segregation (New York: Basic Books, 2016).

35. First National Convention of the Progressive Party, *Report*, Chicago, 5–7 August 1912, 79, 83, Roosevelt papers, Library of Congress.

36. Link and McCormick, *Progressivism*, 42; "Mr. Roosevelt's 'State Socialism,'" *The State*, 9 August 1912, 4.

37. "Mr. Roosevelt's 'State Socialism,'" 4.

38. Charles Henry Pearson, *National Life and Character: A Forecast* (London: Macmillan, 1893), 18.

39. Ibid., 19.

40. Henry Demarest Lloyd, *Newest England: Notes of a Democratic Traveller in New Zealand, with Some Australian Comparisons* (New York: Doubleday, 1900), 8; Victor S. Clark, "Present State of Labor Legislation in Australia and New Zealand," *Annals of the American Academy of Political and Social Science* 33, no. 2 (March 1909): 223.

41. Lloyd, *Newest England*, 1.

42. Henry George, "Australia," *Cosmopolitan* 9 (January 1891): 359.

43. *South Australian Register*, 2 May 1899, 5.

44. Peter J. Coleman, *Progressivism and the World of Reform: New Zealand and the Origins of the American Welfare State* (Lawrence: University Press of Kansas, 1987), 51–60, 156–163.

45. Lloyd, *Newest England*, 1, 5, 7, 8.

46. Clark, "Present State of Labor Legislation in Australia and New Zealand," 223.

47. Maud Wood Park, "Around the World," 12–13, Maud Wood Park Papers, M-133, Schlesinger Library, Harvard University.

48. Jessie Ackermann, *Australia from a Woman's Point of View* (1908; repr., London: Cassell, 1913), 166–168.

49. Susan Magarey, *Unbridling the Tongues of Women: A Biography of Catherine Helen Spence* (Adelaide: Adelaide University Press, 2010); Diane Kirkby, *Alice Henry, the Power of Pen and Voice: The Life of an Australian-American Labor Reformer* (Cambridge: Cambridge University Press, 1991).

50. Alice Henry, *Memoirs*, ed. Nettie Palmer (Melbourne, 1944), 38.

51. Ibid.

52. Ibid., 41.

53. Higgins's letters were preserved by Frankfurter and can be found with the papers of Felix Frankfurter, MSS 47571, reel 40, Library of Congress. Copies can also be found with Higgins's papers, MS 2525, NLA.

54. Henry Bournes Higgins, "A New Province for Law and Order: Industrial Peace through Minimum Wage and Arbitration," *Harvard Law Review* 29, no. 1 (November 1915) [repr. National Consumers League, Minimum Wages Series 14 (New York: National Consumers League, 1915)].

55. Higgins to Frankfurter, 12 December 1914, Frankfurter papers, MSS 47571, reel 40, Library of Congress.

56. Matthew B. Hammond, "Judicial Interpretation of the Minimum Wage in Australia," *American Economic Review* 3, no. 2 (1913): 285; Hammond, "The Minimum Wage in Great Britain and Australia," *Annals of the American*

Academy of Political and Social Science 48 (1913): 22–36; Hammond, "Wages Boards in Australia," *Quarterly Journal of Economics* 29, no. 3 (1915): 563–630.

57. Jerold Waltman, *The Politics of the Minimum Wage* (Urbana: University of Illinois Press, 2000), 14.

58. H. B. Higgins, "Draft Autobiography," Higgins papers, MS 1057 / 3, NLA.

59. Theodore Roosevelt, *The Winning of the West*, vol. 1 (New York: G. P. Putnam's Sons, 1889), 5–6.

60. Ibid., 14.

61. Theodore Roosevelt, "National Life and Character" [repr. from *Sewanee Review*, August 1894], in Roosevelt, *American Ideals and Other Essays Social and Political* (New York: G. P. Putnam's Sons, 1897), 289.

62. Coleman, *Progressivism and the World of Reform*, 52–53.

63. Edward Tregear, "How New Zealand Is Governed," *Arena* 32, no. 181 (December, 1904): 570.

64. Veracini, *Settler Colonialism*, 3.

65. Marilyn Lake, "Between Old World 'Barbarism' and 'Stone Age Primitivism': The Double Difference of the White Australian Feminist Subject," in *Australian Women Contemporary Feminist Thought*, ed. Norma Grieve and Ailsa Burns (Melbourne: Oxford University Press, 1994), 80–91.

66. Sam Gompers, *The Eight Hour Workday: Its Inauguration, Enforcement and Influences*, Eight Hour Series (Washington, DC: American Federation of Labor, 1897), 1–8. See also Lemuel Danryid, *History and Philosophy of the Eight-Hour Movement*, Eight Hour Series (Washington, DC: American Federation of Labor, 1899), 7.

67. Mink, "The Lady and the Tramp," 99; Alice Kessler Harris, *In Pursuit of Equity: Women, Men, and the Quest for Economic Citizenship in 20th-Century America* (New York: Oxford University Press, 2001), 67–70; Fink, *The Long Gilded Age*, 91–118.

68. Marilyn Lake, "The Gendered and Racialised Self Who Claimed the Right to Self-Government," *Journal of Colonialism and Colonial History* 13, no. 1 (Spring 2012), http://search.proquest.com.ezp.lib.unimelb.edu.au/docview /1018692259?accountid=12372; Bell, *Reordering the World*, 39.

69. James Turner, *The Liberal Education of Charles Eliot Norton* (Baltimore: Johns Hopkins University Press, 1999), 51. On laboring men and manliness in the United States, see Gregory L. Kaster, "Labour's True Man: Organised Workingmen and the Language of Manliness in the USA, 1827–1877," *Gender and History* 13, no. 1 (April 2001): 24–46. On the Australian context, see Marilyn Lake, "Socialism and Manhood," *Labour History* 50 (1986): 54–62.

70. Ida M. Van Etten, *The Condition of Women Workers under the Present Industrial System: An Address* (Detroit: American Federation of Labor, 1891), 4.

71. Quoted in Stromquist, *Reinventing "The People,"* 13.

72. See, for example, Walter Lippman, "The Campaign against Sweating," *New Republic* 27 (March 1915): 27.

73. Rodgers, *Atlantic Crossings*; Fink, *The Long Gilded Age*, 92–93.

74. Fink, *The Long Gilded Age*, 93.

75. Ibid., 91.

76. Jane Addams, *Democracy and Social Ethics* (New York: Macmillan, 1902), 228.

77. Matthew Frye Jacobson, *Whiteness of a Different Color: European Immigrants and the Alchemy of Race* (Cambridge, MA: Harvard University Press, 1999); Lake, "The Gendered and Racialised Self."

78. Both Felix Frankfurter and Victor S. Clark worked at different times for the Bureau of Insular Affairs. As law officer between 1906 and 1910, Frankfurter prepared a memorandum for the secretary of war on "Government and Administration of the Philippine Islands."

79. Richard Broome, *Aboriginal Victorians: A History Since 1800* (Sydney: Allen and Unwin, 2005), 184–190; Samuel Murphy, "'They Formed a Little Family as It Were': The Board for the Protection of Aborigines (1875–1883)," in *Settler Colonial Governance in Nineteenth-Century Victoria*, ed. Leigh Boucher and Lynette Russell (Canberra: ANU Press, 2015), 110–112.

80. Victoria, Parl. Deb., sess. 1886, 52, 1810.

81. Victoria, Parl. Deb., sess. 1886, 53, 2912–2913.

82. Frederick E. Hoxie, *A Final Promise: The Campaign to Assimilate the Indians, 1880–1920* (New York: Cambridge University Press, 1995), 70–81; Ellinghaus, *Blood Will Tell.*

83. Tom Holm, *The Great Confusion in Indian Affairs: Native Americans and Whites in the Progressive Era* (Austin: University of Texas Press, 2005), 1–22.

84. Benjamin Madley, "Reexamining the American Genocide Debate: Meaning, Historiography and New Methods," *American Historical Review* 120, no. 1 (2015): 98; Roosevelt speaking to First National Convention of the Progressive Party, Chicago, 6 August 1912, in *Report*, 133.

85. Boyd Cothran and C. Joseph Genetin-Pilawa, introduction to "Forum: Indigenous Histories of the Gilded Age and Progressive Era," *Journal of the Gilded Age and Progressive Era* 14 (2015): 503–511.

86. Linda Gordon, "Putting Children First: Women, Maternalism and Welfare in the Early Twentieth Century," in *US History as Women's History: New Feminist Essays*, ed. Linda Kerber, Alice Kessler-Harris, and Kathryn Kish Sklar (Chapel Hill: University of North Carolina Press, 1995), 63–86.

87. Paula Baker, "The Domestication of Politics: Women and American Political Society, 1780–1920," in Gordon, *Women, the State and Welfare*, 61–77; Marilyn Lake, *Getting Equal: The History of Australian Feminism* (Sydney: Allen and Unwin, 1999), 47–136.

88. Commissioner of Indian Affairs, *Report* (Washington, DC: Office of Indian Affairs, 1894), 19.

89. Lake, *Getting Equal*, 110–135; Fiona Paisley, *Loving Protection? Australian Feminism and Aboriginal Women's Rights, 1919–1939* (Melbourne: Melbourne University Press, 2000); Margaret Jacobs, *White Mother to a Dark Race: Settler Colonialism, Maternalism and the Removal of Indigenous Children in the American West and Australia, 1880–1940* (Lincoln: University of Nebraska Press, 2011).

90. Cathleen D. Cahill, *Federal Fathers and Mothers: A Social History of the United States Indian Service, 1869–1933* (Chapel Hill: University of North Carolina Press, 2011), 6–7; Jacobs, *White Mother to a Dark Race.*

91. Cathleen Cahill, "Marie Louise Bottineau Baldwin," *American Indian Quarterly* 37, no. 3 (Summer 2013): 62–86; Frederick Hoxie, *This Indian Country: American Indian Political Activists and the Place They Made* (New York: Penguin Press, 2012), 225–276.

92. Victor S. Clark, "Chippeway Country," Clark papers, Library of Congress, Box 10.

93. George, "Australia," 360.

94. Victor S. Clark, "Labor Conditions in Australia," *Bulletin of the Bureau of Labor* 56 (January 1905): 243.

95. *Washington Post*, 29 December 1901, 29.

96. *South Australian Register*, 26 July 1893, 6.

97. Tregear, quoted in *Daily Herald* (Adelaide), 19 May 1911, 8.

98. *Report of the First International Woman Suffrage Conference*, 22.

99. F. C. Howe, *Wisconsin: An Experiment in Democracy* (New York: Scribner's, 1912; repr., London: Forgotten Books, 2015), x.

100. H. B. Higgins to Lord Bryce, 7 February 1914, Higgins papers, MS 1057, 1 / 79, NLA.

101. *Report of the First International Woman Suffrage Conference*, 39.

102. It is beyond the scope of this book to explain the differences in political culture between the United States and Australia, but such an inquiry could begin with the classic study by Louis Hartz, *Foundations of New Societies* (New York: Harcourt, Brace and World, 1964). For an illuminating recent study of US constitutional foundations, see Gary Gerstle, *Liberty and Coercion: The Paradox of American Government* (Princeton, NJ: Princeton University Press, 2015).

103. H. B. Higgins to Felix Frankfurter, 8 July 1914, Frankfurter papers, reel 40, Library of Congress; see also H. B. Higgins, "The Rigid Constitution," *Political Science Quarterly*, June 1905, 211–212.

104. Catherine Helen Spence, "Lecture," in *Proceedings of the First Australasian Conference on Charity* (Melbourne,1890), 15–25.

105. Felix Frankfurter to H. B. Higgins, 10 July 1918, Frankfurter papers, reel 40, Library of Congress.

106. Edward Tregear to Victor Clark, 24 July 1903, Clark papers, box 1, Library of Congress.

107. Pearson, *National Life and Character*, 34; Marilyn Lake, "History and the Nation," in *Whitewash: On Keith Windschuttle's Fabrication of Aboriginal History*, ed. Robert Manne (Melbourne: History Black, 2003), 161–169; Jacqueline Rose, *States of Fantasy* (Oxford: Clarendon Press, 1996), 1–77.

108. Hazel Hertzberg, *The Search for an American Indian Identity: Modern Pan-Indian Movements* (Syracuse NY: Syracuse University Press, 1971); Holm, *The Great Confusion in Indian Affairs*, 58–59; Lucy Maddox, *Citizen Indians: Native American Intellectuals, Race and Reform* (Ithaca, NY: Cornell University Press, 2005), 9–10, 90–91; Chadwick Allen, "Introduction:

Locating the Society of American Indians," *American Indian Quarterly* 37, no. 3 (Summer 2013): 3–22; John Maynard, "Fred Maynard and the Australian Aboriginal Progressive Association (AAPA): One God, One Aim, One Destiny," *Aboriginal History* 21 (1997): 73–74; Maynard, *Fight for Liberty and Freedom: The Origins of Australian Aboriginal Activism* (Canberra: Aboriginal Studies Press, 2007).

109. Cothran and Genetin-Pilawa, "Forum," 505.

110. The Australian Aboriginal Progressive Association was succeeded in New South Wales by the Aborigines Progressive Association.

111. Warner, quoted in *Telegraph*, 20 October 1927, in Maynard, "Fred Maynard," 6.

112. Fred Hoxie, *Talking Back to Civilization: Indian Voices from the Progressive Era* (Boston: St. Martin's Press, 2001); Maynard, *Fight for Liberty and Freedom*, 56–117.

1. SELF-GOVERNMENT, DEMOCRACY, AND WHITE MANHOOD

1. Charles Pearson to Charles Eliot Norton, 14 May 1873, Norton papers, MS Am 1088 / 5416, Houghton Library, Harvard University (hereafter Norton papers).

2. Quoted in John Tregenza, *Professor of Democracy: The Life of Charles Henry Pearson, 1830–1894; Oxford Don and Australian Radical* (Melbourne: Melbourne University Press, 1968), 41.

3. Marian Sawer, *The Ethical State: Social Liberalism in Australia* (Melbourne: Melbourne University Press, 2003), 4.

4. On "memories of class rule," see [Charles Pearson], "Young Australia," editorial, *Age*, 11 July 1882; on "the elimination of the native," see Patrick Wolfe, *Settler Colonialism and the Transformation of Anthropology: The Politics and Poetics of an Ethnographic Event* (London: Cassell, 1999), 163; and Patrick Wolfe, "Settler Colonialism and the Elimination of the Native," *Journal of Genocide Research* 8, no. 4 (2006): 387–409.

5. Theodore Roosevelt, "National Life and Character" [repr. from *Sewanee Review*, August 1894], in Roosevelt, *American Ideals and Other Essays Social and Political* (New York: G. P. Putnam's Sons, 1897), 289.

6. Patrick Brantlinger, "'Dying Races': Rationalizing Genocide in the Nineteenth Century," in *The Decolonization of Imagination: Culture, Knowledge and Power*, ed. Nederveen Pieterse and Bhiku Parekh (London: Zed Books, 1995), 43–56; Brantlinger, *Dark Vanishings: Discourse on the Extinction of Primitive Races, 1800–1930* (Ithaca, NY: Cornell University Press, 2003); Marilyn Lake, "History and the Nation," in *Whitewash: On Keith Windschuttle's Fabrication of Aboriginal History*, ed. Robert Manne (Melbourne: Black, 2003), 160–169.

7. Theodore Roosevelt, *The Winning of the West*, vol. 1 (New York: Putnam's, 1889); Francis Parkman, *The Oregon Trail: Sketches of Prairie and Rocky-Mountain Life* (1847; repr., Boston: Little, Brown, 1922); Parkman, *The Conspiracy of Pontiac and the Indian Wars after the Conquest of Canada*, 2 vols. (1851; repr., Boston: Little, Brown, 1922); Parkman, *A Half-Century of Conflict* (Boston: Little, Brown, 1893).

8. Theodore Roosevelt to Francis Parkman, 23 April 1888, in *The Letters of Theodore Roosevelt*, ed. Elting E. Morrison (Cambridge, MA: Harvard University Press, 1951), 142.

9. Wilbur R. Jacobs, *Francis Parkman, Historian as Hero: The Formative Years* (Austin: University of Texas Press, 1991), 81–83.

10. Kermit Vanderbilt, *Charles Eliot Norton: Apostle of Culture in a Democracy* (Cambridge, MA: Belknap Press of Harvard University Press, 1959), 32.

11. Roosevelt, "National Life and Character," 271.

12. Charles Henry Pearson, *National Life and Character: A Forecast* (London: Macmillan, 1893), 16.

13. Ibid., 34.

14. Jacqueline Rose, *States of Fantasy* (Oxford: Clarendon, 1996), 1–15.

15. Pearson, *National Life and Character*, 34; Lake, "History and the Nation," 161–169.

16. On the nineteenth-century ideal of manhood, see Marilyn Lake, "Socialism and Manhood: The Case of William Lane," *Labour History* 50 (1986): 54–62; Gail Bederman, *Manliness and Civilization: A Cultural History of Gender and Race in the United States, 1880–1917* (Chicago: University of Chicago Press, 1995); Kristin L. Hoganson, *Fighting for American Manhood: How Gender Provoked the Spanish-American and Philippine-American Wars* (New Haven, CT: Yale University Press, 1998); Michael Kimmel, *Manhood in America: A Cultural History* (New York: Free Press, 1995); Martin Crotty, *Making the Australian Male: Middle Class Masculinity, 1870–1920* (Melbourne: Melbourne University Press, 2001).

17. Christina Snyder, "The Rise and Fall and Rise of Civilizations: Indian Intellectual Culture during the Removal Period," *Journal of American History* 104, no. 2 (September 2017): 387.

18. James Turner, *The Liberal Education of Charles Eliot Norton* (Baltimore: Johns Hopkins University Press, 1999), 51.

19. Charles Pearson, "Democracy in Victoria," *Fortnightly Review*, May 1879, 688.

20. Francis Parkman, "The Failure of Universal Suffrage," *North American Review* 127, no. 263 (July 1878): 7.

21. Ibid., 10.

22. Marilyn Lake, "The Gendered and Racialised Self Who Claimed the Right to Self-Government," *Journal of Colonialism and Colonial History* 13, no. 1 (Spring 2012), http://search.proquest.com.ezp.lib.unimelb.edu.au/docview/1018692259?accountid=12372.

23. Duncan Bell, *Reordering the World: Essays on Liberalism and Empire* (Princeton, NJ: Princeton University Press, 2016), 39.

24. Marilyn Lake, "Fellow Feeling: A Transnational Perspective on Conceptions of Civil Society and Citizenship in 'White Men's Countries,' 1890–1910," in *Civil Society and Gender Justice: Historical and Comparative Perspectives*, ed. Karen Hagemann, Sonya Michel, and Gunilla Budde (2008; repr., New York: Berghahn, 2011), 256–284.

25. Nicholas Guyatt, *Bind Us Apart: How Enlightened Americans Invented Racial Segregation* (New York: Basic Books, 2016); Paul R. D. Lawrie, *Forging a Laboring Race: The African American Worker in the Progressive Imagination* (New York: New York University Press, 2016); Kevin K. Gaines, *Uplifting the Race: Black Leadership, Politics, and Culture in the Twentieth Century* (Chapel Hill: University of North Carolina Press, 1996).

26. Christopher Harvie, *The Lights of Liberalism: University Liberals and the Challenge of Democracy 1860–86* (London: Allen Lane, 1976); Duncan Bell and Casper Sylvest, "International Society in Victorian Political Thought: T. H. Green, Herbert Spencer, and Henry Sidgwick," *Modern Intellectual History* 3, no. 2 (2006): 207–238.

27. Hugh Tulloch, *James Bryce's American Commonwealth: The Anglo-American Background* (London: Boydell Press, 1988), 4.

28. Ibid., 20.

29. Goldwin Smith to Charles Eliot Norton, 7 November 1863, Norton papers, MS Am 1088 / 6682.

30. Goldwin Smith to Charles Eliot Norton, 25 May 1864, Norton papers, MS Am 1088 / 6682.

31. Goldwin Smith to Charles Eliot Norton, 22 July 1864, Norton papers, MS Am 1088 / 6682.

32. Charles Henry Pearson, "The Story of My Life," in *Charles Henry Pearson: Memorials by Himself, His Wife, and His Friends*, ed. William Stebbing (London: Longmans Green, 1900), 133.

33. Ibid.

34. Charles Eliot Norton to J. B. Harrison, 18 November 1891, Norton papers, MS Am 1088.2, box 5.

35. Vanderbilt, *Charles Eliot Norton*, 54–55.

36. Ibid.

37. Ibid., 56.

38. Ibid., 61.

39. Pearson, "The Story of My Life," 10.

40. Ibid.

41. Ibid., 17.

42. Ibid., 24.

43. Charles Eliot Norton, "The Poverty of England," *North American Review* 109, no. 224 (July 1869): 122–154.

44. Ibid., 123, 149.

45. Vanderbilt, *Charles Eliot Norton*, 105.

46. Charles Pearson to Norton, 5 October 1868, Norton papers, MS Am 1088 / 6716.

47. Vanderbilt, *Charles Eliot Norton*, 106.

48. Norton, "The Poverty of England," 152.

49. Ibid., 154.

50. Smith to Norton, 11 September 1868, Norton papers, MS Am 1088 / 6716.

51. Smith to Norton, 8 October 1868, Norton papers MS Am, 1088 / 6717.

52. Turner, *Liberal Education*, 92.

53. Charles Eliot Norton to John Ruskin, 15 June 1870, CE Norton letters, MS Am 1088.2.
54. Turner, *Liberal Education*, 92, 94, 95.
55. On Pearson's political aspirations, see Tregenza, *Professor of Democracy*, 87–119.
56. Ibid., 118.
57. Henry Sidgwick to Charles Pearson, 8 July [year unclear], Pearson papers, MS Eng misc. c. 386, Bodleian Library.
58. Pearson to Norton, 14 May 1873, Norton papers, MS Am 1088 / 5416.
59. Tregenza, *Professor of Democracy*, 120.
60. Ibid., 41.
61. Turner, *Liberal Education* 72; Vanderbilt, *Charles Eliot Norton*, 33–34.
62. Norton to Parkman, 21 October 1849, Norton letters, MS Am 1088.2, box 5.
63. Norton to Charles Mills, 4 October 1849, Norton letters, MS Am 1088.2, box 5.
64. Pearson, "The Story of My Life," 123.
65. Pearson, *National Life and Character*, 17, 90.
66. Pearson, "On the Working of Australian Institutions," in *Essays on Reform* (London, 1867), 191, 201, 216; on Lowe's attacks on colonial democracy, see Catherine Hall, Keith McClelland, and Jane Rendall, *Defining the Victorian Nation: Class, Race, Gender and the Reform Act of 1867* (Cambridge: Cambridge University Press, 2000), 223–224.
67. Leslie Stephen, "The Political Situation in England," *North American Review*, October 1868, 544–546.
68. Pearson, "Australian Institutions," 191; Stephen, "The Political Situation in England," 545.
69. Pearson, "Australian Institutions," 193.
70. Ibid., 197.
71. Ibid., 199.
72. Ibid., 210.
73. Ibid., 209.
74. Goldwin Smith, "The Experience of the American Commonwealth," in *Essays on Reform* (London, 1867), 218.
75. Ibid., 219.
76. Charles Pearson, "The Land Question in the United States," *Contemporary Review*, September–December 1868, 347–354; Frederick Jackson Turner, "The Significance of the Frontier in American History," in *Annual Report of the American Historical Association for the Year 1893* (Washington, DC, 1894), 199–227.
77. Charles Henry Pearson, *The Higher Culture of Women* (Melbourne: Samuel Mullen, 1875); Tregenza, *Professor of Democracy*, 75–86.
78. Pearson, *The Higher Culture of Women*.
79. Ibid., 19.
80. Charles Pearson papers, Miscellaneous, MS Eng. Misc. c 386, Bodleian Library.
81. Tregenza, *Professor of Democracy*, 53.
82. Ibid.

83. Stuart Macintyre, *A Colonial Liberalism: The Lost World of Three Victorian Visionaries* (Melbourne: Oxford University Press, 1991), 142.
84. Pearson to Norton, 30 June 1868, MS Am 1088 / 5413, Norton papers.
85. Pearson, "The Story of My Life," 124.
86. Pearson to Norton, 30 June 1868, MS Am 1088 / 5143, Norton papers.
87. Pearson, "The Story of My Life," 133–134.
88. Ibid.
89. Ibid., 134–135.
90. *Spectator*, 21 October 1871; *Spectator*, 11 November 1871.
91. *Spectator*, 11 November 1871.
92. Ibid.
93. *Spectator*, 9 March 1872.
94. Ibid.
95. Pearson to Norton, 14 May 1873, MS Am 1088 / 5416, Norton papers.
96. Henry Reynolds, *Forgotten War* (Sydney: NewSouth Books, 2013), 67.
97. Pearson to Norton, 14 May 1873, MS Am 1088 / 5416, Norton papers.
98. Pearson to Norton, 10 August 1874, MS Am 1088 / 5417, Norton papers.
99. Ibid.
100. Ibid.
101. Ibid.
102. Victoria, Parl. Deb., sess. 1878, 28, 9 July 1878.
103. Victoria, Parl. Deb., sess. 1884, 46, 12 August 1884.
104. Victoria, Parl. Deb., sess. 1881, 37, 4 October 1881, 220.
105. Pearson to Norton, 10 August 1874.
106. Victoria, Parl. Deb., sess. 1891, 68, 10 November 1891.
107. Sawer, *The Ethical State*, 4–8; Macintyre, *A Colonial Liberalism*, 152–168.
108. "Australia and the Royal Veto," *Speaker*, 26 April 1890, 458–459.
109. Pearson, *National Life and Character*, 18–19.
110. Henry Demarest Lloyd, *Newest England: Notes of a Democratic Traveller in New Zealand, with Some Australian Comparisons* (New York: Doubleday, Page, 1900), 1.
111. Roosevelt to Pearson, 11 May 1894, Pearson papers, MS English letters, d.190, Bodleian Library.
112. Theodore Roosevelt to Cecil Arthur Spring Rice, 11 August 1899, in *The Letters of Theodore Roosevelt*, vol. 2, ed. Elting E. Morison (Cambridge MA: Harvard University Press, 1951), 1052.
113. Roosevelt, "National Life and Character," 271–285.

2. AN EXPANSIVE STATE WITH SOCIALISTIC TENDENCIES

1. Josiah Royce, "Impressions of Australia," *Scribner's* 9, no. 1 (January 1891): 85.
2. Ibid.
3. Ibid., 86.
4. Josiah Royce, "Reflections after a Wandering Life in Australasia," first paper, *Atlantic Monthly* 63 (May 1889): 685.
5. Royce "Impressions of Australia," 86.
6. Ibid, 87.

7. Ibid., 78, 79.

8. Josiah Royce, "Reflections after a Wandering Life in Australasia," second paper, *Atlantic Monthly* 63 (June 1889): 828.

9. Marilyn Lake, "The Australian Dream of an Island Empire: Race, Reputation and Resistance," *Australian Historical Studies* 46, no. 3 (2015): 410–424.

10. Alfred Deakin, "The Federation of Australia," *Scribner's* 10, no. 5 (November 1891): 16.

11. Lake, "The Australian Dream of an Island Empire," 416–420.

12. Theodore Roosevelt, *The Strenuous Life: Essays and Addresses* (London: Grant Richards, 1902), 18.

13. Vicente L. Rafael, "White Love: Surveillance and Nationalist Resistance in the US Colonization of the Philippines," in *Cultures of United States Imperialism*, ed. Amy Kaplan and Donald E. Pease (Durham, NC: Duke University Press, 1993), 185–218; Warwick Anderson, *Colonial Pathologies: American Tropical Medicine, Race and Hygiene in the Philippines* (Durham, NC: Duke University Press, 2006); Roland Sintos Coloma, "Empire: An Analytical Category for Educational Research," *Educational Theory* 63, no. 6 (2013): 639–658. On progressivism and the administration of empire, see Julie Greene, *The Canal Builders: Making America's Empire at the Panama Canal* (New York: Penguin Press, 2009).

14. Marilyn Lake, "Colonial Australia and the Asia-Pacific Region," *The Cambridge History of Australia*, vol. 1, ed. Alison Bashford and Stuart Macintyre (Melbourne: Cambridge University Press, 2013), 535–559.

15. Ibid.; Roger C. Thompson, *Australian Imperialism in the Pacific: The Expansionist Era, 1820–1920* (Melbourne: Melbourne University Press, 1980).

16. Alan Atkinson, *The Europeans in Australia*, vol. 3, *Nation* (Sydney: UNSW Press, 2014), 105–109.

17. Tracey Banivanua-Mar, *Violence and Colonial Dialogue: The Australian-Pacific Labor Trade* (Honolulu: University of Hawai'i Press, 2007).

18. Deakin to Catherine, 1 November 1879, Catherine Deakin papers, MS 4913, NLA.

19. Deakin to Catherine, 7 November 1879, Catherine Deakin papers, MS 4913, NLA.

20. Deakin to Catherine, 30 October 1879, Catherine Deakin papers, MS 4913, NLA.

21. Ian Tyrrell, *True Gardens of the Gods: Californian-Australian Environmental Reform, 1860–1930* (Berkeley: University of California Press, 1999), 123–124; Jessica B. Teisch, *Engineering Nature: Water, Development and the Global Spread of American Environmental Expertise* (Chapel Hill: University of North Carolina Press, 2001), chap. 3.

22. Deakin travel diary, 6 January 1885, MS 1540 / 2 / 38, s 2–s11, NLA.

23. Ibid.

24. Bob Dye, *Merchant Prince of the Sandalwood Mountains: Afong and the Chinese in Hawai'i* (Honolulu: University of Hawai'i Press, 1997), 198–201.

25. Deakin travel diary, 6 January 1885.

26. Deakin travel diary, 29 January 1885, MS 1540 / 2 / 38, s12–s18, NLA.

27. Marilyn Lake, "'The Brightness of Eyes and Quiet Assurance Which Seem to Say American': Alfred Deakin's Identification with Republican Manhood," *Australian Historical Studies* 38, no. 129 (2007): 32–51.
28. Deakin travel diary, 29 January 1885.
29. Douglas Henry Daniels, *Pioneer Urbanites: A Social and Cultural History of Black San Francisco* (Philadelphia: Temple University Press, 1980), 38–40.
30. John L. Dow, "The Irrigation Commission in America," no. 1, and "From Melbourne to Sacramento," *Age*, 21 March 1885.
31. John L. Dow, "The Irrigation Commission in America," no. 2, *Age*, 25 April 1885.
32. Josiah Royce, *California from the Conquest in 1846 to the Second Vigilance Committee in San Francisco* (Boston: Houghton Mifflin, 1884), 1.
33. Dow, "The Irrigation Commission in America," no. 2, *Age*, 25 April 1885.
34. Deakin travel diary, 12–15 February 1885, MS 1540 / 2 / 38, s28, NLA.
35. Deakin travel diary, 16–27 February 1885, MS 1540 / 2 / 38, s28–s78, NLA.
36. Ibid.
37. Deakin travel diary, 2 February 1885, MS 1540 / 2 / 38, s75–s76, NLA.
38. On the Santa Fe Trail, see Elliott West, *The Contested Plains: Indians, Goldseekers and the Rush to Colorado* (Lawrence: University Press of Kansas, 1998), 88, 119–120.
39. Deakin travel diary, 6 March 1885, MS 1540 / 2 / 38, s101, NLA.
40. *Age*, news report, 6 March 1885.
41. Tyrrell, *True Gardens of the Gods*, 123–124.
42. Geoffrey Serle, *The Rush to Be Rich: A History of the Colony of Victoria, 1883–1889* (Melbourne: Melbourne University Press, 1974), 45–47; Noel G. Butlin, "Colonial Socialism in Australia, 1860–1900," in *The State and Economic Growth*, ed. Hugh G. J. Aitken (New York: Social Science Research Council, 1959), 26–78; Noel Butlin, *Investment in Australian Economic Development, 1861–1900* (Cambridge: Cambridge University Press, 1964); Donald Denoon and Phillipa Mein Smith, with Marivic Wyndham, *A History of Australia, New Zealand and the Pacific: The Blackwell History of the World* (Oxford: Blackwells, 2000); Ian W. McLean, *Why Australia Prospered: The Shifting Sources of Economic Growth* (Princeton, NJ: Princeton University Press, 2013), 80–112.
43. Serle, *The Rush to Be Rich*, 51.
44. Richard Broome, *Aboriginal Victorians: A History since 1800* (Sydney: Allen and Unwin, 2005), 193.
45. Serle, *The Rush to Be Rich*, 55.
46. Helen Page Bates, "State Irrigation in the Australian Colonies" (PhD diss., University of Wisconsin, 1896).
47. Claire H. Hammond, "Helen Frances Page Bates: The First American Woman Ph.D. in Economics," *American Economic Association Newsletter*, March 1991, 9; Karen O'Connor, *Gender and Women's Leadership: A Reference Handbook* (Los Angeles: Sage Reference, 2010), 659. On Ely's School of Economics, Political Science, and History at Wisconsin, see Shelton Stromquist, *Reinventing "The People": The Progressive Movement, the*

Class Problem and the Origins of Modern Liberalism (Champaign: University of Illinois Press, 2006), 30; Leon Fink, *The Long Gilded Age: American Capitalism and the Lessons of a New World Order* (Philadelphia: University of Pennsylvania Press, 2015), 71–78.

48. Helen Page Bates to Richard Ely, 3 May 1902, Ely papers, Wisconsin Historical Society.

49. Helen Page Bates, "Australian Experiments in Industry," *Annals of the American Academy of Political and Social Science* 12 (September 1898): 41; on Ely's students, see Stromquist, *Reinventing "The People,"* 30.

50. Correspondence, Ely papers, Wisconsin Historical Society.

51. F. C. Howe, *Wisconsin: An Experiment in Democracy* (New York: Scribner's, 1912; repr., London: Forgotten Books, 2015), 42, 47, 191.

52. Howe, *Wisconsin*, xii.

53. Bates, "Australian Experiments," 23.

54. Ibid., 11.

55. Royce, "Impressions of Australia," 86.

56. Royce, "Reflections after a Wandering Life," first paper, 682.

57. Josiah Royce to Alfred Deakin, 28 February 1889, Deakin papers, MS 1540 / 1 / 75, NLA.

58. Deakin to Royce, 14 January 1898, Deakin papers, MS 1540 / 1 / 412, NLA.

59. Alfred Deakin, *The Federal Story: The Inner History of the Federal Cause, 1880–1900*, ed. J. A. La Nauze (Melbourne: Melbourne University Press, 1963), 21; see also Deakin's notes, Deakin papers, MS 1540 / 9 / 444, NLA.

60. Deakin travel diary, 5 April 1887, Deakin papers, MS 1540 / 2 / 39, s267, NLA; Deakin, *The Federal Story*, 22–23.

61. Deakin, *The Federal Story*, 23.

62. Deakin papers, folder 15, notes, speeches, etc., MS 1540 / 9 / 444, NLA.

63. Deakin travel diary, 5 April 1887.

64. Theodore Roosevelt to Henry Cabot Lodge, 7 March 1887, in *The Letters of Theodore Roosevelt*, ed. Elting E. Morrison (Cambridge, MA: Harvard University Press, 1951), 126.

65. Ibid.

66. Deakin travel diary, 5 April 1887, MS 1540 / 2 / 39, s258–s263, s316, s331, s358–s359, NLA.

67. Ibid., s350.

68. *Age*, 23 May 1887, news clipping, Deakin papers, MS 1540 / 9 / 477, NLA.

69. Deakin travel diary, 5–24 April 1987, MS 1540 / 2 / 39, s250–s251, s269, s277–s278, s281, s321, NLA.

70. Deakin travel diary, 24 April 1887, MS 1540 / 2 / 39, s310–s311, NLA.

71. *Standard*, news clippings, Deakin papers, MS 1540 / 9 / 479; *Age*, 6 June 1887.

72. Victoria, Parl. Deb., Legislative Assembly, 6 July 1887, 269.

73. Royce to Deakin, 28 February 1889, Deakin papers, MS 1540 / 1 / 73, NLA.

74. Royce, *Philosophy of Loyalty*, 9.

75. Deakin to Dilke (undated), Letterbook, 86, Dilke papers, British Library.

76. J. A. La Nauze, *Alfred Deakin: A Biography*, vol. 1 (Melbourne: Melbourne University Press, 1965), 83.

77. Ibid.

78. Marilyn Lake, "Challenging the 'Slave-Driving Employers': Understanding Victoria's 1896 Minimum Wage through a World-History Approach," *Australian Historical Studies* 45, no. 1 (2014): 87–102.

79. Deakin, in Victoria, Parl. Deb., Legislative Assembly, 12 November 1895, 3148–3149.

80. Florence Kelley, *The Present Status of Minimum Wage Legislation* (New York: National Consumers League, 1913), 6–7; Walter Lippmann, "The Campaign against Sweating," *New Republic*, 27 March 1915, 22.

81. Higgins, in Victoria, Parl. Deb., Legislative Assembly, 12 November 1895, 3129.

82. Deakin, in Victoria, Parl. Deb., Legislative Assembly, 12 November 1895, 3148.

83. Royce, "Reflections after a Wandering Life," second paper, 825.

84. Deakin to Royce, 30 June 1888, Deakin papers, MS 1540 / 1 / 48, NLA.

85. Royce to Deakin, 21 June 1888, Deakin papers, MS 1540 / 1 / 48, NLA.

86. Marilyn Lake, "From Mississippi to Melbourne via Natal," in *Connected Worlds History in Transnational Perspective*, ed. Ann Curthoys and Marilyn Lake (Canberra: ANU Press, 2006).

87. Alfred Deakin, Commonwealth Parl. Deb., House [usually referred to as House of Representatives in Australia], 12 September 1901, 4804.

88. Prescott Hall, in Immigration Restriction League papers, MS Am 2245 (1111), Houghton Library.

89. Frank Parsons, "Australasian Methods of Dealing with Immigration," *Annals of the American Academy of Political and Social Science* 24 (1904): 211.

90. Ibid., 220.

91. First National Convention of the Progressive Party, Chicago, 5–7 August 1912, 33, Roosevelt papers, Library of Congress.

92. Barton minute to Governor General, 28 November 1901, CO 418 / 10 / 479, National Archives of the UK; Roger C. Thompson, *Australian Imperialism in the Pacific: The Expansionist Era 1820–1920* (Melbourne: Melbourne University Press, 1980), 3–4.

93. Barton minute to Governor General, 28 November 1901, CO 418 / 10 / 479, National Archives of the UK.

94. Alfred Deakin, Commonwealth Parl. Deb., House, vol. 6, 19 November 1901, 7411.

95. The first compulsory arbitration bill was introduced by its author, Charles Kingston, federal minister for trade and customs, in 1901, but he resigned over a number of issues, including the exclusion of seamen from its coverage. The final Commonwealth Conciliation and Arbitration Act was passed in December 1904.

96. Alfred Deakin, Commonwealth Parl. Deb., House, no. 31, 30 July 1903, 2862.

97. Stuart Macintyre and Richard Mitchell, eds., *Foundations of Arbitration: The Origins and Effects of State Compulsory Arbitration 1890–1914* (Melbourne: Oxford University Press, 1989); Shaun Goldfinch and Philippa Mein Smith, "Compulsory Arbitration and the Australasian Model of State Development: Policy Transfer, Learning, and Innovation," *Journal of Policy History* 18, no. 4 (2006): 419–445.

98. Henry Demarest Lloyd, *A Country without Strikes: A Visit to the Compulsory Arbitration Court of New Zealand* (New York: Doubleday, 1900).

99. Alfred Deakin, Commonwealth Parl. Deb., House, no. 31, 30 July 1903, 2864.

100. Ibid., 2863.

101. Isaac Isaacs, Commonwealth Parl. Deb., House, no. 35, 26 August 1903, 4266.

102. Alfred Deakin, Commonwealth Parl. Deb., House, no. 31, 30 July 1903, 2868.

103. James Hume Cook, G. B. Edwards, and William Sawers, Commonwealth Parl. Deb., House, no. 34, 20 and 25 August 1903, 3975, 4171–4173; Commonwealth Parl. Deb., House, no. 33, 12 August 1903, 3483.

104. Alfred Deakin, "The Liberal Party and Its Liberal Programme," Speech in Adelaide, 29 March 1906, Deakin papers, MS 1540 / 15 / 1807, NLA.

105. Ibid.

106. Marian Sawer, "Andrew Fisher and the Era of Liberal Reform," *Labour History* 102 (May 2012): 76–79.

107. Commonwealth Parl. Deb., House, 1908, 11925.

108. Deakin, *Morning Post*, 14 April 1908, in *Federated Australia: Selections of Letters to the Morning Post, 1900–1910*, ed. J. A. La Nauze (Melbourne: Melbourne University Press, 1968), 229.

109. Deakin to Whitelaw Reid, 7 January 1908, Secretary of State papers, roll 598, 8758 / 161, US National Archives.

110. Roosevelt to Metcalf, 21 February 1908, Secretary of State, roll 598, 825 / 159, US National Archives.

111. Theodore Roosevelt, *An Autobiography* (New York: Macmillan, 1913), 598.

112. Royce to Deakin, 18 April 1908, Deakin papers, MS 1540 / 1 / 1964, MLA.

113. Ibid.

114. Ibid.

115. Ibid.

116. Ibid.

117. Deakin, final draft, Deakin papers, MS 1540 / 15 / 3912, NLA; *Age*, 24 August 1908.

118. Roosevelt, *An Autobiography*, 589.

119. Link and McCormick, *Progressivism*, 42.

120. Theodore Roosevelt, "Address delivered at Boston, Mass., 27 April 1912 on political issues of Presidential election," US Congressional serial set, 62nd Congress, no. 6177, s.doc.616.

121. "Mr Roosevelt's 'State Socialism,'" *State*, 9 August 1912.

122. Robert Valentine to Dr. Mumford, 18 June 1912, Valentine papers, 8 / 82, Massachusetts Historical Society.

3. PURIFYING POLITICS THROUGH ELECTORAL REFORM

1. Brenda G. McGowan, "Historical Evolution of Child Welfare Services," in *Child Welfare for the Twenty-First Century*, ed. G. P. Mallon (New York: Columbia University Press, 2005), 15; Jennifer Anderson, "Juvenile Courts—an Australian Innovation?," *Adelaide Law Review* 35, no. 2 (2014): 331–359.

2. Catherine Spence, "Autobiography," in *Ever Yours, Catherine Helen Spence*, ed. Susan Magarey with Barbara Wall (Adelaide: Wakefield Press, 2005), 147.
3. James H. Barry, "Biographical Sketch," *Star* (San Francisco), 18 January 1902; Susan Magarey, *Unbridling the Tongues of Women: A Biography of Catherine Helen Spence* (Adelaide: University of Adelaide Press, 2010), xxii.
4. Clarence Hoag and George Hallett, *Proportional Representation* (New York: Macmillan, 1926), 124.
5. Spence, "Autobiography," 146.
6. Alfred Cridge, preface to *Proportional Representation Including Its Relation to the Initiative and Referendum*, pamphlet first published as supplement to *Hope and Home*, 21 October 1893, repr. with an appendix by Robert Tyson (San Francisco: Star Press, 1904).
7. Spence, "Autobiography," 147.
8. Magarey, *Unbridling the Tongues of Women*, 143.
9. Spence, "Autobiography," 279.
10. Catherine Spence, "Diary," in Magarey with Wall, *Ever Yours, Catherine Helen Spence*, 292.
11. *South Australian Register*, 26 July 1893, 6.
12. *South Australian Register*, 5 July 1893, 6.
13. Catherine Helen Spence, "The Democratic Ideal," *Champion*, 23 May 1896, 207.
14. Susan Magarey with Barbara Wall, introduction to Magarey with Wall, *Ever Yours, Catherine Helen Spence*, 12.
15. *South Australian Register*, 26 July 1893, 6.
16. Magarey, *Unbridling the Tongues of Women*, 9.
17. Josiah Royce, *California: From the Conquest in 1846 to the Second Vigilance Committee in San Francisco: A Study of American Character*, American Commonwealths Series, ed. Horace E Scudder (Boston: Houghton Mifflin, 1886).
18. Frankfurter to Higgins, 25 July 1918, Frankfurter papers, reel 40, Library of Congress.
19. *South Australian Register*, 26 July 1893, 6.
20. Richard H. Dana, "The Practical Working of the Australian Voting System in Massachusetts," *Annals of the Academy of Political and Social Science* 2 (May 1892): 733–750; Lionel Fredman, *The Australian Ballot: The Story of an American Reform* (East Lansing: Michigan State University Press, 1968); J. Morgan Kousser, *The Shaping of Southern Politics: Suffrage Restriction and the Establishment of the One-Party South, 1880–1910* (New Haven, CT: Yale University Press, 1974); Shelton Stromquist, *Reinventing "The People:" The Progressive Movement, the Class Problem, and the Origins of Modern Liberalism* (Urbana: University of Illinois Press, 2006), 68.
21. Kousser, *The Shaping of Southern Politics*, 53–55.
22. Arthur S. Link and Richard L. McCormick, *Progressivism* (Chicago: Harlan Davidson, 1983), 27–66; Martha Derthick and John J. Dinan, "Progressivism and Federalism," and Jerome M. Mileur, "The Legacy of Reform: Progressive Government, Regressive Politics," in *Progressivism and the New Democracy*, ed. Sidney M. Milkis and Jerome M. Mileur (Amherst: University

of Massachusetts Press, 1999), 81–102, 265; Stromquist, *Reinventing "The People,"* 34–36; 67–69; R. Todd Laugen, *The Gospel of Progressivism: Moral Reform and Labor War in Colorado, 1900–1930* (Boulder: University Press of Colorado, 2010), 1–5; Amel Ahmed, *Democracy and the Politics of Electoral System Choice* (New York: Cambridge University Press, 2013), 115.

23. Douglas J. Amy "The Forgotten History of the Single Transferable Vote in the United States," *Representation* 34, no. 1 (1996): 15; Kathleen L. Barber, *Proportional Representation and Election Reform in Ohio* (Columbus: Ohio State University Press, 1995).

24. George C. Brodrick, ed., *Essays on Reform* (London: Macmillan, 1867).

25. C. H. Spence, preface to *A Plea for Pure Democracy: Mr. Hare's Reform Bill Applied to South Australia* (Adelaide: W. C. Rigby, 1861).

26. Spence, *A Plea for Pure Democracy*, 1.

27. *South Australian Register*, 2 November 1893, 6.

28. Tony Ballantyne, "Remaking the Empire from Newgate: Wakefield's *Letter from Sydney*," in *Ten Books That Shaped the British Empire: Creating an Imperial Commons*, ed. Antoinette Burton and Isabel Hofmeyr (Durham, NC: Duke University Press, 2014), 29–49.

29. Magarey, *Unbridling the Tongues*, 28.

30. Robert Foster, Rick Hosking, and Amanda Nettlebeck, *Fatal Collisions: The South Australian Frontier and the Violence of Memory* (Adelaide: Wakefield Press, 2001), 1–28.

31. Lorenzo Veracini, *Settler Colonialism: A Theoretical Overview* (London: Palgrave, 2010), 3.

32. Magarey, *Unbridling the Tongues*, 28.

33. Ibid.

34. Goldwin Smith, "The Experience of the American Commonwealth," in *Essays on Reform*, ed. George C. Brodrick (London: Macmillan, 1867), 218–219.

35. *South Australian Register*, 10 May 1881, 6.

36. C. H. Spence, "A Californian Political Economist," *Victorian Review* 4, no. 20 (1 June 1881): 130.

37. Spence, "Autobiography," 155.

38. *South Australian Register*, 4 April 1893, 5.

39. Magarey, *Unbridling the Tongues*, 126.

40. For more on the later influence of Florence and Rosamond Davenport Hill as advocates of boarding out and their book *Children of the State*, see Shurlee Swain, "Florence and Rosamond Davenport Hill and the Development of Boarding Out in England and Australia: A Study in Cultural Transmission," *Women's History Review* 23, no. 5 (2014): 744–759.

41. Frances Power Cobbe, "The Philosophy of the Poor-Laws and the Report of the Committee on Poor Relief," *Fraser's* 70 (1864): 373–394.

42. Ibid., 387.

43. Ibid.

44. Swain, "Florence and Rosamond Davenport Hill," 748–749.

45. Alfred Deakin to Charles Dilke, [1894], Dilke papers, Letterbook, 83, British Library.

46. Ibid.

47. *South Australian Register*, 4 April 1893, 5.

48. Ibid.

49. Robyn Muncy, *Creating a Female Dominion in American Reform, 1880–1935* (New York: Oxford University Press, 1994); Marilyn Lake, *Getting Equal: The History of Australian Feminism* (Sydney: Allen and Unwin, 1999), 19–45.

50. Gail Bederman, *Manliness and Civilization: A Cultural History of Gender and Race in the United States, 1880–1917* (Chicago: Chicago University Press, 1995), 31.

51. Theodore Roosevelt to James Brander Matthews, 8 June 1893, in *The Letters of Theodore Roosevelt*, vol. 1, ed. Elting E. Morison (Cambridge MA: Harvard University Press, 1951), 320.

52. *South Australian Register*, 21 August 1893, 6.

53. Lucy Maddox, *Citizen Indians: Native American Intellectuals, Race and Reform* (Ithaca, NY: Cornell University Press, 2005), 2–3.

54. Richard White and Patricia Nelson Limerick, "Frederick Jackson Turner and Buffalo Bill," in *The Frontier in American Culture*, ed. James Grossman (Berkeley: University of California Press, 1994), ProQuest Ebook Central, https://ebookcentral.proquest.com/lib/unimelb/detail.action?docID =223337.

55. Ibid.

56. Simon Pokagon, "The Red Man's Greeting," in *Talking Back to Civilization: Indian Voices from the Progressive Era*, ed. Frederick Hoxie (Boston: Bedford, 2001), 29.

57. Ibid., 31–33.

58. Ibid., 32.

59. Robert Rydell, *All the World's a Fair: Visions of Empire at American International Expositions, 1876–1916* (Chicago: University of Chicago Press, 1984), 38–71.

60. Bederman, *Manliness and Civilization*, 31.

61. Catherine Helen Spence, "Lecture," in *Proceedings of the First Australasian Conference on Charity* (Melbourne, 1890), 15–25.

62. Ibid.

63. Spence, "Autobiography," 103.

64. *Adelaide Register*, 26 July 1893, 6.

65. *General Exercises of the International Congress of Charities, Correction and Philanthropy, Chicago, June, 1893* (Baltimore: Johns Hopkins Press, 1894), 294.

66. Ibid., 300.

67. Ibid.

68. Ibid., 301.

69. Ibid., 293.

70. Spence, "Autobiography," 150.

71. Rev. Anna Garlin Spencer, "Advantages and Dangers of Organization," in *The Congress of Women: Held in the Woman's Building, World's Columbian Exposition, Chicago, USA, 1893*, ed. Mary Kavanaugh Oldham Eagle (Chi-

cago: Monarch, 1894), 171; Muncy, *Creating a Female Dominion*; Kathryn Kish Sklar, "The Historical Foundations of Women's Power in the Creation of the American Welfare State, 1830–1930," in *US History as Women's History: New Feminist Essays*, ed. Linda K. Kerber, Alice Kessler-Harris, and Kathryn Kish Sklar (Chapel Hill: University of North Carolina Press, 1995).

72. Spencer, "Advantages and Dangers of Organization," 172.

73. Spence, "The Democratic Ideal," 207.

74. Ibid.

75. *South Australian Register*, 2 November 1893, 6.

76. Catherine Spence, "Effective Voting: The Only Effective Moralizer of Politics," *Arena* 10 (November 1894): 774.

77. *South Australian Register*, 2 November 1893, 6.

78. *South Australian Register*, 12 October 1893, 6.

79. Ibid.

80. *South Australian Register*, 2 November 1893, 6.

81. Catherine Helen Spence, "Notes Political and Social of Ten Months in America," *Christian Advocate*, 23 August 1894, 554.

82. *South Australian Register*, 16 October 1893, 6.

83. Spence, "Notes Political and Social," 544.

84. *South Australian Register*, 26 February 1894, 6.

85. Amy, "The Forgotten History," 13.

86. Catherine Helen Spence, "Address on Effective Voting," in *The Congress of Women: Held in the Woman's Building, World's Columbian Exposition, Chicago, USA, 1893*, ed. Mary Kavanaugh Oldham Eagle (Chicago: Monarch, 1894), 459.

87. Stoughton Cooley, "The Proportional Representation Congress," *Annals of the American Academy of Political and Social Science* 4 (November 1893): 112; Kathleen Barber, *A Right to Representation: Proportional Representation Systems for the Twenty-First Century* (Columbus: Ohio State University Press, 2000), 32; Amel Ahmed, *Democracy and the Politics of Electoral System Choice: Engineering Electoral Dominance* (New York: Cambridge University Press, 2013), 115.

88. Cooley, "The Proportional Representation Congress," 113–114.

89. Eldon J. Eisenbach, *The Lost Promise of Progressivism* (Lawrence: University Press of Kansas, 1994), 117–118.

90. Cooley, "The Proportional Representation Congress," 115.

91. *South Australian Register*, 16 October 1893, 6.

92. Ibid.

93. Kevin G. Gaines, *Uplifting the Race: Black Leadership, Politics and Culture in the Twentieth Century* (Chapel Hill: University of North Carolina Press, 1996), 36–37.

94. *South Australian Register*, 16 October 1893, 6.

95. Cooley, "Proportional Representation Congress," 117.

96. *South Australian Register*, 16 October 1983, 6.

97. *South Australian Register*, 3 January 1894, 6.

98. Ibid.

99. Spence, "Autobiography," 150.

100. *South Australian Register*, 3 January 1894, 6.
101. Ibid.
102. *South Australian Register*, 26 February 1894, 6.
103. *South Australian Register*, 3 January 1894, 6.
104. Catherine Helen Spence, "Diary," in Magarey with Wall, *Ever Yours, Catherine Helen Spence*, 232.
105. Magarey with Wall, introduction to Spence, "Diary," 222.
106. Joan T. Mark, *A Stranger in Her Native Land: Alice Fletcher and the American Indians* (Lincoln: University of Nebraska Press, 1988).
107. Spence, "Diary," 14 January 1894, 232.
108. Spence, "Autobiography," 153.
109. Oliver Wendell Holmes Jr., "Blackbook of Reading," Special collections, MS 4075a, Harvard Law Library.
110. Theodore Roosevelt to Charles Pearson, 11 May 1894, Pearson papers, MS English letters, folios 187–191, d.190, Bodleian Library.
111. Spence, "Autobiography," 152.
112. Ibid., 152–153.
113. *South Australian Register*, 17 May 1894, 6.
114. *South Australian Register*, 7 August 1894, 5–6.
115. Spence, "Autobiography," 156.
116. *South Australian Register*, 17 May 1894, 6.
117. Spence, "Effective Voting," 770.
118. C. H. Spence, "An Australian's Impressions of America," *Harper's New Monthly Magazine* 89 (June–November 1894): 245.
119. Spence, "Effective Voting," 771.
120. John Commons, *Proportional Representation* (New York: T. Y. Crowell, 1896), 101, 143.
121. Spence to Alice Henry, 7 November 1900, Letters by Catherine Helen Spence to Alice Henry, 1900–1910, transcribed by Dr. Barbara Wall, PRG 88 / 7 / 1, State Library of South Australia. My thanks to James Keating for alerting me to this source.
122. Emily Parmely Collins to Catherine Spence, 30 September 1902, enclosed in Spence to Alice Henry, 18 November 1902, Letters by Catherine Helen Spence to Alice Henry, 1900–1910, PRG 88 / 7 / 23, State Library of South Australia.
123. Ibid.
124. Ahmed, *Democracy and the Politics of the Electoral System*, 114–116.
125. Catherine Spence to Alice Henry, 7 January 1901, Correspondence between Spence and Henry, PRG 88/ 7 / 2, State Library of South Australia.

4. FEDERAL IDEALISM AND LABOR REALISM

1. Albert Bushnell Hart, *National Ideals Historically Traced, 1607 to 1907: The American Nation; A History*, vol. 26 (New York: Harper and Brothers, 1907), 133.
2. Frankfurter to Stimson, quoted in Joseph P. Lasch, ed., *Diaries of Felix Frankfurter* (New York: W. W. Norton, 1975), 13.

3. Frankfurter to Higgins, 25 July 1918, Frankfurter papers, reel 40, Library of Congress; Gerard Henderson to Higgins, 26 August 1915, Higgins papers, MS 1057 / 238, NLA.

4. H. B. Higgins, "A New Province for Law and Order: Industrial Peace through the Minimum Wage and Arbitration," *Harvard Law Review* 29, no. 1 (November 1915): 14.

5. Higgins, quoted in Felix Frankfurter and James M. Landis, "The Business of the Supreme Court of the United States: A Study in the Federal Judicial System," *Harvard Law Review* 38, no. 8 (June 1925): 1009.

6. H. B. Higgins, "The Rigid Constitution," *Political Science Quarterly* 20, no. 2 (June 1905): 203–222.

7. F. W. Taussig to H. B. Higgins, 11 April 1916, Higgins papers, MS 1057 / 234, NLA.

8. M. B. Hammond, "Judicial Interpretation of the Minimum Wage in Australia," *American Economic Review* 3, no. 2 (1913): 285.

9. "The Legislative Minimum Wage," *Harvard Law Review* 31, no. 7 (May 1918): 1013–1017.

10. Alfred Deakin to Josiah Royce, 5 June 1892, Deakin papers, 1540 / 1 / 412, NLA.

11. Bernhard Ringrose Wise, *The Making of the Australian Commonwealth, 1889–1900* (London: Longmans Green, 1913), 25.

12. See for example W. G. Buss, "Andrew Inglis Clark's Draft Constitution, Chapter III of the Australian Constitution and the Assist from Article III of the Constitution of the United States," *Melbourne University Law Review* 33 (2009): 718–801.

13. John Williams, "Andrew Inglis Clark: 'The Republic of Tasmania,'" in *Makers of Miracles: The Cast of the Federation Story,* ed. David Headon and John Williams (Melbourne: Melbourne University Press, 2000), 55; Robert French, "Inglis Clark: A Living Force," in *"The Truest Patriotism": Andrew Inglis Clark and the Building of an Australian Nation,* Papers on Parliament 61, ed. Rosemary Laing and David Headon (Canberra, ACT: Department of the Senate, 2014), 113.

14. Albert Bushnell Hart papers, HUG 4448.6, box 10, Harvard University Archives.

15. Albert Bushnell Hart, *An Introduction to the Study of Federal Government* (Boston: Ginn, 1891); Hart to Clark, 18 October 1899, Clark papers, C4 / C197, University of Tasmania Archives.

16. Hart to Clark, 18 October 1899, Clark papers, C4 / C197, University of Tasmania Archives.

17. Hart to Clark, 14 April 1900, Clark papers, C4 / C198, University of Tasmania Archives; Hart to Clark, 6 June 1900, Clark papers, C4 / C199, University of Tasmania Archives.

18. President and fellows of Harvard College: Certificate, Clark papers, C4 / 200, University of Tasmania Archives.

19. John Reynolds to Mark de Wolfe Howe, 10 March 1947, Oliver Wendell Holmes papers, ALEPH 601674 / HULPR ACZ6483, Harvard Law Library.

20. James Warden, "Andrew Inglis Clark Deserves to Be Remembered across the Great Divide," in Laing and Headon, *The Truest Patriotism,*" 50.
21. *Proceedings and Debates of the Australasian Federation Conference, Melbourne, 1890* (Melbourne, 1890), 36.
22. Williams, "Andrew Inglis Clark," 47.
23. F. M. Neasey and L. J. Neasey, *Andrew Inglis Clark* (Hobart: University of Tasmania Law Press, 2001), 36.
24. William Harkness to Clark, 28 September 1898, Clark papers, C4 / C195, University of Tasmania Archives.
25. George Dewey to Clark, 29 July 1898, Clark papers, C4 / C46, University of Tasmania Archives.
26. Thomas Gossett, *Race: The History of an Idea in America* (1963; repr., New York: Oxford University Press, 1997), 314; Paul Kramer, *The Blood of Government: Race, Empire, the United States and the Philippines* (Chapel Hill: University of North Carolina Press, 2006); Marilyn Lake and Vanessa Pratt, "'Blood Brothers': Racial Identification and the Right to Rule: The Australian Response to the Spanish-American War," *Australian Journal of Politics and History* 54, no. 1 (2008): 16–27.
27. *Centennial Exhibition, Official Catalogue* (Philadelphia: J. R. Nagle & Co., 1876), 182.
28. Andrys Onsman, "Truganini's Funeral," *Island* 96 (Autumn 2004): 39–52.
29. Peter Hulme, *Remnants of Conquest: The Island Caribs and Their Visitors, 1877–1998* (Oxford: Oxford University Press, 2000), 16.
30. Quoted in John Reynolds, "AI Clark's American Sympathies and His Influence on Australian Federation," *Australian Law Review* 32, no. 3 (1958): 62.
31. Wayne Hudson, *Australian Religious Thought* (Melbourne: Monash University, 2016), 93–131.
32. Williams, "Andrew Inglis Clark," 49.
33. Stefan Petrow, "Andrew Inglis Clark as Attorney-General," in *A Living Force: Andrew Inglis Clark and the Ideal of Commonwealth*, ed. Richard Ely with Marcus Haward and James Warden (Hobart: Centre for Tasmanian Historical Studies, 2001), 36–70.
34. Clark to Edward Ivey, quoted in Williams, "Andrew Inglis Clark," 52.
35. John Reynolds to Howe, 28 September 1947, Holmes papers.
36. W. Rumble, "Legal Realism, Sociological Jurisprudence and Mr. Justice Holmes," *Journal of the History of Ideas* 26, no. 4 (1965): 564–566.
37. Nicholas Aroney, "Imagining a Federal Commonwealth: Australian Conceptions of Federalism, 1890–1901," *Federal Law Review* 30, no. 2 (2002); J. A. La Nauze, *The Making of the Constitution* (Melbourne: Melbourne University Press, 1972), 18–19.
38. E. A. Freeman, *Greater Greece and Greater England; and George Washington the Expander of England* (London: Macmillan, 1886).
39. *Official Report of the National Australasian Convention Debates*, Sydney, 11 March 1891, 243, citing Edward Augustus Freeman, *The History of Federal Government from the Foundation of the Achaian League to the Disruption of the United States* (London: Macmillan, 1863), repr. as *The History*

of Federal Government in Greece and Italy, 2nd ed., ed. J. B. Bury (London: Macmillan, 1893).

40. Marilyn Lake, "EA Freeman: Liberal Race Historian," in *Race, Nation and Empire: Making Histories, 1750 to the Present,* ed. Catherine Hall and Keith McClelland (Manchester: Manchester University Press, 2010).

41. Andrew Inglis Clark, "Federal Government: The Commonwealth of Australia, No. 2," in *The Making of the Commonwealth,* ed. Scott Bennett (Melbourne: Cassell, 1971), 101.

42. Alfred Deakin, "The Federation of Australia," *Scribner's* 10, no. 5 (November 1891): 561.

43. Charles Dilke, "The Commonwealth of Australia," *Forum* 11 (June 1891): 393.

44. Quoted in Aroney, "Imagining a Federal Commonwealth."

45. John Hirst, *The Sentimental Nation: The Making of the Australian Commonwealth* (Melbourne: Oxford University Press, 2000).

46. *Debates of the Australasian Federal Convention,* second session, Sydney, 2–24 September 1897, 10 September, 1897, 349.

47. H. B. Higgins, *The Australian Commonwealth Bill . . . Essays and Addresses* (Melbourne: Atlas Press, 1900).

48. Higgins, "The Convention Bill of 1898," in Higgins, *The Australian Commonwealth Bill,* 10–11.

49. Higgins, preface to *The Australian Commonwealth Bill.*

50. Higgins, *The Australian Commonwealth Bill,* 32.

51. Clark, "Federal Government"; *Daily Telegraph* (Launceston), 31 October 1900, 6.

52. H. B. Higgins, "Australian Ideals," *Austral Light,* 1 January 1902, 9.

53. Clark, *Studies in Constitutional Law,* 20–21.

54. Clark to Holmes, 26 October 1901, Clark papers, C4 / C211 (3).

55. David W. Blight, *Race and Reunion: The Civil War in American History* (Cambridge, MA: Belknap Press of Harvard University Press, 2002).

56. Holmes to Clark (undated), Clark papers, C4 / C210.

57. Julius Weinberg, *Edward Alsworth Ross and the Sociology of Progressivism* (Madison: State Historical Society of Wisconsin, 1972), 136–138.

58. Ibid., 136–137.

59. Felix Frankfurter, *Mr. Justice Holmes and the Constitution* (Cambridge, MA: Dunster House Papers, 1927), 8.

60. Ibid., 6.

61. Edward A. Purcell Jr., *Brandeis and the Progressive Constitution: Erie, the Judicial Power, and the Politics of the Federal Courts in Twentieth Century America* (New Haven, CT: Yale University Press, 2000), 165–168.

62. Higgins, "The Rigid Constitution," 210.

63. Ibid., 211.

64. Ibid., 203.

65. Ibid.

66. Ibid., 205.

67. Ibid., 206.

68. Ibid., 207.

69. Ibid., 211–212.

70. Ibid., 221.

71. Ibid.

72. H. H. Champion to H. B. Higgins, 9 November 1907, Higgins papers, MS 1057 / 149, NLA.

73. Vida Goldstein, "Socialism of Today—an Australian View," *Nineteenth Century and After*, September 1907, 408–410, cited in John Lack and Charles Fahey, "The Industrialist, the Trade Unionist and the Judge: The Harvester Judgment of 1907 Revisited," *Victorian Historical Journal* 79, no. 1 (June 2008): 11–12.

74. M. B. Hammond, "Judicial Interpretation of the Minimum Wage in Australia," *American Economic Review* 3, no. 2 (June 1913): 259.

75. H. B. Higgins, "Address to the Millions Club," Sydney, 1 June 1917. Copy in Frankfurter papers, reel 40.

76. Melvin I. Urovsky, *Louis D. Brandeis: A Life* (New York: Pantheon Books, 2009), 212–222.

77. Josephine Goldmark, *Impatient Crusader: Florence Kelley's Life Story* (Urbana: University of Illinois Press, 1953), 157.

78. Alpheus Thomas Mason, *Brandeis: A Free Man's Life* (New York: Viking Press, 1956), 245–253.

79. Felix Frankfurter, "Hours of Labor and Realism in Constitutional Law," *Harvard Law Review* 29, no. 4 (February 1916): 353–373.

80. Urofsky, *Louis D Brandeis*, 217.

81. "Brandeis," in *The New Republic Book: Selections from the First Hundred Issues* (New York: Republic, 1916), 160.

82. Progressive Party Platform of 1912, Roosevelt papers, Library of Congress.

83. Joseph A. McCartin, *Labor's Great War: The Struggle for Industrial Democracy and the Origins of Modern American Labor Relations, 1912–1921* (Chapel Hill: University of North Carolina Press, 1997), 51–53; Nelson Lloyd Dawson, *Louis D. Brandeis, Felix Frankfurter and the New Deal* (Hamden, CT: Archon Books, 1980), 2–3.

84. Higgins travel diary, 1914–1915, Higgins papers, MS 1057 / 3, NLA.

85. Paul A. Freund, *Felix Frankfurter: Reminiscences and Reflections* (Cambridge, MA: Harvard University Press, 1982), 6.

86. Michael E. Parrish, *Felix Frankfurter and His Times: The Reform Years* (New York: Free Press, 1982), 5.

87. Felix Frankfurter, "Government and Administration of the Philippine Islands," Memorandum for the Secretary of War, Frankfurter papers, Library of Congress.

88. Joseph P. Lash, *From the Diaries of Felix Frankfurter* (New York: W. W. Norton, 1975), 12.

89. Higgins to Holmes, in H. N. Hirsch, *The Enigma of Felix Frankfurter* (New York: Basic Books, 1981), 41.

90. Higgins, "Draft Autobiography," 138, Higgins papers, MS 1057 / 3, NLA.

91. Higgins travel diary, 1914–1915, 30 June 2014, Higgins papers, MS 1057 / 3, NLA.

92. Higgins travel diary, 1914–1915, 1 July 1914, Higgins papers, MS 1057 / 3, NLA.

93. Higgins to Frankfurter, 8 July 1914, Frankfurter papers, reel 40, Library of Congress.

94. Higgins to Frankfurter, 4 December 1915, Frankfurter papers, reel 40, Library of Congress.

95. Gerard C. Henderson to Higgins, 13 April 1915, Higgins papers, MS 1057 / 233, NLA.

96. Henderson to Higgins, 26 August 1915, Higgins papers, MS 1057 / 238, NLA.

97. Frankfurter to Holmes, 11 November 1915, in *Holmes and Frankfurter: Their Correspondence, 1912–34,* ed. Robert Mennel and Christine L. Compston (Hanover, NH: University Press of New England, 1996), 39.

98. H. B. Higgins, "A New Province for Law and Order: Industrial Peace through the Minimum Wage and Arbitration," *Harvard Law Review* 29, no. 1 (November 1915): 14.

99. Ibid., 15.

100. Ibid., 19.

101. Ibid., 23–25.

102. Learned Hand, "The Hope of the Minimum Wage," *New Republic,* 20 November 1915, 66–68.

103. Herbert Croly, "Unionism and Anti-Unionism," in *The New Republic Book* (New York: Republic, 1916), 163.

104. Higgins to Frankfurter, 12 December 1914, Frankfurter papers, reel 40, Library of Congress.

105. Ibid.

106. Higgins to Frankfurter, 21 December 1920, Frankfurter papers, reel 40, Library of Congress.

107. Felix Frankfurter, "New Labor Ideas Taught by War," *New York Times,* 15 December 1918, 8.

108. Samuel Crowther, "Who Wants a Living Wage?," *Collier's,* 30 December 1922, 8.

109. Adkins v. Children's Hospital of the District of Columbia, 261 U.S. 525 (1923).

110. Holmes to Higgins, 3 August 1926, Higgins papers, MS 1057 / 2 / 546, NLA.

111. Dawson, *Brandeis, Frankfurter and the New Deal,* 47–85; Alice Kessler-Harris, *In Pursuit of Equity: Women, Men and the Quest for Economic Citizenship in 20th Century America* (New York: Oxford University Press, 2001), 101–107.

5. WOMAN SUFFRAGE AS AN OBJECT LESSON

1. Vida Goldstein, "Autograph Book," Goldstein papers, 67, Fawcett Library, London.

2. Maud Wood Park, "Around the World," Maud Wood Park Papers, M-133, Schlesinger Library, Harvard University.

3. Goldstein, "Autograph Book."

4. Ibid.

5. Ibid.; "Our Delegate," *Australian Woman's Sphere* 2, no. 22 (10 June 1902).

6. *Report of the First International Woman Suffrage Conference* (Washington, DC, 12–18 February 1902) (New York: NAWSA, 1902), 22.

7. Ibid., 39.

8. Clare Wright, "'A Splendid Object Lesson': A Transnational Perspective on the Birth of the Australian Nation," *Journal of Women's History* 26, no. 4 (2014): 16.

9. National American Woman Suffrage Association (NAWSA), 36th Annual Convention, *Proceedings*, 11–17 February 1904, Papers 324.06, vol. 36, Schlesinger Library, Harvard University (hereafter *Proceedings*).

10. NAWSA, 36th Annual Convention, "Declaration of Principles," in *Proceedings*, 20.

11. *Report of the First International Woman Suffrage Conference*, 39.

12. Josephine Henry, "800,000 Women Are Enfranchised: The Great Victory for Woman Suffrage Which Was Recently Won in Australia Discussed by a Woman," *Bluegrass Blade* (Lexington, KY), 20 July 1902, 4, repr. in *Commercial Tribune* (Cincinnati, OH), 20 July 1902, 8.

13. Ibid.

14. H. B. Higgins, "The Rigid Constitution," *Political Science Quarterly* 20, no. 2 (June 1905): 203–222.

15. Helen Irving, *To Constitute a Nation: A Cultural History of Australia's Constitution* (Melbourne: Cambridge University Press, 1997), 176–195.

16. Ida Husted Harper, "Franchise for Women," *Washington Post*, 17 January 1904, 10.

17. Ibid.

18. Marilyn Lake, "The Gendered and Racialised Self Who Claimed the Right to Self-Government," *Journal and Colonialism and Colonial History* 13, no. 1 (Spring 2012), http://search.proquest.com.ezp.lib.unimelb.edu.au/docview/1018692259?accountid=12372.

19. Ibid.

20. Nancy Cott, "Early Twentieth Century Feminism in Political Context: A Comparative Look at Germany and the United States," in *Suffrage and Beyond: International Feminist Perspectives*, ed. Caroline Daley and Melanie Nolan (Auckland: Auckland University Press / Pluto Press, 1994), 247; Nancy Cott, *The Grounding of Modern Feminism* (New Haven, CT: Yale University Press, 1987).

21. Lake, "Gendered and Racialised Self"; Catherine Bishop and Angela Woollacott, "Business and Politics as Women's Work: The Australian Colonies and the Mid-Nineteenth Century Women's Movement," *Journal of Women's History* 28, no. 1 (2016): 84–106.

22. On woman suffrage in Australia, see Audrey Oldfield, *Woman Suffrage in Australia: A Gift or a Struggle* (Melbourne: Cambridge University Press, 1992); Kirsten Lees, *Votes for Women: The Australian Story* (Sydney: Allen and Unwin, 1995); Marilyn Lake, *Getting Equal: The History of Feminism in Australia* (Sydney: Allen and Unwin, 1999).

23. Irma Sulkunan, "An International Comparison of Women's Suffrage: The Cases of Finland and New Zealand in the Late Nineteenth Century," *Journal of Women's History* 27, no. 4 (Winter 2015): 88–111.

24. Seth Koven and Sonya Michel, eds., *Mothers of a New World: Maternalist Politics and Welfares States in Comparative Perspective* (New York: Rout-

ledge, 1993); Linda Gordon, "Putting Children First: Women, Maternalism and Welfare in the Early Twentieth Century," in *US History as Women's History: New Feminist Essays*, ed. Linda Kerber, Alice Kessler-Harris, and Kathryn Kish Sklar (Chapel Hill: University of North Carolina Press, 1995), 63–86.

25. Jessie Ackerman, *Australia from a Woman's Point of View* (London: Cassell, 1913), 209; S. M. Marilley, "Frances Willard and the Feminism of Fear," *Feminist Studies* 19, no. 1 (Spring 1993): 123–146; Marilyn Lake, "Frontier Feminism and the Marauding White Man," in *Nation, Empire, Colony: Historicizing Gender and Race*, ed. Ruth Roach Pierson and Nupur Chaudhuri (Bloomington: Indiana University Press, 1998), 94–105.

26. Oldfield, *Woman Suffrage in Australia*, 139; see also Judith Smart, "Modernity and Mother-Heartedness: Spirituality and Religious Meaning in Australian Women's Suffrage and Citizenship Movements, 1890s–1920s," in *Women's Suffrage in the British Empire: Citizenship, Nation, Race*, ed. Ian Christopher Fletcher, Laura E. Nym Mayhall, and Philippa Levine (London: Routledge, 2000), 51–67.

27. Oldfield, *Woman Suffrage in Australia*, 140.

28. Lake, *Getting Equal*, 145–146.

29. Jill Roe, "'Testimonies of the Field': The Coming of Christian Science to Australia, c. 1890–1910," *Journal of Religious History* 22, no. 3 (October 1998): 314–319.

30. Patricia Grimshaw, *Women's Suffrage in New Zealand* (Auckland: Auckland University Press, 1972).

31. Susan Magarey, *Unbridling the Tongues of Women: A Biography of Catherine Helen Spence* (Adelaide: University of Adelaide Press, 2010), 154–155.

32. Oldfield, *Woman Suffrage in Australia*, 40.

33. Ibid., 39.

34. Spence to Alice Henry, Catherine Helen Spence Correspondence, South Australian Public Library.

35. Ibid.

36. *Australian Woman's Sphere* 2, no. 18 (10 February 1902): 136.

37. Ibid.

38. *Australian Woman's Sphere* 2, no. 19 (10 March 1902): 156.

39. Ibid.

40. *Australian Woman's Sphere* 2, no. 22 (10 June 1902): 181–182; *Australian Woman's Sphere* 2, no. 23 (10 July 1902): 189–190.

41. *Washington Post*, 17 February 1902, 12.

42. *Report of the First International Woman Suffrage Conference*, 39.

43. Irving, *To Constitute a Nation*, 175.

44. Ibid., 171–195.

45. Ibid., 179.

46. "The Australian Woman in Politics," *The Woman's Journal*, 1 March 1902, 66.

47. Ibid.

48. Ibid.

49. Oldfield, *Woman Suffrage in Australia*, 64.

50. Marilyn Lake, "Between Old World 'Barbarism' and 'Stone Age Primitivism': The Double Difference of the White Australian Feminist Subject," in *Australian Women Contemporary Feminist Thought*, ed. Norma Grieve and Ailsa Burns (Melbourne: Oxford University Press, 1994), 80–91; Louise Michele Newman, *White Women's Rights: The Racial Origins of Feminism in the United States* (New York: Oxford University Press, 1999), 116–131; Patricia Grimshaw, "Reading the Silences: Suffrage Activists and Race in Nineteenth-Century Settler Societies," in *Women's Rights and Human Rights: International Historical Perspectives*, ed. Patricia Grimshaw, Katie Holmes, and Marilyn Lake (London: Palgrave, 2001), 31–48.

51. Marilyn Lake and Henry Reynolds, *Drawing the Global Colour Line: White Men's Countries and the International Challenge of Racial Equality* (Cambridge: Cambridge University Press, 2008), 101.

52. Ibid., 111–112.

53. *Australian Woman's Sphere* 2, no. 20 (10 April 1902): 165–166.

54. Vida Goldstein, *To America and Back, January–July 1902* (Sydney: Australian History Museum, 2002), 31.

55. Marilyn Lake and Vanessa Pratt, "'Blood Brothers': Racial Identification and the Right to Rule: The Australian Response to the Spanish-American War," *Australian Journal of Politics and History* 54, no. 1 (2008): 16–27.

56. Theodore Roosevelt, *An Autobiography* (New York: Macmillan, 1913), 598.

57. *The New Idea*, 1 October 1902, 194.

58. *Australian Woman's Sphere* 2, no. 28 (10 December 1902): 242.

59. *Australian Woman's Sphere* 2, no. 21 (10 May 1902): 173–174.

60. Ibid.

61. *New York Herald*, 1 March 1902.

62. *Australian Woman's Sphere* 2, no. 20 (10 April 1902): 165–166.

63. *Australian Woman's Sphere* 2, no. 21 (10 May 1902): 173–174.

64. *Australian Woman's Sphere* 2, no. 22 (10 June 1902): 181–182.

65. Ibid.

66. Ibid.; *Boston Advertiser*, 12 April 1902.

67. Sharon Hartman Strom, "Leadership and Tactics in the American Woman Suffrage Movement: A New Perspective from Massachusetts," *Journal of American History* 62, no. 2 (September 1975): 296–297.

68. *Australian Woman's Sphere* 2, no. 21 (10 May 1902): 173–174.

69. *Australian Woman's Sphere* 2, no. 23 (10 July 1902): 189–190.

70. Ibid.

71. Ibid.

72. *Chicago Daily Tribune*, 29 May 1902, 12.

73. Ibid.

74. Ibid.; *Australian Woman's Sphere* 2, no. 23 (10 July 1902): 189–190.

75. *Australian Woman's Sphere* 2, no. 24 (10 August 1902): 197.

76. Ibid.

77. *New Idea*, 1 October 1902, 194.

78. *Woman Voter* 29 (12 April 1912): 6.

79. Carrie Chapman Catt, *The Enfranchisement of Women*, container 10, Carrie Chapman Catt papers, Library of Congress; Catt, "The Outlook for Woman Suffrage," *Citizen*, 4 June 1903, 4.

80. *New York Tribune*, 14 June 1902, 7.

81. *Australian Woman's Sphere* 3, no. 29 (10 January 1902): 250.

82. *New York Times*, 17 December 1903, 6.

83. *New York Times*, 29 December 1907, 5.

84. *Idaho Daily Statesman*, 19 May 1907, 24; see also "New Zealand's Experience," in NAWSA Political Equality Series, III, 6, 1907, Schlesinger Library.

85. Marilyn Lake, "State Socialism for Australian Mothers: Andrew Fisher's Radical Maternalism in Its International and Local Contexts," *Labour History* 102 (May 2012): 64–65.

86. *Harper's Weekly*, 2 July 1904, 1006.

87. Diane Kirkby, *Alice Henry: The Power of Pen and Voice; The Life of an Australian-American Labor Reformer* (Cambridge: Cambridge University Press, 1991), 70.

88. An American Sociologist, "Progress towards Equality," *Independent* 55 (11 June 1903), 1384.

89. Park, "Around the World," 4.

90. Ibid., 5.

91. *Argus*, 18 October 1909, 9.

92. *Argus*, 25 October 1909, 8.

93. Park, "Around the World," 12–13.

94. Ibid.

95. Carrie Chapman Catt, "Political Parties and the League of Women Voters," in *For the Public Record: A Documentary History of the League of Women Voters*, by Barbara Stuhler (Westport, CT: Greenwood Press, 2000), 27.

96. Maud Wood Park, "Five Questions," in Stuhler, *For the Public Record*, 33.

97. Ibid., 34.

98. "Planks to Be Presented by the National League of Women Voters," in Stuhler, *For the Public Record*, 35.

99. Carrie Chapman Catt, "Minutes of Conference," in Stuhler, *For the Public Record*, 42.

100. Carrie Chapman Catt to Maud Wood Park, "Easter Sunday, 1922," in Stuhler, *For the Public Record*, 68.

101. Quoted in Josephine Goldmark, *Impatient Crusader: Florence Kelley's Life Story* (Urbana: University of Illinois Press, 1953), 93.

6. MOTHERS OF THE NATION

1. *General Exercises of the International Congress of Charities, Correction and Philanthropy, Chicago, June, 1893* (Baltimore: Johns Hopkins Press, 1894), 294–300.

2. Catherine Helen Spence, "Lecture," in *Proceedings of the First Australasian Conference on Charity, Melbourne, 11–17 November, 1890* (Melbourne: Government Printing Office, 1890), 15–25.

3. Theodore Roosevelt, "Address," in *Proceedings of the Conference on the Care of Dependent Children*, Washington, DC, January 25–26, 1909 (Washington, DC: Government Printing Office, 1909), 35.

4. Theodore Roosevelt, "Special Message," in *Proceedings of the Conference on the Care of Dependent Children*, 5.

5. *Proceedings of the Conference on the Care of Dependent Children*, 48.

6. Ibid., 49–50.

7. Joanne L. Goodwin, *Gender and the Politics of Welfare Reform: Mothers' Pensions in Chicago, 1911–1929* (Chicago: University of Chicago Press, 1997), 111.

8. Mary McDougall Gordon, "Australia and New Zealand," in *Children in Historical and Comparative Perspective*, ed. Joseph M. Hawes and N. Ray Hiner (Westport, CT: Greenwood Press, 1991), 121.

9. Mark H. Leff, "The Mothers' Pension Movement in the Progressive Era," *Social Service Review* 47, no. 3 (September 1973): 397–410.

10. Goodwin, *Gender and the Politics of Welfare Reform*, 87–104.

11. Gwendolyn Mink, "The Lady and the Tramp: Gender, Race and the Origins of the American Welfare State," in *Women, the State and Welfare*, ed. Linda Gordon (Madison: University of Wisconsin Press, 1990), 110.

12. Catherine Spence, "Diary 14 January 1894," in *Ever Yours, Catherine Helen Spence*, ed. Susan Magarey and Barbara Wall (Adelaide: Wakefield Press, 2005), 232.

13. Brenda J. Child, *Boarding School Seasons: American Indian Families, 1900–1940* (Lincoln: University of Nebraska Press, 2000), 66–67; Jacqueline Fear-Segal and Susan D. Rose, *Carlisle Indian Industrial School: Indigenous Histories, Memories, and Reclamations* (Lincoln: University of Nebraska Press, 2016).

14. Jane Addams, *Democracy and Social Ethics* (Chicago, 1902), 228; Mink, "Lady and the Tramp," 103–104.

15. George M. Frederickson, *The Black Image in the White Mind: The Debate on Afro-American Character and Destiny* (New York: Harper and Row, 1971), 263–266; Marilyn Lake and Henry Reynolds, *Drawing the Global Colour Line: White Men's Countries and the International Challenge of Racial Equality* (Cambridge: Cambridge University Press, 2008), 59–64.

16. Michael McGerr, *A Fierce Discontent: The Rise and Fall of the Progressive Movement in America, 1870–1920* (New York: Free Press, 2003), 206.

17. Robert Valentine, "The People of the United States . . . ," Valentine family papers, 12 / 99, Massachusetts Historical Society.

18. Ibid., 5.

19. David Wallace Adams, *Education for Extinction: American Indians and the Boarding School Experience, 1875–1928* (Lawrence: University Press of Nebraska, 1995); Patrick Wolfe, "After the Frontier: Separation and Absorption in US Indian Policy," *Settler Colonial Studies* 1 (2011): 13–40.

20. Valentine, "The People of the United States . . . ," Valentine family papers, 12 / 99, 6, Massachusetts Historical Society.

21. For comparisons of indigenous and non-indigenous child welfare policies in Australia, see Naomi Parry, "Such a Longing: Black and White Children in

Welfare in New South Wales and Tasmania, 1880–1940" (PhD thesis, University of New South Wales, 2007); Naomi Parry, "Stolen Childhoods: Reforming Aboriginal and Orphan Children through Removal and Labour in New South Wales, 1909–1917," *Revue d'histoire de l'enfance "irreguliere"* 14 (2012): 141–163.

22. *The Problem of Indian Administration: Report of a Survey made at the request of Hon Hubert Work, Secretary of the Interior and submitted to him, 21 February, 1928* (Baltimore: Johns Hopkins Press, 1928), ch. 9.

23. Margaret Jacobs, *White Mother to a Dark Race: Settler Colonialism, Maternalism and the Removal of Indigenous Children in the American West and Australia, 1880–1940* (Lincoln: University of Nebraska Press, 2009), 26.

24. Child, *Boarding School Seasons*, 49.

25. Robyn Muncy, *Creating a Female Dominion in American Reform, 1890–1935* (New York: Oxford University Press, 1994), 38.

26. Child, *Boarding School Seasons*, 35–37.

27. Lilian Locke-Burns, "State Provision for Mother and Child," *Labor Call*, 26 June 1919.

28. Marilyn Lake, "State Socialism for Australian Mothers: Andrew Fisher's Radical Maternalism in National and International Contexts," *Labour History* 102 (May 2012): 55–70.

29. Muncy, *Creating a Female Dominion*; Linda Gordon, "Putting Children First: Women, Maternalism, and Welfare in the Early Twentieth Century," in *US History as Women's History: New Feminist Essays*, ed. Linda K. Kerber, Alice Kessler-Harris, and Kathryn Kish Sklar (Chapel Hill: University of North Carolina Press, 1995), 63–86; Seth Koven and Sonya Michel, eds., *Mothers of a New World: Maternalist Politics and the Origins of Welfare States* (New York: Routledge, 1993); Marilyn Lake and Katie Holmes, eds., "Maternal Citizenship, 1900–1920," in *Freedom Bound II* (Sydney: Allen and Unwin, 1995), 1–35; Lake, "State Socialism for Australian Mothers."

30. Rose Scott on the Women's Political Education League, Scott papers, MS 38 / 41, Mitchell Library.

31. *Woman Voter*, 29 (19 October 1912): 6.

32. *Proceedings of the Conference on the Care of Dependent Children*, 44.

33. John Murphy, *A Decent Provision: Australian Welfare Policy, 1870 to 1949* (London: Ashgate, 2011), 58–59.

34. Ibid., 99–101.

35. *Age*, 6 September 1912.

36. Commonwealth Parl. Deb., House, 25 September 1912, 3446.

37. *Philadelphia Enquirer*, 4 August 1912.

38. Marilyn Lake, "The Independence of Women and the Brotherhood of Man: Debates in the Labour Movement over Equal Pay and Motherhood Endowment in the 1920s," *Labour History* 63 (November 1992): 1–24.

39. Marilyn Lake, *Getting Equal: The History of Feminism in Australia* (Sydney: Allen and Unwin, 1999), 116–135.

40. Henry J. Harris, *Maternity Benefit Systems in Certain Foreign Countries*, Legal Series no. 3 (Washington, DC: Government Printing Service, 1919)

[also printed in US Children's Bureau, *Bulletin*, no. 57, Washington, DC (1919)].

41. Harris, *Maternity Benefit Systems*, 18.

42. Quoted in Seth Koven and Sonya Michel, introduction to Koven and Michel, *Mothers of a New World*, 20.

43. Muncy, *Creating a Female Dominion*, 39.

44. Fiona Paisley, *Loving Protection? Australian Feminism and Aboriginal Women's Rights, 1919–39* (Melbourne: Melbourne University Press, 2000).

45. Jane E. Simonsen, *Making Home Work: Domesticity and Native American Assimilation in the American West, 1869–1919* (Chapel Hill: University of North Carolina Press, 2006), 71–75.

46. Shurlee Swain, "'The Supervision of . . . Babies Is Women's Work, and Cannot Be Rightly Done by Men': Victorian Women's Organisations and Female Child Welfare Inspectors, 1890–1915," *Victorian Historical Journal* 79, no. 2 (2008): 314–327.

47. Catherine Spence, letter to the editor, *Australian Woman's Sphere* 1, no. 7 (March 1901): 60.

48. Lake, *Getting Equal*, 58–59.

49. Ibid., 59.

50. Ibid., 61–62.

51. Gordon, "Putting Children First," 64.

52. Theodore Roosevelt, "Call for the Conference," in *Proceedings of the Conference on the Care of Dependent Children*, 15.

53. Roosevelt, "Memorandum," in *Proceedings of the Conference on the Care of Dependent Children*, 16.

54. *Proceedings of the Conference on the Care of Dependent Children*, 216–218.

55. Ibid., 99–101.

56. Ibid., 100.

57. Muncy, *Creating a Female Dominion*, 47.

58. Ibid., 53.

59. Lake and Holmes, *Freedom Bound II*, 8–12; Shurlee Swain and Renate Howe, *Single Mothers and Their Children: Disposal, Punishment and Survival in Australia* (Melbourne: Cambridge University Press, 1995); Richard Broome, *Aboriginal Victorians: A History Since 1800* (Sydney: Allen and Unwin, 2005), 188–193.

60. Frederick E. Hoxie, *A Final Promise: The Campaign to Assimilate the Indians, 1880–1920* (1984; repr., New York: Cambridge University Press, 1995).

61. Ibid., 67.

62. Ibid.

63. Margaret Jacobs, "Maternal Colonialism: White Women and Indigenous Child Removal in the American West and Australia, 1880–1940," *Western Historical Quarterly* 39 (Winter 2005): 462.

64. "Education for Indian Girls," *Woman's Journal*, 19 January 1901, 1.

65. Lake, *Getting Equal*, 47–136; Louise Newman, *White Women's Rights: The Racial Origins of Feminism in the United States* (New York: Oxford University Press, 1999), 116–131; Paisley, *Loving Protection?*; Victoria Haskins,

Matrons and Maids: Regulating Indian Domestic Service in Tucson, 1914–1934 (Tucson: University of Arizona Press, 2012), 1–17.

66. Haskins, *Matrons and Maids*, 5–6.

67. Francis Paul Prucha, *The Great Father: The United States Government and the American Indians*, vol. 2 (Lincoln: University of Nebraska Press, 1984), 700.

68. Ibid., 703.

69. *Annual Report of the Commissioner of Indian Affairs to the Secretary of the Interior, 1893* (Washington DC: Government Printing Office, 1893), 20.

70. Child, *Boarding School Seasons*, 12–13.

71. *Annual Report of the Commissioner of Indian Affairs*, 10–11.

72. Child, *Boarding Schools Seasons*, 47.

73. Ibid., 65.

74. Patricia Grimshaw, Marilyn Lake, Ann McGrath, and Marian Quartly, *Creating a Nation* (Melbourne: McPhee Gribble, 1994), 291.

75. Lake, *Getting Equal*, 83.

76. Anna Haebich, *Broken Circles: Fragmenting Indigenous Families 1800–2000* (Fremantle: Fremantle Arts Centre Press, 2000), 290.

77. Ibid., 290–291.

78. Margaret Tucker, *If Everyone Cared* (Melbourne: Grosvenor Press, 1977), 90–93.

79. Lake and Holmes, *Freedom Bound II*, 12.

80. Haebich, *Broken Circles*, 163.

81. Judith Elton, "Comrades or Competition? Union Relations with Aboriginal Workers in the South Australian and Northern Territory Pastoral Industries, 1878–1955" (PhD thesis, University of South Australia, 2007), 123–128.

82. Ibid.

83. Lake, *Getting Equal*, 110–135.

84. Ibid., 129.

85. Jacobs, *White Mother to a Dark Race*, 404.

86. Ibid., 393.

87. Francis Leupp, speech, c. 1908, as recorded by Valentine, 9 May 1912, Valentine papers, 12 / 38.

88. Robert Valentine to Dr. Mumford [undated], 14, Valentine papers, 8 / 82.

89. Ibid., 14.

90. *The Problem of Indian Administration*, ch. 9.

91. Marie Baldwin, "Modern Home-Making and the Indian Woman," quoted in Jacobs, *White Mother to a Dark Race*, 322.

92. Cathleen D. Cahill, "Marie Louise Bottineau Baldwin: Indigenizing the Federal Indian Service," *American Indian Quarterly* 37, no. 3 (Summer 2013): 63–86.

93. Ibid., 72.

94. Ibid., 77.

95. Jacobs, *White Mother to a Dark Race*, 322.

96. Child, *Boarding School Seasons*, 54.

97. Ibid., 19, 25, 49, 54.

7. LABOR INVESTIGATORS CROSS THE PACIFIC

1. Henry Demarest Lloyd, interview by the *Australian Worker*, 20 May 1899, 4.

2. Edward Tregear, *The Aryan Maori* (Wellington: G. Didsbury, Government Printer, 1885); Tony Ballantyne, *Orientalism and Race: Aryanism in the British Empire* (London: Palgrave, 2002).

3. Henry Demarest Lloyd, *Newest England: Notes of a Democratic Traveller in New Zealand, with Some Australian Comparisons* (New York: Doubleday, 1900), 5.

4. On immigration restriction laws across the Australasian colonies, see Marilyn Lake and Henry Reynolds, *Drawing the Global Colour Line: White Men's Countries and the International Challenge of Racial Equality* (Cambridge: Cambridge University Press, 2008), 15–45; W. Pember Reeves, *State Experiments in Australia and New Zealand*, 2 vols. (London: Grant Richards, 1902), 2:354.

5. Reeves, *State Experiments in Australia and New Zealand*, 2:359. See also Tony Ballantyne, "Writing Out Asia: Race, Colonialism and Chinese Migration in New Zealand History," in *East by South: China in the Australasian Imagination*, ed. Charles Ferrall, Paul Millar, and Keren Smith (Wellington: Victoria University Press, 2005), 87–109.

6. Peter Coleman, *Progressivism and the World of Reform: New Zealand and the Origins of the American Welfare State* (Lawrence: University Press of Kansas, 1987), 49.

7. "An American Publicist," *Sydney Morning Herald*, 27 January 1899, 4; *South Australian Register*, 19 January 1899, 4.

8. Lloyd, *Newest England*, 8.

9. K. R. Howe, "Tregear, Edward Robert," in *Dictionary of New Zealand Biography*, http://www.TeAra.govt.nz/en/biographies/2t48/tregear-edward-robert.

10. Edward Tregear to Henry Demarest Lloyd, 5 September 1899, Henry Demarest Lloyd correspondence on microfilm, Reel 7, Baillieu Library, University of Melbourne.

11. Henry Demarest Lloyd, *A Country without Strikes* (New York: Doubleday, 1900), 15.

12. Richard Mitchell, "State Systems of Conciliation and Arbitration: The Legal Origins of the Australasian Model," in *Foundations of Arbitration: The Origins and Effects of State Compulsory Arbitration, 1890–1914*, ed. Stuart Macintyre and Richard Mitchell (Melbourne: Oxford University Press, 1989), 93–99.

13. Edward Tregear, "Old Age Pensions," *Independent* 23 (March 1899): 799–802; Edward Tregear, "Progress in New Zealand," *Independent* 52 (July–December 1900): 1716–1719; Edward Tregear, "New Zealand Social and Industrial Experiments," *Amalgamated Engineers' Journal* 6, no. 4 (April 1902): 2–8; Edward Tregear, "Recent Humanisitic Legislation in New Zealand," *Arena* 37 (January–June 1907): 366–374.

14. Lloyd, *A Country without Strikes*, 15.

15. Reeves, *State Experiments in Australia and New Zealand*; Lloyd, *A Country without Strikes*, xiv.

16. Reeves, quoted in Lloyd, *A Country without Strikes*, xv.

17. Lloyd, *Newest England*, 1.

18. Ibid., 7–9.

19. Henry Demarest Lloyd to Florence Kelley, 18 October 1899, Series 1, correspondence, box 62, Kelley papers, New York Public Library.

20. Henry Demarest Lloyd to Richard Ely, 10 November 1900, Richard Ely papers, Wisconsin Historical Society.

21. Richard Ely to Henry Demarest Lloyd, 12 November 1900, Richard Ely papers, Wisconsin Historical Society.

22. Coleman, *Progressivism and the World of Reform*, 51, 230n10; "Australasian Cures for Coal Wars," *Atlantic Monthly* 90, no. 102 (November 1902): 667–674.

23. Lloyd, "Australasian Cures for Coal Wars," 672–674.

24. Leon Fink, *The Long Gilded Age: American Capitalism and the Lessons of a New World Order* (Philadelphia: University of Pennsylvania Press, 2015), 92.

25. Alfred Deakin, Commonwealth Parl. Deb., House, 1903, 2862–2863.

26. *New York Sun*, two-page review (undated), news clippings, box 1, Victor S. Clark papers, Library of Congress.

27. *New York Times*, 24 November 1906, news clippings, box 1, Clark papers.

28. Victor Clark, "Chippeway Country," box 10, poems and stories, Clark papers.

29. Victor Clark, "High-Tide Wilson," box 10, poems and stories, Clark papers.

30. Victor Clark, "Unmonopolized," 1908, box 10, poems and stories, Clark papers.

31. Clinton B. Fisk to Major Clark, 15 March 1880, box 2, Clark papers.

32. Ibid.

33. R. H. Pratt to Major Clark, 27 June 1894, box 2, Clark papers.

34. "To President Roosevelt," reference for Victor Selden Clark, 10 January 1902, box 1, Clark papers.

35. Senate Document, 363, Report by Victor Selden Clark, box 1, Clark papers.

36. Emma S. Colcleugh, "Porto Rico," newspaper clippings, box 1, Clark papers.

37. Newspaper clipping, no name or date, newspaper clippings, box 1, Clark papers.

38. Victor Selden Clark, "Labor Conditions in Cuba," *Bulletin of the Department of Labor* 41 (July 1902): 663–793.

39. Tregear to Clark, 24 June 1903, box 1, Clark papers.

40. Howe, "Tregear, Edward Robert"; K. R. Howe, *Singer in a Songless Land: A Life of Edward Tregear, 1846–1931* (1991; repr., Auckland: Auckland University Press, 2013), e-book.

41. Edward Tregear, *The Maori Race* (London: A. D. Willis, 1904).

42. Tregear to Clark, 21 July 1904, box 1, Clark papers.

43. Tregear to Clark, 24 July 1903, box 1, Clark papers.

44. Ibid.

45. Ibid.

46. Ibid.

47. Ibid.

48. Ibid.

49. Ibid.

50. Ibid.
51. Ibid.
52. Tregear to Clark, 3 November 1903, box 1, Clark papers.
53. Victor S. Clark, "Labor Conditions in Australia," *Bulletin of the Department of Labor* 56 (January 1905): 9–243.
54. Tregear to Clark, 8 April 1904, box 1, Clark papers.
55. Ibid.
56. Edward Tregear, "Industrial Arbitration in New Zealand," *Independent* 55 (1903): 1908–1910; Edward Tregear, "How New Zealand Is Solving the Problem of Popular Government," *Arena* 32 (1904): 569–577.
57. Fink, *The Long Gilded Age*, 101, 117.
58. Gwendolyn Mink, "The Lady and the Tramp: Gender, Race and the Origins of the American Welfare State," in *Women, the State and Welfare*, ed. Linda Gordon (Madison: University of Wisconsin Press, 1990), 99.
59. Tregear to Clark, 21 July 1904, box 1, Clark papers.
60. Victor S. Clark, "Labor Conditions in New Zealand," *Bulletin of the Department of Labor* 49 (November 1903): 1176.
61. Clark, "Labor Conditions in Australia."
62. V. S. Clark, *The Labor Movement in Australasia: A Study in Social Democracy* (New York: Henry Holt, 1906); *Nation*, 18 April 1907, newspaper clippings, box 1, Clark papers.
63. *Bankers' Magazine*, February 1907, newspaper clippings, box 1, Clark papers.
64. *Boston Times*, 16 March 1907, newspaper clippings, box 1, Clark papers.
65. *Athenaeum*, 16 March 1907, newspaper clippings, box 1, Clark papers.
66. Lake and Reynolds, *Drawing the Global Colour Line*, 190–191.
67. Newspaper clippings (untitled and undated), box 1, Clark papers.
68. Ibid.
69. *Toronto Globe*, 3 December 1908, and *New York Tribune* (undated), newspaper clippings, box 1, Clark papers.
70. Victor S. Clark, "The Canadian Industrial Disputes Investigation Act of 1907," *Bulletin of the Department of Labor* 76 (May 1908): 657–658.
71. Ibid., 667.
72. Ibid., 662.
73. Ibid., 678.
74. Newspaper clippings, *Chicago Evening Post*, quoted in advertisement for *The Labor Movement in Australasia*, box 1, Clark papers.
75. Fink, *The Long Gilded Age*, 108, 111–112.
76. William Reynolds Vance, "The Kansas Court of Industrial Relations with Its Background," *Yale Law Journal* 30 (1920–1921): 457.
77. Ibid., 466–468.
78. Ibid., 473, 476.
79. *Journal of Political Economy*, April 1907; *The Dial*, 1 May 1907, newspaper clippings, box 1, Clark papers.
80. National Consumers League, *Report*, Tenth Annual Session of the Council, Providence, Rhode Island, 2 March 1909, 16–18; *Report*, Consumers' League of Oregon, January 1913, 10–11; Florence Kelley, National Conference of Charities and Correction, *Proceedings* (July 1913), 3.

81. National Consumers League, *Report*, Tenth Annual Session of the Council, "Label"; Kathryn Kish Sklar, "Two Political Cultures in the Progressive Era: The National Consumers' League and the American Association for Labor Legislation," in *US History as Women's History: New Feminist Essays*, ed. Linda K. Kerber, Alice Kessler-Harris, and Kathryn Kish Sklar (Chapel Hill: University of North Carolina Press, 1995), 43–50.

82. Kelley, Conference of Charities and Correction, *Proceedings*, 3.

83. National Consumers League, *Report*, Tenth Annual Session of the Council, 18.

84. Ibid., 33.

85. Henry W. Macrosty, "State Arbitration and the Minimum Wage in Australasia," in *Trade Unionism and Labor Problems*, ed. John Commons (Boston: Ginn, 1905), 195–221.

86. Marilyn Lake, "Challenging the "Slave-Driving Employers": Understanding Victoria's 1896 Minimum Wage through a World-History Approach," *Australian Historical Studies* 45, no. 1 (2014): 87–102.

87. Walter Lippman, "The Campaign against Sweating," *New Republic*, 27 March 1915, repr. by the National Consumers League in *Capital and Labor*, New York Public Library, TDB p.v.62, 22.

88. Ibid., 27–28.

89. Massachusetts, Commission on Minimum Wage Boards, *Report* (January 1912).

90. *Philadelphia Enquirer*, 5 January 1913, 9.

91. Ibid.

92. Higgins travel diary, 1914–1915, 24 June 1914, Higgins papers, MS 1057 / 3, NLA.

93. "Justice Higgins on Mr Valentine," *New Republic*, 7 April 1917, 296; Higgins travel diary, 1914–1915, 19–23 June 1914.

94. Alice Henry, "The Living Wage," *Life and Labor* 3 (7 July 1913): 1.

95. Ibid.

96. M. B. Hammond, "Judicial Interpretation of the Minimum Wage in Australia," *American Economic Review* 3, no. 2 (June 1913): 285.

97. Hammond to Andrews, 14 August 1911, correspondence files, series 5001, box 4, AALL papers, Kheel Center, Cornell University.

98. Andrews to Singer, 17 August 1911, AALL papers.

99. Hammond, "Judicial Interpretation," 259.

100. Andrews to Hammond, 23 August 1911, AALL papers.

101. In addition to "Judicial Interpretation," see "Wages Boards in Australia: IV Social and Economic Results of Wages Boards," *Quarterly Journal of Economics* 29, no. 3 (May 1915): 563–630; M. B. Hammond, "Where Life Is More than Meat: The Australian Experience with Wages Boards," in "The Case for the Minimum Wage," ed. Florence Kelley, special issue, *Survey* 33, no. 19 (February 1915): 495–502; M. B. Hammond, "The Regulation of Wages in New Zealand," *Quarterly Journal of Economics* 31, no. 3 (May 1917): 404–446.

102. Hammond, "Judicial Interpretation," 285.

103. Higgins to Hammond, 25 July 1913, Higgins papers, MS 1057 / 208, NLA.

104. Hammond, "Judicial Interpretation," 262.

105. Craig Phelan, *William Green: Biography of a Labor Leader* (Albany: State University of New York Press, 1989), 43.

106. Learned Hand, "The Hope of the Minimum Wage," *New Republic* 20 (November 1915): 67.

107. Florence Kelley, "The Status of Legislation in the United States," in Kelley, "The Case for the Minimum Wage," 487.

108. Ibid., 489.

109. Louis Brandeis, "The Constitution and the Minimum Wage," in Kelley, "The Case for the Minimum Wage," 492.

110. Ibid., 493.

111. Josephine Goldmark to H. B. Higgins, 28 August 1917, Higgins papers, MS 1057 / 526, NLA.

112. Alice Kessler-Harris, *In Pursuit of Equity: Women, Men and the Quest for Economic Citizenship in 20th Century America* (New York: Oxford University Press, 2001), 31.

113. Mary Gilmore to H. B. Higgins, 17 July and 30 July 1909, Higgins papers, MS 1057 / 156 / 7, NLA; Higgins to Mary Gilmore, 26 July 1909, Higgins papers, MS 1057 / 158, NLA. For the classic critique of Higgins's sexism, see Edna Ryan and Anne Conlon, *Gentle Invaders: Australian Women at Work, 1788–1914* (Melbourne: Thomas Nelson, 1975).

8. INDIGENOUS PROGRESSIVISM CALLS SETTLER COLONIALISM TO ACCOUNT

1. Hazel Hertzberg, *The Search for an American Indian Identity* (Syracuse, NY: Syracuse University Press, 1971), 38; Kyle T. Mays, "Transnational Progressivism: African Americans, Native Americans and the Universal Races Congress of 1911," *American Indian Quarterly* 37, no. 3 (2013): 247.

2. Charles A. Eastman, "The North American Indian," in *Papers on Interracial Problems Communicated to the First Universal Races Congress Held at the University of London, July 26–29, 1911*, ed. Gustav Spiller (London: King and Son, 1911), 373–376; Charles Eastman to Carlos Montezuma, 27 January 1911, quoted in Mays, "Transnational Progressivism," 247.

3. Eastman, "The North American Indian," 369–375.

4. Frederick E. Hoxie, ed., *Talking Back to Civilization: Indian Voices from the Progressive Era* (Boston: Bedford, 2001), 2. Eastman's books include *Indian Boyhood* (1902), *Old Indian Days* (1907), *The Soul of an Indian* (1911), *Indian Child Life* (1913), and *From the Deep Woods to Civilization* (1916).

5. Gustav Spiller, "The Problem of Race Equality," in Spiller, *Papers on Interracial Problems*, 38.

6. Mays, "Transnational Progressivism," 258.

7. Marilyn Lake and Henry Reynolds, *Drawing the Global Colour Line: White Men's Countries and the International Challenge of Racial Equality* (Cambridge: Cambridge University Press, 2008), 251–256.

8. Ibid., 258.

9. Ibid., 251–259.

10. Franz Boas, "The Instability of Human Types," in Spiller, *Papers on Interracial Problems*, 99–103.
11. W. E. B. Du Bois, "The Negro Race in the United States of America," in Spiller, *Papers on Interracial Problems*, 364.
12. Eastman, "North American Indian," in Spiller, *Papers on Interracial Problems*, 376.
13. Lake and Reynolds, *Drawing the Global Colour Line*, 249–250, 255–256.
14. Eastman, "The North American Indian," 374.
15. Ibid., 376.
16. Mays, "Transnational Progressivism," 246.
17. K. Tsianina Lomawaima, *They Called It Prairie Light: The Story of the Chilocco Indian School* (Lincoln: University of Nebraska Press, 1996).
18. Joane Nagel, *American Indian Ethnic Revival: Red Power and the Resurgence of Identity and Culture* (New York: Oxford University Press, 1997), 116.
19. Mays, "Transnational Progressivism," 253.
20. Chadwick Allen, "Introduction: Locating the Society of American Indians," *American Indian Quarterly* 37, no. 3 (2013): 9.
21. Hertzberg, *The Search for an American Indian Identity*, 36.
22. Ibid., 37.
23. Helen Hunt Jackson, *A Century of Dishonor: A Sketch of the United States Government's Dealings with Some of the Indian Tribes* (New York: Harper and Brothers, 1881).
24. Philip J. DeLoria, "Four Thousand Invitations," *Indian American Quarterly* 37, no. 3 (Summer 2013): 27–28, 32.
25. Ibid., 28.
26. Letter to Charles Parker, quoted in Lucy Maddox, *Citizen Indians: Native American Intellectuals, Race and Reform* (Ithaca, NY: Cornell University Press, 2005), 9–10.
27. See also K. Tsianina Lomawaima, "The Mutuality of Citizenship and Sovereignty: The Society of American Indians and the Battle to Inherit America," *American Indian Quarterly* 37, no. 3 (2013): 333–345. On opposition to Wild West shows, see Chauncey Yellow Robe, "The Menace of the Wild West Show," *Quarterly Journal* 2 (1914), in Hoxie, *Talking Back to Civilization*, 115–118.
28. Allen, "Locating the Society," 4.
29. Ibid., 5.
30. Ibid., 6.
31. Hertzberg, *The Search for American Indian Identity*, 60.
32. R. G. Valentine, "Address to the Employees and Students of the Sherman Institute," 1, November 1911, Felix Frankfurter papers, microfilm reel 119, Library of Congress.
33. Hertzberg, *The Search for American Indian Identity*, 61.
34. Ibid.
35. Ibid., 65.
36. Christina Stanciu, "An Indian Woman of Many Hats: Laura Cornelius Kellogg's Embattled Search for an Indigenous Voice," *American Indian Quarterly* 37, no. 3 (Summer 2013): 94–108.

37. Laura Cornelius Kellogg, "Some Facts and Figures on Indian Education," *Quarterly Journal* 1 (1913), in Hoxie, *Talking Back to Civilization*, 53–55.

38. Ibid.

39. Cathleen D. Cahill, "Marie Louise Bottineau Baldwin: Indigenizing the Federal Indian Service," *American Indian Quarterly* 17, no. 3 (Summer 2013): 68–69.

40. Cahill, "Baldwin," 83.

41. Frederick Hoxie, *This Indian Country: American Political Activists and the Place They Made* (New York: Penguin, 2012), 257–258.

42. K. Tsianina Lomawaima, "The Society of American Indians," *Oxford Research Encyclopedia of American History*, May 2015, 2, Americanhistory .oxfordre.com.

43. Hertzberg, *The Search for an American Indian Identity*, 111.

44. Society of American Indians, Legal Aid Committee, "An Appeal to the Nation," *Quarterly Journal* 1 (1913), in Hoxie, *Talking Back to Civilization*, 102–107.

45. Ibid., 104.

46. Ibid., 102.

47. Arthur C. Parker, "Certain Important Elements of the Indian Problem," *Quarterly Journal* 3 (1915), in Hoxie, *Talking Back to Civilization*, 99.

48. Ibid., 101.

49. John Maynard, *Fight for Liberty and Freedom: The Origins of Australian Aboriginal Activism* (Canberra: Aboriginal Studies Press, 2007), 59–67.

50. John Maynard, "In the Interests of Our People: The Influence of Garveyism on the Rise of Australian Aboriginal Political Activism," *Aboriginal History* 29 (2005): 17.

51. Ibid., 13.

52. Ibid., 14.

53. Ibid., 17.

54. Maynard, *Fight for Liberty*, 54.

55. Ibid., 81, 91–92, 112.

56. Ibid., 47.

57. Ibid., 52.

58. *Daily Guardian*, 7 May 1925, 1.

59. *Daily Guardian*, 24 April 1925, 1; *Daily Guardian*, 7 May 1925, 1.

60. Maynard, *Fight for Liberty*, 99.

61. *Daily Guardian*, 24 April 1925, 1.

62. Charles A. Eastman, "The Indian Plea for Freedom," in Hoxie, *Talking Back to Civilization*, 132.

63. Hoxie, *This Indian Country*, 284.

64. Robert Yellowtail, "Address in Defense of the Rights of the Crow Indians, and the Indians Generally, Before the Senate Committee on Indian Affairs, 9 September, 1919," in Hoxie, *Talking Back to Civilization*, 136–137.

65. Ibid., 137.

66. Erez Manela, *The Wilsonian Moment: Self-Determination and the International Origins of Anticolonial Nationalism* (New York: Oxford University Press, 2007).

67. Karin L. Huebner, "An Unexpected Alliance: Stella Atwood, the Califor-nian Clubwomen, John Collier, and the Indians of the Southwest, 1917–1934," *Pacific Historical Review* 78, no. 3 (2009): 347.

68. John Maynard, "On the Political 'Warpath'—Native Americans and Austra-lian Aborigines after the First World War," *Wicazo Sa Review: A Journal of Native American Studies* 32, no. 1 (2017): 48–62. See also the Mission Indian Federation website, http://www.missionindianfederation.com/. My thanks to John Maynard for alerting me to MIF and its "home rule" aspirations.

69. Francis Paul Prucha, *The Great Father: The United States Government and the American Indians* (Lincoln: University of Nebraska Press, 1984), 798; Huebner, "An Unexpected Alliance," 350.

70. Huebner, "An Unexpected Alliance," 354.

71. Margaret D. Jacobs, *Engendered Encounters: Feminism and Pueblo Cul-tures, 1879–1934* (Lincoln: University of Nebraska Press, 1999), 18, 112, 124; Huebner, "An Unexpected Alliance," 344.

72. *Santa Fe New Mexican*, 6 November 1922, in Hoxie, *Talking Back to Civi-lization*, 173–174.

73. Hoxie, *Talking Back to Civilization*, 174.

74. Jacobs, *Engendered Encounters*, 14–15, 71–72; on Elsie Clews Parsons see Desley Deacon, *Elsie Clews Parsons: Inventing Modern Life* (Chicago: Uni-versity of Chicago Press, 1997).

75. John Collier, "The Experiment in Milwaukee," *Harper's Weekly*, 12 August 1911, 11–12.

76. Pucha, *The Great Father*, 955.

77. Ibid., 956.

78. Huebner, "An Unexpected Alliance," 340.

79. Stanciu, "An Indian Woman," 107.

80. Ibid., 101.

81. Deloria, "Four Thousand Invitations," 28.

Acknowledgments

This book has been long in the making, and I have accrued many debts.

I wish to thank the many colleagues and friends who shared their expertise, time, references, and sometimes their own libraries. Historical scholarship is forged collectively in dinner conversation and email exchange, as well as in seminar rooms and institutional archives.

I was fortunate to have generous interlocutors both close to home and across the world. They challenged me to think deeply and to write clearly. I wish to thank Warwick Anderson, the late Tracey Banivanua-Mar, Eileen Boris, Dorothy Sue Cobble, Clare Corbould, Nancy Cott, Phil Deloria, Kat Ellinghaus, Leon Fink, David Goodman, Julie Greene, Pat Grimshaw, Catherine Hall, Vicky Haskins, Dave Headon, Jill Jensen, James Keating, Paul Kramer, Sophie Loy-Wilson, Charlotte Macdonald, Susan Magarey, John Maynard, Kyle Mays, Sonya Michel, Nell Musgrove, Marian Quartly, Henry Reynolds, Doug Rossinow, Tim Rowse, Kim Rubenstein, Marian Sawer, Judy Smart, Shurlee Swain, Ian Tyrrell, and John Williams. I also thank the organizers and audiences at the LAWCHA conference in New York in 2013; the National History Center seminar at the Woodrow Wilson Center in Washington, DC, in February 2014; and the American History and Transnational and Global History Joint Seminar at the University of Oxford in December 2014, who provided memorable feedback. Special thanks to Ben Mountford and Jay Sexton.

For their long-term example and support, I owe a particular debt to Michael Roe, Graeme Davison, and Desley Deacon, three mentors who have engaged with my interest in transnational American-Australian history and acted as sounding boards over the long haul. I also thank Stuart Macintyre, who read the entire manuscript and offered much informed advice and many useful suggestions.

I researched and wrote this book while on an Australian Professorial Fellowship, awarded by the Australian Research Council (ARC) to research the international history of Australian democracy. I thank the ARC for its generous funding, without which a project such as this would not have been possible. Australian researchers are fortunate to enjoy this distinctive national investment, which funds international scholarship, extensive travel, research in far-flung libraries and archives, and well-qualified research assistance. This project has benefited greatly from the superb research assistance provided by Lee-Ann Monk and Rosemary Francis. Their cheerful and conscientious work was invaluable.

Online resources make so many records more easily accessible, but there is nothing like reading letters in their original form. Much of this book is based on reading personal correspondence. I am grateful for the assistance of archivists and librarians in Australia and in the United States for making this possible, especially at the National Library of Australia (NLA), the Library of Congress, the New York Public Library, the Massachusetts Historical Society, the Harvard University Archives, the Schlesinger Library, and the Wisconsin Historical Society archives. I am especially grateful to my sister, Pamela Gatenby, for her professional assistance at the NLA and her and Ross's warm hospitality in Canberra.

I completed this book at the University of Melbourne, where Trevor Burnard, as head of the School of Historical and Philosophical Studies, invited me to convene a program we called Australia in the World, a series of public lectures, seminars, and symposia, for which I curated thirty events over three years. The series supported the visits of wonderful local and international scholars to Melbourne and provided a stimulating research environment conducive to thinking about the Australian past in larger historical frameworks. I thank the support of colleagues at the University of Melbourne—Trevor Burnard, Joy Damousi, Kate Darian-Smith, David Goodman, Pat Grimshaw, Ara Keys, Samia Khatun, and Andy May—for their engagement with this series, and Emma Shortis and Liam Byrne for their elegant and efficient administrative support.

On behalf of the University of Melbourne, I undertook an exchange visit to the University of North Carolina, at Chapel Hill, in 2016, where I taught classes and spoke to seminars in history about my work in progress. I thank Fitz Brundage, Kyle Mays, and Susan Pennybacker, in particular, for stimulating conversation and debate, and Karen Hagemann for her generous hospitality.

At Harvard University Press, the work of transforming a manuscript into a book was made easier by David Armitage's encouragement in the early stages, two very useful readers' reports, attentive text editing, and Joyce Seltzer's superb editorial guidance. Her creative input was essential to realizing the final outcome.

Writers generally leave acknowledgments to family to the end. This is because we recognize that their support underpins all the rest. My family increased suddenly from four to eleven during the gestation of this book, and life became more complicated as five little ones made their appearance. The joy they provided was a welcome distraction and a source of happiness, even as family care needs rapidly expanded. I am thus especially mindful of my family's support of my writing and their generosity during busy times.

Special thanks to Sam, Kath and Dave, and Jess and Lachie. I hope you enjoy the book. Welcome to future readers Matilda, Mia, Henry, Larry, and baby Anna.

Index

www.ingramcontent.com/pod-product-compliance
Lightning Source LLC
Chambersburg PA
CBHW051727260326
41914CB00031B/1779/J